Cuban Revolution in America

Justice, Power, and Politics

COEDITORS

Heather Ann Thompson
Rhonda Y. Williams

EDITORIAL ADVISORY BOARD

Peniel E. Joseph
Matthew D. Lassiter
Daryl Maeda
Barbara Ransby
Vicki L. Ruiz
Marc Stein

The Justice, Power, and Politics series publishes new works in history that explore the myriad struggles for justice, battles for power, and shifts in politics that have shaped the United States over time. Through the lenses of justice, power, and politics, the series seeks to broaden scholarly debates about America's past as well as to inform public discussions about its future.

More information on the series, including a complete list of books published, is available at http://justicepowerandpolitics.com/.

Cuban Revolution in America

HAVANA AND
THE MAKING OF A
UNITED STATES LEFT,
1968–1992

Teishan A. Latner

THE UNIVERSITY OF NORTH CAROLINA PRESS | CHAPEL HILL

© 2018 The University of North Carolina Press
All rights reserved

Designed by April Leidig
Set in Arno by Copperline Book Services, Inc.

The University of North Carolina Press has been a member of the Green Press Initiative since 2003.

Cover illustration: Fidel Castro speaking to members of the Venceremos Brigade. Photo by George Cohen.

Library of Congress Cataloging-in-Publication Data
Names: Latner, Teishan, author.
Title: Cuban revolution in America : Havana and the making of a United States Left, 1968–1992 / Teishan A. Latner.
Other titles: Justice, power, and politics.
Description: Chapel Hill : The University of North Carolina Press, [2017] | Series: Justice, power, and politics | Includes bibliographical references and index.
Identifiers: LCCN 2017033404| ISBN 9781469635460 (cloth : alk. paper) | ISBN 9781469659206 (pbk. : alk. paper) | ISBN 9781469635477 (ebook)
Subjects: LCSH: Cuba — History — Revolution, 1959 — Influence. | New Left — United States. | United States — Foreign relations — Cuba. | Cuba — Foreign relations — United States.
Classification: LCC F1788 .L3393 2017 | DDC 327.7307291 — dc23
LC record available at https://lccn.loc.gov/2017033404

For my parents,
Laurie and Joel Latner

A billboard on a Havana street in May 1972 reads "Freedom for Angela Davis."
Photo by John van Hasselt/Corbis.

Contents

Acknowledgments xi

Introduction. Cuban Revolution in America 1

1 *Venceremos* Means "We Will Win":
  The Venceremos Brigades, Cuba, and the U.S. Left 27

2 Missiles, in Human Form:
  Cuba and the Specter of Foreign Subversion in America 75

3 Revolution in the Air:
  Hijacking, Political Protest, and U.S.-Cuba Relations 123

4 *Joven Cuba* inside the Colossus:
  The Antonio Maceo Brigade and the Making of a
  Cuban American Left 153

5 Assata Is Welcome Here:
  Black Radicalism, Political Asylum, and the
  Diplomacy of Exile and Freedom 199

Epilogue. Unfinished Revolutions 265

Notes 273

Bibliography 317

Index 335

Figures

vi   "Freedom for Angela Davis" billboard

36   Members of the Venceremos Brigade pose while working in the sugarcane fields, December 1969

40   Fidel Castro and members of the Venceremos Brigade pause while cutting sugarcane together on Christmas Day, 1969

52   Satirical advertisement in the pages of *Tricontinental*

64   Venceremos Brigade members and Cuban representatives hold a joint panel discussion, International Women's Day, March 7, 1970

85   Poster, 1980, depicting global support for the Cuban revolution striking back against U.S. power

87   Venceremos Brigade members and Vietnamese delegates from the National Liberation Front embrace in December 1969

111   "We will destroy imperialism from the outside; they will destroy it from the inside," poster, 1968

135   Image celebrating African American militancy and black nationalism

149   A December 1972 cartoon from the *Buffalo Evening News*

164   The spring 1978 cover of *Areíto*

178   Antonio Maceo Brigade members visit the José Martí Mausoleum

178   Members of the Antonio Maceo Brigade with Ramón Castro

179   Antonio Maceo Brigade members with Fidel Castro after a meeting with Castro and other Cuban officials, 1978

212   "Free all political prisoners," poster, 1968

212   "Freedom for the Wilmington 10," poster, ca. 1971

213   "Power to the People — George," poster, ca. 1971

220 "Solidarity with the African American people," poster, 1968

236 Charlie Hill photographed in Old Havana, August 2015

241 Assata Shakur in Havana, 1998

246 Nehanda Abiodun in Havana, 2006

262 Joint FBI and New Jersey State Police poster for Assata Shakur issued on May 2, 2013

Acknowledgments

Many debts were accumulated in the writing of this book. In Cuba, I was aided in innumerable ways by the kindness and generosity of friends, colleagues, and strangers, who opened their homes, shared meals, and agreed to be interviewed. I especially thank René Tamayo, who was instrumental in locating key contacts and setting up interviews. Nehanda Abiodun, patron saint to a legion of foreign students and academics, and Charlie Hill, the longest remaining U.S. political exile in Cuba, both provided key insights into my topic. My gratitude also goes to Roberto Zurbano and Tomás Fernández Robaina for sharing their perspectives, as well as to the staff at the Instituto Cubano de Amistad con los Pueblos (ICAP), especially Vladimir Falcón, Orlaida Cabrera, Hugo Govín, and José Estévez Hernández. Friends such as Pavel Fuentes Contreras and Jessica Piedra Díaz helped interpret the complex realities of daily life in Cuba, and Jesús Arboleya, Rafael Betancourt, William Potts, Conner Gorry, and Antonio Pérez were interlocutors at key moments. Given the sensitive nature of some of my research, I also thank all those in Havana and its vicinities who spoke to me off the record or on condition of anonymity. Finally, I acknowledge Assata Shakur, whose comments during a brief conversation many years ago provided one of the early sparks that compelled me to take up this research.

At the University of North Carolina Press, I had the good fortune to work with Brandon Proia, who guided the manuscript through the long process of review and revision with enthusiasm and encouragement, and the press's excellent production team. Many thanks as well to Heather Ann Thompson and Rhonda Y. Williams, editors of the Justice, Power, and Politics book series, for their interest in the project. Two anonymous reviewers provided thoughtful critiques of the manuscript at various stages, greatly improving it.

Some of the ideas and arguments that appear in this book were first tested in professional forums. The Center for Black Studies Research at the University of California, Santa Barbara, where I was a Research Associate as I was completing the manuscript, provided crucial support and a forum for intellectual growth, and I am indebted to director Diane Fujino for her mentorship and comments on my work; to Jonathan Gómez for his insights, and to the amazing students in the Transformative Pedagogy Project for their commitment and brilliance. At New York University's Center for the United States and the Cold War, where I was a Postdoctoral Fellow during a key phase of research and revision, I gratefully acknowledge the support of then-director Timothy Naftali. I also appreciate Ana María Dopico and Ada Ferrer for their comments to an early version of chapter 5, and the staff of the Tamiment Library, especially Michael Koncewicz. My thanks also to Sowande' Mustakeem and her students at Washington University in St. Louis, as well as the Department of History and African & African American Studies Program there for giving me the opportunity to present my work.

Portions of this research were also presented on panels at meetings of the American Historical Association, the Society for Historians of American Foreign Relations, the Organization of American Historians, the American Studies Association, the Pacific Coast Branch of the American Historical Association, and the UC-Cuba Academic Initiative, and I especially appreciate the comments of Michael Allen, Anita Casavantes Bradford, Robin Derby, David Farber, Ada Ferrer, Van Gosse, Lillian Guerra, Ivette N. Hernandez-Torres, and Martin Klimke.

Several colleagues generously took the time to critique sections of the manuscript, including Dan Berger, Barry Carr, Anita Casavantes Bradford, Raúl A. Fernández, Roxanne Dunbar-Ortiz, John Gronbeck-Tedesco, Sara Julia Kozameh, Ben V. Olguín, Marc D. Perry, Rubén G. Rumbaut, Sarah J. Seidman, Devyn Spence-Benson, James Shrader, Henry Louis Taylor, Jasmin A. Young, and Mark Redondo Villegas. An earlier version of chapter 3 was published as an article by *Diplomatic History*, and I am grateful to Devyn Spence-Benson, Van Gosse, and Emily Rosenberg for their comments to that manuscript, and to Komozi Woodard and Sean Malloy for their comments to a manuscript derived from chapter 5. Former participants of the Venceremos Brigade and Antonio Maceo Brigade generously reviewed chapters or agreed to be interviewed, and I gratefully acknowledge Raul Alzaga, Rafael Betancourt, Eduardo Santana Castellon, Dennis Duncanwood, Mariana Gaston, Albor Ruíz, Rubén G. Rumbaut, Tony Ryan, Louis Segal, and Mirén Uriarte. Charles McKelvey, Amberly Alene Ellis, Kaeten Mistry, and Jay Davis also provided assistance or sounding boards at key times for topics related to the study of Cuba.

I am especially grateful to Winston A. James, my esteemed committee chair and adviser at the University of California, Irvine, for his unflagging support at every stage. Sohail Daulatzai was an invaluable mentor, and Jon Wiener provided valuable feedback. My affiliation with the UC-Cuba Academic Initiative provided key support for my work on Cuba within the University of California system, and I owe a tremendous debt to then-director Raúl A. Fernández.

Numerous faculty in UC Irvine's Department of History aided me in important ways, and I especially acknowledge Sharon Block, Alice Fahs, Alex Borucki, Mark LeVine, Jessica Millward, and Rachel O'Toole, as well as Laura Mitchell, department chair for much of my time there. Beyond the Department of History, I am grateful to Glen Mimura for his support from within the School of Humanities. I likewise owe a debt of gratitude to UC Irvine's Program in African American Studies, which offered me five years of teaching assistantships, profoundly impacting my research and teaching. I especially thank Bridget Cooks, Jared Sexton, and Tiffany Willoughby-Herard for their support, and Frank Wilderson for sharing his research with me. I thank also the legion of UC Irvine graduate students with whom I alternately debated, relied upon, commiserated, and laughed with throughout the journey of doctoral work, especially Mark Redondo Villegas, Daniel McClure, Raul Pérez, Danielle Vigneaux, and Martha Arguello. My interest in Cuba first took scholarly form at Temple University, and I thank David Farber, who supervised an MA thesis, and Harvey Neptune and Kenneth L. Kusmer for their support there.

Outside UC Irvine, others did much to aid this research. K. Wayne Yang was an invaluable mentor, offering writing critiques and hosting dinners for stray neighborhood graduate students. Mark A. Sanders provided introductions to two key contacts in Cuba. Sowande' Mustakeem was an unflagging source of advice and encouragement, and Ruth Reitan generously shared her knowledge and key resources. Deep appreciation also goes to Luis Esparza and Antonio Prieto-Stambaugh, friends and intellectuals extraordinaire, who hosted a two-month writing retreat, complete with homegrown coffee, at their home outside Xalapa, Mexico, during my final months of dissertating.

I am also indebted to the assistance of numerous archives and libraries. The staff at the FBI's Record/Information Dissemination Section handled my Freedom of Information Act (FOIA) requests with professionalism. While my FOIA requests to the CIA usually resulted in some variant of the dreaded "we can neither confirm nor deny...," the agency ultimately provided a small number of valuable materials for which I am grateful. The staff of several archives provided helpful assistance, and I acknowledge Rosa Monzon-Alvarez and Esperanza de Varona at the Cuban Heritage Collection at the University of Miami; Kathryn DeGraff at DePaul University's Special

Collections; Azalea Camacho at the Special Collections & Archives at California State University, Los Angeles; and the staff at the Lourdes Casal Library at the Center for Cuban Studies in New York. Several people also lent materials from their personal archives, including Dennis Duncanwood, Iraida H. López, Timothy Naftali, and Rubén G. Rumbaut. For providing and licensing images, I gratefully acknowledge Raúl Alzaga; George Cohen; Lincoln Cushing; Nils Grossien and the Jerry Berndt Estate; the Tamiment Library and Robert F. Wagner Labor Archives; University Archives & Special Collections at the Joseph P. Healey Library, University of Massachusetts Boston; and the *Buffalo News*.

I never could have completed this research without the financial support of several institutions. A research grant from the Society for Historians of American Foreign Relations allowed me to make an initial research trip to Cuba in 2012. At UC Irvine, grants from the International Center for Writing and Translation, the Humanities Center, the Center for Citizen Peacebuilding, and the Department of History supported research trips to Havana, Miami, Chicago, College Park, New York, Philadelphia, and Berkeley. The UC Irvine Office of the Chancellor awarded me a dissertation completion fellowship in my final year, permitting me the unaccustomed freedom of six months of unfettered writing time. During two crucial years after my graduate-school career, postdoctoral research positions at New York University's Center for the United States and the Cold War and the Center for Black Studies Research at the University of California, Santa Barbara provided key financial support.

Thomas Jefferson University has offered a supportive and collegial professional home, and I gratefully acknowledge Barbara Kimmelman, Valerie Hanson, Katharine Jones, Tom Schrand, David Rogers, Marcella L. McCoy-Deh, Evan Laine, Ryan Long, Stacey Van Dahm, Marilisa Navarro, and the Office of the Provost for their support as I finished the manuscript.

Finally, I am grateful to my parents, Laurie and Joel Latner, whose love and support helped me keep my feet on the path, and to whom this book is dedicated.

Cuban Revolution in America

Introduction

Cuban Revolution in America

IN AUGUST 1967, Stokely Carmichael stood before a crowd of 1,500 Cubans and foreign delegates during the summit of the Organization of Latin American Solidarity (OLAS) in Havana. Convened at the peak of Cuba's efforts to foment left-wing revolution in Latin America and drawing representatives from twenty-seven countries in the hemisphere, the conference aimed to codify a broad position of support for revolution in the Americas. Although focused on Latin America, the conference drew delegates from across the insurgent Third World, as well as a number of leftist dissidents from the United States and Europe.

Linking the fate of African Americans confronting the vestiges of Jim Crow to that of Latin Americans struggling against the legacy of foreign domination, Carmichael, a veteran organizer with the Student Nonviolent Coordinating Committee (SNCC), offered a message of solidarity to the assembled delegates. "We look upon Cuba as a shining example of hope in our hemisphere. We do not view our struggle as being contained within the boundaries of the United States as they are defined by present day maps. Instead, we look to the day when a true United States of America will extend from Tierra del Fuego to Alaska, when those formerly oppressed will stand together, a liberated people."[1]

Positioning the U.S. black freedom movement within larger hemispheric forces in opposition to U.S. influence in the Americas and articulating an internationalist vision of Black Power — the phrase that he had popularized in Mississippi — Carmichael's speech evinced the global gaze of a growing number of black radical activists during the late 1960s, a gaze that had followed the arc of Cuba's evolving revolution with pointed interest. Dismantling formal segregation on the island shortly after its triumph in 1959, when desegregation was still several years away in the American South, and initiating nationwide campaigns of literacy and land reform, the changes wrought by the revolutionary upheaval had benefited Afro-Cubans, the poorest and most marginalized of the island's population, disproportionately. The Cuban press, in turn, had propagandized in support of the radicalizing U.S. civil rights movement, accusing Washington of failing to live up to its Cold War rhetoric. African Americans, survivors of slavery, racial terrorism, and Jim Crow, had lived under "400 years of fascism," as Carmichael had written in the Cuban periodical *Tricontinental*, not liberal democracy.[2] Police violence against unarmed black demonstrators in Mississippi and Alabama was front-page news in Cuba — evidence, Cuban journalists charged, of the poverty of America's claims to moral authority as the self-anointed leader of the free world.

At OLAS, Carmichael lost no time in entering the fray, linking black liberation at home to decolonization abroad with his famous oratory fire. "We share with you a common struggle; we have a common enemy. Our enemy is white Western imperialist society.... Our struggle is to overthrow this system which feeds itself and expands itself through the economic and cultural exploitation of nonwhite, non-Western peoples."[3]

The response from U.S. officialdom was swift. As the U.S. State Department pledged to confiscate Carmichael's passport for violating the U.S. travel ban on Cuba, calls came for the revoking of Carmichael's U.S. citizenship as punishment for what some termed his "traitorous" critique of America from the shores of the nation's primary Cold War adversary in the hemisphere.[4] Fidel Castro came to his guest's defense, however, offering the SNCC leader formal political asylum in Cuba and calling on the Cuban people to help protect Carmichael from "the repression of the imperialists." Reading aloud from a condemnatory *New York Daily News* editorial entitled "Stokely, Stay There" before an audience of Cubans at Havana's Chaplin Theater on August 10, Castro began: "We would indeed be honored if he wished to remain here..." before being cut off by applause. "He must know that, whatever the circumstances, this country will always be his home."[5]

Carmichael, however, would soon voice doubts about Cuba's own claims to racial democracy. The 1959 revolution, he pointed out, had not entirely eradicated Cuba's legacy of racism, one that remained imbedded in the island's history of colonization, slavery, and foreign domination. Carmichael had already been critical of Cuban calls for Americans to forge a united, multiracial movement, writing in the Cuban periodical *Tricontinental* that the "subconscious racism of white workers," not black nationalism, prevented poor people in the United States from uniting to fight for economic justice. In Cuba, however, these divisions were precisely what Cuba's revolutionary history had sought to overcome. The vision of José Martí, the nineteenth-century philosophical architect of Cuban nationalism, had encouraged black, mixed-race, and white Cubans to unite and stand as one, embracing a raceless national imaginary as they fought and died together for a free Cuba.

To most Cubans, the revolutionary process of the late 1950s was the fulfillment of Martí's dream of racial unity in the service of national self-determination. But to Carmichael, it was a revolution cut short. True, the revolutionary process had made Cuba more racially equitable than ever before in its history—more so than any other nation in the western hemisphere—but the leadership had also opposed race-specific measures to address inequalities that remained. Institutional racism, Castro declared in 1962, had been vanquished, and public debate about racism in Cuban society all but ceased. Returning to the United States, Carmichael became outspoken in his opposition to communism, which, he contended, conceived of white supremacy as an outgrowth of capitalist exploitation and failed to address the ontology of antiblack racism. "It is our humanity that is at stake," he told an audience in Oakland. "It is not a question of dollars and cents."[6]

Yet despite the discordance between his vision of race-first black nationalism and the Cuban dream of racially egalitarian socialism, Carmichael's rift with Cuba's revolutionary leadership was short-lived. Relocating to Guinea in 1969 in a self-imposed exile from America's boiling racial cauldron, Carmichael soon reestablished ties with Havana. He worked closely with Cuban officials at the embassy in Conakry, and praised the Caribbean nation's support of Third World liberation movements thousands of miles away. The congruence between their broader goals, including a shared commitment to African decolonization, eclipsed Carmichael's lingering unease with the Cubans' confidence in structural approaches to achieving racial equality.

In his memoirs, written in the mid-1990s as he was undergoing cancer treatment in Cuba, Carmichael opined that "Africans have a lot to thank the Cubans for," a reference to Havana's already legendary aid to anticolonial movements throughout the continent, particularly in Angola and Namibia, where massive Cuban military interventions costing the lives of several thousand Cuban soldiers contributed to the fall of apartheid rule in neighboring South Africa. Looking back on his time in Cuba in 1967, Carmichael now modified his earlier characterization of Cuba, declaring that nowhere on the island had he witnessed "signs of racism or extreme poverty," only the "lingering *effects* of racism and poverty. Those couldn't be eliminated in eight years." Cuba, he maintained, had inspired him with the "humanistic idealism of their revolution.... My support for which has never wavered over the years."[7]

Carmichael's encounter with Cuba in 1967 was the prelude to a dramatic increase in engagements between American leftists and the island during the coming months and years. Traveling alone and with organized delegations, several thousand American dissidents had defied the U.S. travel ban by the end of the decade, reaching Cuba to witness the socialist experiment unfolding on Florida's doorstep. The Cuban Revolution captured the imaginations of Americans,[8] in part because its social achievements resonated with the hopes of a generation that had come of age during the rising expectations of the era. Channeling the island's material wealth and human capital into a socialist system, Cuba's revolution had enshrined education, health care, housing, and food not as "social services" but as universal human rights to which all Cubans were entitled. In the age of the Great Society and the War on Poverty, when public support in the United States for a robust welfare state was still strong, Cuban socialism guaranteed state provision of basic human needs on a mass scale, making Cuba the only nation in Latin America with no endemic hunger, malnutrition, or homelessness. In the era of the Vietnam War, as Americans reeled at televised images of the conflict's human toll and the tide of mainstream public opinion turned against the war, Cuba publicly accused Washington of crimes against humanity and sent aid to the Vietnamese liberation forces, as it had aided anticolonial insurgencies and revolutionary movements across Africa and Latin America. In the era of Women's Liberation, as American women fought for control over their own bodies and demanded that left-wing political movements envision gender as a category of liberation together with race and class, Cuban women claimed the Cuban Revolution as their own despite its patriarchal contours, demanding new independence in the home and the workplace and claiming rights to abortion, which had been decriminalized in Cuba several years before *Roe v. Wade*. In the age of civil rights and Black Power, the Cuban government lionized SNCC and the Black Panther Party, going as far as to provide formal political asylum to Panther leaders such as Eldridge Cleaver and Huey P. Newton, and played an important role in the international campaign to keep radical intellectual Angela Davis out of prison in the early 1970s.

In turn, the Cuban government cultivated alliances with American leftists for reasons of both radical altruism and geopolitical pragmatism. Havana lent its support to U.S. radicals in the late 1960s as an expression of internationalist solidarity with those working for social justice in its northern neighbor, but also as a counterpoint to Washington's efforts to isolate Cuba within the world system. As a small nation living in the shadow of a superpower, the ethos of revolutionary internationalism allowed Cuba to forge subaltern political networks beyond the reach of U.S. power. Within this geopolitical imperative, Havana's relationships with the U.S. Left assumed a special importance. Cuba's leaders understood that strengthening U.S. protest movements could hinder America's anticommunist war effort in Indochina and reduce the threat of an attack on Cuba.

Although Havana never directly sought to foment revolution within the United States, the island's leaders perceived that the rising tide of social upheaval in its northern neighbor provided a bulwark against U.S. hostility. Cuba, like all nations, needed allies abroad, and Havana's relations with U.S. leftists grew in the fertile ground that lay between solidarity and realpolitik. Positioning itself as a leader of global antiimperialist revolution and facing a proximate hostile superpower, Cuba's alliances with left-wing Americans became intertwined with Havana's foreign policy and national security aims, which sought allies abroad and the undermining of Washington's capacity to isolate Cuba diplomatically and assault it militarily.

Irresistible Revolution

Carmichael's ambivalent engagements with Cuba, spanning three decades, suggests the tremendous possibility and hope embodied within the Cuban Revolution for American leftists, as well as its limits. Indeed, support for Cuba within the U.S. Left was hardly reliable. Just as Cuba's initial independence from the Soviet sphere had won it admirers among the New Left during the revolution's early years, Cuba's later economic dependence upon the Soviet bloc, and with it, the inevitability of ties between Havana and Moscow, led to disillusionment among some former supporters. Fidel Castro's decision to back the Soviet invasion of Czechoslovakia in August of 1968, for instance, sparked widespread criticism within the U.S. Left, presaging concern over government censorship of Cuban intellectuals and artists during the 1970s.

Moreover, while the Cuban Revolution's framing of freedom and human rights through the concept of radical democracy had allowed it to guarantee the basic material wellbeing and the political participation of the majority, this conceptualization of liberty and rights did not extend to classic metrics of western liberal democracy such as property rights, free enterprise, and individual liberty. Metaphorically characterizing the defense of the revolution's social gains as a David and Goliath struggle between an island nation and the capitalist superpower to its north, Cuba's revolutionaries attempted to jettison the values of individualism and capitalism and champion those of collectivity and socialism. But other freedoms, including those of expression and the protection of political minorities, also fell victim to a climate of fear created by sabotage and counterrevolutionary campaigns, many of them sponsored within the United States, as well as the authoritarian tendencies of some revolutionary leaders. Limits on individual liberty and political freedom would become the Cuban Revolution's Achilles heel within the capitalist world and, at certain moments, within Cuba itself.[9]

And there were policies more troubling still. Cuban state persecution against those conceptualized as "social deviants," including gender nonconforming and gay men, whose identities were perceived as a threat to the nation's masculinist body politic, and some religious devotees, including Jehovah's Witnesses, whose beliefs against military service and inoculations made them objects of suspicion, ruptured the allure of Cuba's revolution for some North Americans. Policies such as these, which reached their peak in the mid-1960s with the creation of the *Unidades Militares de Ayuda a la Producción* — "military units to aid production" — which functioned as agricultural labor camps where several thousand political dissidents, gay men, and religious devotees were sent for "rehabilitation" until the camps were denounced and closed — remained a stain upon the aura of the Cuban Revolution for years and was a source of vigorous debate within the U.S. Left.

Similarly, Cuba's notorious "gray period" of 1971–1976 was interpreted by some previously sympathetic U.S. supporters of Cuba as an ominous veer toward crude Soviet-style authoritarianism. These years, characterized by a stifling of creative and intellectual expression on the island, leading to the exile or imprisonment of a number of key artists and intellectuals who were accused of undermining the revolution, including the famed poet Heberto Padilla, strained the goodwill of some of Cuba's allies in the United States and around the world. These dislocations of solidarity reinforced a series of binaries. While Cuba's most ardent supporters in the United States constructed Cuba in idealized terms, flattening the contradictions and failures of the revolutionary process in ways that left them unprepared to understand the new nation's complex and ever-evolving realities, Cuba's staunchest left-wing critics simply reduced the revolution to a sum of its contradictions.

These binaries of perception reveal much about Cuba's singular place in the U.S. radical imaginary. From 1959 until well after the decline of the Cold War, the Cuban revolutionary project remained the most consistent foreign influence on left-wing radicalism in the United States. Cuba in the American radical imaginary served as a symbolic home of global revolution, in all of its contradictions, a usable history whose achievements and failures simultaneously inspired and cautioned. In the uniquely intertwined histories of the two nations, the relationship between Cuba and American left-wing social movements provides an underexplored avenue through which to understand the significance of post-1959 Cuba within American political thought.

Cuba's influence on American activists has been perhaps most palpable in the transformative experience of travel to the island itself. Participating in volunteer labor brigades, international conferences, fact-finding missions, and political tourism, Americans witnessed Cuba's socialist process firsthand. There too, Americans encountered not only Cuba's revolution, but also the outliers of decolonization and leftist social transformation worldwide. Indeed, Americans were not the only radicals traveling to the island during the 1960s to witness the nation's transformation, as attested to by a global literature of testimony and memoir written by foreign travelers in Cuba.[10] As journalist and SNCC activist Elizabeth Sutherland Martínez reported it, Cuba was the "youngest revolution" in a world still in the throes of decolonization and anti-imperial rebellion, a new nation whose intersectional radicalism held lessons for social change at home.[11] In the heady incandescence of the sixties era, when anything seemed possible, global leftists read the Cuban Revolution as a sign that revolutionary social transformation was possible in a troubled world.

Cuba's internationalism reached its first peak with the Tricontinental Conference of January 1966, a series of encounters that drew thousands of revolutionaries from around the world. The most important gathering of representatives of communist and nonaligned states and the Third World since the Bandung conference of 1954, the Tricontinental sought to unify the insurgent nations of Africa, Asia, and Latin America in support of self-determination and revolution through armed struggle. Imagining Cuba as a portal to foreign political movements, Americans traveled to Cuba to forge direct relationships with both Cubans and members of insurgent African, Asian, European, and Latin American movements, who were also traveling to Cuba. "Havana in the 1960s, like Paris in the 1790s and Moscow in the 1920s," Richard Gott observes, became "a revolutionary Mecca, the epicenter of a changing and optimistic world."[12]

In the American radical imaginary, Havana thus became a global radical public where Americans could mingle with foreign activists and revolutionaries. Travel to Cuba frequently resulted in personal transformation, radicalizing individual activists in ways that would reverberate deeply within U.S. radical circles. Several dozen Americans lived in Cuba for years or decades as residents, dedicating themselves to the island's revolutionary project and its daily life.[13] Key political formations of the era, including SNCC, the Black Panthers, Students for a Democratic Society (SDS) and the Young Lords

Party sent contingents to Cuba for international conferences and to meet with Cuban officials and representatives of foreign movements. U.S.-based communist formations such as the Socialist Workers Party and the Communist Party U.S.A. (CPUSA) also sent contingents of activists to Cuba.

Throughout these relations, cultural production played a critical role in disseminating Cuban revolutionary ideology globally and imbuing it with meaning. In a parallel to the infiltration of Cuban dance and music into North America in decades past, by the 1960s the allure of Cuban revolutionary culture exerted a singularly conspicuous influence on the U.S. Left. Internationalist iconography, including photographs, political art, and printed slogans produced by massive Cuban publishing operations and disseminated into the United States through subterranean political networks, created a public transcript of the island's revolution and appeared in the pages of key left publications such as *Ramparts* and *The Black Panther* during the late 1960s. Radio Havana Cuba dedicated several running programs to Cuba's North American allies — including the legendary *Radio Free Dixie*, hosted by advocate of armed black self-defense Robert F. Williams during his Cuban exile from an FBI dragnet; and *On the Ten Millions Trail*, dedicated to the New Left volunteers of the Venceremos Brigade, who were in Cuba contributing to the island's sugar harvest — that were beamed around the world, and deep into the United States, on a powerful signal. Cuban government-sponsored entities such as the literary institute *Casa de las Américas* and the Organization of Solidarity with the People of Asia, Africa, and Latin America (OSPAAAL), whose iconic political posters heroizing global insurgent movements became widely available in the United States, rendered Cuban revolutionary ideology in vivid hues.

Cuban cultural production, including OSPAAAL's quadrilingual and globally distributed journal, *Tricontinental*, which Carmichael later claimed was regarded as "a bible in revolutionary circles" stateside, provided textual bridges between Cuba and American radicals, giving American leftists access to a cultural *lingua franca*, one that they used to reinterpret their own social conditions within a global context. If, as the eminent Cubanist historian Louis A. Pérez has argued, Cuba's place in the imaginary of American empire has been mediated in large part through representation and metaphor, then the alternative posed by Cuban revolutionary cultural production exerted a potent counternarrative, capturing the imaginations of U.S. leftists and influencing their political thought and activist praxis.[14]

Drawing together many of these expressions of solidarity and communication was the Venceremos Brigade. Formed by New Left antiwar activists and incorporating a broad spectrum of the era's protest movements, including women's liberation, SNCC, the Black Panther Party, SDS, and elements from Puerto Rican, Chicano/a, and Asian American activist movements, it sent the largest activist delegations of the era. Volunteering in agricultural and construction projects to support the island's development, and publicizing the Cuban Revolution's social gains in literacy, education, and health care, the Venceremos Brigade sought to build a grassroots counterpoint to the Washington consensus of antagonism toward the island. Becoming the largest Cuba solidarity organization in the world, its work reverberated into an impressively wide range of social justice movements, from feminist movements of the 1970s to the Latin American solidarity movements of the 1980s, to the U.S. Black Left. Enduring for over four decades, the Venceremos Brigade had become, as Elizabeth Martinez put it in 1999, a "unique pillar" of the U.S. Left — the focus of chapter 1 of this book.[15]

The significance of encounters between American dissidents and Cuba was not lost on U.S. officialdom. Outrage over Carmichael's comments in Havana in 1967 was the opening salvo in a series of prolonged campaigns by the FBI, CIA, local law enforcement, and politicians to portray travel to Cuba by leftwing dissidents as a threat to U.S. national security. Alleging covert Cuban involvement in left-wing political bombings, espionage, street demonstrations, and growing public interest in socialism, U.S. officials claimed that Cuba's relationship with American radicals posed an internal security threat. Lurid media coverage focused in particular on the Venceremos Brigade, denounced on the Senate floor as "missiles in human form" and accused of receiving training in guerrilla warfare and espionage by the Castro government.

The imagined perils of contact between Cuba's revolutionaries and American radicals, however, lay in their ideological, not military, nature. In 1976, the FBI summed up a decade of investigations into ties between U.S. leftists and Havana during the previous decade, concluding that the communist nation had been the single greatest foreign influence on domestic radicalism during the 1960s. Whereas the FBI had once warned of communist ideology smuggled into U.S. society from the Soviet Union during the red scares of the previous decade, by the late 1960s the bureau's focus had shifted to a Caribbean island less than 100 miles away. "For the youthful revolutionary a new model of successful revolution existed — Havana," the FBI contended, in which "the example of the Cuban revolution became the guide" for left-wing movements such as the Venceremos Brigade and the Black Panther Party, the story that is the subject of chapter 2 of this book.[16]

Yet the Cuban government also regarded some of its most zealous American admirers with dismay and suspicion. Carmichael's presence in Cuba in 1967 had barely receded from the national news before American encounters with

Cuba again made headlines, this time as dozens of Americans began hijacking aircraft to the island beginning in January 1968. Seeking political asylum, sanctuary from criminal charges, contact with Third World revolutionary movements, and simple adventure, hijackers often framed air piracy as an act of political protest. Cuban immigration officials were not always convinced, however, and imprisoned many hijackers as suspected spies and common criminals. Making ninety attempts to reach Cuba in commandeered aircraft in five years, a rate higher than all other global hijacking incidents combined, American air piracy ultimately forced the U.S. and Cuban governments into an unprecedented series of diplomatic negotiations. Viewing the hijackings as a liability, the Cuban government moved to counter its "outlaw" mystique in the American popular imaginary, entering into a rare diplomatic collaboration with Washington in 1973 to end the hijacking surge — the subject of chapter 3.

By the mid-1970s, left-wing politics were in decline — or so it seemed. If street protests in the United States now rarely drew crowds of tens of thousands, it was also true that progressive organizations were also more likely to be institutionalized, had developed more sophisticated political analyses, and were more likely to be globally oriented.[17] As the Venceremos Brigade now become a stable, pro-Cuba solidarity organization, sending work contingents to Cuba every summer throughout the decade, a wide variety of other left-leaning political, cultural, and academic groups sent delegations of activists to Cuba, including the Center for Cuban Studies in New York, *The Black Scholar* journal (based at Temple University), and the CPUSA. Amid the short-lived détente in U.S.-Cuba relations under the Carter administration, Cuba solidarity activists in the United States renewed their push for the normalization of diplomatic relations and the end of the embargo and travel ban. This time, leverage came from an unexpected quarter: Cuban American communities, long considered dependable hotbeds of hawkish anticommunism, whose voters had been successfully courted by the Republican Party.

Cuban American progressives and intellectuals, the subject of chapter 4 of this book, played a pivotal role in resetting the island's relationships with its diaspora. In 1977, a movement of young exilic Cubans in cities across the nation, including the anti-Castro strongholds of Miami, Florida, and Union City, New Jersey, began defying the anticommunist leaders of their parents' generation to seek reconciliation with the nation of their birth. Shaped by their experiences in the African American civil rights and anti–Vietnam War movements, and their contact with Puerto Rican, Dominican, and Chicano/a social movements, these émigré youth rejected the hardline anti-Castroism that prevailed within Cuban American communities.

In the brief warming of diplomatic relations encouraged by the Carter administration, visits to Cuba by progressive and left-wing Cuban Americans, traveling as the Antonio Maceo Brigade, helped catalyze a critical shift in the Cuban government's relations with its diaspora. Although U.S.-Cuba relations had cooled again by the end of the decade, prompted by Washington's disapproval of Cuba's robust aid to anticolonial movements in Southern Africa, the Antonio Maceo Brigade's efforts left an indelible mark. Reverberating in exilic Cuban political and intellectual circles for years, the Maceo Brigade's activism created an unprecedented space for Cuban American progressive politics, initiating an early precursor to the growing openness among Cuban Americans toward reconciliation with the Cuban government. These early fractures within the seemingly unified front of hardline anti-Castroism within Cuban American communities, long a causal factor in Washington's punitive foreign policy toward post-1959 Cuba, would later have significant implications for the eventual warming of U.S.-Cuba relations in 2014.

But with the dawning of the Reagan Revolution, the politics of the global Cold War again darkened. The acceleration of anti-Cuba rhetoric within U.S. officialdom in the 1980s signaled the renewal of U.S.-Cuba hostilities, and with it, the relationship between Cuba and American dissidents again became imbricated within U.S. foreign relations. Classified by the Reagan administration as a State Sponsor of Terrorism in 1982, Cuba's continuing support, both real and purported, for left-wing movements and governments in Africa and Central America became Washington's primary justification for the hardening of the U.S. embargo. In 1987, news reports revealed that Assata Shakur, a former Black Panther who had escaped from a New Jersey prison, was living in Cuba as a protected political exile. Shakur's presence on the island triggered renewed scrutiny of one of the most electric elements of Cuba's relationship with the American Left: the Castro government's consistent provision of formal political asylum to U.S. dissidents — the subject of chapter 5.

Imprisoned in connection to a 1973 killing of a New Jersey State Trooper, although her supporters disputed the evidence against her, Shakur, who had been previously classified by the Cuban government as a U.S. political prisoner, became a global cause célèbre. While Cuba's provision of asylum for left-wing American political asylees and fugitives wanted on criminal charges had been a thorn in the side of local U.S. law enforcement agencies and the State Department for years, news of Shakur's asylum in Cuba initiated a political process that transformed the return of U.S. asylees into one of Washington's essential requirements for the normalization of diplomatic relations. Cuba's provision of political asylum to Shakur and other U.S. dissidents now became imbricated within U.S.-Cuba relations. In turn, the fate of Shakur and other 1960s-era political exiles on the island became wedded to the future of the Cuban Revolution. Unbowed, Cuba asserted its sovereign right to grant sanctuary to those it believed to be facing legitimate political persecution. In doing so, Havana signaled its continued willingness to support social justice movements within the borders of its northern neighbor, especially the remnants of the black freedom struggle, even at significant political cost, long after the end of the sixties and the decline of the Cold War itself.

Cuba and American Radicalism

The Cuban Revolution was one of the formative events of the turbulent global 1960s era, one that reverberated deep into North America. The rebels' victory against a U.S.-supported dictatorial regime on New Year's Day in 1959 was the opening salvo in an era that would be scarred by war in Vietnam and transformed by domestic protest. For a generation of Americans, the events unfolding in the Caribbean, and Washington's response to them, would be the first inkling that their government's Cold War calculus was animated by forces other than neighborly goodwill.[18] Cuba's revolution prompted new critiques of U.S. power in the world and suggested new radical possibilities at home. As historian Van Gosse has contended, the impact of Cuba's revolution was an early spark that helped set off "the era of renewed social and political struggle known as 'the sixties'" north of the Florida Straits.[18] The significance of Cuba's revolution for American leftists was due in large part to the perception that the island's popular insurgency against the dictatorial government of Fulgencio Batista represented a departure from both Cold War liberalism and the orthodoxies of the Old Left, suggesting a new heterodox left politics oriented away from the precedent of Soviet communism, with its shadow of totalitarianism, and toward liberation movements in the rising Third World.[20]

Widely perceived as a political transformation imbued with humanistic ideals, the Cuban Revolution elicited significant interest within the U.S. intellectual Left.[21] Marxist theorists Paul Sweezy and Leo Huberman, who had distanced themselves from Soviet communism, became early, if critical, supporters of the Cuban Revolution, writing and coauthoring a series of articles and books evaluating the evolving revolution.[22] Iconoclastic sociologist C. Wright Mills's forceful defense of the revolution, entitled *Listen, Yankee: The Revolution in Cuba,* drawing upon all-night conversations with Fidel Castro, and journalist Robert Scheer and sociologist Maurice Zeitlin's *Cuba: An American Tragedy* became key texts for a generation hungry for information on the revolution south of Florida.[23]

Left-wing intellectuals and writers were prominently represented among the first broad-based U.S. support coalition for Cuban Revolution, the Fair Play for Cuba Committee (FPCC), formed in New York in April 1960 to lobby for recognition of Cuba's right to self-determination amid mounting U.S.-Cuba tensions during the Kennedy era. Fair Play's multiracial cast of members and supporters, which included writers, Marxist and black radical intellectuals, and members of the cultural left, including James Baldwin, Amiri Baraka, Carleton Beals, Truman Capote, Harold Cruse, Waldo Frank, Allen Ginsberg, Lawrence Ferlinghetti, Norman Mailer, Jean-Paul Sartre, and William Appleman Williams, attempted to shield Cuba's revolution from rising U.S. animus with editorials and political organizing, composing one of the first multiracial, truly anti-imperialist formations of the American sixties era.[24]

For American leftists, Cuba, more than any other nation, came to symbolize the liberation of the rising decolonized world and of new formulations of social transformation born of Third World resistance to foreign domination and colonial legacies. Whereas orthodox Marxism conceptualized a global industrial working class — those with their hands on the levers of the capitalist means of production — as the human engine of revolution, the Cuban insurgency had relied upon the energies of those positioned outside the formal industrial system, including rural peasants, students, and intellectuals. Indeed, for the largely student-based U.S. New Left of the early 1960s, the critical role played by students at the University of Havana in the 1959 revolution mirrored their own class positionality, whose political potential the Old Left had dismissed. As Fredric Jameson has observed, the Cuban Revolution "announce[d] the impending 60s as a period of unexpected political innovation rather than the confirmation of older social and conceptual schemes."[25]

If communism as practiced in the Soviet Union and China had come to represent totalitarianism and millions dead, Cuba's "tropical Marxism" had avoided the state violence that had come to be associated in the public mind with both communist regimes and with Cuba's capitalist Latin American neighbors. Despite documented authoritarianism and a formidable internal security apparatus, Cuba had no death squads or extrajudicial executions and had created one of the most secure societies in the world. Following the Bay of Pigs invasion, when Fidel Castro declared his adherence to communism for the first time and Havana began to publicly align itself with the Soviet Union, Cuba attained increasing support from the U.S. Old Left. Although the appeal of Cuba's revolution in North America, with its promise of a new socialism less fettered to the Soviet and Chinese ideological models, came at a time when the CPUSA's resonance with younger radicals was sagging, leader Gus Hall, a stalwart supporter of Moscow, readily acknowledged Cuba's appeal. In a letter to Fidel Castro, Hall spoke of the "prestige and influence of the Cuban revolution" within America, and of "a new generation of youth [that] is growing up ... inspired by the seeming miracle of your revolution."[26]

By the late 1960s, Cuba's revolution had solidified a wide base of support within the multifaceted U.S. Left, becoming its most conspicuous global ideological influence. In his influential study of SDS, the largest formation of the New Left, scholar Kirkpatrick Sale observed that among the group's various foreign influences and contacts, which included student movements in Europe and Vietnamese insurgents and diplomats, "by far the most important international turn was toward Cuba," which had quickly become a source of both inspiration and collaboration even after the revolution's formal turn toward communism after 1961.[27] SNCC organizer and writer Elizabeth Sutherland Martínez's journalistic report on Cuba, published in 1969 as a book entitled *The Youngest Revolution*, similarly illustrated the way in which American and global activists perceived the radicalism of the Cuban Revolution as a potential blueprint for bringing into being a new society based upon economic, gender, and racial equality.[28]

The Cuban Revolution's symbolic realignment of the global locus of revolutionary theory away from Europe and toward the Third World captured the imaginations of U.S. activists and intellectuals of color, who looked to the decolonizing world as a source of inspiration and radical theory. Scholar Cynthia A. Young locates a key foundation for diverse articulations of 1960s radicalism among globally-oriented U.S. activists of color during the 1960s — a "U.S. Third World Left"— within the debates about race, identity, and culture spurred by Cuba's 1959 revolution.[29] African American, Asian American, and Latino/a radicals embraced transnational identities that allowed them to view themselves not as domestic racialized minorities but as members of a global majority. Transcending the geographic and conceptual limits of the nation-state, these activists located their domestic struggles for racial and economic justice within a larger geopolitical context of decolonization and national self-determination.[30] These activists of color conceptualized their movements not only within the East-West binaries of the Cold War, but within a North–South framework forged of decolonization and Third World revolution.

Cuba's revolution loomed especially large within the U.S. black radical imaginary. As historian Kevin Gaines notes, black radical intellectuals such as W. E. B. Du Bois and Julian Mayfield were "powerfully drawn to the utopian sites of radical hope exemplified by Ghana and the Cuban Revolution" in the late 1950s.[31] Although Malcolm X had followed the development of the Cuban Revolution with pointed interest, he was particularly impressed with Fidel

Castro, with whom he conversed during the Cuban premier's stay at Harlem's Hotel Theresa in September of 1960, telling a reporter that "I am very interested in Cuba... the only white person that I have really liked was Fidel."[32]

Armed revolution in Cuba and Algeria provided the global backdrop for Malcolm X's insistence that Africans in America were not bound to the doctrines of nonviolence.[33] Cuba's revolution, like Algeria's two years later, signaled that armed struggle was a legitimate tactic of anticolonial liberation, announcing the dawning global 1960s as the era of the ballot *and* the bullet in the struggle for national liberation in the Third World.[34] Like Ghana in the late 1950s, travel to revolutionary Cuba allowed U.S. black radicals to interact directly with a global radical public, forging people-to-people ties in Cuba between the subjects of North America's "internal colonies" and the Third World.[35]

Imagining post-1959 Cuba as a sanctuary from U.S.-style white supremacy and an opportunity to forge political connections with African diasporic and global anticolonial movements, African American perceptions of the new Cuba's racial project paralleled earlier renderings of the island by U.S. Pan-Africanists, who understood the island nation as a vital part of the African diaspora, one whose fate was bound up with that of black North Americans. The circulations of African-descended people between Cuba and the United States in the early and mid-twentieth century had influenced black radical politics in the United States long before Cuba's 1959 revolution.[36]

Later encounters between African Americans and Cuba occurred as black activists, artists, and intellectuals traveled to Cuba to evaluate the revolution's claims to have forged a break with the island's racial past.[37] While Cuba's bid to transcend the color line through revolution was not unique — over two dozen nations in the global south had declared formal independence from European colonialism by the mid-1960s — the importance of Cuba's revolution within the U.S. black radical imaginary was enabled by its close geographical proximity to the United States, its large population of people of African descent, and long-standing ties between the two nations facilitated by slavery, trade, empire, and cultural exchange. A 1960 visit to Cuba organized by FPCC, whose founding members were approximately one-third African American, included then beat poet LeRoi Jones (later to become Amiri Baraka), advocate of black armed self-defense Robert F. Williams, social critic Harold Cruse, and writers John Henrik Clarke, Julian Mayfield, and Sarah Wright. The trip, which was planned to coincide with a commemoration of the rebel victory over the U.S.-supported Batista dictatorship, allowed the travelers to witness the early stages of the new nation's social experiment, which had visibly empowered

Afro-Cubans, profoundly affecting the American visitors' ideas about the possibilities for antiracist social change stateside. The trip radicalized LeRoi Jones, who wrote that "the idea of 'a revolution' had been foreign to me"[38] and summed up his Cuban experience years later as "a turning point in my life."[39]

In Cuba, the legendary advocate of black armed self-defense, Robert F. Williams, already known on the island for his leadership in armed confrontations with the Ku Klux Klan in North Carolina, noted the presence of high-ranking black military commander Juan Almeida in Fidel Castro's army and was stunned at the sight of armed black men from the rebel army and militias in the streets of Havana. In 1961, after the FBI sought to arrest Williams on trumped-up kidnapping charges in North Carolina, Williams fled to Cuba, were he was granted formal political asylum.[40] Although Williams would later question the Cuban government's commitment to full racial equality for Afro-Cubans despite the revolution's antiracist agenda, Cuba's revolutionary experiment initially offered Williams, who considered himself a political refugee from Jim Crow white supremacy, a glimpse of a "shrine of hope ... three weeks of the only freedom I have ever known."[41]

By the 1970s, as evidence that Cuba's social programs had significantly ameliorated racial disparities in health, education, and housing became widely publicized, Cuban socialism figured within the political imaginations of a wide range of African American intellectuals, activists, and public officials, some of whom participated in delegations to Cuba to evaluate race relations on the island or traveled there for conferences. A sojourn to the socialist island, it seemed, had an uncanny ability to clarify personal political commitments. Writer and filmmaker Toni Cade Bambara credited a 1973 trip to Cuba as an experience that solidified her belief that writing was the tool with which she could effect positive change in the world. Speaking with filmmaker Louis Massiah, Bambara recalled that after the trip, "I began to think that writing could be a way to engage in struggle, it could be a weapon, a real instrument for transformation politics."[42] Writer Alice Walker, who also traveled to Cuba during this period, became a lifelong supporter of Cuba's efforts to build a society based upon economic and racial justice as a result. Writing in the *New York Times* in 1977, Walker recounted a meeting with a Cuban Institute for Friendship Among the People (ICAP) worker that had reminded her of a family member. "Before the Cuban Revolution," Walker wrote, "Pablo Diaz had been like my father, a man who might have belonged to any country, or to none, so poor was he."[43]

If the impulse to seek foreign horizons and new theoretical inspirations is as universal a claim as can be made about the youth of the global sixties era, white Americans at times sought to align themselves with Cuba's revolution for somewhat different reasons. As scholar Laura Pulido observes, youth of the 1960s became radicalized for different reasons, often in ways that were linked to their racial positionality within American society. As a young "rebel with a cause," the image of Castro as a ruggedly independent and idealistic leader resonated with American cultural tropes of the 1950s, particularly for young white men. A "great going out into the world" by politicized white youth, disaffected with their social location in a deeply unequal world, drew some of them physically to Cuba in the late 1950s as it would bring others into the segregated American South as civil rights volunteers a few years later.[44]

Support for the Cuban Revolution among white Americans was evident early in the insurgency against Batista. Journalist Herbert Matthews, in his sympathetic account of the *fidelista* rebel campaign for the *New York Times* in 1957, portrayed Castro as akin to a modern-day Robin Hood, one who was seizing the destiny of the nation away from a despot on behalf of the dispossessed. "Here," wrote Matthews, "was an educated, dedicated fanatic, a man of ideals, of courage and of remarkable qualities of leadership."[45] Longtime activist and writer Tom Hayden credited the Cuban Revolution as one of the key events that propelled him into a lifetime of politics.[46] Images of the guerillas' triumphant march into Havana on New Year's Day in 1959, broadcast worldwide, solidified the revolution's image as a popular victory against tyranny.

Years later, Todd Gitlin's canonic memoir of the sixties era would proceed less than two pages before invoking the moment: "We saw the black-and-white footage of bearded Cubans wearing fatigues, smoking big cigars, grinning big grins to the cheers of throngs deliriously happy at the news that Batista had fled; and we cheered too. The overthrow of a brutal dictator, yes. But more, on the face of the striding barbudos surrounded by adoring crowds we read redemption—a revolt of young people, underdogs, who might just cleanse one scrap of earth of the bloodletting and misery we had heard about all our lives. From a living room in the Bronx we saluted our unruly champions."[47]

For many white Americans, the revolution's leaders seemed both foreign and familiar. Certainly, romantic portrayals of the Cuban rebels as independent, bearded outlaws resonated with Beat-era tropes of revolt against the conformity and alienation of straight, clean-cut America, soon to blossom into the cultural rebellion of hippiedom, whose shaggy devotees uncannily resembled Castro's longed-haired rebels of the Sierra Maestra. But the resonance between the white New Left and the Cuban Revolution was above all about the perception of a shared political worldview. Although critics derided the New Left's embrace of Ernesto "Che" Guevara as the reckless romanticization of a Third World communist by privileged white middle-class students far removed from the grim realities of revolution, the identification between the New Left and Guevara requires a more rigorous consideration. Guevara's political evolution displays unexpected parallels with that of white American leftists who had found inspiration in Cuba, and the arc of Guevara's youthful path to radicalization mirrored that of many middle-class radicals in the United States. Born to a politically progressive, middle-class Argentine family of Irish and Basque origins, with aspirations to become a doctor, Guevara's social upbringing on the higher rungs of Argentine society was not dissimilar to that of a number of white U.S. radicals.

Cast in this light, Guevara's social positionality as a young man bears resemblance to the mostly white, middle-class members of SDS, who described themselves reflectively in their 1962 Port Huron Statement as those "bred in at least modest comfort, housed now in universities, looking uncomfortably to the world we inherit."[48] Coming of age in an elevated economic and racial position relative to his surroundings, Guevara, too, witnessed poverty and oppression not as part of his lived experience, but after he had left home to travel through South America, a journey of personal transformation, chronicled in diary entries, that would eventually be published as *The Motorcycle Diaries*. There, in the heart of *América*, the stark inequality that he witnessed profoundly affected him. For Guevara, it was a radicalizing experience not unlike that of white college students from the U.S. North who joined the Freedom Rides and civil rights marches of the Deep South. Witnessing extreme injustice, while incidental to their own range of lived experiences, nevertheless impelled them to seek a new social consciousness, convincing them to side with the oppressed. Guevara has more in common with white, middle-class American radicals traveling to Cuba than at first meets the eye.[49]

Organized expressions of American leftist solidarity with Cuba waned for several years after 1963, due in no small part to the discovery that Kennedy assassin Lee Harvey Oswald had been a member of FPCC. Indeed, U.S. Senate hearings had earlier revealed that FPCC received funds from the Cuban government to pay for a *New York Times* advertisement seeking to dispel misconceptions about the Cuban Revolution circulating in the U.S. press, allowing critics to charge that FPCC was a Cuban front.[50] Although the veracity of Oswald's connection to FPCC was soon cast into doubt — Oswald, in fact, had not been known to the Committee's national office when he apparently appointed himself the sole member of the New Orleans chapter that he had founded[51] — a cloud hung over the group's legacy.

Members of the U.S. Left continued to engage Cuba after the disbanding of the FPCC in the mid-1960s, albeit on a far smaller scale. The CPUSA retained cordial relations with Havana throughout the decade, sending delegations of party members to Cuba and laying the foundations for the island's substantial support for the "Free Angela Davis" movement of the early 1970s after Davis, a CPUSA member, was accused of aiding a California courthouse shootout.[52] The Progressive Labor Party sent a solidarity contingent of students to the island in 1964, a group which included Max Stanford, the leader of the Revolutionary Action Movement, and Ernie Allen, founder of the Soul Students Advisory Council.[53] In 1965, Robert F. Williams left Cuba for political exile in China, citing the Cuban government's unwillingness to support his ambitions for armed rebellion in the United States, ending the first phase of the historical engagement between Cuba and the African American freedom movement.

Yet a new phase of American leftist engagement with Cuba would soon begin. Stokely Carmichael's proclamation of solidarity with Cuba's revolution from the stage at OLAS was the forerunner to a series of encounters between the multiracial American Left and Cuba at the end of the decade. These encounters, involving thousands of protagonists amid an increasingly volatile political climate domestically and globally, would exert a far greater impact on both the contours of U.S. radicalism and on U.S.-Cuba diplomatic relations than anything that had come before. It is this high point of the arc of relations between the Cuban Revolution and the U.S. Left, from roughly 1968 through the decline of the Cold War, that this book examines.

Overview

In its broadest terms, *Cuban Revolution in America* is about the relationship between post-1959 Cuba and American left-wing social movements. It merges three primary areas of historical and interdisciplinary inquiry: the social, cultural, and diplomatic interplay between the United States and Cuba within the geopolitical context of the global Cold War; the tumult of the "long sixties" in America and the multifaceted, multiracial protest and social justice movements that arose out of it; and the understudied influence of decolonization and Third World nationalist and anti-imperialist ferment upon American life and politics. Beginning in the tumult of the late 1960s and concluding after the decline of the Cold War, this book explores how Cuba's global image as an idealized model of Third World self-determination, racial equality, and socialist redistribution inspired left-wing Americans to formulate themselves as global political actors beyond the geographical and conceptual bounds of the U.S. state, as they linked their demands for domestic social justice to global resistance to U.S. power in the world. Focusing in particular on the experiences of four distinct groups of Americans who forged relationships with Cuba, including solidarity activists, airplane hijackers, Cuban American progressives, and African American political exiles, I seek to show how left-wing American encounters with Cuba created a counterpoint to U.S. power while influencing U.S.-Cuba diplomatic relations.

This book is also about how Cuba functioned in the American radical imaginary. For the U.S. multiracial Left, Cuba stood as an idealized terrain of liberatory possibility and radical hope, one that seemed to offer an alternative to capitalism, racism, and U.S. global hegemony, as well as a portal to global radicalism and Third World revolution. Yet in conceiving of Cuba in this way, Americans at times relied upon romanticized constructions of the Cuban nation and its revolution that flattened the complexity of the island's history, culture, and politics.

Cuban Revolution in America has three primary goals. First, it seeks to contribute to a rapidly expanding body of scholarship that has globalized the study of the "long" sixties era by illuminating the transnational relationships between the social movements and nation-states that animated the era.[54] While much of this scholarship has focused on the linkages between movements in North America and Europe, a growing number of studies have foregrounded the centrality of the decolonizing world. Third World revolution became part of the imaginary of First World protest and social upheaval, and America in the 1960s, these scholars have argued, cannot be fully understood outside of the influence of the Third World.[55]

America in the sixties, however, also cannot be understood outside of the singular significance of the Cuban Revolution. Scholars of U.S. social movements during the "long" 1960s have repeatedly argued that Cuba's revolution was a key influence that informed, and in some cases helped to initiate, elements of a new leftism in America, one that was increasingly oriented away from the precedent of the Soviet Union and toward the insurgent Third World. The Cuban Revolution's reception within the U.S. intellectual left of the late 1950s and early 1960s, including the response by organizations such as FPCC and in intellectual and leftist circles associated with publications such as *Monthly Review*, has already been the subject of scholarship.[56] A significant body of work has also examined the relationship between the Cuban Revolution and the African American freedom struggle during this early period.[57]

But whereas these studies have emphasized the Cuban Revolution's role in the formation of the early New Left and the U.S. Third World Left, few have examined Cuba's significance beyond the formative period of the early 1960s.[58] Ample evidence indicates that Cuba's influence became more significant, not less so, by the end of the decade and beyond. I argue that Cuba's influence was greater in the late 1960s in part because left-wing movements in the United States became larger, more radicalized, more globally oriented, and more internationalist in ways that brought them more frequently into engagement with the proximate Caribbean revolution. While the U.S. Left in the early 1960s became divided over the question of socialism in Cuba, an ideological orientation that became increasingly apparent in mid-1961, by the late 1960s, the question was settled: Cuba had joined the communist world. Thus, those Americans willing to support Cuba from the mid-1960s onward were far more likely to be politically radical—a departure from the mixed liberal-progressive milieu of Cuba's earlier U.S. supporters.

Although left-wing social movements contracted again in the 1970s, Cuba nonetheless remained the most consistent foreign influence on U.S. leftism well into the 1990s, a prominence that was only eclipsed, for a time, by interest in left-wing popular movements in Central America in the 1980s in the context of the Sandinista Revolution in Nicaragua and left-wing insurgencies in Guatemala and El Salvador against U.S.-supported dictatorships. By the mid-1990s, the Zapatista movement in Chiapas, Mexico, had also captured the imagination of the U.S. Left, particularly within those sectors that had long been critical of the hegemony of the Cuban state within the island's revolution. Broadening the scope of the "ties of singular intimacy" that have been the conceptual focus of many previous studies of Cuba and the United States to include U.S. protest movements and political dissent, this book seeks to reveal the transnational encounters that have linked modern Cuba inseparably with American left-wing radicalism.

Relations between left-wing Americans and post-1959 Cuba have always been deeply imbricated within the larger structure of U.S.-Cuba diplomatic relations in the context of the Cold War. Accordingly, *Cuban Revolution in America* also seeks to build upon scholarship that has examined interactions between the two countries at the level of the state by focusing on the role that left-wing activists played in influencing U.S.-Cuba diplomatic relations. As such, I seek to add a crucial "nonstate" element to evaluations of Cold War diplomacy between Washington and Havana, a relationship that has most commonly been framed by the workings of two intransigent governments.[59] I argue that the protest politics of the late-sixties era collided with U.S.-Cuba relations through both the direct advocacy of activists working for changes in foreign policy and the reactions of the U.S. and Cuban governments to transnational encounters between Americans and Cuba. Although locked in a diplomatic impasse, left-wing Americans forced the U.S. and Cuban governments into an unprecedented series of dialogues, culminating most dramatically in a 1973 antihijacking agreement.

Indeed, the phenomenon of hijacking itself was a direct consequence of Washington's policy of diplomatic antagonism toward Cuba, which had ruptured the normal diplomatic channels of reciprocity, characterized by the absence of embassies and active extradition treaties, rendering the island an attractive sanctuary for Americans on the lam. The antihijacking agreement foreshadowed the mild thaw in relations during the coming Carter era, an opportunity that Cuban American progressive activists seized to leverage changes to both Washington's and Havana's policy on travel to the island by Cuban exiles in the United States, and to negotiate the release of Cuban political prisoners.

In the 1990s, American leftists again influenced U.S. policy, and indeed the very core of Washington-Havana relations itself, as the U.S. government increasingly used Cuba's provision of political asylum to American radicals as a justification for the maintenance and intensification of its economic, diplomatic, and covert war against the communist government in Havana. By focusing on these intersections between the American Left and Cuba, this book reveals a hidden narrative of U.S.-Cuba relations during the global Cold War.

Finally, *Cuban Revolution in America* pays particular attention to how racial and ethnic identity shaped left-wing American engagements with Cuba. Focusing upon the experiences of African Americans, exilic Cubans, and white Americans, I seek to show how their perceptions of Cuba's revolution — and especially, their (re)encounters with the island itself — contrasted in ways that were conditioned by social positionality and diverging experiences of race and nation. African American leftists, the political bloc that has provided the Cuban Revolution with its most consistent base of U.S. support since the late 1950s, regarded Cuba as a potential sanctuary from U.S. racism and an ally in the struggle for full citizenship and black freedom within America. In turn, the Cuban government sought to cultivate support in African American communities in its northern neighbor as a matter of both genuine antiracist solidarity and strategic geopolitics.

Unsurprisingly, the politics of coalition between Cuba and African Americans have sometimes been fraught with contradiction, ambivalence, and misunderstanding. While the U.S. government's resistance to full black equality, in both the 1960s and in succeeding decades, allowed the Cuban government to expose America's Cold War Achilles heel before the eyes of the world, public disagreements between the Cuban government and several prominent U.S. black activists, including Robert F. Williams, Stokely Carmichael, and Eldridge Cleaver, provided Washington with rare, if short-lived, victories in its global war of image with Havana, allowing U.S. newspapers and politicians to construct counternarratives to Cuba's image of racial equality and solidarity with global black liberation.

The contemporary persistence of antiblack racism in Cuba, as well as the Cuban government's suppression of the efforts by a small but vocal group of Afro-Cuban activists and intellectuals who have called for race-based solutions to racial inequality, continues to highlight the cracks within the Cuban Revolution's significant antiracist accomplishments — cracks that have been opportunistically exploited by U.S. opponents of the Cuban government who have used the persistence of racial inequality in Cuba to attack the legitimacy of the revolutionary project itself. Although Cuba has been curiously marginal to most academic studies of the import of the Cold War for U.S. racial politics, a significant body of work has examined the global dimensions of the African American freedom struggle, especially during the Cold War, and it is to this body of work that this book speaks as well.[60]

Cuban Revolution in America is formed around five interlocking chapters, each representing a distinct case study. Chapter 1 examines the origins of the Venceremos Brigade, a New Left international solidarity organization that began sending multiracial groups of volunteers to Cuba in 1969 to participate in agricultural and construction projects. Seeking to create people-to-people ties between Americans and Cubans in an effort to undermine Cold War mistrust between the nations, the Brigade articulated an anti-imperialist "foreign policy" of the multiethnic U.S. Left. The Brigade's delegations, which emphasized physical labor and solidarity work, constituted a kind of "radical Peace Corps" as an explicit counterpoint to the remnants of Kennedy's Alliance for Progress. I argue that the group's solidarity politics sometimes depended, however, upon the construction of Cuba in idealized terms, ignoring contradictions within the revolutionary project and evidence of authoritarian and antidemocratic tendencies. Nonetheless, the Brigade soon became the largest Cuba solidarity organization in the world. By creating a lasting relationship of solidarity between the Cuban government and left-wing Americans that continues to this day, the Brigade laid the foundations for future relationships between U.S. leftists and Latin America in the 1970s and 1980s, including in El Salvador and Nicaragua, that would have meaningful consequences for U.S. foreign policy in the region.

Building upon my examination of the Venceremos Brigade, chapter 2 illuminates the U.S. government's portrayal of travel to Cuba by American dissidents as a threat to national security. Focusing on FBI and CIA investigations of the Venceremos Brigade, as well as other left-wing formations such as the Black Panther Party, I evaluate the U.S. government's claims that Cuba was indoctrinating its American visitors with transplanted Soviet communism and indigenous Cuban revolutionary theory, training them in guerrilla warfare and terrorism, and recruiting them as spies for Havana. I argue that although U.S. government agencies failed to present credible evidence of these claims, its efforts nonetheless highlighted the prevailing anxiety within U.S. law enforcement and national security apparatuses that Cuba was an *internal*, ideological threat to the United States, as well as an external, military one.

Moreover, while the FBI's claims against the Brigade were spurious, Cuba did promise limited military training to members of the Black Panther Party, while several academic supporters of Cuban sovereignty later admitted to conducting high-level espionage for Havana, including from within the State Department, in an effort to aid Cuba in defending itself from hostile U.S. policies. While this facet of U.S.-Cuba relations has significant implications for understanding Cold War relations between the two nations, it has never been explored in published scholarship. As mutual espionage allegations between the United States and Cuba continue to pose an impediment to normal diplomatic relations, this chapter provides new historical context for these contemporary debates.

Chapter 3 examines the rise of airline hijackings to Cuba by U.S. citizens. Seeking political asylum, sanctuary from racism, participation in Third World liberation movements, haven from criminal charges, and apolitical adventure, Americans hijacked more planes to Cuba during this period than all other global hijacking incidents combined. I argue that American hijackers seeking to reach Cuba were also strongly attracted by the Caribbean island's "outlaw mystique" in the American cultural imaginary. Constructing Cuba as both a lawless space for the realization of personal revolutionary adventure, and as a portal to Third World liberation movements within the geopolitical context of the Cold War and decolonization, American hijackers formulated themselves as political refugees from a racist and capitalist America, even as some hijackers reproduced age-old fantasies of imperial entitlement by demanding that Cuba welcome them as comrades. Influencing U.S.-Cuba relations and resulting in unprecedented diplomatic collaboration between Havana and Washington to produce a mutual antihijacking agreement, the hijacking outbreak of 1968–73 marks the unlikely meeting point where political protest movements, the African American freedom struggle, and U.S.-Cuba relations collided in the late 1960s.

Chapter 4 examines the buried history of the Antonio Maceo Brigade, a coalition of Cuban American students, young professionals, and activists in the United States and Puerto Rico who advocated the normalization of U.S. relations with Cuba. Facing violent opposition from anti-Castro Cuban exiles in Miami, Union City, New Jersey, and New York, many of the group's members were openly supportive of the Cuban Revolution yet sometimes critical of the Cuban government. The group's diverse demands included both the end of U.S. bellicosity toward their homeland and the release of 3,600 political dissidents from Cuban prisons. I argue that the Maceo Brigade's bold activism created an unprecedented early political space for Cuban American progressive politics, challenging for the first time the exile community's public image of right-wing political homogeneity.

Yet the Antonio Maceo Brigade's impact was also international. As left-wing Cuban American youth traveled to Cuba and forged new relationships with the island that they had left as children, their presence helped initiate a brief but pivotal shift in the Cuban revolutionary government's historically strained relationship with the post-1959 diaspora. The group's trajectory complicates prevailing scholarly and popular narratives that emphasize Cuban American anti-Castroism, revealing an early precursor to the exile community's contemporary shift toward favoring the normalization of U.S. relations with Cuba.

Chapter 5 examines the community of U.S. political expatriates residing in Havana and the influence of their presence there upon U.S.-Cuba relations. Focusing on Cuba's provision of formal political asylum to African American radicals, the chapter traces this phenomenon through the story of Cuba's most famous foreign asylee, former Black Panther Assata Shakur. Accused of killing a New Jersey State Trooper in 1973, Shakur escaped from a U.S. prison and fled to Cuba in 1984, where she was granted formal sanctuary. As U.S. officials called for her extradition, Shakur defiantly characterized Cuba as a modern "palenque." As U.S. diplomatic and law-enforcement pressure on Cuba to extradite Shakur and other U.S. radical exiles in Cuba mounted in the 1990s, the U.S. Department of State began to insist that the return of the exiles — with Shakur always given highest priority — constituted a precondition for the normalization of diplomatic relations and the removal of Cuba's much-contested designation as a "State Sponsor of Terrorism." Shakur's case demonstrates the wedding of Washington's antipathy toward the Cuban Revolution with its persistent efforts to destroy grassroots black liberation politics. Conjoined now within the discourse of "antiterrorism," Washington's hostility toward both Cuban socialism and the legacy of the Black Panther Party suggests the durability of these antagonisms long after the decline of the civil rights, Black Power, and Cold War eras to which they are normally linked.

Although *Cuban Revolution in America* is intended to fill a scholarly lacuna, it makes no pretense of being comprehensive. Indeed, many of the historical engagements and protagonists examined briefly in the following pages could well be the subject of book-length studies in their own right. Others are overlooked entirely. In choosing a focus within an exceedingly long and complex set of histories, much is necessarily omitted, and silences inevitably arise.[61] I hope that this book will be not the final word but the beginning of further inquiry, scholarship, and debate.

1

Venceremos Means "We Will Win"
The Venceremos Brigades, Cuba, and the U.S. Left

I envy you. You North Americans are very lucky. You are fighting the most important fight of all—you live in the heart of the beast.
—**Ernesto "Che" Guevara,** attributed

I grew up an Okie, and could really appreciate people having a concrete floor instead of dirt. Cuba was a beacon to the world for me.
—**Roxanne Dunbar-Ortiz,** *Outlaw Woman*

IN AUGUST 1970, the Venceremos Brigade commissioned a fundraising advertisement in *Ramparts*, a glossy magazine of politics and letters that had become the unofficial cultural organ of the New Left. The ad featured an ink illustration of menacing armed men running through a forest, juxtaposed against an image of Cuban workers placidly harvesting sugarcane. Underneath was the fundraising appeal: "The U.S. Government Sends Mercenaries and Death to Cuba: What Are You Sending?"[1]

The Venceremos Brigade had made headlines the previous winter by sending a delegation of 216 American volunteers to Cuba, in violation of the U.S. travel ban, to participate in the island's sugarcane harvest. There they worked side-by-side with Cuban students, workers, and revolutionaries, including Fidel Castro himself, as well as volunteer brigades from across the Third World and Europe. Social justice movements in the United States had elicited coverage in the Cuban press for years, so when *Granma*, Cuba's largest newspaper, ran a front-page article about the Venceremos Brigade's arrival, it was opposite a feature story on the Los Angeles Police Department's armed assault upon the regional headquarters of the Black Panther Party that same day, which had provoked a ferocious four-hour gun battle. The Venceremos Brigade, *Granma* explained, had come "in solidarity with the Cuban Revolution" and consisted of members of Students for a Democratic Society (SDS), the Black Panthers, and organizations representing Chicano/as and Puerto Ricans. Noting that the Brigade had drawn its participants from throughout the multiethnic U.S. Left, *Granma* proclaimed that the group represented "a concrete form of opposition to Washington's attempts to strangle the Cuban Revolution."[2] The CIA took note, sending a bulletin of its own two weeks later. Echoing *Granma*'s characterization, the Agency noted that the Brigade was composed of "radicalized American youth, all sharing pro-Castro sentiments and opposing what they term U.S. imperialism."[3]

Fashioning itself as kind of a radical Peace Corps for the civil rights and antiwar generation, the Venceremos Brigade hoped to undermine the atmosphere of Cold War mistrust by allowing Americans to witness Cuban society with their own eyes. Borrowing their name, *Venceremos*, meaning "we shall win," from a Cuban revolutionary slogan, the Brigade's organizers launched chapters in a dozen U.S. cities in a bid to create a grassroots counterweight to the Cold War stalemate that had gripped U.S.–Cuba relations since the early 1960s. As an anti-imperialist answer to John F. Kennedy's Alliance for Progress, which sought to erode Soviet and Cuban influence in Latin America through the soft power of development and economic aid, the Venceremos Brigade embodied a form of grassroots soft power, one that created a nonstate route through which Americans could directly support Cuban self-determination through symbolic aid and volunteerism.

Contrasting their vision of a world shaped by transnational solidarity and people-to-people aid against the venality of corporate militarism and global capitalism, members of the Brigade took rhetorical aim at U.S. foreign policy. In news releases and public statements, the activists condemned U.S. diplomatic policies that, since the early 1960s, had sought to isolate Cuba within the world system. They denounced the CIA's sabotage campaigns on the island, which had accelerated markedly during the Nixon era, as well as Washington's willingness to allow paramilitary attacks by Cuban exiles to proceed unhindered from South Florida.[4] The Brigade criticized the U.S. trade embargo against Cuba that, while designed to suffocate the island's state-run economy, had inflicted its deprivation primarily upon the Cuban people.

Most of all, the Brigade challenged the ban on travel to Cuba by U.S. citizens, a policy initiated in January 1961, after Washington broke off diplomatic relations with Havana.[5] Although the U.S. travel ban existed seemingly in direct violation of the UN's Universal Declaration of Human Rights, Article 13 of which asserted that "Everyone has the right to leave any country, including his own, and to return to his country," the Kennedy administration had justified the ban under the 1917 Trading with the Enemy Act, which grants the

President the authority to suspend all financial transactions, including those related to travel, with enemy nations.[6] But the ban's true purpose, members of the Venceremos Brigade argued, was not merely to keep U.S. currency out of Castro's coffers. It was also designed to keep Americans from witnessing revolutionary Cuba for themselves — and thereby judging for themselves the evils or merits of a socialist society. Breaking this "information blockade" would therefore become one of the group's primary political projects.

Arriving on the island on December 8, 1969, 216 American *brigadistas* who composed the first contingent of the Venceremos Brigade traveled at the invitation of the Cuban Institute for Friendship Among the People (ICAP) to labor in support of the ambitious *zafra de los diez millones* — the historic 10 million tons harvest, slated for 1970 — on which Cuba had gambled its hopes of economic development. Three months later, in late February, a delegation of 687 American recruits replaced them, staying on the island until late April. Another contingent of 409 arrived in August 1970, this time to tend newly planted fields of citrus trees on the Isla de la Juventud off Cuba's southwestern coast. By the early 1970s, the Brigade, which now traveled to the island yearly and whose volunteer efforts focused increasingly on the construction of houses, was well established as the most prominent pro-Cuba solidarity group in the United States and among the largest in the world. Sponsoring workshops and cultural events across the United States, the Brigade described itself as a "year-round, multiracial political education project which attempts to contribute to the political formation of the U.S. people through the development of anti-imperialist consciousness."[7]

Formed amid the tumult of the Vietnam War era, the Brigade situated itself within the multiethnic U.S. Left's blossoming internationalist imaginary, one that was increasingly linking demands for domestic racial and economic justice to global resistance to U.S. militarism. Hoping to steer the "foreign relations" of the broad U.S. Left toward a politics of Third World solidarity, the activists of the Brigade framed its transgressions of Washington's ban on travel to Cuba as an act of civil disobedience against the hubris of U.S. exceptionalism and an affirmation of North American solidarity with the people of nations living in the shadow of U.S. power. Volunteering their labor in the service of Cuban socialism and working alongside both Cubans and volunteers from around the world, *brigadistas* formulated themselves as internationalist political actors on the global terrain of anti-imperialism, representatives of a dissident movement deep within the "heart of the empire."

Yet the Brigade's objectives were as much local as they were global. In showing their solidarity with global left-wing movements, *brigadistas* hoped to glean insights from political movements abroad that could be incorporated into political struggles at home. Reflecting upon its origins in 1974, the Brigade's self-fashioning exemplified the way in which large sections of the multifaceted U.S. Left continued to identify with Cuba's revolution, a decade after its rise to power, as a symbol of the potentials of revolutionary political transformation, one whose social gains in the arenas of health, education, racial equality, and economic justice served as a potential model for building a more egalitarian society at home:

> We, who participated in the civil rights movement, the battles for self determination of Black, Chicano, Native American and Puerto Rican People, the student protests, the anti-war movement, the fight for women's liberation, could never again be convinced that our society could be healed without deep and fundamental change. We began to look outside the borders of the United States toward those who were already building societies of justice, equality and human dignity: we were ready to learn from their examples.[8]

The Brigade's efforts to craft a foreign policy of the American movement through direct contact with the Cuban Revolution remains an underexplored episode within global linkages of left-wing U.S. radicalism during the "long" sixties era, as U.S. leftists increasingly framed their political visions in global terms, looking abroad — and especially southward — for inspiration. The prevailing notion of "the Third World as the future," as historian Odd Arne Westad has observed, made Africa, Asia, and Latin America part of the imaginary of the European and American New Left at a time when First World radicals were looking for alternatives to the perceived moral bankruptcy of their own societies.[9] And yet, remarkably little scholarship has examined the most influential of Third World revolutions within the imagination of the multiethnic U.S. Left. Cuba's well-publicized achievements in social welfare, its defiant insistence on diplomatic equality in its dealings with the United States, and its prestige as a supporter — and sometimes a sponsor — of armed revolutionary and anticolonial movements in the Third World contributed to the island nation's outsized significance for U.S. protest movements. The Venceremos Brigade's search for inspiration, usable political theory, and global belonging in Cuba provides a glimpse into the Third World gaze of many U.S. radicals during the late 1960s, and the ways in which its focus upon the Caribbean nation during the 1960s and 1970s helped crystallize this internationalism into a tangible "nonstate foreign policy" of the multifaceted American Left.

These transnational encounters were not without ambivalence and contradiction, however. In seeking to defend Cuba's revolution, members of the

Brigade at times flattened the complexity of the Cuban Revolution's successes and failures in an effort to articulate a cohesive counterpoint to Washington's position of unrelenting antagonism. Likewise, American activists in Cuba sometimes experienced misunderstandings with their hosts, as Americans and Cubans alike sought to span the cultural, historical, and linguistic gulfs that separated them. Yet the Brigade's greatest obstacle in the early years was often itself. The early brigades experienced debilitating factionalism and interpersonal rifts, especially along the lines of race, sexual identity, and gender. While the tensions did not paralyze their solidarity work and the Brigade soon consolidated itself into the largest — and ultimately the longest-lived — Cuba solidarity organization in the world, the internal fractures evident during the early years at times revealed significant differences between the political ideologies of the Cuban government and those of its American supporters. As the largest U.S.-Cuba solidarity organization of its era, one that has continued to send a delegation to Cuba every year from 1969 up to this writing in 2017, the trajectory of the Venceremos Brigade brings the complexity of the American Left's engagement with the Cuban Revolution into vivid relief.

Building a North American Brigade

On January 2, 1969, 1 million Cubans—or one-eighth of the nation's population — crammed into Havana's Plaza de la Revolución to listen to Fidel Castro commemorate the tenth anniversary of the ousting of Fulgencio Batista and the beginning of a massive reorganization of Cuban society. Cuba's revolution, Castro emphasized, had come far, but the nation's sagging economy threatened to nullify that progress. Laughter erupted in the crowd near the Cuban leader when he announced that the coming year would have eighteen months instead of twelve, and that the New Year and Christmas holidays would therefore have to be postponed.

The rearranged calendar would be Cuba's "year of decisive effort" that sought to mobilize the nation's entire population in an all-out labor campaign to produce a record sugar harvest.[10] Sugar, the quintessential source of foreign currency for Cuba since the colonial era, had by the early 1960s become de-emphasized as the government attempted to diversify the economy and leave behind both the risks of a monoculture economy and the stigma of a crop associated with slavery and foreign dependence. By mid-decade, however, amid the stark economic realities of the struggling new nation and a sobering lack of alternatives, sugar once again regained prominence as the only viable source of foreign exchange. The Cuban government had settled upon a staggering production goal: a record 10 million tons of sugar, whose sale at the highly favorable rates extended by the Soviet Union would inject much needed cash into the economy. The harvest campaign, which would culminate in 1970, assumed the atmosphere of a war for the preservation of the revolution.[11]

Among the foreigners present in the Plaza that day were a number of Americans, including a contingent from SDS, which had been invited by Cuba's Mission to the United Nations in New York to witness the anniversary. This was not SDS's first time in Cuba. Small contingents from the group had traveled to the island previously in the decade, most recently a year earlier, when a group that included Carl Davidson, Dave Dellinger, Todd Gitlin, and Tom Hayden attended the Cultural Congress of Havana in January 1968.[12]

Unbeknownst to anyone then, however, the SDS delegation of 1969 would have a far-reaching impact on relations between the Cuban government and the multifaceted U.S. Left. Arriving via Yugoslavia and Mexico to circumvent the U.S. travel ban, the SDS delegation was installed with other foreign delegates at the Havana Libre, the hotel that had formerly been the opulent Havana Hilton in the Vedado district of the city before it had been nationalized and renamed. In the daytime, Cuban hosts guided the Americans on bus tours where they were shown revolution's development efforts: acres of newly planted citrus fields, brand new schools and hospitals, cattle farms, and the ubiquitous sugar fields. Impressed, the visitors wondered what American sympathizers could do to support the nation's efforts.

Carl Oglesby, an SDS activist who had secured his travel expenses to Havana by agreeing to cover the anniversary of the revolution for *Life* magazine, was the first to formulate the idea of Americans volunteering their labor in Cuba.[13] The delegation, Oglesby hoped, would be akin to an "illegal Peace Corps," as he put it, one that would be broad-based enough to incorporate "good, old fashioned, regular Americans as well as students," church groups, and trade unions.[14] Oglesby proposed the idea on behalf of the SDS delegation to Carlos Rafael Rodríguez, Cuba's ambassador to the United Nations.

Upon returning to the United States, however, Oglesby was promptly dismissed from the project by SDS's new National Committee, which was now controlled by the group's Weathermen faction. He had been accused, he later wrote, of trying to lead the rapidly radicalizing organization into alliances with liberal and mainstream groups. The Cuban volunteer project would proceed, SDS's new leadership made clear, only if Oglesby recused himself. Cuban officials, dismayed by Oglesby's ousting and the growing factionalism within SDS, decided to cancel the project. According to Oglesby, Ambassador Rodríguez agreed to move forward on the sole condition that Oglesby stay discreetly involved. Meeting with Rodríguez in secret to review the project's progress, which had been enthusiastically approved by Fidel Castro, without the knowledge of SDS's national organizers for the first year, Oglesby remained closely involved with the development of the organization that he had envisioned.[15]

The Venceremos Brigade rapidly gained momentum. True to Oglesby's original blueprint, organizers of the first brigade set about trying to recruit a broad delegation of volunteers that would, as the application form stated, be "representative of the radical movement in this country — black and third world people, white working class youth, students, drop-outs, returned GIs."[16] The mostly white organizers took pains to broaden the leadership and, by 1970, the organization's core would be formed around a multiracial leadership collective and an activist theory that stressed leadership by activists of color as a necessary prerequisite to principled solidarity with Cuba and the broader post-colonial world. This emphasis on domestic "Third World leadership," in the terminology of the Brigade, would help shape the group's trajectory from the early 1970s onward, as delegations soon became majority African American, Latino/a, Asian American, and Native American.

The Brigade is notable as one of the few organizations of the era that prioritized the bridging of the New Left and U.S. Third World Left, white activists with activists of color, as a precondition for a viable politics of North American solidarity with the Third World. Organizing itself into a National Committee and a series of regional organizing committees, the Brigade's activists formed working relationships with a wide range of activist groups. Regional and local committees raised money to fund their activities by holding concerts and screening Cuban films or American-made documentaries about the island. In New York, where many of the largest of the group's travel contingents originated, a sizable crowd attended a screening of Saul Landau's 1969 documentary *Fidel*; in New Orleans, the group's screening of the same film was physically attacked by anti-Castro Cuban exiles.[17]

The origins of the Brigade, rooted in both a broad-based vision of grassroots collaboration and the sectarianism that characterized the implosion of SDS, would influence the group's trajectory for years after its formation. But for the group's organizers, its initial growth out of the ashes of the white New Left's most prominent organization provided an unlikely opportunity to craft a new kind of activism. The weakening of key movement organizations of the late 1960s, they observed, had left in their wake a political vacuum. As key organizations such as SDS, SNCC, and the Black Panther Party lost vitality or were weakened by internal conflicts and government repression, former members had fewer organizational channels through which to remain politically engaged. While an estimated 2 million people across the nation had participated in the October 15th Moratorium protests in 1969 against the Vietnam War — reportedly among the largest demonstrations in world history — single-day mobilizations did not necessary translate into the creation of sustainable social movements.

Thus the formation of the Brigade grew out of conditions within the largely white New Left, as organizations such as SDS sought new ways to channel the enormous social energy of an awakened protest generation. As the group's National Committee explained, "thousands of young people politicized by [the antiwar movement] were still committed to the struggle — searching for new forms of political activity. Especially with the demise of SDS came a mass disorientation: what do we do? Where do go from here?"[18] For some activists the answer, figuratively speaking, lay abroad. The global gaze of many American leftists during the late 1960s was also a search for fresh inspiration and new models upon which to base movements built from the failures of old ones. For the Brigade, volunteer work in Cuba provided an opportunity for a rudderless movement to redefine itself. It was a utility that Brigade organizer and University of Michigan anthropology student Julie Nichamin readily acknowledged. "One of the most important aspects of the Venceremos Brigade project," Nichamin wrote, "was the contribution it could make in pulling SDS together organizationally and politically."[19]

The Brigade's vision would therefore be as much about the reconstitution of the U.S. Left as it would be about supporting Cuban national self-determination. But Cuba's revolutionary allure also provided a more existential foil. For some, a sojourn to the island promised an antidote to the perceived alienation of modern American life, an opportunity to witness a society that seemed to be so different from America, one mobilized around the communitarian goals of collective welfare and social equality instead of capitalist individualism and competition. In the eyes of American visitors, the Cubans they met seemed to evince a patriotic pride and a rooted sense of national identity that left-wing Americans lacked. As one U.S. professor visiting Cuba in 1969 opined, "I would say that a young person in the U.S. feels exactly opposite of what a young person in Cuba feels. There, a young person finds himself lost, alienated, in the Marxist sense of the word and totally divorced from the center of action."[20]

Young Americans returning from Cuba with the Brigade later echoed this sentiment, explaining that traveling to Cuba had allowed them to situate their local movements for social justice within a larger geopolitical continuum, one in which tangible victories had been achieved. As one *brigadista* put it,

"I come back from Cuba feeling much less isolated. We are not a few hundred thousand valiant but impotent souls struggling alone within the wasteland of Amerika — we are part of an international movement."[21] Travel to Cuba and exposure to an alternate political system, some Americans hoped, would allow them to redefine their activism and re-imagine the possibilities for social transformation in the United States against the hopeful backdrop of Cuba's revolutionary experiment. As one *brigadista* wrote: "All of those old dreams that we had written off as being utopian can be seen not as fantasies, but as victims of our own pessimism."[22]

Like other left-wing Americans opposing U.S. foreign policy in Asia and Latin America, members of the Brigade grappled with the ideological dilemma of how they could most effectively support Third World self-determination from their peculiar positionality as anti-imperialists living inside the empire. In addition to its adoption by New Left formations such as SDS, the politics of transnational solidarity had been embraced by communist organizations such as the Socialist Workers Party (SWP), which had also sent a delegation to Havana for the tenth anniversary of the revolution. The group, hosted by ICAP, stayed in Cuba for four weeks, visiting a wide variety of Cuban public institutions, encounters that were chronicled in the newspaper affiliated with the party, *The Militant*.[23] Yet the SWP, despite its dedication to "solidarity politics" in support of the Cuban Revolution, was also committed to a politics of bitter factionalism with other communist formations and with the New Left, preventing it from forming a broad-based coalition in support of Cuba.[24] In this respect, the Venceremos Brigade represented the first broad-based Cuba solidarity movement since the Fair Play for Cuba Committee (FPCC) of the early 1960s.[25]

The Brigade's model of international solidarity represented a new amalgamation of the era's prevailing theories about the nature of principled solidarity across differentials of racial and national power. Although the Brigade was now multiracial in composition, the Brigade's initial organizers, who produced much of the early literature, were white. Their search for "concrete work" mirrored the contemporaneous dilemmas of white "mother country radicals," as Black Panther Party cofounder Huey Newton dubbed the organization's white supporters, to identify the proper means to aid black liberation as nonblacks.[26] Although forming important alliances with white radical organizations in the 1960s, the Panthers simultaneously insisted that whites desiring to take a stand against white supremacy should do so primarily from within their own communities, where they could leverage much-needed financial resources and place pressure on the racial status quo from within, a

Members of the Venceremos Brigade in the sugarcane fields, December 1969. Photo by George Cohen.

position that Stokely Carmichael had also articulated at the Organization of Latin American Solidarity (OLAS) conference in Havana in 1967.[27] Instead of staying home to pressure the U.S. government to normalize relations with Cuba, however, the Brigade endeavored to forge direct ties to Cuba's revolutionary project. In turn, they hoped to "import" ideas from revolutionary Cuba back into the United States to nurture domestic social justice movements. The Brigade's efforts to form a political relationship with Cuba were ultimately refracted through the prism of both the group's evolving multiracial composition, which necessitated a conscious grappling with the dynamics of interracial coalition.

Unalienated Labor

Arriving by air from Mexico City on December 8, 1969, the first contingent of the Venceremos Brigade landed in the early morning darkness at Havana's José Martí Airport. As Cuban journalists photographed them and a trio of musicians serenaded them, ICAP workers offered them daiquris and then shuttled them to an international solidarity work camp in Aguacate, Havana Province, at the site of a sugar mill that had once been owned by a U.S. company but was now named for nineteenth-century Cuban revolutionary leader

Rubén Martínez Villena. The camp director was Javier Ardizones, an ICAP officer who would later serve as Cuba's ambassador to Italy. Large canvas tents on raised wooden frames composed the dormitories, and as with most agricultural labor camps around the island, the site included a sports and recreation center, an indoor facility for meetings and entertainment, an open-air movie theater, and a medical facility. There they would be joined by fifty-nine members of a Cuban volunteer youth work brigade, composed of members of Cuba's Young Communist League, and would be instructed in the use of machetes for harvesting by Reynaldo Castro Yedra, a Cuban who had become akin to a revolutionary celebrity after being anointed Cuba's "National Labor Hero" for his ability to cut record amounts of sugarcane.[28]

The Americans divided up into seven sub-brigades composed of American, Cuban, and, eventually, Vietnamese volunteers who would labor together, as one Cuban journalist put it, "without the stimulus of monetary interest."[29] While daytimes would be spent in the cane fields under the hot sun, evenings would be devoted almost exclusively to entertainment, often courtesy of some of Cuba's most acclaimed music and dance troupes, including Hermanos Bravo and El Conjunto Folklórico Nacional de Cuba — the National Folkloric Group of Cuba.[30]

Stateside, however, the Brigade's organizers had worked hard to dispel any notion that the delegations would be a tropical variant of radical tourism. Indeed, the defining characteristic of the trips would be volunteer labor. The group's recruitment literature urged U.S. activists, many of them radicalized through their experiences in the civil rights and antiwar movements, to translate their internationalist theory into praxis and commit themselves to a more tangible, *physical* stand in support of Third World self-determination. Viewing themselves as representatives of an inchoate but definable U.S. Left, *brigadistas* endeavored to express their solidarity with international struggles and voice their opposition to U.S. power in the hemisphere directly, with their bodies and with their labor. In the words of two organizers, *brigadistas* would "gain direct experience with a Third World socialist revolution and a greater understanding of 'revolution' as something which entails much more than guns in the hills, something which means hard work every day."[31]

The orientation of the Venceremos Brigades toward physical labor coincided with a shift among some sectors of both the New Left and the U.S. Third World Left to construct a theory/praxis binary, one that deemphasized the role of reflection and political education within social movements and instead placed an emphasis on "action." The Brigade's organizers hoped that participants from U.S. social movements would have the opportunity to move beyond intellectual understandings of social change and gain firsthand knowledge of life in a socialist society. Explaining their ideology in 1971, representatives of the Brigade contended that the trips had "expanded the concept of solidarity by doing concrete work while we were in Cuba. Precisely the most dynamic experience of the Brigada Venceremos is that political consciousness is transformed into productive work; and it is this concrete work itself which becomes the common denominator for a revolutionary. You are either working or you're not."[32]

In its initial recruiting efforts, the Brigade emphasized that the trips would be an opportunity for Americans to support the Cuban Revolution physically, not with rhetoric or protests, but with their bodies. In this way, the Brigade sought to initiate a new model of solidarity travel that contrasted with earlier contact between U.S. leftist organizations and the Cuban Revolution. Whereas organizations such as the Fair Play for Cuba Committee had primarily sent journalists and intellectuals to the island to witness the nascent revolution, the Brigade sought to engage with the island's revolution not as observers, but as laborers and direct participants.[33]

Cuba's socialist system utilized both material and moral incentives to mobilize the substantial labor forces necessary to drive the nation's development projects. Believing that the economic liberation of the Cuban nation was a cause worth fighting for, millions of Cubans participated enthusiastically in the everyday work of building the revolution. Nonetheless, the hours afforded in normal workdays were not always sufficient to meet the nation's substantial production needs. For this, volunteerism was required. Absent a profit-driven labor market and with only small incentives for personal material gain, Cuba's interpretation of the communist idea of "socialist emulation" conceptualized collective labor as a liberating force and encouraged individual and group labor channeled for collective benefit. Prizes, defended merit titles, media attention, honorary appointments in local and national political organizations, social pressure, and the popularity of the revolutionary government itself encouraged extremely high levels of volunteer participation from Cubans.[34] In the context of the 1970 sugar harvest, however, popular participation became a war for the revolution's very survival and the defense of the nation's gains against the encroaching legacy of underdevelopment and foreign domination. As historian Louis A. Pérez has observed, the 1970 *zafra* was "guerrilla warfare all over again.... Production metaphors borrowed freely from guerrilla vernacular. The harvest was conceived in military terms."[35]

The Cuban emphasis on collective labor now assumed an importance comparable to the unity required for battle. Che Guevara, a chief architect of the nation's theory of socialist collectivity, embodied in Cuba's goal of building a "New Man," had argued that "isolated individual endeavor, for all its purity of ideals, is of no use, and the desire to sacrifice an entire lifetime to the noblest of ideals serves no purpose if one works alone, solitarily, in some corner of America, fighting against adverse governments and social conditions which prevent progress."[36] Cuba's volunteer brigades combined Guevara's invocation to selfless labor in the service of socialist collectivity, an effort to which all were expected to contribute, with metaphors of armed insurgency borrowed from the vernacular of global anti-imperialist revolution. Cutting sugarcane along with the Venceremos Brigade during the harvests of 1960 and 1970 were representatives of Cuba's island-wide Youth Centennial Column, fully 40,000 volunteers strong; and a Cuban "women's agricultural battalion" of almost 300 that was named after Haydee Tamara Bunke — better known in Cuba as *Tania La Guerrillera* — an Argentine-born Cuban intelligence agent and guerrilla and the only female member of Che Guevara's band during its fateful 1967 incursion into Bolivia, where she was killed.[37]

Volunteer delegations from foreign nations, such as the Guerrilleros de Bolivia "millionaire brigade," so-named because they had cut 1 million *arrobas* of cane, and the Chullima Riders Volunteer Workers Brigade, composed of North Korean youth, labored side by side with the American *brigadistas* in the nation's new war of economic liberation.[38] Cuban press coverage of the Brigade was frequently featured alongside news of other international delegations visiting Cuba from around the world, whose labor exploits were celebrated as evidence of the international support for Cuba's ongoing revolution.[39]

Most of the volunteers in Cuba's battle against underdevelopment, however, were Cuban. Billboards throughout the countryside throughout 1969 and 1970 trumpeted the harvest as a life-and-death battle against the legacy of underdevelopment and declared *"Los Diez Millones Van!"* — the ten million [tons] are going! Large sectors of the national economy were reorganized to bring factory workers, farmers, and urban professionals into the fields, "working guerilla style,"[40] as tens of thousands of Cubans from all walks of life mobilized into the countryside as the first Venceremos Brigades arrived. Even after the 1970 harvest, the motley composition of the Cuban volunteer labor force was apparent to the Americans. As activist and scholar Roxanne Dunbar-Ortiz recalled her participation in the third Venceremos Brigade on the Isla de la Juventud, an island south of the Cuban mainland: "The Cubans supervising us and working beside us were teachers, students, civil servants, doctors, accountants — the proverbial blind leading the blind. The officials administering the brigade expected us to decide everything democratically; they

Fidel Castro and members of the Venceremos Brigade pause while cutting sugarcane on Christmas Day, 1969. While Cuban officials regularly performed manual labor alongside Cuban workers and volunteer brigades and sometimes labored alongside visiting foreign delegations, Castro's extended visit to the VB camp signaled the importance the Cuban leadership placed upon the Americans' presence on the island. Photo by George Cohen.

didn't give orders, and at any rate, they knew no more about citrus production than we did."[41]

Collaborative and democratically enacted physical labor in Cuba was promoted as an instrument of revolutionary social transformation, one that could break down latent class barriers and instill in Cubans of widely varying educational backgrounds and skill sets an appreciation of the dignity of the humblest of work and an awareness of the necessity of all labor, from the janitorial to the scientific, to the nation's survival. High-ranking Cuban officials and members of the armed forces endeavored to set an example in the nation's war against underdevelopment by cutting cane and performing manual labor alongside Cuban brigades and foreign volunteers, posing for photos at agricultural fields, factories, and docks that were published in the Cuban press.[42] Fidel Castro, Raúl Castro, and Che Guevara completed regular labor shifts in fields and factories long after 1959.[43]

When Fidel himself visited the Venceremos Brigade camp and cut sugarcane with the Americans for seven hours on Christmas Day 1969, his presence prompted the *brigadistas* to reconsider the relationship between class divisions and political disaffection. His labor in the fields, the Cuban leader explained to them, was "an antidote for 'bureaucratitis' and 'bourgeoisitis.'"[44] As one *brigadista* noted wryly: "you'll never find Nixon out there chopping cotton."[45]

U.S. feminist writer Margaret Randall, who lived in Cuba for eleven years beginning in 1969 and raised her four children there, came to see socialist emulation as a theory and practice by which Cubans developed qualities of collectivity, mutual aid, and democratic decision-making: "Children who were trained from a young age in emulation rather than competition developed a sense of solidarity foreign to most children in capitalist societies. Emulation ... meant that those involved decided collectively on their goals and then helped one another achieve them. Thus, in the school setting, collective analysis was encouraged. A child good in math was expected to help one who had trouble in that subject but excelled in history, and she in turn would offer help in her area of expertise. This way everyone succeeded."[46]

In the Brigade, radicalized Americans, some already self-identifying as socialists, reflected upon their opportunity to witness a socialist labor system, one whose production logic was oriented toward the public good instead of individual gain. Julian Rizo, the ICAP coordinator of the Brigade's activities while it was on the island, explained that the differences between the Marxist concepts of concrete versus abstract labor reveal themselves "when the members of a society start to understand that progress will come about only as a result of their work, and that they are working for themselves as a people, they are starting to eliminate the alienating characteristics that work formerly had."[47]

For the North Americans, the experience was sometimes revelatory. Isidro Martínez, a member of the Puerto Rican Socialist Party who had traveled to Cuba to help build houses as a member of the sixth Venceremos Brigade explained that, "for once in my life it was really good to know that the sweat of my labor wasn't going to enrich some capitalist but rather it was going to the benefit of workers like myself." Working as a laborer in Puerto Rico, he said, had been an exploitative and dead-end job. Having dropped out of college in Puerto Rico because he could not afford tuition, Martínez was impressed with the Cuban educational system that, in contrast to the American, ensured uniform access to education regardless of economic background. Cuba's attempts to erase class divisions through education and labor, he contended, had "breached the capitalist gap between the categories of student and worker."[48]

The Brigade's volunteerism earned the organization high accolades in Cuba. *Granma* repeatedly chronicled the group's work efforts, documenting the weight of sugarcane harvested, citrus trees tended, and fruit harvested.[49] Radio Havana Cuba, which hosted a program about the Brigade titled *On the Ten Millions Trail* in 1970, featured interviews with American *brigadistas* and chronicled their harvesting feats for a global audience of listeners in English and Spanish. When the Americans reached their first production goal of 1 million *arrobas* of harvested cane, the station noted their "exemplary gesture of solidarity and friendship, which will never be forgotten in our country."[50] Although a substantial portion of the participants on the first three Venceremos Brigades were middle-class students with no prior experience with physical labor and had to be trained for the arduous task of harvesting sugarcane by hand — cane-cutting has a deserved reputation as a singularly backbreaking occupation in Cuba and elsewhere — the Americans excelled. In January 1970, when the Brigade was honored at a ceremony in which a high-ranking Communist Party official of Havana Province presented the Americans, together with the fifty-nine Cubans working with them, with a banner of recognition after they harvested their first 1 million *arrobas* of cane, the achievement was front page news in *Granma*.[51] Jaíme Crombet, First Secretary of the National Committee of the Young Communist League in Cuba, praised the Brigade's work with the Cuban and Vietnamese delegations as an act of "profound moral and revolutionary significance," one symbolic of the potential for global solidarity to overcome the intertwined brutality of militarism and capitalist inequality, one capable of creating "a more just society, a superior society where man will no longer be a beast attacking other men." The attitude of the Americans, Crombet admitted, had been a "pleasant surprise," an "example of the moral values that exist in a great part of the U.S. people."[52]

Fidel Castro personally praised the third delegation to an audience of thousands of Cubans in September 1970, at no less an event than the ten-year anniversary of the establishment of the Committees for the Defense of the Revolution (CDRs), created in 1960 as a neighborhood surveillance network amid a wave of counterrevolutionary bombings, sabotage, and terrorism. On a stage with President Osvaldo Dorticós, Minister Carlos Rafael Rodríguez, Foreign Minister Raúl Roa, and Secretariat Member Blas Roca, Castro singled out the American brigade as "a splendid movement of great revolutionary and internationalist content, and an expression of the sentiments and the moral reserves of the best people of the United States."[53] Interrupted by applause from the crowd, Castro detailed the group's exploits using his legendary photographic memory in lieu of notes:

> This brigade also is a millionaire brigade. You ask how, since the harvest is over? Do you ask how there can be a millionaire brigade on the Isle of Pines, where there is no sugarcane? Well, they fertilized 1,095,187 citrus plants in an area of 570 *caballerias*. They also fertilized 450 kilometers of windbreaks in 28,799 work hours. They harvested 5,389 *quintals* of lemons in 18,518 work hours. They planted 21,681 grapefruit plants, 3,903 orange plants, and transplanted 6,803 orange trees in 10,627 work hours. This is a total of 13 *caballerias* freshly planted. And six *caballerias* replanted. They worked 3,938 hours inspecting their plants. They irrigated 32,903 plants, unloaded 7,599 plants, filled 8,208 holes for planting, in addition to working 512 hours on construction projects at Loma de Sierra de Caballo, on the Isle of Pines television antenna, and 960 hours building a kindergarten in Gerona. They lost 3,821 hours because of rain, which is an insignificant figure.[54]

The Cuban staff also sang the praises of the Brigade. For Orlaida Cabrera, an ICAP officer who worked as a liaison for the first delegation in 1969, the arrival of the Venceremos Brigade was accompanied by unexpected emotions. "The arrival of the Americans showed us as Cubans that we were not alone," she recalled in 2015, becoming misty-eyed. "The Venceremos Brigade broke the isolation that the U.S. government had tried to impose on Cuba."[55] Before the arrival of the Brigade, she had never met an American. While solidarity brigades from around the world had been coming to Cuba for a decade, the American delegations had a distinct importance, one that affirmed to Cubans that they had friends even within the empire to the north. Cabrera's biography parallels that of many Cubans who embraced the 1959 Cuban Revolution as their own. A black Cuban girl born to a poor family, her mother had worked as a maid in the home of a wealthy white family while her father sold newspapers. On more than one occasion she was forced to miss school because she had no shoes to wear. With the rebel victory against Batista in 1959, her parents became involved in the revolutionary process: her father, she remembers, was away for weeks at a time cutting sugarcane in volunteer brigades. Cabrera's deep investment in the Cuban Revolution and pride in its achievements mirrored the idealism of a generation of working class Cubans.

Cabrera was enrolled in the University of Havana studying sociology when someone told her about ICAP. Since its founding in 1960, the institute had been Cuba's official liaison to foreign solidarity organizations, participating in outreach activities abroad and coordinating delegations of activists and volunteers to Cuba. *Bohemia*, Cuba's oldest magazine, had included a regular section in the mid-1960s entitled "Amigos de Cuba" providing short profiles of supporters of the revolution's supporters abroad. "I don't like foreigners" was Cabrera's first reaction upon learning of an open position at ICAP. But she signed up with the organization anyway and promptly fell in love with the labor of transnational solidarity. The first delegation that she helped coordinate was from Japan. When ICAP formally created a "North American Section," the branch of the institute that would henceforth be responsible for coordinating solidarity from supporters in the United States and Canada, Cabrera, who had studied English as a university student, became one of its officers.

Although Cabrera also became involved with coordinating solidarity initiatives in Africa and eventually became ICAP's director for Africa and the Middle East, the grassroots transnationalism of the Venceremos Brigade would remain especially close to her heart. "In the camps, Americans and Cubans learned to see each other as comrades in a common struggle for humanity, and Washington could not stop it. The Americans helped us, and we helped them become more free as they learned that they could be part of the struggle of the oppressed."[56]

Indeed, despite their prodigious volunteer efforts, the contributions of the early American brigades were ultimately as much symbolic as material.[57] Part of this lay in the Brigade's public flouting of the U.S. travel ban, and in the highly potent Cold War symbolism of American dissidents coalescing with global revolutionaries in Cuba. Indeed, in 1969 and 1970 the Venceremos Brigade made front-page news throughout the United States, where their transgressions of the embargo ignited a firestorm of media controversy and political condemnation from U.S. officialdom. At the CDR rally, Castro reminded the audience of this significance: "[I]t must be said that the imperialists are in no way pleased and that they become hysterical when they know about the presence of these North American youths in our country. These are the youths who risk the ire of the imperialists and the consequences of this revolutionary gesture toward our people."[58] Five months earlier, when Castro announced during a speech that the 10 million ton harvest had fallen short, at 8.5 million tons, he acknowledged, to applause, the "young people from capitalist countries, youths from socialist countries, two brigades of North American youths" who had aided in the effort.[59]

Nonetheless, it is unlikely that the contributions of the foreign brigades recouped Cuba's costs in hosting them. Several dozen or several hundred guests had to be housed, fed, transported, and looked after for weeks on end.[60] The early Venceremos Brigades received several-week tours of the island, from

Havana to Santiago de Cuba at the eastern end of the island. This exercise too was laden with symbolic significance, and their progress was chronicled in the state-run media for Cubans and foreign readers alike to witness.[61] Traversing the island by bus, the Americans visited historic sites, listened to former rebel fighters recount their experiences in the armed phase of revolution, and retraced Che Guevara's steps up a mountain to the guerrilla leader's former stronghold. Especially, however, their Cuban hosts made sure that the Americans witnessed the revolution's social programs up close. At hospitals, schools, farms, sports centers, neighborhood clinics, construction sites, dairies, universities, and daycare centers, the Americans met Cubans who were participating directly in the forging of the new socialist society. On the way, they traveled through provincial capitals and small towns, sleeping in school dormitories or camping in portable tents. In a few places, "feasts of lobster or crab or sea bass awaited us," one *brigadista* recalled, and the groups visited the white sand beaches of Varadero, formerly Cuba's premier resort area that now drew vacationing, working-class Cuban families instead of wealthy foreigners.[62]

As honored guests, the Americans in Cuba were treated well—an experience made possible at great expense and likely by the labor and sacrifice of many dozens of Cubans. The greatest significance of the Venceremos Brigades ultimately lay not in their material contributions to the Cuba's development but in their forging of a long-term relationship of solidarity between the multifaceted U.S. Left and the government of Cuba. Likewise, the power of the delegations lay in their ability to radicalize Americans through the transformative potentials of travel and the symbolism of global solidarity.

Travel and Transformation

Traveling illegally to Cuba, especially for a group endeavoring to publicly breach the U.S. travel ban as an act of civil disobedience, required navigating through a sea of legal and logistical obstacles. The Johnson administration began prosecuting American citizens for violating the U.S. travel ban in 1964, setting in place a policy that would become the defining feature of relations between American citizens and the island for the next half-century. The policy had found an early opponent in President Kennedy, who argued that lifting the ban would be "more consistent with our views as a free society."[63] For Kennedy's successor, however, the ban was consistent with the administration's view that Cuba must be isolated within the hemisphere.

By 1968, with the travel ban aggressively enforced, Americans endeavoring to reach Cuba without U.S. government authorization were forced to travel surreptitiously through a third country. Mexico was the simplest route due to proximity, if not geopolitics. Officially, Mexico was the only Latin American nation that had refused to break off diplomatic relations with Cuba after the Organization of American States voted to terminate relations with Cuba in 1964, a position of reluctant neutrality necessitated by the political strength of the Mexican Left.

Unofficially, however, Mexico cooperated closely with Washington to assist in Cuba-related efforts ranging from the Bay of Pigs invasion to monitoring travel to the island.[64] The Mexican government reported the names of U.S. citizens traveling to the island to the U.S. State Department, and allowed CIA agents full latitude to photograph members of the Venceremos Brigade at the airport in Mexico City. Mexican customs officials stamped "Mexico D.F. CUBA" on the passports of Americans and, until 1976, also used stamps reading *Salio Para Cuba* (went to Cuba) and *Llego de Cuba* (arrived from Cuba).[65] Mexican officials had occasionally deported Americans attempting to reach Cuba, often placing them on the first flight out of the country, sometimes to another continent. In one case, an American companion of Angela Davis was placed on a plane that ended up in Paris.[66]

Other routes existed to Cuba, of course. Although the first contingent of the Venceremos Brigade arrived by air, they returned by sea aboard the *Luis Arcos Bergnes*, a repurposed Cuban cattle ship. Prohibited by the embargo from docking in the United States, the ship instead headed for the Canadian port of Saint John, New Brunswick, where members of the Venceremos Brigade's second contingent were waiting to take their places as the ship returned to Cuba.

Getting to Saint John presented its own challenges. To thwart surveillance at the border and in Canada, the Organizing Committee decided that the second contingent of the Brigade, which would arrive in Cuba in late February 1970, would pose as skiers bound for Quebec. However, the travelers proved inexpert in the art of disguise. Making their way from New York City to Saint John, New Brunswick, in buses rented under a false name—"Skimasters"—the group was nonetheless met at the border by a waiting assemblage of FBI agents and reporters. The ruse quickly unraveled. The hapless travelers were carrying no alpine equipment, and their suitcases contained bikinis, shorts, and other suspiciously tropical gear.[67] Upon their return, the news media lampooned the group, with the *Chicago Tribune* running an article gleefully titled: "So How Was the Skiing in Cuba?"[68] Although the Brigade made a few more half-hearted efforts to thwart the FBI and local police, surveillance and petty harassment remained a fact of travel for the group throughout the 1970s.[69]

The Venceremos Brigade's sea route to Cuba presented other problems. Seasickness beset many of the travelers, who had never traveled by sea. As it entered international waters, the ship was buzzed repeatedly by an U.S. Air

Force fighter plane that streaked low enough for the *brigadistas* to see the pilot's face. The overflights soon stopped, however, and the winter air grew warmer as the ship neared the Caribbean.

Once safely on the island, however, many members of the Venceremos Brigade experienced a transformative moment in their political lives of many participants. Cuba's transformative power was due to a variety of factors. Prominent among them was the opportunity afforded by solidarity travel for activists to meet left-wing volunteers from around the world. Encountering the island's global radical public, Americans in Cuba came to see U.S. movements for social justice not as isolated struggles, but as small currents within a broader sea of global social change.

In this sense, the transformational capacity of travel to Cuba lay as much in the Caribbean nation's status as a confluence of global movements as it did with the particulars of the revolution's social achievements. Cuba's status as a hub of international leftism had impressed earlier American travelers to Cuba, such as the Beat writer LeRoi Jones. Traveling to Cuba in 1959 as part of a delegation of black writers sponsored by FPCC, Jones wrote of being challenged to politicize his hitherto largely apolitical writing by a group of visiting Mexican students and poets as they shared a train ride through the Cuban countryside. In the contagious excitement and revolutionary incandescence of Havana in the months following the revolution, Jones underwent a transformation from Beat to Black Nationalist. Returning to New York, Jones soon departed from Greenwich Village's largely white avant-garde artistic scene.[70] Cuba, it may be said, is where LeRoi Jones first began to transform into Amiri Baraka, and where the political path that would define him thereafter first revealed itself to him. Reflecting on the trip years later, he recalled:

> I carried so much back with me that I was never the same again. The dynamic of the revolution had touched me. Talking to Fidel or Juan Almeida, the black commander of the revolutionary army, or to the young minister of agrarian reform, Nuñez Jiménez, or Jaime or Rubi or Pablo Fernández. Seeing youth not just turning on and dropping out, not just hiply cynical or cynically hip, but using their strength and energy to *change* the real world — that was too much. The growing kernel of social consciousness I had was mightily fertilized by the visit.[71]

A decade later, American visitors to Cuba, particularly those from the U.S. Third World Left, also noted that the island's impact on them owed much to their exposure to the nation's global radical public. Longtime radical journalist Elizabeth "Betita" Martinez, who traveled to Cuba in 1967 to interview Cubans about the new society that they were building, published her report as a book, *The Youngest Revolution*, its title a reference to the popular perception, in North America and globally, of Cuba as an insurgent leader in a world still in the throes of decolonization and anti-imperial rebellion.

Stokely Carmichael, a lead organizer for SNCC, similarly recalled that the confluence of global leftists at the OLAS meeting in Havana in 1967 crystallized his conceptualization of the global context of the domestic African American freedom struggle and the interconnections between local and global movements. Carmichael later recalled that in Cuba "the international struggle became tangible, a human reality, names, faces, stories, no longer an abstraction, and our struggle in Mississippi or Harlem was part and parcel of this great international and historical motion."[72]

Scholar and activist Angela Davis echoed the sentiments of numerous American travelers to Cuba, reflecting later that her weeks on the island in July and August of 1969 had been a foundational moment in her political development. As a member of a delegation of the Communist Party USA, Davis and her companions met with Cuban officials and workers, contributed their labor to the 10 million tons *zafra*, and toured the island's socialist development projects. "The Cuban trip," she later wrote, "had been a great climax in my life. Politically I felt infinitely more mature, and it seemed that the Cubans' limitless revolutionary enthusiasm had left a permanent mark on my existence."[73] Davis's sister, Fania Jordan, would travel to Cuba with the third delegation of the Venceremos Brigade the next year.

Not surprisingly, the potential of Cuba's global radical public to politicize American visitors became a central feature of the Brigade's delegations. The organization's recruitment brochures noted that Americans in Cuba would "have the opportunity to work with revolutionaries from such places as Guinea Bissau, Indochina, and Uruguay."[74] A significant feature of the Brigade would therefore be the opportunity to communicate across the national, cultural, and ideological gulfs that separated American leftists from their counterparts abroad, allowing U.S. activists to resituate themselves and their movements within a broader global terrain of political struggle. The camps for foreign volunteers in Cuba often functioned as transnational public spheres beyond the orbit of the U.S. power — although mediated by the Cuban state — where global leftists mingled, coalesced, and exchanged ideas. The camps where American volunteers lived and worked were structured in ways that allowed visitors to interact with their global counterparts through shared activities, "encounter meetings," and lectures about political movements and events abroad.

For other Americans, the encounters were opportunities to make their political movements known to Cubans and to other international volunteers.

Leroy Mills, a Native American activist from Franks Landing, Washington, and the director of the Survival of the American Indian Association, traveled to Cuba with the Brigade with the hope of making Cubans aware of the "struggle of the native American," a population facing a legacy of colonization and underdevelopment whose nature, he noted, shared continuities with the history of the island. "What has happened [in Cuba]," Mills explained, "would be good for the Indians in the U.S."[75]

The global radical public afforded by the volunteer camps allowed activists from far-flung movements across North America to connect with each other in unexpected ways. Miriam Ching Louie, who traveled with the Brigade's first delegation in time to celebrate her nineteenth birthday in Cuba, reflected later that one significant outcome of her trip had been the opportunity to coalesce with activists from across the U.S. Third World Left. "In the wake of Martin Luther King's assassination, Watts, rebellions burning across the face of urban America and Indian Country and full-scale U.S. intervention in Southeast Asia," Louie later wrote, "the Brigade enabled us to hook up with young bloods from communities of color across the U.S."[76]

Encountering Global Revolution

The confluence of global radicalism on display within Cuba's volunteer camps existed against the backdrop of the internationalism of Cuba's revolutionary project itself.[77] The 10-million-ton *zafra*, American volunteers were reminded, had been dedicated symbolically to the "heroic Vietnamese people" who were resisting Washington's war of aggression.[78] Visual representations of Cuban internationalism, whose ethos of solidarity with the world's downtrodden had become a pillar of Cuban identity, were immediately apparent to the *brigadistas*. Commercial advertising no longer existed on the island, and the giant billboards had now been emblazoned with colorful agitprop that juxtaposed images from Cuba's history of national liberation struggle, dating back to the nineteenth century, with depictions of modern anticolonial movements from around the world and quotations from a global pantheon of revolutionary leaders from Africa, Asia, and Latin America.

Overshadowing all global conflicts in the late 1960s was the war in Indochina. The Cuban government had lent significant material and moral support to the Vietnamese National Liberation Front, and Cuba's state-sponsored media chronicled the deadly human cost of the war relentlessly in the state-sponsored press. Updates were broadcast continuously on radio and television, including during the Venceremos Brigade's visits, quickly catching the attention of the *brigadistas*.[79]

Depictions of the war, and of the heroism of Vietnamese resistance in the face of the world's most advanced military apparatus, also preoccupied Cuban cultural production throughout the era. *79 primaveras*, a 1969 filmic portrait of the life of Hồ Chí Minh directed by acclaimed Cuban filmmaker Santiago Álvarez, vividly depicted the human devastation of war, while also suggesting that the increasing fragility of the U.S. war effort was due in part to the U.S. antiwar movement, including its radical internationalist wing. Set to a score featuring the music of the American rock group Iron Butterfly, the film included footage of antiwar demonstrators marching and facing off with police, some holding placards that situated their U.S. protest alongside the two most visible Third World influences within U.S. social justice movements at the time: "Vietnam, Watts: it's the same struggle!" and "Avenge Che!"[80]

Billboards made explicit the Cuban government's support of North Vietnam against the U.S. intervention through slogans and images that emphasized the interconnections between Cuba's struggle for self-determination in the face of U.S. imperial bellicosity in the Caribbean and Vietnam's efforts to repel the U.S. occupation in Asia. Louis Segal, a twenty-year-old white Berkeley man who had participated in demonstrations against the Vietnam War before joining the Brigade, recalled his first impression of Cuba as his group of Americans left the airport outside Havana:

> I remember vividly driving down the highway toward where we would be staying, and there was a huge billboard that said "*Como en Vietnam*"—like in Vietnam—and it showed a huge *machetero* in vivid polychromatic colors cutting sugarcane, attacking it with a sense of purpose. And the guy on the billboard had a 'thought balloon' that depicted a Vietnamese National Liberation Front member fighting against jets that were streaming against the sky, and he too was in a green field not unlike the green sugarcane field that the *machetero* was in, except that this NLP fighter was up against jets that were bombing his homeland. That really made an impression on me because it was public didactic art against a war that I was fully against, and it had supplanted advertising. It was saying, there's a war going on, and it's a global war, and there's an analogue between what we do in Cuba, cutting sugarcane for the harvest, the 10 million tons to kick-start Cuban development and self-sufficiency, and the effort against the Vietnam War and our support of Vietnam's people.[81]

The symbolic linking of Cuban and Vietnamese self-determination was evident even in the naming of villages, streets, sports and military facilities, and industry. Visiting the Cuban village of Ben Tre, established in 1969 in the Cuban province of Artemisa, the *brigadistas* learned that it had been named for a South Vietnamese town — Bến Tre — whose destruction a U.S. Army major, interviewed by an American reporter, had tried to explain in words that soon became symbolic of the Pentagon's cold calculus of counterinsurgency: "It became necessary to destroy the town to save it."[82] Nguyễn Văn Trỗi, a National Liberation Front fighter executed for attempting to assassinate U.S. Secretary of Defense Robert McNamara in 1963, became the namesake of a Cuban shoe factory and a stadium. Other Cuban villages bore names such as "Free Algeria," in honor of the anticolonial struggle that had freed the nation from French colonial rule, while also marking the beginning of Cuba's military and humanitarian involvement in the African continent during the coming three decades.[83]

American visitors marveled at seeing billboards and murals depicting heroes of the Cuban Revolution side by side with those from leftist movements from around the world. White *brigadista* Cleo Gorman remembered encountering Cuban streets bearing names such as Avenida Patrice Lumumba, prompting him to write in his journal: "With whom do U.S. citizens have such a close connection? De Gaulle in Chicago? Rockefeller in L.A.? We are so far from this kind of political consciousness, we who live on Plumtree Road."[84] Visiting Cuba in 1976, educator Jonathan Kozol discovered that a newly built rural school had been named "Martyrs of Kent," after four students killed by members of the Ohio National Guard as they protested the recently announced air bombings of President Nixon's Cambodian Campaign.[85]

Cuba's conspicuous replacement of the iconography of consumer capitalism with revolutionary propaganda also captivated the American visitors. Arriving in Cuba, the complete absence of advertising was almost as striking as the brightly hued agitprop that had replaced it across the island. Visiting a few months before the Brigade arrived, Angela Davis noted the repurposed billboards that had once been used to sell consumer products. "I felt a great satisfaction knowing that the Cubans had ripped down these trademarks of global exploitation and had replaced them with warm and stirring symbols that had real meaning for the people. The sense of human dignity was palpable."[86] As *brigadista* Chris Camarano wrote, "All over the place are magnificent posters — right where some of our most garish advertisements would be. Office buildings in Havana have huge signs reading '*Patria O Muerte — Venceremos!*' or '*Hasta la Victoria Siempre.*' Farmhouses have homemade murals of Che on their walls."[87] The charged political imagery, coupled with the Cuban media's detailed coverage of global leftist movements, produced a rich public pedagogy in which everyday life became relentlessly politicized. The Cubans that the *brigadistas* met were often knowledgeable about a wide range of events occurring outside Cuba, including those in the United States, and sometimes

A satirical advertisement in the pages of *Tricontinental* is illustrative of the magazine's gleeful lampooning of U.S. allies and business interests with agitprop that often sought to accentuate linkages between capitalism, colonization, and white supremacy. *Tricontinental* no. 7, July-August 1968.

had detailed knowledge of social movements there. "Farmers I meet on the road, who are busily picking up horseloads of cane leaves for their cows, stop to chat," wrote Camarano, "and I find they know about the Panthers."[88]

Some visitors had already encountered Cuba's audacious brand of political lampoonery. The quarterly periodical *Tricontinental*, which was printed in four languages and distributed globally, often satirized advertisements by transnational corporations on the inside of the magazine's back cover. In one adaptation of an advertisement that had run in *The Economist*, a caption read, "In Brazil too, you have a friend at Chase Manhattan . . . a 'friend' who leaves the following balance in Brazil: 200 children die daily from hunger; 15,874,000 illiterates over 15 years of age; 60% increase in the cost of medicines; 2,500,000 people suffer from chronic starvation."[89] Another advertisement for South African Airways had been modified to invite travelers to participate in "an unforgettable vacation in the land of apartheid, where Africans are massacred, where prisons overflow with patriots fighting against white racists."[90] And in another, Bank of America ostensibly advertised the services of its "man-on-the-spot" in La Paz, Bolivia, a briefcase-carrying white man identified as a "commodities expert, a foreign exchange specialist, an economist, a diplomat, a political scientist, a reporter, a tax expert, a business consultant, a banker ... in short, an imperialist agent."[91]

Many *brigadistas*, particularly those who were white, traced their personal politicization to their participation in the anti–Vietnam War movement. All of the Americans, however, had been impacted in some way by the daily media images of the war's carnage. In their journal entries and letters, Americans in Cuba recalled being jolted by their face-to-face meetings with the Vietnamese National Liberation Front fighters and diplomats who visited the volunteer camps and worked side by side with Americans in the fields during the late 1960s and early 1970s. Thousands of miles removed from the horror of war in Vietnam, most American antiwar activists had never had the opportunity to meet the victims of the U.S. occupation. The Vietnamese representatives implored the *brigadistas* to continue to build the antiwar movement in the United States. "Your country is trying to kill our people, destroy our nation which is no larger than one of your states," a National Liberation Front captain told members of the second Venceremos Brigade in Cuba. "We will fight to victory and we are thankful for your support."[92]

Cuba's campaign of solidarity with Vietnam, expressed in the slogan *como en Vietnam*—like in Vietnam—symbolized the Cuban people's solidarity with the Vietnamese resistance to U.S. occupation, and their identification with Vietnam's fate at the hands of U.S. power as a reality that was inherently linked with their own. Cuba had been providing free medical care and university scholarships to thousands of Vietnamese soldiers and orphans, and although there was a milk shortage on the island during the late 1960s, Cuba nonetheless sent shipments of powdered milk to Vietnam. ICAP coordinator Julian Rizo explained Cuba's policy to the Americans as one of internationalist sacrifice. "We give what we have little of and need ourselves, not what we can easily spare."[93]

In the terrible context of the war, with its human devastation in Vietnam and social upheaval in the United States, the act of North Americans traveling to a forbidden nation to meet representatives of a faraway specter —Vietnamese communist revolutionaries—was a significant experience for Americans, Vietnamese, and Cubans alike. As Miriam Ching Louie, who traveled with the first Brigade, put it: "I met all my 'enemies'— all those revolutionaries.

That affected me for years."[94] *Brigadista* Tarnel Abbot wrote of her meeting with a young Vietnamese delegate from Hanoi who was visiting the village of Ben Tre in Cuba. "We spoke in very broken Spanish. In Spanish her name is Margarita, and she is twenty-two years old. We talked about her family and my family. She was very excited and emotional — she held my arm a while. We talked and never stopped smiling. Her brother is also here. She told me that I was like a sister to her and that after we have our revolution in the U.S. we should come and visit Vietnam. I almost started crying."[95]

A white working class *brigadista* named Pat Ruckert, whose brother had been a GI in Vietnam, was assigned to work in the sugarcane fields with Huỳnh Văn Ba,[96] a Vietnamese diplomat with a military background who had served twenty-five years fighting against Japanese, French, and now American invasions. Ruckert, instructed by his brother to convey a message to the Vietnamese delegates should the opportunity arise, communicated his sibling's apologies for "having participated in a war against his people" in Vietnam. Gesturing toward his boots, he told Huỳnh that the boots he was wearing "were worn by my brother while fighting your people; they are now worn by me working beside you in the cane fields of Cuba."[97]

The Americans were sometimes surprised — and perhaps not a little relieved — to find that the people who had felt the sting of U.S. military power most acutely readily differentiated between the American government and its citizens.[98] The Cuban media continually covered the meetings between the Brigade and delegates from Vietnam, Cambodia, and Laos, emphasizing the symbolic import of these transnational encounters as evidence that solidarity could trump militarism.[99]

The catharsis of the encounters with the Vietnamese delegates notwithstanding, the Americans seemed more at ease relating to the Cubans. For all its foreignness, Cuba's history had been closely intertwined with that of the United States for a century, constituting what President William McKinley had once called "ties of singular intimacy."[100] The imperial imagination of the U.S. state and the long series of political and cultural interactions between Cuba and the United States had created a familiarity among the neighboring nations that helped shape popular American perceptions of Cuba. Writer Susan Sontag claimed that while Cuba's revolution was uniquely "accessible" to Americans, a "barrier of exoticism" kept the Americans from fully comprehending the Vietnamese revolution.[101] Todd Gitlin, too, found a shared sensibility with the Cubans. "Even our poetic styles — loose-jointed rhythms, [Bertolt] Brecht's bluntness, [Jorge Luis] Borges beat-skipping — seemed similar," unlike "the culturally alien Vietnamese" who the Americans had met in Bratislava.[102]

As historian Judy Tzu-Chun Wu contends, American antiwar activists who traveled to Vietnam in the 1960s at times perceived members of the Vietnamese liberation movement through a lens that she calls "radical orientalism." Idealizing the Vietnamese movement's resistance to U.S. domination, American antiwar activists nonetheless constructed a vision of a revolutionary "East" that was dichotomous with a corrupt "West," one that was sometimes informed by reductive, binary notions of cultural difference.[103] American leftists, women and men, both white and of color, idealized the Cuban Revolution in a variety of ways. Many idealizations were based, ultimately, on hope: the hope that Cuba was effectively eradicating institutional racism; the hope that Cuban society was moving toward gender equality; or the hope that all the world's people would one day, like the Cubans, have enough to eat, and have a right to education, health, and a place to live. Ultimately, the social gains of Cuba's evolving revolution nurtured the hope among Americans that meaningful forms of social change might be possible elsewhere in the world, including in the United States. Translating Cuba's successes into a North American context, particularly within their own movements for social transformation, however, proved to be one of the Brigade's greatest challenges.

Conflicts of Coalition, Potentials of Solidarity

With their sojourn in Cuba drawing to a close, the first delegation of the Venceremos Brigade that had arrived in December of 1969 boarded the *Luis Arcos Bergnes* and sailed north for six days, reaching Saint John, New Brunswick, in frigid weather on the morning of February 12, where the second delegation awaited them, along with a group of reporters. The two delegations held a brief meeting, allowing the first group to answer questions from those who would soon be boarding the ship and taking their place at the Rubén Martínez Villena solidarity camp. The arriving group left a written communiqué offering advice, and a pointed word of caution: "Cane cutting itself is perhaps less difficult than working with others to reach specific common goals... individualism, in its diverse forms, can be extremely harmful to collective productive work."[104]

The bulk of the second contingent of the Brigade, nearly 500 participants, arrived in Havana harbor on February 19. Over 100 more would arrive by plane, making this delegation — 687 in all — the largest before or since. Several hundred Cubans lined the dock, some bearing a banner reading "Welcome, Venceremos," as the group was serenaded live by the Tata Güines Orchestra.[105] The brigade was soon installed in the Rubén Martínez Villena camp, as the Cuban and international press — which included reporters from

Mexico, the Soviet Union, and the United States — chronicled their work in the cane fields, some of which had been performed side by side with volunteer contingents from North Korea and Vietnam. At a press conference on the occasion of the Brigade's harvesting of 3 million *arrobas* of cane, for which they were presented with a "bronze titan" banner named for legendary nineteenth-century, Afro-Cuban independence leader Antonio Maceo, representatives of the group contended that the opportunity to work with radical volunteers from around the globe in the service of Cuban self-determination had given them confidence that "a new type of relationship between the progressive and revolutionary sectors of the United States" and Cuba was possible, one based upon "joint friendship and effort instead of on racism and exploitation."[106]

Despite their production achievements and the heady affirmation of transnational solidarity, however, Cuba as a transcendent space for U.S. radicals had limits. Participants in the Venceremos Brigades of 1969 and 1970 repeatedly lamented their failure to "act collectively" as a disciplined unit, claiming that the problem derived from their upbringing in a capitalist society that rewarded individual achievement over collective gain. It was an explanation that, for many participants, seemed to explain their difficulty in adapting to the rigors of physical labor in a socialist country.[107] At times, it seemed to some *brigadistas* in the Venceremos Brigades of 1969 and 1970 that they were hindered by their own invisible yet inescapable American-ness, a quality that, they imagined, rendered them prone to a kind of "individualism" that was antithetical to socialism and unity.

Yet the Brigade's greatest impediment in Cuba was often interpersonal. Tensions among *brigadistas* surfaced regularly enough to interfere with the coherence of the early delegations and occasionally complicated their relationships with their Cuban hosts.[108] Despite the Brigade's aspirations to function as a unified representative body of the American Left, the organization drew its membership from an inchoate constellation of social movements encompassing a wide range of identities, political ideologies, and social positionalities that defied any notions of a single, unified Left. The first three delegations in particular were notorious for divisive splits as activists from diverse socioeconomic, sexual, gender, and racial backgrounds tried to live together in canvas tents for weeks at a time in the tropical heat — "Sartre's version of hell," as one *brigadista* put it.[109]

Factional tendencies remained an element of the brigades to some degree for years. As Harry Maurer, a journalist for *The Nation* traveling with the Brigade as an observer in the summer of 1977, noted, "If the brigadistas tended to gaze upon Cuba with adoring eyes, they did not feel the same about one another.... The faction-ridden state of the movement was obvious."[110] The Brigade's efforts to ensure that a broad cross-section of the American movement would be represented in Cuba, while often successful, created other challenges once the delegations were assembled. Some participants wondered whether the ideological diversity of the delegations was viable. Margot Adler, a member of the first brigade, recalled that the motley group included both "Quakers committed to total nonviolence as well as at least a dozen Weathermen, who viewed their sojourn in Cuba as part of an effort to recruit members for the coming struggle back home."[111]

As ICAP officer Hugo Govín later recalled, "we could see the differences within the U.S. movement reflected within the American delegations."[112] Nonetheless, the Cuban staff usually refrained from providing direct advice on ideological matters. The Cubans in the camps would freely share their views with the Americans, but the official ICAP position was to allow the Americans latitude to work out their internal differences on their own.[113]

The social dynamics of the first three delegations were deepened additionally by the Brigade's decision to admit a number of recruits with no activist background at all. For other participants, Cuba was their first prolonged negotiation of the fraught politics of interracial, intergender, and intersocioeconomic class coalition. Reflecting upon the issue in an internal paper, the Bay Area regional committee noted that "problems such as racism, cultural chauvinism and sexism which exist among the US people do not simply disappear because North Americans have touched socialist soil. Most often, these problems are accentuated."[114]

Indeed, it was the politics of identity that most complicated their unity while in Cuba. With several hundred Americans — approximately 50 percent women, 60 percent white, and 40 percent people of color,[115] and of diverse class backgrounds and ideological and political convictions — living in cramped tents for weeks on end, the first three delegations experienced divisive splits.[116] As one participant on the second brigade put it: "We... heard rumors that a lot of racial tension had soured the first Brigade, which for some reason shocked us. I guess it was because of our naïve and unconscious assumption that the bitter and disheartening factionalism souring our little white radical scene in Durham had been left behind at the bus depot."[117]

The third Brigade, too, was wracked by the petty theft of personal items and even physical confrontations between *brigadistas*. Some participants attributed the problems to the Brigade's hasty recruitment of a number of poorly vetted individuals who had no prior activist experience and knew little about Cuba. Their presence reflected the Brigade's experiment with using travel to

Cuba as a means of politicizing nonactivists. "Some who'd joined the brigade seemed to regard it as a free vacation in the Caribbean and had had no idea they would have to work," one *brigadista* later wrote.[118] Confronted with the adversity of hard labor, the tropical heat, rugged outdoor living conditions, and routine interpersonal tensions, a few Americans refused to work or became disruptive. The Cuban coordinators eventually sent a number of such Americans home. As mysterious thefts proliferated during the first weeks of the third delegation in September 1970, paranoia grew that U.S. government agents, who were known to have infiltrated the Brigade, might be contributing to the mischief.[119] As fears of sabotage grew and an aura of suspicion and insecurity began to pervade the camp, Julian Rizo switched his civilian clothes for a Cuban military uniform and began to wear a pistol.[120]

It remains unknown whether agents provocateurs may have instigated or exacerbated some of the Brigade's early conflicts in Cuba. It is well established that assets from the FBI and local U.S. police forces had infiltrated the Brigade and, as detailed in the next chapter, the FBI eventually compiled over 20,000 pages of files on the group. At least one perpetrator of a serious incident — a physical attack on a gay man — in a Brigade camp was later revealed to be an undercover FBI agent.[121] ICAP staff, for their part, suspected that agents provocateurs were behind several incidents. "There was much trouble in the camps," remembers ICAP officer Orlaida Cabrera, although the Cubans had little concrete evidence that the problems were being caused by saboteurs. "At the time, we never knew whether the disruptive people were agents or just people who were not ready for life in Cuba. There was no way to know."[122]

Hugo Govín, an ICAP officer who also lived and worked with the Americans in the camps during this period, remembers suspecting that agents provocateurs were present in the camps. On one occasion, two *brigadistas* on the first 1969 trip seemed to make a point of bitterly disagreeing with each other on ideological matters and provoking arguments with others in the camp. After the American delegation disembarked in Canada following their time in Cuba, however, Govín was surprised to see the two young men leaving together in a car.[123] Until the bureau's files on the Brigade are released in their entirety, it is impossible to determine with certainty the role that U.S. government infiltrators may have played. Documents pertaining to the Brigade obtained from the FBI through the Freedom of Information Act, contain numerous references to the presence of informants and infiltrators but are heavily excised, and do not reveal whether any of the bureau's assets caused the disturbances.

FBI provocations notwithstanding, it is also clear that genuine tensions existed in the Brigade's work camps.[124] More than any other factor, racial tension complicated the Brigade's attempts during its early years to become a coherent representation of what the National Committee optimistically termed the "American movement." As scholar Laura Pulido has shown, the way in which African American, Asian American, Latino/a, and white activists arrived at political consciousness during the 1960s was conditioned by their divergent lived experiences of race.[125] For some *brigadistas,* Cuba was their first substantive experience with cross-racial, cross-ethnic living and political work. Americans in Cuba at times "encountered" one another as domestic foreigners in ways that paralleled their encounters with Cubans and volunteers from other nations.

The ethnic as well as global contours of the global radical public present in the volunteer camps also held unexpected productive potentials. African American, Asian American, and Latino/a *brigadistas,* in particular, formed themselves into racial caucuses within the Brigade to discuss the meaning of the Cuban Revolution in relation to their own political subject status as racialized groups within the U.S. nation. These caucuses could then articulate their solidarity with Cuba and representatives of other Third World nations simultaneously as American dissidents and as members of subaltern, internally colonized, or racially oppressed populations within the body of the empire. The Brigade's organically formed Puerto Rican Caucus, for instance, presented a statement to a visiting North Vietnamese delegation that reflected upon their position as both beneficiaries of the American imperium and as subjects of it vis-à-vis colonization. Using the example of Puerto Rican GIs who fought for U.S. interests in Vietnam, the *brigadistas* communicated their hope that "the future meetings between the people of Puerto Rico and Vietnam will not be as enemies on the battlefield but as comrades in the same trenches."[126]

Conceptualizing U.S. Latino/a, African American, and Indigenous communities as "internal colonies" resonated with Cuban understandings of the ethnic makeup of the colossus to the north. *Granma* referred to the Brigade as being composed of both U.S. citizens and "Latin Americans residing inside the United States," and *Granma* and other Cuban media and periodicals had regularly detailed the histories of Africans, Native Americans, Chicanos/as, and immigrants from throughout the hemisphere and the world, histories intermingled with the forces of empire, colonization, slavery, and migration.[127] When a *brigadista* identified as "Melva" from California explained her ethnic identity to a Cuban reporter thusly—"I was born on Mexican territory occupied by Yankee imperialism"—her invocation of colonialism and empire to describe her positionality within North America would have been recognizable to Cuban readers.[128]

To the Cuban coordinators of the Brigade, however, the propensity of the Americans to emphasize their ethnic and racial identities over political ideology was puzzling. "We knew that in 1969, U.S. blacks were at the highest point of their confrontation with the U.S. government on the question of race," remembers Orlaida Cabrera. "But we felt that blacks could not do it themselves. They needed allies. We saw blacks and Puerto Ricans meeting by themselves, and we didn't understand."[129] Unversed in the nuances of U.S. racial politics, the Cuban ICAP hosts who lived and worked in the camps, many of whom were Afro-Cuban, were confounded by the formation of racial caucuses in the camps and the tendency of American activists of color to organize themselves by race.[130] The Cubans were generally uneasy with the use of race as a political organizing principle in the camps, an attitude that was also reflected in the Cuban press. Coverage of the group in *Granma* tended to highlight the multiracial composition of the brigades, making almost no mention of racial tensions. While they did not interfere with the caucuses, the Cuban ICAP staff responded unenthusiastically to the racial nationalist ideologies espoused by black and brown North Americans and their white supporters. "ICAP's message to the U.S. people who wanted to know our ideas about social change in their country was always about unity," remembers Hugo Govín, himself Afro-Cuban, who often fielded questions from the *brigadistas* about race in Cuba. "The objective should be creating unified political movements powerful enough to stop the aggression against Vietnam and Cuba and to fight for the rights of all people in the U.S."[131]

The incongruities in political theory were often mutual. Many black American *brigadistas* praised the Cuban government's successes in breaking down structures of institutional racism, particularly in the arenas of education, health care, and housing. Racial violence, including lynching, which claimed victims in the United States throughout the 1960s, was unknown in Cuba. There could be no doubt that the Americans had come from a far more racially segregated society, one that was significantly more unequal than the new nation the Cubans were building. This fact alone influenced the perceptions of both groups in ways that were both conscious and not. Nonetheless, visual evidence of what appeared to be lingering antiblack racism, including the predominance of white Cubans in high government offices and the apparent concentration of Afro-Cubans in manual labor positions could not, it seemed, be simply explained away as the imperfections of a young revolution that had not yet had time to overcome three centuries of segregationist heritage. As the Third World Caucus of the first Brigade in 1969 explained in a statement, "a lot of [U.S.] Third World people — black people in particular — felt there was discrimination here in the camp, that all of the black people they have seen are either athletes, entertainers, in the Army, or working in the kitchen, which are very stereotyped positions for black people in the U.S."[132] Cuban racial attitudes, in all their complexity, could be disquieting to American eyes. Margaret Randall, a white woman living in Cuba during the period, wrote of being shocked to witness a black Cuban teacher asking her students to form two lines, one for students with "good" hair and one for "bad" hair, reinforcing her conviction that overcoming racism, in Cuba or the United States, had to be a structural *and* cultural process. The Cuban government was neglecting the latter.[133]

The Cuban government's guiding political framework, explicitly Marxist in its analysis of race, prescribed that racism and racial inequality could be ameliorated only with the eradication of capitalism. The end of exploitation, Cuban revolutionary theory contended, would undermine the structural basis that ultimately upheld racial inequality.[134] During his visit to the Brigade camp, Fidel Castro explained that desegregation in Cuba and the transfer of the land and property of the wealthy elite into the public domain via the government had "dealt a tremendous blow to the main basis of discrimination in our country. But this does not mean that the simple change in structure eliminates *prejudice*. Some of the attitudes of the superstructure of the old society inevitably persist in the new society."[135] While several Afro-Cubans confirmed to the Americans that the resilience of racism on the island was quite real, they nonetheless remained confident that the structural remedies to institutional racism — in Cuba or elsewhere — would eventually bring about racial equality both institutionally and culturally.

This theoretical position, some black American *brigadistas* argued, allowed some white Americans in the brigades to conveniently rationalize their pushing of the "race question" aside in favor of class struggle, allowing them to escape the implications of their own racial position as beneficiaries of a white-supremacist society. In the aftermath of the Brigade delegations of 1969 and 1970, the group's National Committee ultimately echoed the Cuban government's official position on race, contending that although racial strife on the camps had been debilitating, its source lay ultimately in the material relations of their society. "We live in a society which creates these things in order to exploit us more successfully ... they will not disappear until capitalism is destroyed."[136]

Brigadistas occasionally found their Cuban hosts unprepared to understand

American attitudes about racial divisions, both within social justice movements and in Cuba's volunteer camps. The North Americans at times felt that the Cubans were unresponsive to the anger of African American, Asian American, and Latino/a Brigade members who charged that some white American radicals, despite their pronouncements of solidarity with the Third World, had not fully confronted their own ingrained racism and racial privilege. *Brigadista* Bernard Hughes wrote that he suspected the racialized camp environment had made black *brigadistas* cognizant of "just how deep racist attitudes went when they found themselves with progressive, radical whites — the whites who were supposed to be committed to changing this country — who were not liberated from their racist heritage."[137]

Gendered tensions similarly manifested themselves in the Brigade camps, often in ways that mirrored those within U.S. social movements stateside. Women *brigadistas*, some of whom had actively confronted misogyny within leftist movements at home as women's liberation gathered momentum as a political and cultural force in the late 1960s, were often angered by the lack of priority that male Americans gave gender equality in the Brigade camps. Women's demands that gender be taken seriously as a legitimate arena of political struggle often faced challenges from both Americans and Cubans, and both men and women. Adopting a class-based analysis, some male *brigadistas* saw gendered power and the oppression of women — in a word, patriarchy — as emanating primarily from the gendered divisions of labor and power within capitalist production.

The first two brigades, in particular, struggled to attain a balance between production goals and the distribution of labor by sex. In Cuba, cutting sugarcane had traditionally been a male occupation. Female Cuban laborers in turn piled it and performed other labor related to the harvest. A number of American women in the first brigade initially balked at what they considered to be an arbitrary division of labor by sex. All forms of labor might have equal status under socialism in theory, but in practice the distribution of labor often became arranged in ways that reinforced traditional gendered inequalities. The ICAP leadership gave the Americans latitude to decide the issue for themselves. After meeting for three days, a caucus of women in the Brigade ultimately decided that they "were not going to try to tell the Cubans how to cut their own sugarcane."

Nonetheless, the event forced the Americans to grapple with what their politics of gender meant in the context of Cuba's emphasis on collective, society-wide gain over the politics of individual liberation. Wrote one female *brigadista*: "The Cubans said that anyone could cut, but in many cases it has worked out that slow cutters pile the cane that others cut, since both things have to be done. And because it is the women who are not used to heavy physical labor as the men, they often end up with the piling. It has been a long road, to get to the point where men don't feel superior because they are the cutters, and in many brigades the problem has not been solved."[138] But the ICAP staffers encouraged the Brigade to vote on the issue, and the women were soon cutting sugarcane side by side with the men. While individual motivations for advocating for and approving the change likely varied, there is no doubt that, as the Brigade's production goal of 1 million *arrobas* began to loom, the gendered division of labor increasingly appeared both arbitrary and counterproductive, alluded to in *Granma*'s coverage of the Brigade.[139] On January 18, 1970, for instance, the newspaper's lengthy article on the progress of the Brigade featured a series of photographs, one showing both male and female *brigadistas* learning how to use a machete, and another showing another mixed male/female group gathering hewn cane, with the caption: "[T]he important work of piling."[140]

Other experiences in Cuba challenged Americans to rethink their conceptualizations of labor versus entertainment, and "bourgeois" versus "revolutionary" culture, and what, exactly, women's liberation should look like in socialist society. By the late 1960s, hundreds of thousands of Cuban women had received military instruction, and were increasingly common in manual-labor occupations. Forty percent of Cuban women had attained higher education by 1972,[141] and many had entered work sectors that had been historically male. Cuban women benefited significantly from the provision of universal education and health care during the first two decades of the revolution in ways that, by 1980, had equalized racial gaps in education and virtually all key health indicators among Cubans.[142] Socialism, Margaret Randall argued in her 1974 book, *Cuban Women Now*, had made the nation's women better off than their counterparts in the United States. Although some Cuban women entered traditionally feminized labor sectors such as teaching, the broad distribution of women throughout the country in the famed 1961 literacy campaign, as well as more recent deployments of teachers into the countryside in the late 1960s, allowed Cuban women to achieve new independence from the confines of gendered domestic labor and to level new political demands for equality within the workforce.[143]

But while Cuba's success in addressing some areas of gendered inequality was well known among the American brigades, the Americans were surprised to find that many Cuban women seemed to have little interest in jettisoning what some Americans considered to be traditional feminine gender norms.

Venceremos Brigade members and Cuban representatives hold a joint panel discussion on the occasion of International Women's Day, March 7, 1970. Courtesy of the Tamiment Library and Robert F. Wagner Labor Archives.

As one *brigadista* explained: "One of the hardest things for us to take was the Cuban entertainers who came to the camp. Most of the women in these singing groups seemed to us to come out of old Miami (or Havana) nightclubs. They frequently had bleached blond hair and tight-fitting skirts, and relied on sexual gestures and flirtation with the audience. We knew that when not entertaining, these women were probably dedicated revolutionaries, doing hard work. The incongruity was hard to deal with.... Good, bad, liberated, nonliberated — our categories didn't work."[144]

Yet there was also significant resonance between U.S. and Cuban feminist visions. Like American women, Cuban women also struggled to overcome traditional gender mores. On at least one occasion an American woman, acting as an ally to an influential Cuban leader, may have helped initiate public reflection on the issue. Margaret Randall writes in her memoir that near the beginning of her eleven years living in Cuba, Haydée Santamaría, a Cuban revolutionary who participated in the armed struggle phase of the revolution before founding the renowned Havana literary institute Casa de las Américas, asked her to sit on an otherwise all-male panel to elect Havana's annual Carnival queen. The outspoken Randall had been chosen, Santamaría later told her, because she suspected that Randall would regard the exercise as sexist and objectifying — and would "find a way to move us a bit closer to stopping those terrible contests."¹⁴⁵ Judges typically asked contestants questions about politics and global events, but the event remained essentially a beauty pageant. Sure enough, Randall composed an essay critiquing the contest's emphasis on judging women by physical characteristics instead of their participation in social change. The next day, *Granma* printed it on the front page, resulting in much public discussion. As Randall recalls Santamaría telling her later: "The armed struggle part of revolution is relatively easy. It is changing society, changing the old values and replacing them with new ones, that's hard."¹⁴⁶

The Cuban government's attempts to institutionalize gender equality through the protection of women's reproductive rights affected some members of the Venceremos Brigade in deeply personal ways. One *brigadista*, who had become pregnant while in Cuba, received an abortion while the group was passing through Santiago de Cuba on their tour of the island. Contrasting the popular attitude and institutional stance toward abortion in Cuba, which had been decriminalized in 1965, with those in the United States, which was still in the pre–*Row v. Wade* era, she credited both the Cuban staff at the hospital and her American comrades in the Brigade with allowing her to assume ownership of her body in a way that had not been possible in the United States:

> In Cuba, I was free, psychologically as well as practically, to choose. No one asked how I happened to get pregnant; no one asked whether I was married; no one asked why I didn't want the baby. People simply assumed my right to choose and then helped me to effect that choice. It was all a perfectly normal and natural process. This experience has liberated me, because it has given me my first complete understanding of my rights — not privileges or special favors, but rights regarding my body and my life.¹⁴⁷

The assumed freedom of women to control their bodies and their sexuality, however, did not necessarily translate into other forms of sexual freedom in either Cuba or the Brigade. Struggles over the meaning of gender in the early Venceremos Brigades achieved a particularly divisive manifestation amid a pattern of antigay discrimination and homophobic antagonism within the organization that demonstrated, in stark terms, the limits of the Brigade's vision for a new society domestically as well as the Americans' understanding of Cuba itself. Freedom of sexual orientation and the right to love freely, the Brigade's central leadership made clear, would not be part of that vision. Gay and lesbian *brigadistas* who joined the early delegations frequently experienced an environment of alienation from other Americans in the Brigade's camps. The Brigade's National Committee ultimately issued a statement declaring that critiques by *brigadistas* of the post-1959 Cuban government's notoriously negative stance toward homosexuality amounted to a form of "cultural imperialism," in which Americans ostensibly attempted to inculcate Cubans with "bourgeois" sexual values. The Brigade's Central Committee went as far as to claim, without any evidence, that "in general, homosexuals in Cuba have not participated in the revolutionary process...and are essentially parasites in the revolution." Maintaining that "the Cuban people had already opened a full discussion on homosexuality' and had concluded that "homosexuality in Cuba is a social pathology left over from the decadent bourgeois order," the Brigade's Central Committee echoed the antigay stance of moral hardliners in the Cuban government while also demonstrating a willful misreading of Cuban society and history.[148]

According to historian Ian Lekus, the Brigade's National Committee ultimately adopted — apparently on their own, and not at the bidding of their Cuban hosts — a "don't ask, don't tell" policy toward gay men and women who wanted to join the delegations to Cuba, demanding that they hide their sexual identities if they wished to participate.[149] ICAP workers were aware of the antigay persecution in the camps and often disapproved, but apparently did nothing to intervene, regarding it as an internal matter that the Americans had to decide for themselves.[150] Although the Cuban government's infamous practice of sending gay and gender-nonconforming men to the *Unidades Militates de Ayuda a la Producción* — Military Units to Aid Production — a series of work camps where political dissidents, those who refused to work, and "antisocial" individuals (primarily gay men, or those who appeared as such to police) had been discontinued before the Brigades arrived, rumors of the practice had already sullied the revolution's reputation for some visiting North Americans.[151] In 1965, the poet Allen Ginsberg had been expelled from Cuba for speaking out against the government's ban on the smoking of marijuana, its intellectual censorship and, especially, its persecution of gay men.[152]

The Cuban government's morality drives against gay and gender-nonconforming individuals, peaking in the the 1960s but persisting in milder forms for two decades, has cast a shadow over the reputation of the Cuban Revolution for decades among gay and lesbian leftists and their allies.[153] Although homophobia was endemic to the United States as well during this period, including within the New Left and Black Power movements — and indeed, to nations throughout Latin America and the world — North American leftists in Cuba were often shocked by the government's stance on homosexuality precisely because they had assumed that Cuba would be different. As scholars such as Rafael Rojas and Lillian Guerra have demonstrated, the often narrow political and cultural orthodoxies of the Cuban state facilitated a climate in which political and sexual minorities could experience significant social ostracism and political persecution. While not unique to the post-1959 era within Cuban history, this tendency was nevertheless significantly heightened by the Cuban state's need to consolidate its power during the 1960s, particularly amid a climate of constant U.S. interference, when it felt under siege by enemies real and imagined, a tendency that intensified during the 1970s with the deepening of the nation's ties to the Soviet Union.[154]

Ironically, the same year that Ginsberg was deported from Cuba as a political undesirable, the FBI and CIA opened files on him for his illegal travels to Cuba and classified him as "potentially dangerous."[155] Homophobic antagonism against gay and lesbian *brigadistas* during the organization's early years revealed the ways in which unity within the American movement was hindered by its own lack of vision, highlighting in painful ways the tendency of some Americans to simplify the complexity of Cuban society to suit their own expectations and ideologies.

Like the Cuban government, the Brigade's leadership eventually jettisoned its overtly antigay stance. Organizers were known in later years to apologize publicly for the group's earlier homophobia. Views on the politics of sexuality in Cuba also varied within cultural and political organizations, which were composed of individuals who often held nuanced views on many social issues, and significant ideological latitude sometimes existed, particularly within cultural and intellectual organizations. For instance, although organizations like OSPAAAL did not make gay liberation a primary part of their cultural production, the September-October issue of *Tricontinental* in 1971 featured a full-page "wanted poster" for Richard Nixon that had been modified to contain information about repression against the Gay Liberation Movement. The poster, which condemned Nixon for the crimes of "genocide; homicide; conspiracy," had a dialogue box drawn into it which forced Nixon to "speak" a press release titled "Los Angeles GLF Sues Police Department," which condemned the police for "violation of the group's civil rights." The release read, in part: "The suit, citing the Constitutional guarantees of free assembly and equal protection of the law, points out that an inordinately high number of pigs have shown up at gay-ins and that the police have selectively discriminated against gays by selectively enforcing a city ordinance against distributing leaflets in Griffith Park."[156]

In other words, gay and gender-nonconforming people were being harassed in Los Angeles in 1971 in a remarkably similar fashion to the way they were harassed in Havana. It is unclear whether this protest art produced by OSPAAAL was intended to draw attention to the injustice of antigay harassment, or to relieve Cuba of some responsibility by pointing out that similar harassment occurred in the United States. Nonetheless, the fact that gay people were depicted as victims of injustice solely because they were gay in the pages of *Tricontinental* demonstrates that ideological uniformity was by no means a given within Cuban institutions. By the 1990s, the official stance toward homosexuality within the Cuban state itself began to shift significantly, embracing some policies on sexual freedom that were among the most progressive in Latin America. In 2010, Fidel Castro personally accepted responsibility for state repression against gays and lesbians in Cuba in the 1960s and 1970s, and the government has continued to assume a number of progressive stances on the issue.[157]

Fractures within the early Venceremos Brigade delegations put on full display the precarious nature of coalition across yawning gulfs of identity and ideology. Yet the ability of the Brigade's participants to wrestle productively with these contradictions through dialogue, as well as the institutionalization of key changes to the organization, convinced some participants that coalition among fractious U.S. social justice movements was possible. The living conditions of the Brigade camps bore an inadvertent resemblance to the "encounter groups" of the era, in which people of different racial backgrounds would intensively discuss their differences face to face, a practice that had gained popularity in progressive circles during the late 1960s.

Similarly, identity-based caucuses encouraged a kind of intragroup "consciousness-raising" of the kind that had been popularized by U.S. feminists.[158] The experience of Cuba provided Americans with a mirror with which to self-reflexively assess the state of the American Left. According to core Brigade organizers Carol Brightman and Sandra Levinson, "what happened to the *brigadistas* in Cuba, the way they responded to the challenges of that daily struggle in the *campamento*, gives us more insight into the strengths and weaknesses of our movement than any single activity in the United States."[159]

Inside the Colossus in the 1970s and Beyond

Writing in the early 1970s, scholar Kirkpatrick Sale surmised that the Venceremos Brigade had already become "one of the most imaginative enterprises ever undertaken by the American left."[160] Although tested by internal strife, indeed birthed in the midst of one of the most culturally tumultuous periods of the long 1960s era, the Venceremos Brigade was remarkable for organizations of the era in that it did not implode. Instead, it grew into one of the most dynamic and longest-lived grassroots organizations of the era. Sending Americans to Cuba every year throughout the 1970s, the group continued its unique model of people-to-people exchange, irrespective of the shifting diplomatic tides between Havana and Washington.

The experience of the early delegations subsequently led to changes in recruitment practices to favor participants who were firmly engaged in political activism. New recruits in particular, whatever their movement or ideological location, were required to have "a defined position of support for the Cuban revolution."[161] It was a move away from a model of solidarity travel in which politically inexperienced recruits would become radicalized through their experiences in Cuba. In a January 1971 letter to the Brigade's National Committee, the Puerto Rican organization Movimiento Pro Independencia announced its resignation from the Brigade due, in part, to the Brigade's incorporation of nonactivists. "It has been our experience that the non-movement people are simply 'tripping' (as you call it) and do not integrate into the struggle upon their return. There are very few exceptions to this to warrant their inclusion."[162] The Movimiento critique echoed the concerns of some Brigade organizers, who had pointed out the contradictions inherent to a political project that simultaneously sought to provide everyday Americans with a firsthand glimpse of Cuba, yet also sought to forge stronger connections between Cubans and U.S. activists already committed to social justice work. "Due to the weak and often apolitical basis of that international orientation," the group's National Committee wrote, "many people who gravitated toward the brigade were doing so for rather confused reasons."[163] In the years to come, the Brigade would now focus on building delegations composed exclusively of committed activists.

With its travel mission thus redefined, the Brigade also sought to clarify its purpose at home. The Brigade's model of travel activism, the national organizers decided, would be complemented by a reinvigorated campaign of public education and print culture aimed at countering the mainstream media's portrayals of Cuba, beginning with the perspectives of Americans who had seen the island firsthand. In 1971, a collective within the organization compiled journal entries and letters from the first two delegations into an edited collection, published by Simon and Schuster in 1971 as *The Venceremos Brigade: Young Americans Sharing the Life and Work of Revolutionary Cuba*, excerpts of which were published in the Cuban quarterly *Tricontinental*.[164] Discontinuing the newsletter *Turquino* in 1972, the Brigade published a series of other pamphlets throughout the 1970s in an attempt to inform the U.S. public of its work, provide basic information about the Cuban Revolution and the nation's ongoing socialist development, and provide information about pertinent struggles elsewhere in the Third World. The newsletter *Venceremos*, initiated in 1973, featured news about left-wing movements worldwide and updates on U.S.-Cuba relations from a Cuban perspective. Many of the articles were reproduced from Cuban periodicals. In 1974, the Brigade also briefly published a pamphlet series called *Cuba Va* as a record of its activities. The first issue reintroduced the Brigade as "an educational project which since 1969 has directed its efforts toward developing solidarity with the Cuban Revolution and the struggles against U.S. domination in the Third World."[165] The Brigade conceptualized its political advocacy as another means of breaking the U.S. government's blockade against the island, a policy that, the group maintained, sought to isolate Cuba from the world while also isolating Americans from their Caribbean neighbor.

While remaining radical in its rhetoric, the Brigade's goals during the 1970s centered increasingly upon public education through the experiential learning of solidarity travel. As the effervescence of the sixties era dimmed, the group's goal of creating "revolutionary consciousness" in the United States for the purpose of domestic transformation was gradually superseded by the more modest goals of encouraging broad public opposition to the U.S. embargo, support for the normalization of diplomatic relations, and support for socialism in America. Yet this too articulated a radical reconceptualization of U.S.-Cuba diplomatic relations, one that understood a more benevolent U.S. presence in the world as fundamentally dependent upon social justice at home. Writing in 1971, Carol Brightman and Sandra Levinson outlined a new model of domestic political transformation through which people in the United States could simultaneously support self-determination for Cuba and social justice in America:

> We want a new social order in which the United States contributes its vast technological resources to the alleviation of human misery, not its perpetuation, and to the liberation of people everywhere from the corruption of capitalist overdevelopment as well as from the tyranny of underdevelopment. To bring this new world into being, we must confront the institutions which preserve an aging empire, with revolutionary institutions which extend the power of all peoples to determine their collective destinies.[166]

The Brigade's campaign of print culture peaked in the mid-1970s with the publication of a series of booklets examining different aspects of Cuban society and politics. In 1975, the group's Educational Commission published a booklet entitled, *Only the People Can Perform Miracles: Health Care in Cuba*. An overview of the nation's health system, including in the arenas of maternity and occupational health, it contrasted Cuba's provision of high-quality, universal health care with conditions before the revolution which, the group's activists noted, were "comparable to health care in much of Latin America today, or to the situation in the ghettoes and barrios and Indian reservations in the United States ... a privilege of the rich and upper middle classes."[167] The Brigade also published speeches by Fidel Castro in booklet form, including an English/Spanish speech outlining Cuba's military intervention in support of the leftist Movimento Popular de Libertação de Angola (MPLA) against a U.S.-backed invasion by South Africa,[168] and another entitled *Angola: African Giron (Bay of Pigs)—April 1976*.[169] The Brigade's 1976 booklet, *Democracy in Cuba*, a detailed overview of the nation's governing system, examined socialist "participatory democracy" within Cuban society through mass membership organizations. Focusing on the neighborhood CDRs, the Federación de Mujeres Cubanas (FMC), and the workings of the Cuban electoral system, the authors contrasted massive popular electoral participation in Cuba — 98 percent of Cuba's eligible voters, for example, had turned out on February 15, 1976, to ratify the nation's new constitution by a margin of 97.7 percent — with the 7 percent voter turnout in the U.S. primary elections that same year.[170]

In 1978, in the aftermath of Cuba's intervention in Angola, the Brigade published its definitive statement on race in Cuba as a booklet entitled *Free and Equal: The End of Racial Discrimination in Cuba*. Authored by Terry Cannon, a former SNCC member who traveled to Cuba with the Brigade in 1971, and Johnnetta Cole, a professor of anthropology at the University of Massachusetts, both members of the Brigade's National Committee, the booklet argued that Cuba exemplified a nation "where the institutions of racism have been seriously weakened or eliminated altogether" through the initiative of the revolutionary government to break down racial discrimination.[171] Evaluating Cuba's pre-1959 history, Cannon and Cole emphasized the role of U.S. and Spanish domination in creating the institutional framework for formal racial segregation in Cuba through the empowerment of a wealthy, largely white elite, and highlighted the role of worker's organizations and communists in the nation's history of antiracist struggle. "Racist ideology," they claimed, "failed to imbed itself deeply in the peasantry and working class," in which interracial collaboration had long existed.[172]

The heart of the booklet was a series of excerpted interviews with a distinguished group of North Americans who had visited Cuba, some of them for the sole purpose of witnessing the island's race relations: Edward Boorstein, an economist who had worked for the Federal Reserve Board, the government of Germany, and Cuba's Ministry of Foreign Commerce, and had been an economic adviser to Chilean president Salvador Allende; Reggie Boorstein, an employee with *Prensa Latina*'s New York office who had previously worked in Cuba in the early 1960s and in Chile before the 1973 coup; Robert Chrisman, an essayist, scholar, and founding publisher of *The Black Scholar* who had first visited Cuba in 1971; Robert Davidson, an activist with Citizens for Participation in Political Action who had been a factory worker when he traveled to Cuba with the 8th contingent of Brigade; Ronald V. Dellums, a California Congressman who had traveled to Cuba in 1977, where he met with Fidel Castro; Phyl Garland, a professor of journalism at Columbia University who had traveled to Cuba with a delegation of African-American artists; Helen Rodríguez-Trías, Associate Director of Pediatrics at Roosevelt Hospital in New York who had visited Cuba at the invitation of the Ministry of Public Health; and Jacquelyn Stanton, a professor of education at the University of Massachusetts who had visited Cuba with the ninth contingent of the Brigade.

Reflecting upon their experiences in Cuba, the speakers contrasted Cuba's successes in ameliorating many forms of institutional racism with persisting racial inequality in the United States in areas such as education and health care. Although the booklet has been critiqued for understating the persistence of racism in Cuba, many of their findings comport with later studies of race in Cuba.

As historian Alejandro de la Fuente has argued, indicators of racial inequality in Cuba in the areas of health and education, arenas where the Cuban Revolution has been most successful, suggest the comparative uniqueness of the revolution's achievements in relation to other multiracial nations. According to de la Fuente, "in the early 1980s, Cuba's black and mulatto population was probably the only one in the hemisphere whose members could expect to live to more or less the same age as their white countrymen," far exceeding both the United States and Brazil.[173] Cuba's partial transcendence of its racial past provided the American visitors with a model for imagining the eradication of institutional racism in their own country.

THE VENCEREMOS BRIGADE continued to send a delegation to the island every summer throughout the 1970s, 1980s, 1990s, and into the new millennium. The Brigade's trips increasingly averaged two to four weeks, and arrived by plane instead of ship. As with earlier delegations, these brigades also performed agricultural or housing construction work, although not sugarcane harvesting, which became increasingly mechanized during the 1970s. A disproportionate portion of the participants continued to come from California and New York, followed by the Northeast and the Southwest regions, although activists, workers, and students from throughout the nation joined the Brigade.

Although the Brigade was a key antecedent of later, much larger, more pluralistic mobilizations of Americans against U.S. policy in the world in the 1970s and 1980s, these movements, most notably the varied Latin American solidarity movements, sought primarily to change U.S. foreign policy toward nations such as Chile, El Salvador, Guatemala, and Nicaragua, emphasizing less the transformation of U.S. society itself.[174] There is evidence that the Brigade's bid to shape the "foreign policy" of the American Left by bringing it into contact with Cuba's revolution reverberated within left-wing social justice movements in the United States in important ways. Writing in 1999, Elizabeth Martinez observed that, thirty years after its founding, the Brigade remained a "unique pillar of the U.S. Left." Much of this impact, she argued, was a result of the continuing activism of the group's alumni. "It is rare not to encounter one or two wherever you find motion in the U.S."[175] In the years following the first delegation in 1969, hundreds of veterans of the Brigade's "radical Peace Corps" turned up throughout the spectrum of U.S. left-wing politics. While it is not surprising that many *brigadistas* went on to be active in multifaceted movements concerning U.S. foreign policy during the 1970s and 1980s, particularly those related to Washington's involvement in Latin America,[176] the Brigade's legacy includes a substantial activist presence elsewhere. Alumni of the Brigade include attorney Michael Ratner, longtime head of the Center for Constitutional Rights; legendary Japanese American civil rights activist Yuri Kochiyama; attorney Fania E. Davis, the sister of Angela Davis; and numerous academic scholars, including Michael Kazin, Ben V. Olguín, Daniel Widener, and Roxanne Dunbar-Ortiz.

The Brigade's domestic impact is also illustrated by the role that it played in the upsurge of Marxism in leftist circles during the 1970s. Formed around the organization's avowedly communist National Committee, the Brigade helped disseminate Third World variants of Marxism, principally those originating in Cuba, among the broad U.S. Left.[177] As scholar Max Elbaum has observed, the Brigade's public education programs and its creation of opportunities for activists to interact directly with Cuban communists "popularized socialism and Marxism" to a wide range of activists in the United States. By prioritizing the recruitment of young people of color, the Brigade also served as a vehicle through which the racial nationalism of many young activists was augmented by socialism through travel to Cuba.[178] Whereas the Brigade had begun as an outgrowth of the largely white New Left, by the 1980s most delegations and the group's leadership were majority people of color, often of working class background, a characteristic that would endure for the next two decades. Although not examined in any published studies of activism in U.S. communities of color, the Brigade exists firmly within the constellation of activist formations that scholar Cynthia A. Young has conceptualized as a "U.S. Third World Left."[179] Finally, a significant number of alumni from the 1969 and 1970 delegations, although disillusioned with the Brigade's stance on gay liberation, became active in feminist and antihomophobia work upon their return.[180] *Brigadistas* were also prominent among the West Coast founders of the historic Third World Women's Alliance in 1971.[181] While the radicalizing potentials of travel to Cuba were evident well before 1969 — indeed, this was one of the primary legacies of earlier Cuba solidarity movements in the United States, including the activism of the Fair Play for Cuba Committee — the Brigade created a particularly fertile environment for the development of radical consciousness. Activists from a broad spectrum of grassroots political movements lived and worked together in close quarters for weeks at a time, where they exchanged ideas, argued and bickered, and frequently broke down barriers and challenged themselves to rethink basic assumptions about each other and the ideologies that they held. These struggles and transformations reverberated into their political work upon returning stateside. Many activists credited their experiences in the Brigade with crystallizing their personal politics and launching them into a lifetime of political engagement. Others who were already firmly rooted in left-wing activities returned with a renewed hopefulness born of witnessing the capacity of everyday Cubans to treat adversity with optimism and overcome great odds with the humor and ingenuity born of the belief that human exploitation was not inevitable.

2

Missiles, in Human Form
Cuba and the Specter of Foreign Subversion in America

All this has internal repercussion in the United States; propitiates the resurgence of an element which is being minimized in spite of its vigor by all imperialist forces: class struggle even within its own territory. How close we could look into a bright future should two, three or many Vietnams flourish throughout the world.
—**Che Guevara,** 1967

The revolutionary who has committed his destiny under the banner of Marxism-Leninism establishes his identity with a world center of revolution (in this instance Havana).... He ceases to be merely "domestic" when he adopts his international identity as a revolutionary.
—**Federal Bureau of Investigation,** 1976

IN THE SPRING OF 1970, James O. Eastland, the arch segregationist senator from Mississippi, held forth on the Senate floor to condemn the rising specter of Cuban communism inside the United States. "We intend to light the shadows that surround this vicious operation — to drive from those shadows the missiles — in human form — which have been fashioned on that Communist island and fired at America," the Senator warned. "We want our people to be aware of the direct chain which reaches from Cuba into our cities, our campuses, our conventions, our lives — and which threatens the life of this Republic."[1]

The "vicious operation" that Eastland referred to was the Venceremos Brigade. A left-wing humanitarian organization that sought to forge people-to-people ties between Americans and Cubans to undermine Cold War mistrust, participants of the Brigade had defied the U.S. travel ban to show their support for Cuban self-determination and the social gains of the nation's ongoing socialist revolution. To the Venceremos Brigade's organizers, the delegations, which drew their members from the burgeoning antiwar, Black Power, Puerto Rican independence, Chicano/a, women's liberation, and labor movements, testified to the broad-based support that the Cuban Revolution had managed to accrue within the United States.[2] To key U.S. officials, however, the Venceremos Brigade had the hallmarks of a conspiracy of foreign subversion.

Ties between Havana and the Venceremos Brigade, as well as constitutive groups such as the Black Panther Party and the Weather Underground offshoot of Students for a Democratic Society (SDS), would become a preoccupation of the FBI and CIA during the late 1960s and throughout the next decade as officials charged that ties between the U.S. Left and Havana represented a threat to U.S. internal security. An indefatigable cold warrior, Eastland had already distinguished himself with an uncanny ability to discern communism virtually everywhere he looked. Its influence, the senator claimed, lurked behind civil rights organizing in the South, and he had worked to expose it.[3] In reality, communists had not played a prominent role in southern organizing against white supremacy since the 1930s.[4] But although the socialist and communist movements that rose in interwar America, cresting in the Great Depression, had been largely subdued by state repression during the McCarthy era, by the mid-1960s, Marxist theory, and indeed communism itself, had again gained credibility within a broad spectrum of the Left. This time, the allure of Marxism shined most brightly not from the Soviet Union, but from the Third World. Cuba's revolution captured the imagination of the global Left in 1959 and, in doing so, helped realign radicalism in the United States in ways that would have a significant impact on the "long" 1960s era.[5] Cuba would now claim center stage for a generation of American radicals who looked to the decolonizing world for inspiration and political theory. As scholars of U.S. social movements in the long 1960s era have often argued, Cuba's revolution was a key influence that informed elements of a new leftism in America that was increasingly oriented away from the Soviet Union and toward revolutionary precedents in the Third World.[6] By the mid-1970s, the FBI had reached a similar conclusion, contending that Cuba had become the primary global inspiration of the U.S. Left. Cuba, not the Soviet Union or China, now represented the most potent global locus of radical theory: a living Third World socialist experiment, one that had persisted for a decade despite U.S. efforts to unseat it. "For the youthful revolutionary," one bureau report observed, "a new model of successful revolution existed — Havana," in which "the example of the Cuban revolution became the guide." Instead of the Old Left's decades-old blueprint, there now existed "another center of world revolution . . . that would rival Moscow and Peking." Havana was "where the youthful revolutionary [can] learn at first hand how to create revolution."[7] Cuba was thus imagined as the new epicenter of radicalism for the 1960s era, and the primary foreign benefactor of left-wing dissent and subversion in North America.

Senator Eastland's invocation of the Cuban Missile Crisis through his likening of Venceremos Brigade participants to "missiles" illustrates the manner in which key U.S. officials regarded Cuba's threat to America in the late 1960s and 1970s to be not only military, but ideological. Cuba, they warned, had replaced Soviet military hardware, "aimed at America" during the October 1962 crisis, with American leftist dissidents bent on deploying Cuban revolutionary theory to subvert America from within. Accused of collaborating with their nation's primary foreign adversary in the hemisphere, American dissidents who traveled to Cuba during the late 1960s became a lightning rod for state fears that the American Left was being influenced by foreign powers.

In October of 1970, the *Long Island Press* ran an investigative series entitled "Cuba: School for U.S. Radicals." The series, authored by journalists Georgie Ann Greyer and Keyes Beech, noted that the stream of American leftist travelers to Cuba had included a lengthy list of well-known American activists and intellectuals — a veritable "who's who of the American radical movement."[8] The series paid special attention to the Venceremos Brigade. The organization, the FBI noted, was the largest single group of Americans to travel to the Caribbean nation since its 1959 revolution. According to the CIA, the Brigade was composed of "radicalized American youth, all sharing pro-Castro sentiments and opposing what they term U.S. imperialism."[9] As the Americans coalesced with Cuban officials and held meetings with Vietnamese National Liberation Front representatives, U.S. officials warned of the perils of allowing impressionable young people to consort with communists and revolutionaries. As an indication of the risk, the U.S. State Department pointed to a number of high-profile American radicals, including members of the Weather Underground Organization and the Black Panther Party, who had participated in protest actions in the United States after their meetings with revolutionaries in Cuba. As one State Department official put it: "Name any disturbance in the United States — on campus, in the streets, anywhere — and I'll name you the leaders of it who have been to Cuba."[10]

Scrutiny of the Venceremos Brigade took three primary forms. First, the Brigade, which referred to itself increasingly as a "political education project" during the early 1970s, was accused of being a vehicle for the dissemination of Cuban political propaganda within America. Second, U.S. officials claimed that Cuba was secretly training Brigade members in guerrilla warfare. Finally,

U.S. officials charged that the Cuban intelligence apparatus was exploiting the Brigade as an opportunity to recruit Americans as spies, or as a means of implanting Cuban-born operatives inside the United States. These claims, in various forms, created the primary contours of the U.S. government's campaign of surveillance and disruption against the Brigade and other American radicals who formed close relationships with Cuba.

WHILE THE U.S. GOVERNMENT'S perception of Cuba as an external military threat to the United States has been extensively studied in scholarship, little attention has focused on the ways in which Cuba also functioned within the imaginary of U.S. officialdom as a threat to *internal* security in the context of the global Cold War and the social tumult of the 1960s era. Indeed, while much scholarship has examined Cuban revolutionary internationalism, particularly Havana's aid to leftist movements beyond its shores, little critical attention has examined Cuban support for radicalism within North America. Concern over Cuba's support for leftist revolutionary movements in Latin America in the 1960s, and in Africa in the 1960s and 1970s, ranked as one of the primary preoccupations of the State Department and CIA with regard to U.S.-Cuba relations, and the ceasing of Havana's revolutionary internationalism was among the most strenuously sought demands of successive U.S. presidential administrations, from Kennedy to Reagan.[11] Examining claims of Cuban influence inside the United States brings a key aspect of U.S.-Cuba state relations into conversation with the history of the U.S. Left during the long 1960s era.

Similarly, the U.S. government's investigation of pro-Cuba solidarity activities in the United States contributes to our understanding of how Washington deployed political discourses of "foreign influence" to justify repressive measures against domestic dissent. As is well known, the FBI's Counter Intelligence Program of the 1960s, popularly known as "Cointelpro," sought to disrupt civilian opposition to the Vietnam War and attempted to destroy radical currents within the African American freedom movement and other grassroots formations. The FBI's covert operations deployed a variety of repressive tactics against left-wing social movements, much of it carried out against political activists who had been organizing in an expressly legal and nonviolent manner. Charges that American dissidents were being controlled ideologically — and perhaps aided materially — by a hostile foreign power provided U.S. intelligence and local law enforcement agencies with an additional pretext for surveillance of domestic dissent activities, which they sought to paint in the red light of communist subversion.

Yet the specter of Cuban influence within the United States was not simply a FBI and CIA fantasy. Indeed, the American government's investigation of the Venceremos Brigade and other U.S. left-wing social movements illuminates several unexpected facets of Cuban revolutionary internationalism through its intersection with U.S. radicalism. Che Guevara's famous "Message to the Tricontinental," addressed to the First Solidarity Conference of the Peoples of Africa, Asia, and Latin America (OSPAAAL) in Havana in January 1966 and published the following April in OSPAAAL's globally circulated magazine, *Tricontinental*, is generally regarded as a call for Third World solidarity with Vietnamese resistance to American military aggression. Nonetheless, Guevara's invocation of global solidarity with the Vietnamese cause also spoke indirectly to the First World — and by extension, the U.S. Left — by inviting north-south solidarity in the anticolonial struggle and raising the possibility of direct participation by radicals of the north. "To die under the flag of Vietnam," Guevara wrote, "would be equally glorious and desirable for an American, an Asian, an African, even a European."[12]

Although the antiwar movement in early 1966 was but a shadow of the broad-based protest movement that would emerge two years later, the rising death toll among U.S. troops was already fueling intense public disillusionment with the war effort. As Guevara observed, "All this has internal repercussion in the United States; propitiates the resurgence of an element which is being minimized in spite of its vigor by all imperialist forces: class struggle even within its own territory."[13]

Guevara thus suggested presciently that the United States would be forced from the field of war in Vietnam not only by the military defeat, but by the rupture of domestic popular unity required for sustaining the war effort. Cuba sought to hasten these developments by supporting the U.S. radical Left. Organizations such as the Black Panther Party, the Student Nonviolent Coordinating Committee (SNCC), and the Weather Underground, all of which forged strong relationships with Cuba, repeatedly echoed Guevara's call for anti-imperialist struggle inside the empire. As an amalgamation of these movements, the Venceremos Brigade attempted to crystalize Guevara's vision of north-south solidarity into a sustained praxis of direct engagement with Cuba.

Finally, U.S. government anxiety regarding the U.S. Left's engagements with Cuba yields insights about the relationship between state, popular, and academically generated histories of social movements. Since the FBI has compiled an estimated 23,000 pages of surveillance[14] on the Venceremos Brigade, an organization largely overlooked by historians, I argue that these surveillance records represent a kind of "state history" of dissent. FBI files are undertheorized in their function as historical archives, and the FBI has been underscrutinized in its role as archivist and historical biographer. Locked away in vaults and storerooms, classified files represent a vast and subterranean incarcerated archive, one that can be paroled to the public record, and thus historical memory, by the Freedom of Information Act. This is accomplished after it has been determined by review that the release of the information poses no remaining danger to the state. FBI files on the Brigade provide an underexamined avenue through which to understand the relationship between social movements, state power, and knowledge production, and a window through which we may peer into hitherto concealed aspects of U.S.-Cuba relations during a period of intense social upheaval.

Foreign Influence, Domestic Dissent

In June 1970, President Nixon convened a meeting of top national security staff to encourage interagency coordination to address domestic dissent. "Certainly hundreds, perhaps thousands, of Americans — mostly under 30 — are determined to destroy our society," Nixon told those assembled. "They are reaching out for the support — ideological and otherwise — of foreign powers and they are developing their own brand of indigenous revolutionary activism."[15]

Nixon's linking of foreign and domestic radicalism, while perhaps characteristic in form of the paranoia that would become a hallmark of his dealings with perceived political enemies, nevertheless evinced continuity in substance with previous administrations. State repression against political dissent in America, from the Red Scares, to the FBI's efforts to undermine Martin Luther King Jr., to the bureau's efforts to disrupt antiwar organizations, to its war against Black Power, was often predicated upon the assertion that domestic social movements were being influenced by foreign powers. That these expressions of political dissent became a focus of the CIA, and not merely domestic agencies such as the FBI, illustrates the way in which the U.S. state viewed homegrown radicalism within a larger international imaginary during the Cold War.

Eastland's investigation of the Venceremos Brigade in 1970 was not the senator's first encounter with U.S. supporters of the Cuban Revolution. In fact, he had chaired Senate hearings a decade earlier on the activities of the Fair Play for Cuba Committee (FPCC), whose founding members had taken out a full-page advertisement in the *New York Times* entitled "What is really happening in Cuba?" Intended to dispel inaccuracies being circulated in the U.S. press regarding the revolution, the ad had initiated the formation of the

FPCC and galvanized widespread support for Cuba among leftists and liberal intellectuals against the backdrop of a quickly gathering storm of anti-Castro animus from Washington. But the advertisement had been paid for in part by the Cuban government. Faced with a fundraising shortfall, FPCC had obtained funds through Raúl Roa Kouri, a Cuban diplomat stationed at the Cuban Mission to the United Nations in New York and the son of Raúl Roa, Cuba's foreign minister.[16] Although no similar Cuban funding for the Venceremos Brigade's activities in the United States has ever been documented, the FPCC advertisement lent credibility to the U.S. government's claims that the Brigade was being financed by Havana.

Moreover, the Cuban government had actively propagandized in support of social justice movements inside the United States, providing U.S. officials with ample reason to accuse Cuba of at least rhetorical encouragement for social upheaval in the United States. If treatments of U.S. life and culture within the Cuban media tended to focus on themes of "alienation" and materialist superficiality,[17] they also celebrated artists and performers who challenged these norms. Santiago Álvarez's acclaimed 1964 film *Now* set moving images of the U.S. civil rights movement to a haunting song by Lena Horne, for instance, and in 1969 the magazine *El Caimán Barbudo* profiled the protest music of U.S. folks singers Joan Baez, Bob Dylan, and Pete Seeger, and reprinted an English-language notice advertising a new book about Woodie Guthrie that identified the singer as a "prophetic singer" and a "killer of fascists."[18]

Cuban news and cultural organs therefore insisted upon celebrating progressive elements within U.S. society even as they lambasted negative ones. Attention to world affairs in Cuban periodicals and newspapers such as *Granma*, *Bohemia*, and *Tricontinental* included regular coverage of protest movements in North America, especially mobilizations against the war in Vietnam, police brutality against African Americans, and repression of student mobilizations.

Violent episodes of repression of political dissidents by the U.S. state allowed the Cuban government to counterbalance U.S. charges of political repression in Cuba, and to dispute the exceptionalism of U.S. claims to moral superiority over Cuba concerning the rights of political dissidents. The killing of four students by Ohio National Guardsmen during an antiwar protest at Kent State University on May 4, 1970, for instance, prompted a flurry of condemnatory Cuban media attention.[19] The incident prompted large demonstrations by students in Havana in solidarity with the victims, with *Granma* running photos of the protests, which the newspaper numbered at 10,000 people. In one photo, Cuban students lead a march with a banner reading "Apoyamos lucha de los estudiantes norteamericanos"—we support the struggle of the

North American students—while in another, students stand on the main steps of the University of Havana carrying large photo portraits of the dead U.S. students. The march led to San Lázaro and Prado Streets, where Cuban student Rubén Batista Rubio, shot by police, had become in 1953 the first student martyr in the campaign against the Batista government.[20]

The Cuban press lionized in particular the African American freedom struggle, providing regular coverage of the civil rights and Black Power movements and devoting significant coverage to urban rebellions, institutional racism, and conditions of urban racial inequality.[21] Cuba's Organization of Solidarity with the People of Asia, Africa, and Latin America (OSPAAAL) published a series of iconic posters depicting repression against African Americans and black radical icons, including a poster depicting the death of George Jackson, which used images and text to artistically defend the right of racially oppressed people to fight for liberation inside the United States, including through force of arms. Fidel Castro personally lauded the burgeoning protest movements in the imperial power to the north, and encouraged Cubans to support en masse "our brothers the black people, of our brothers the students and of our brothers the workers of the United States." In speeches before tens of thousands, the Cuban leader identified North American dissidents as an essential component of the global struggle against imperialism and capitalist exploitation.[22]

The U.S. state's campaign to discredit the Venceremos Brigade thus emerged amid a climate of acute anxiety regarding the global ties, real and imagined, of U.S. social change movements, which had grown large enough for the U.S. government to regard as a genuine threat to both domestic security and to Washington's foreign policy objectives. By the early 1970s, these anxieties had begun to come to light in a series of public scandals over surveillance and domestic political repression, touched off in part by the Watergate affair beginning in 1972. In December 1974, the *New York Times* broke the story that the CIA had conducted a "massive, illegal domestic intelligence operation during the Nixon Administration against the antiwar movement and other dissident groups in the United States."[23] In violation of its charter, a special unit in the CIA had targeted at least 10,000 American citizens using a variety of techniques, including break-ins to offices and homes, wiretapping, and inspection of mail. The CIA alleged that the wide array of targets, which ranged from antiwar activists to members of Congress, had been influenced by "foreign agents" from nations such as the Soviet Union, North Vietnam, and North Korea.

Although Cuba was not mentioned, the *New York Times* article was the first public revelation that the CIA had conducted operations against American citizens on American soil. The CIA, whose 1947 charter explicitly forbade it from conducting domestic law enforcement or internal security functions, had nonetheless deployed a range of illegal intelligence gathering techniques against individuals who had not been accused of any crime. An unnamed government intelligence official acknowledged the implications of the program with regard to domestic dissent: "If you're an agent sitting in Paris and you're asked to find out whether Jane Fonda is being manipulated by foreign intelligence services, you've got to ask yourself who is the real target. Is it the foreign intelligence services or Jane Fonda?"[24]

Documents declassified in 2001 provide additional depth to the 1974 public revelations of CIA spying. In particular, they confirm that state anxieties about the purported influence of communism in America played a significant role in legitimizing repression of political dissent well into the 1960s and 1970s, long after the Red Scare era. A November 1967 CIA report entitled "International Connections of U.S. Peace Groups" profiled eight American antiwar organizations and a civil rights organization suspected of having "significant international communist contacts."[25] Contact, however, did not necessarily connote direct collaboration, but merely association or ideological influence. The report contained a plethora of unverified claims. The National Mobilization Committee to End the War in Vietnam, alleged the report, had been penetrated by communists, and Chairman David Dellinger and Vice Chair Jerry Rubin had "known and associated with Communists."[26] Students for a Democratic Society worked closely on college campuses with the "Communist-controlled W. E. B. Du Bois Clubs of America," the report maintained, but managed themselves to resist direct communist control.[27] The Radical Education Project, SDS's research and publishing arm, "keeps in touch with the Viet Cong and African nationalists," according to the report.[28] The Student Nonviolent Coordinating Committee expounded its concepts of "guerilla warfare and racial violence" at every opportunity, the CIA alleged, while SNCC activist Stokely Carmichael "traveled extensively throughout the Third World" including, most suspiciously, to Vietnam and Cuba.[29] The group Women Strike for Peace, according to the report, had "known communists" in its association, some of whom maintained contact with Hanoi.[30]

Only one group, Tri-Continental Information Center, was accused of actually collaborating with communists in the United States.[31] Another, War Resistors League, was accused not of consorting with communists but of having a "long record of helping pacifists and ... assisting US servicemen who wish to desert their posts."³² Finally, the Bertrand Russell Peace Foundation was accused of failing to "take an objective approach to international problems," preferring instead to engage in "agitation against alleged US 'imperialism' and the advocacy of 'Che Guevara' type revolutionary movements."³³

That the CIA, the most powerful intelligence agency in the world, authorized itself to investigate a wide range of domestic American political organizations, most of them explicitly pacifist or nonviolent, is testament to the degree to which key government and security agencies during the late 1960s believed that organized protest movements in the United States represented a credible threat to the stability of the nation.

Yet the Venceremos Brigade differed from the aforementioned organizations in important respects. From its inception, the Brigade's purpose was explicitly international in scope, and it openly supported Cuban communism, both ideologically and by virtue of its insistence that Cuba had a right to embrace any political system that it chose. As a transnational leftist organization seeking to build bridges between U.S. social justice movements and Cuba by bringing American activists to the island to see a functioning socialist society for themselves, the Brigade linked what they maintained was their constitutionally guaranteed right of free association to Cuba's right of national self-determination. As a December 1969 Situation Information Report from the CIA observed:

> While most Americans spend year-end holidays at home or with friends, and several thousands more devote themselves to low-key, hometown antiwar vigils, sing-ins, and peace demonstrations, another much smaller group will be hacking and stacking sugar cane in Cuba's Havana Province. These will be predominantly Black Panthers and members of Students for a Democratic Society, plus other radicalized American youth, all sharing pro-Castro sentiments and opposing what they term U.S. imperialism.³⁴

As most of the CIA's documents pertaining to the Brigade remain classified, it is not known whether the agency continued to investigate the Brigade after 1969. However, a variety of other high-level security agencies and local police departments conducted investigations of their own. In one September 1973 report, the FBI alleged that the Brigade might be involved in violations of a variety of laws which the bureau organized according to a series of keywords: "rebellion or insurrection," "seditious conspiracy," "advocating overthrow of the government," "passport and visa matter," "foreign influence," "internal security," and "espionage," as well as "registration of persons who

Cuban cultural production consistently took aim at Washington's punitive diplomatic policies toward Cuba. In this 1980 poster produced by OSPAAAL, however, global support for the Cuban revolution is depicted as a force capable of striking back against U.S. power. Courtesy of Docs Populi.

have knowledge of, or received instruction or assignment in, espionage, counterespionage, or sabotage service or tactics of government of foreign country or foreign political party."[35]

An analysis of the FBI's investigation of the Brigade and others who aligned themselves with Cuba provides a window into the U.S. government's efforts to prove its first charge against the organization: that the Brigade was a conduit for the dissemination of Cuban political propaganda within the United States.

"Missiles" as Propagandists

American sympathizers with the Cuban Revolution had long claimed that the U.S. government's travel embargo was motivated in part by Washington's desire to prevent its citizens from witnessing Cuba's socialist project with their own eyes. U.S. travelers in Cuba, the activists contended, reached their own conclusions about the revolution's merits and failures, free from the filter of the U.S. media.

Almost a decade before the Venceremos Brigade earned the ire of Senator Eastland, the case of journalist William Worthy, a foreign correspondent for the *Baltimore Afro-American* and *CBS News* and a member of the Fair Play for Cuba Committee, had become a lightning rod for debates about the travel ban and freedom of association after he was indicted in 1962 for entering the United States from Cuba without a passport.[36] The U.S. State Department had earlier refused to renew Worthy's passport in 1957 after he had defied the U.S. ban on travel to communist nations to report from China, the Soviet Union, and Hungary.[37] Worthy, a former Nieman Fellow at Harvard University and Ford Fellow in African Studies, was charged with violating the 1951 Immigration and Nationality Act, making him the first U.S. citizen ever indicted under its terms.[38] Undeterred, Worthy crisscrossed the United States in hundreds of public speaking events and interviews providing firsthand accounts of Cuba's revolution.[39]

Worthy's legal case became a cause célèbre, spawning an international movement to keep him out of jail and inspiring the Phil Ochs protest song "The Ballad of William Worthy." With his reporting from Cuba, which drew upon extensive interviews with Cuban citizens and leaders, including Fidel Castro, Worthy had become a bridge between the Cuban Revolution and the United States Left, helping to solidify widespread support for the Cuban Revolution among African Americans and the New Left. Although the prosecution of Worthy focused on his passport violation, the political subtext of the trial was clear. The mainstream press played up Worthy's left-wing political connections, and the U.S. Senate Internal Security Subcommittee, chaired by Senator Eastland, had already released a report entitled "Cuba and the American Negro" claiming that Worthy "displayed a marked hostility to the United States and its laws."[40] Worthy, a celebrated black radical internationalist, a lauded journalist, and an associate of Malcolm X and Robert F. Williams, had publicly aligned himself with Cuba's revolution at the height of the Caribbean Cold War and had shattered the information blockade.[41]

When the Venceremos Brigade arrived in Cuba in 1969, the U.S. government's response revealed the ways in which the policing of both travel and speech were used to frame the alleged threat of foreign subversion. For the FBI, much of this framing focused upon the question of political association. The international composition of Cuba's camps for foreign solidarity volunteers, organized by Cuba's Instituto Cubano de Amistad con los Pueblos (ICAP), reflected Cuba's status as a hemispheric confluence of radicalism. It was an environment that replicated Havana's status circa 1960 as

Venceremos Brigade members and Vietnamese delegates from the National Liberation Front embrace in December 1969. For many Americans, meeting Vietnamese soldiers, all of whom had engaged in combat against U.S. occupation forces, was a deeply significant experience. For U.S. officialdom, however, such images suggested collusion between American dissidents and Vietnamese insurgents. Photo by Jerry Berndt; courtesy of the Jerry Berndt Estate.

a "transnational counterpublic," as scholar Todd Tietchen has termed it, in which visiting American intellectuals and artists mingled with a global array of visiting leftists.[42]

A decade later, Americans in the international volunteer camps interacted with their counterparts from around the world, volunteers and delegates from leftist organizations who had similarly come to witness Cuba's revolution for themselves. FBI reports noted that Brigade members in Cuba during September of 1970 encountered volunteer brigades from nations including Bolivia, Brazil, El Salvador, Laos, and Zambia, whose delegates gave public talks on the effects of U.S. military and economic policies on their countries.[43] Members of the Brigade's fifth trip to the island in the spring of 1972, the FBI noted, performed work alongside an international delegation of volunteers from fifty-two nations who endeavored, like the Americans, to show solidarity with Cuba and provide volunteer support to the nation's socialist programs. As a token of solidarity, the North Vietnamese contingent presented each member of the

Brigade with rings that they said had been fashioned from aluminum salvaged from the wreck of the 3,000th U.S. military plane shot down over Vietnam.[44]

For the FBI, these encounters between American leftists and global radicals in Cuba raised the possibility that Americans might be recruited by agents of a foreign power, carrying out Cuban propaganda aims within the United States and becoming ventriloquists for Cuban revolutionary theory.

The FBI sought to authenticate its claims through a variety of methodologies, including analysis of Brigade literature and press accounts, direct surveillance, investigations of individual members, and mail interception. Most valuable, however, was the testimony of informers. Like innumerable leftist organizations in the late 1960s, the Brigade had been infiltrated by various agencies, including both local police departments and the FBI, whose files on the Brigade are filled with excisions protecting the identity of infiltrators.

Well aware that their activities were being scrutinized, the Brigade encouraged noncooperation with law enforcement, but to no avail. Surveillance was often difficult to avoid, and the group's efforts to keep police and federal agents at bay were ineffectual. Although the Brigade went as far as to publish recommendations in their pamphlets detailing what to do when contacted by investigators, transcriptions of the guidelines were subsequently reproduced in FBI reports.[45] When Brigade organizers distributed a National Lawyers Guild pamphlet entitled "I Ain't Singing Charlie or What To Do When the FBI Calls" to Brigade members upon their return to the United States, the text of it was transcribed faithfully into an FBI report.[46]

Surveillance functioned as a kind of panoptic gaze: although activists were aware of being watched, they could not ascertain the depth of the gaze's penetration or determine exactly what was perceived.

For the FBI, proving that the Brigade was propagandizing for a foreign government first required demonstrating that Brigade members were adherents of a foreign ideology. In addition to direct surveillance, FBI reports frequently endeavored a kind of "literature review" of pamphlets, articles, and organizational statements in order to demonstrate the Brigade's adherence to Cuban or Vietnamese revolutionary theory. As scholar Carole Boyce Davies has observed, U.S. government legal cases against American communists and other dissidents during the Cold War era were frequently constructed around "literary evidence," in which the state assembles a dissident's writings and speeches as proof of the individual's intellectual subversion.[47] Such investigative methods followed a familiar Cold War script, in which state apparati collected samples of dissidents' political statements from the public domain or procured them from dissidents' private lives through surveillance.

Although the object of Davies's analysis is Claudia Jones, a Trinidad-born black radical journalist who was deported from the United States in 1955 as a result of her leadership in the Communist Party U.S.A., it also brings into focus the experience of U.S.-born feminist writer Margaret Randall, who in 1984 was ordered deported by the U.S. Immigration and Naturalization Service (INS). Randall, a white U.S. citizen, had received Mexican citizenship in 1967, and went on to live in Cuba for eleven years and Nicaragua for four, moving back to the United States in 1984.

However, upon applying to become a permanent resident of the United States, an INS court invoked the 1952 McCarran-Walter Act, which allowed the government to bar immigrants suspected of being subversives from entering the country. The INS's evidence against Randall consisted almost solely of her prodigious writings, 2,744 pages of which had been reviewed by the immigration judge.[48] According to the INS District Director, the writings had gone "far beyond mere dissent, disagreement with, or criticism of the United States or its policies." Randall's "associations with, and her activities and writings in support of the communist dominated governments of Cuba, North Vietnam, and Nicaragua," the INS ruled, "warrant the denial of her application."[49]

Paralleling state investigations of William Worthy, Claudia Jones, and Margaret Randall, the FBI's scrutiny of the Venceremos Brigade sought to demonstrate the presence of ideological subversion through an engagement with the group's literary production. While some written material on the Brigade was provided by informants or anonymous citizens, the FBI's agents also acted as amanuenses to monitor press reports and media stories, including those appearing in obscure political publications, a task that required knowledge of both the mainstream and underground press. An October 1973 report by the bureau included summaries of the Brigade's announcements in publications by Third World Women's Alliance, a group affiliated with SNCC, in which the Brigade described itself as "an Anti-Imperialist Political Education Project."

The Brigade's self-portrayal of its engagement in public radical pedagogy became, for the FBI, evidence of particular interest. Transcriptions of Brigade literature, often in the form of recruiting pamphlets, similarly appeared in FBI reports as exhibits of the group's subversive ideology. The Brigade's newsletter, *Turquino*, often contained a "political objectives section" that outlined the group's current ideological perspectives. Typical goals included "facilitating dialogue among different U.S. movement groups," "educat[ing] the U.S. movement to an anti-imperialistic consciousness" and "support[ing] and aiding Cuban propaganda programs." This information served as both evidence of intent to engage in subversive activity and as a summary of the group's political beliefs.[50]

The FBI's literature review also contained transcriptions of articles from mainstream publications that were critical of the Brigade. The conservative Washington, D.C., magazine *Human Events* alleged in October 1972 that the Brigade had been sent to Cuba for a variety of unsavory purposes, including "agitation" and "training for guerrilla warfare." Referencing one of the Brigade's calls for applicants for an upcoming delegation, the paper concluded that, "clearly, from this list of stringent requirements, recruits for the fifth contingent were not being sent to Cuba to cut sugarcane. Castro has plenty of native workers for that."[51]

Such extensive accumulations of print material on the Brigade ultimately transformed the FBI into both archivist and "biographer." Considering the dearth of scholarly or popular writing about the Brigade, the bureau's copious reporting, including the amassing of thousands of pages of surveillance material, remains the most extensive archive of the group ever produced, surpassing that of any university's holdings.[52] Yet counternarratives persist even within the body of the state's archive. Evaluating the FBI's files on Claudia Jones, who was ultimately deported from the United States as a result of her political activism, Davies contends that Jones's extensive FBI file became, "ironically, one of the most significant of her biographical documents," one that could ultimately refute the power of the state's body of literary evidence deployed in its attack upon her. Although the state's archive "sought to contain the life of Claudia Jones," Davies notes, "the material itself is so powerful and so honest that it transforms these same files into a massive documentation project, producing instead of destroying its subject."[53]

The productive, regenerative, and re-humanizing potentials of state surveillance, however inadvertent, are apparent in a lengthy report on the Brigade issued in 1973 as a result of the "Theory and Practice of Communism" hearings conducted by the U.S. House of Representatives, Committee on Internal Security, in 1972. The report, running almost 400 pages and printed in monograph form by the U.S. Government Printing Office, consists of several sections of informant testimony, witness statements, and a lengthy appendix of photos, diary entries from informers, and reproductions of the Brigade's writings. The Committee's chair, Claude Pepper, the indefatigable anti-Castro representative from Florida, explained the purpose of the hearings: "Did these Brigades consist of humanitarians who merely assisted the Cuban people in cutting sugarcane, building houses, and harvesting fruit? Or have citizens of the United States been imported by Castro to be indoctrinated in communist propaganda and the techniques of revolution? Do the Brigades constitute a threat to the internal security of the United States?"[54]

In the transcribed testimony, the Committee questions recently returned Brigade members concerning the nature of the group's work in Cuba and how they raised money, which Cubans and foreigners they met in the camps, and the backgrounds of the participants. In one section of the report, the Committee hears testimony from Dwight Douglass Crews, an informant working for the Jefferson Parish Sheriff's office in Louisiana who, posing as a left-wing activist, had joined the Brigade and traveled to Cuba in spring 1972. Crews stated that he had been assigned to work with a group of Cuban students to build a new town in the countryside. As Crews explained, "there was a drive on within Cuba to provide houses for all of the people."[55] It would be "a fairly large town with all types of facilities for people who were to live there." A quarter mile away, he said, a brigade of youth volunteers from other countries was at work building a high school.[56] Photos reproduced in the report indeed show Crews and other American members of the Brigade constructing concrete houses. Some Americans pose together or smile arm in arm with Cuban workers and Vietnamese volunteers.

Although intended to be incriminatory, the photos and testimony contained in the report inadvertently confirm the Brigade's humanitarian mission of support for Cuban development, in ways that mirror the group's own public representations of itself. Indeed, the Committee's bound, book-like report bears similarities to the Brigade's own edited collection of interviews, essays, diary entries, poems, and photographs. Published by Simon and Schuster the year before as *Venceremos Brigade: Young Americans Sharing the Life and Work of Revolutionary Cuba*, the 400-page book, edited by a collective from the Brigade, documents the experiences of Americans on the first three of the Brigade's trips. Although the Committee's report does not mention *Venceremos Brigade* and may not have been compiled in response to its publication, the release of the report by the U.S. Government Printing Office less than a year after the publication of *Venceremos Brigade* suggests an effort to deploy a counternarrative to the Brigade's successful articulation of itself in the public sphere as a radical humanitarian organization.

The Brigade's political literature assumed another significance in FBI reports. Brigade members, the reports noted, viewed themselves as advocates for the Cuban Revolution within the United States. Viewing much of the mainstream press's coverage of the communist nation as tainted by bias and imperial hubris, the Brigade sought to provide the American public with an alternate perspective, one that was unabashedly anti-imperialist and prosocialist.

Emphasizing the success of the revolution's social programs and condemning the U.S. travel ban and trade embargo, Brigade members conducted a public education campaigns aimed at countering misrepresentations about life in a socialist society. Brigade pamphlets emphasized Cuba's provision of free education, free health care, and subsidized housing and food, all guaranteed as universal human rights in Cuba. The Brigade argued that communism, far from making Cubans unfree, had allowed them to attain a different kind of freedom, one that was foreign to Americans, who had been inculcated with notions of a western liberal democracy that equated freedom solely with individual liberty, free enterprise, and private property rights. According to a transcription of an internal Brigade letter provided by an FBI informant in November 1971, public education had become the Brigade's "primary political objective." In disseminating political literature and posters and holding speaking engagements, the FBI contended that the Brigade was developing itself into "one of the major vehicles in this country for disseminating information and propaganda on Cuba and the liberation struggles taking place throughout the underdeveloped world."[57]

The trope of the Brigade as a vector for the spread of Marxism and Third World revolutionary theory inside the United States persisted in U.S. media reports and law enforcement documents for years. At the 1972 House Committee on Internal Security hearings in Miami, which paid special attention to the Brigade's public efforts to disseminate a favorable image of Cuba inside the United States, official witnesses described the organization's print culture in similar terms. Miami television news editor Manolo Reyes, for instance, claimed that the Brigade had achieved several goals, including serving as a "propaganda tool for Castro and international communism against the United States," bringing "revolutionary propaganda into the United States," and using the trips as opportunities for U.S. activists to "increase their militant dedication through training, indoctrination, and some physical labor."[58] As evidence, Reyes presented slides of three leaflets produced by the Brigade's Chicago chapter. One, an invitation to a public screening of Saul Landau's 1968 film *Fidel*, showed a collage of photos of Cubans under a caption that read "Who Are These People?" Underneath appeared block text:

> THEY ARE THE PEOPLE OF REVOLUTIONARY CUBA, WHO IN 11 YEARS HAVE CHANGED THEIR COUNTRY FROM A STARVING COLONY OF U.S. IMPERIALISM INTO A LAND OF 8 MILLION PEOPLE WORKING TOGETHER WITH INCREDIBLE SPIRIT AND ENERGY TO BUILD A NEW SOCIETY — A SOCIETY WHERE SURVIVAL IS A HUMAN RIGHT AND WHERE THE "NEW MAN AND NEW WOMAN" CAN DEVELOP TO THEIR FULLEST HUMAN POTENTIAL.[59]

To FBI eyes, the Brigade's willingness to ventriloquize Cuban characterizations of its revolution rendered the organization little more than a front for the Cuban government. The Brigade, the FBI claimed, was controlled by Cuban intelligence officers and answered directly to Havana. This chain of command was ostensibly accomplished through control of the Brigade's national organizers who, as one report claimed, were carefully "selected by the Cuban government."[60]

While the FBI's reports contained no evidence to support this charge, it is also true that statements by Brigade members could be interpreted in ways that reinforced perceptions of Cuban control. In a February–March 1970 issue of the leftist San Francisco paper *The Movement*, reproduced within an FBI report, Brigade leader Julie Nichamin explained that Cuban leadership of the Brigade was essential because the group was engaged in agricultural projects that the Americans had no experience with. "There was no way," Nichamin argued, "of conceiving American leadership of the Venceremos Brigade" because only Cubans could lead a Cuban project in Cuba which, she pointed out, the Americans were there to support, not lead. Most importantly, said Nichamin, Cuban *communist* leadership was necessary for teaching Americans to "become better communists."[61]

Although some *brigadistas* were certainly communists in the ideological sense, Nichamin's use of the word "communism" in this case referenced the principles of collectivity and "socialist emulation" around which work projects in Cuba were organized, and did not necessarily indicate strict adherence to communist ideology. Brigade members, as the FBI was well aware, evinced a variety of political orientations, and some were critical of Marxism. Similarly, the Brigade's intentional deference to "Cuban leadership" while on Cuban soil did not mean that Cubans controlled the group's activities in the United States, as the Brigade's publications make clear. Members of the Brigade saw themselves as supporters of Cuban self-determination, not its leaders. While the Brigade's organizers deferred to ICAP officials in order to plan the delegations in a manner that would best suit Cuba's development needs, the Americans were clearly equal partners in this process.

Existing in tandem with allegations of Cuban control of the Brigade was the charge that Cuba exploited the presence of American supporters as political capital on the international stage of the Cold War. FBI reports submitted between 1969 and 1974 included sections entitled "propaganda value to the Cuban government" containing transcriptions of articles in the Cuban press and summaries of other media programs that covered the Brigade's activities in Cuba. While the FBI reports do not explain the sections' rationale, the "propaganda value" thesis with regard to the Brigade was widespread among U.S.

government and media observers. In June 1973, the State Department surmised that the presence of the Brigade in Cuba, where Americans expressed "solidarity with the Cuban revolution and opposition to U.S. policy," had been exploited by the Cuban government to "score propaganda points with both domestic and overseas audiences."[62]

Foreign solidarity delegations, of course, undoubtedly offered the Cuban government publicity benefits. Covered heavily in the Cuban media, the presence of foreign supporters of the revolution on the island enabled Havana to demonstrate that its revolution continued to garner global support. The presence of U.S. volunteers, as American citizens opposing their own government's policies, held a potent symbolism, one that both Havana and Washington recognized. A 1984 CIA report entitled "Cuba: Castro's Propaganda Apparatus and Foreign Policy" contended that solidarity groups from the United States, particularly the Brigade, "are usually portrayed by the Cuban media as typical of the idealistic youth who have rejected the anti-Castro political judgments of Washington."[63] Foreign delegations, especially from its adversary to the north, represented for Cuba a public relations victory in the war of ideology between American capitalism and Cuban communism.

"Missiles" as Guerrillas in America

Eastland's characterization of Venceremos Brigade members as human "missiles," however, also had a more literal meaning. Throughout the 1960s, the CIA and FBI repeatedly accused the Cuban government of attempting to export its revolution into the United States through the training and arming of left-wing radical groups, in much the same way that the CIA had provided military training to anti-Castro Cuban exiles. Conjured by law enforcement agencies and the tabloid press, the specter of Cuban aid to armed left-wing groups in the United States became an arena of "fantasy projection" and paranoia, in which anxiety about left-wing political violence against the U.S. government, whether primarily rhetorical and symbolic, as in the case of the Black Panthers, or actualized, as in the case of the Weather Underground, fed upon prevailing state fears that linked domestic radicalism with foreign enemies.[64] Speaking at press conferences in Cuba, which were often attended by members of the Cuban, U.S., and international press, Venceremos Brigades participants repeatedly denied the allegations emanating from their home country.[65] Eastland's Senate floor speech of 1970, in which he accused the Brigade of subversion, drew from a deep well of CIA and FBI accusations that Cuba was inculcating American leftists in the dark arts of radicalism.

And yet, the notion that Cuba might be aiding armed revolutionaries inside its northern neighbor was not entirely fantastical. Indeed, Fidel Castro had claimed Cuba's right to do precisely that in response to Washington's policy of funding, training, and arming opponents of the revolutionary government, which had launched hundreds of attacks upon Cuba and its embassies, personnel, and civilians abroad. In response, Castro in 1964 issued the "Declaration of Santiago," in which he claimed that if foreign nations such as the United States, in collusion with its right-wing Latin American allies, had a right to intervene in Cuba's internal affairs, then Cuba would claim the same right in the offending countries. Listing a range of violations of Cuban sovereignty, Castro warned that "if the pirate attacks being carried out from U.S. territory and that of other nations on the rim of the Caribbean does not cease, as well as the training of mercenaries to carry out acts of sabotage against the Cuban revolution, and also the sending of agents, arms, and explosives into Cuba, the Cuban people will conclude they have the same right to help, with all the resources they believe suitable, the revolutionary movements in all those nations which engage in such intervention in the internal affairs of our country."[66]

The sociologist C. Wright Mills had whimsically invoked precisely this possibility of Cuban support for armed struggle inside the United States in his 1960 book *Listen, Yankee: The Revolution in Cuba*. Drawing upon all-night interviews with Fidel Castro and written in the voice of a Cuban revolutionary ostensibly speaking through Mills to a North American audience, the narrator claimed that "we Cuban revolutionaries don't really know just exactly *how* you could best go about this transforming of your Yankee imperialism. For us, with our problems, it was simple: In Cuba, we had to take to our 'Rocky Mountains'— you couldn't do that, could you? Not yet, we suppose.... (We're joking—we suppose. But if in ten years, in five years—if things go as we think they might inside your country, if it comes to that, then know this, Yankee: some of us will be with you. God almighty, those are great mountains!)."[67]

A decade later, with the United States mired in an increasingly unpopular and costly war in Vietnam, Cuban billboards and political posters proclaimed that U.S. imperial ambitions would be repelled not only by armed struggle in the Third World, but by the citizens of the empire itself. In one handwritten message photographed and reproduced in *Verde Olivo*, the official organ of Cuba's armed forces that featured news and opinion on national and world events, Brigade organizer Julie Nichamin affirmed that the group's members would arrive home from Cuba with a renewed commitment to "destroy the imperialist monster from within, just as the people of the world are destroying imperialism from without."[68] Although Nichamin's statement, written after a meeting between Vietnamese and Venceremos Brigade delegates at a solidarity meeting, is a Guevaraist invocation of the responsibility of U.S. leftists to cripple the war effort at home through protest, not a call for actual armed struggle within the United States, the statement was ambiguous enough to allow for mischaracterization.

It is important to restate at this juncture that no material Cuban support for armed revolution inside the United States has ever been proven — although, as will be argued later, Cuba may have provided weapons training to several members of the Black Panther Party at training grounds in Cuba and Canada. Nonetheless, it is clear that the specter of Cuban training for left-wing North Americans provided intrigue for the intelligence community and fodder for tabloid headlines.

The engagement between the Venceremos Brigade and Cuba that began in 1969 concentrated all of these themes, causing alarm in the United States and abroad. In June 1973, the American Embassy in Lisbon noted in a message to the U.S. State Department that the South African magazine *To The Point* had run an article earlier that month entitled "Venceremos Brigade, composed of 2,000 Americans, now training for armed action in Portuguese Guinea."[69] Cuban aid to the nation that would become Guinea-Bissau upon independence had, since 1966, been instrumental in the military successes of the African Party for the Independence of Guinea and Cape Verde (PAIGC), led in part by the legendary military leader and radical theoretician Amílcar Cabral until his death in 1973, just months before the nation achieved independence from Portuguese colonial rule.[70]

Guinea-Bissau had figured prominently in the internationalist dreams of African American radicals such as Charlie Hill and Michael Finney, members of the U.S.-based Republic of New Afrika, who hijacked a plane to Cuba in 1971 in part because they believed that the Cuban government would help them join an anticolonial movement on the African continent.[71] However, aspiring North American guerrillas such as Hill and Finney were rebuffed by the Cubans, who were not willing to assume the political risks of training U.S. citizens for a foreign conflict. Representatives of Guinea-Bissau may have had similar concerns.[72] Although the *To The Point* story had not yet appeared in the Portuguese press, the American embassy requested further information to allow it to field inquiries.[73] Although Secretary of State William Rogers replied that "the Department had no information to confirm the highly doubtful story," he noted that:

> Venceremos Brigades do exist.... Since late 1969 groups of young Americans have organized themselves into symbolic brigades and traveled annu-

ally to Cuba without U.S. passports, ostensibly to cut sugar cane or work in other projects and learn about the Cuban revolution at first hand. Roughly 2,000–2,500 in all have gone since 1969. This year only 200 at the most have been in Cuba at any one time... While to the best of our knowledge the magazine article is wrong, the possibility obviously cannot be excluded that individual U.S. citizens who have been in Cuba with the Venceremos Brigades may at some time or another turn up in Portuguese Guinea with the PAIGC.[74]

U.S. officials had expressed concern about the Cuban internationalist presence in Africa since the early 1960s. While Cuban involvement in Algeria and the Congo had not caused great alarm in Washington, due to the assumption that the operation would be of little consequence, the issue would increasingly inject tension into U.S.-Cuba relations throughout the 1970s, when Cuba's military involvement in Angola's anticolonial conflict became massive, with consequences reverberating throughout southern Africa.[75] Even then, fears of involvement by U.S. leftists in African affairs, facilitated by Cuba, persisted. In 1976, following the Cuban-assisted Angolan independence from Portuguese colonial rule, the U.S. Embassy in Lagos, Nigeria reported to the U.S. State Department that the *New Nigerian* newspaper had carried a story in February about a "discreet meeting" in Cuba between several dozen U.S. left-wing organizations and high-ranking members of the People's Movement for the Liberation of Angola (MPLA), the socialist anticolonial political party, led by Agostinho Neto, that Cuba had supported during the conflict. According to the article, the participating U.S. organizations, which included the National Congress of Black Lawyers, the Women's International League for Peace and Freedom, the Washington Committee on Africa, the Puerto Rican Socialist Party, and the Venceremos Brigade, allegedly discussed "plans for possible support from American groups for MPLA."[76]

In reality, the meeting was far less conspiratorial. The encounter in question was actually a seminar hosted by ICAP in Havana in February 1976, at the request of the MPLA, to forge ties with members of the U.S. progressive community, especially from "the Black community, and ... the peace and antiwar movement," and other organizations that had taken affirmative positions on the issue of Angolan independence. The U.S. delegation ultimately solidified a program of support for the new nation, including grassroots organizing efforts to provide medical and agricultural aid, lobbying Congress to support recognition of the revolutionary government and avert a U.S. embargo, and a public relations campaign to dispel myths about the MPLA, supported by publications such as *The Black Scholar* and *Freedom Ways Magazine*.[77]

The dissonance between state paranoia and actualized solidarity in transnational encounters between African and Cuban revolutionaries and American progressives reveals much about the official anxieties, among both Washington's security apparatus and among America's allies in Africa, that lay at the heart of the surveillance of U.S. activists traveling to the island. Cuba, it was clear, continued to function as a transnational hub where global left-wing movements coalesced beyond the reach of the U.S. state, with unknown potentials. Certainly, the potential for insurrectionary collaboration was present in the volunteer camps, in which Venceremos Brigade members sometimes encountered global revolutionaries. Historian Michael Kazin, who participated in the 1969 contingent of the Brigade, recalls his meeting with one member of the Viet Cong: "I had a halting, although pleasant conversation, with one of them — a young man about my age. But the conversation ended shortly after I asked him what the large tricolor medal on his chest signified. The soldier beamed and then responded, in English: 'Twenty Yankees killed!'"[78]

Despite the State Department's strong doubts that Cuban-trained Americans were planning to aid the anticolonial movement in West Africa, other U.S. government entities were not as convinced. To FBI eyes, the Brigade seemed to have similar ambitions at home. The FBI's investigation of the Brigade frequently centered upon allegations that some of the group's members had received military instruction or guerrilla warfare training while in Cuba. These allegations, based largely upon the claims of U.S. police informants or Cuban defectors, constituted one of the most inflammatory charges leveled against the Brigade, even if most such claims were tenuous from the beginning. During the House Committee's Theory and Practice of Communism hearings in 1972, witness Manolo Reyes testified that:

> Sources of the Cuban underground have released information that members of the fifth contingent of the Venceremos Brigade that went to Cuba from March to May of this year went to a very special place in Cuba. This is Cayajabos, in Pinar del Río Province, in the western part of the island, where the largest terrorism training camp is located. This vast guerrilla training camp is under the command of Osmani Cienfuegos and is for foreign guerrilla men from Africa, Asia, and Latin America. The existence of this training camp was brought to my attention by an eyewitness who is a recent defector of the Castro regime.[79]

Reyes, however, did not identify the eyewitness nor make reference to any other evidence supporting his claim. Witness Dwight Douglass Crews later testified at the same hearings that during the trip that he participated in, "to my knowledge, no Brigade person received any military training."[80] In fact, the Brigade never went to Pinar del Río that year, and Crews maintained that the pro-Cuba activities of the Brigade had been oriented primarily toward generating and disseminating propaganda in support of Cuba's social programs. While outlining his question about the camps to Crews, Representative Richardson Preyer characterized Reyes's claims as "hearsay ... he hadn't seen anything."[81] FBI informants, for their part, also noted that they had witnessed no evidence of "any member of the Brigade receiving guerrilla warfare training or training in espionage."[82]

Nonetheless, some zealous members of the Brigade may indeed have glibly tried to glean tips about how to foment armed struggle in the United States. Cuban translator Juanito Ortega, interviewed by a Brigade member in 1970 regarding his opinion of the American visitors, expressed his respect for the American volunteers, but observed that "some people actually thought they were going to come here and ask any Cuban our opinion on how to carry out guerrilla tactics."[83] Police informants reported similar events. According to one informant, members of the fourth Brigade in the spring of 1971 organized themselves into caucuses, drawing up plans of political action for their return to the United States, collectively agreeing to "stress action over theory and do whatever is necessary, including engage in violence, where appropriate, to bring about revolution." However, the source admitted that no Cubans had been present at the meeting. Moreover, the source claimed, the Cuban staff had "scoffed ... [at the] allegations of the American Government that they gave guerrilla warfare training to Brigade participants."[84]

Brigade members returning from Cuba repeatedly reported that the Cuban officials encouraged them only to continue to build a broad-based protest movement against the Vietnam War, not to engage in violent actions. Indeed, when the Weather Underground staged the "days of rage" actions in Chicago in October 1969 — timed to coincide with the two-year anniversary of Che Guevara's death — in which baseball bat–wielding activists swept through an affluent district of the city, smashing car windows and storefronts before being subdued by a brutal police counterattack, the Cubans reportedly expressed disapproval.[85]

Even the Black Panther Party's metaphorical invocations of revolutionary violence were met with criticism. Although the Panthers were widely admired in Cuba, Cuban officials repeatedly expressed doubts about the group's ability to carry out an armed campaign in the heart of the most powerful nation on earth. ICAP staffer Hugo Govín remembers the dismay among some of the

Cuban staff after they heard black and white Brigade members singing lines from a famous Panther protest song: "pick up the gun, pick up the gun, pick up the gun and put the pigs on the run."[86] Although the song was primarily a call to self-defense against police violence in African American communities, not an appeal for offensive violence, this subtlety was not always apparent to the Cubans. "To us, that was irresponsible," recalls Govín.[87]

When asked their opinion of direct action and political violence in the United States, the Cuban ICAP hosts in the camps repeatedly suggested to the Americans that the best way to create social change was organize the people in their own communities. The Cuban Revolution, explained the Cubans, some of whom were ex-fighters in the guerrilla campaign against the Batista government, had been a *social* process as much as a military one.[88] Interviewed in April 1971 on Radio Havana Cuba, whose broadcasts were monitored by the CIA, several Brigade members affirmed that the Cuban Revolution, to them, represented "much more than armed struggle."[89]

FBI reports do claim, however, that Brigade members may have been informally encouraged to foment armed struggle within the United States by the North Vietnamese delegates. The Venceremos Brigade regularly met with and worked side by side with members of the National Liberation Army of Vietnam, fighters and strategists who had served with distinction in battles with U.S. occupation forces. According to one informant, an aide to Nguyen Miah Phoung, the Ambassador of the Provisional Revolutionary Government of the Republic of South Vietnam, allegedly told Brigade members that Americans who considered themselves revolutionaries should "play along with the peace demonstrators, but do their own side acts of bombing and violent activities, and that the peace demonstrators will learn that these violent acts are more effective than demonstrations and will join the revolutionaries in acts of terrorism."[90]

But this claim warrants skepticism. According to the same bureau report, a Brigade member giving a public post-trip talk in the United States related participating in a meeting with the Vietnamese delegation during the same period in Cuba but stated that although "Weatherman faction members of SDS.... wanted to hear that violence was the only way to revolution ... the Vietnamese indicated that mass demonstrations were the way."[91]

Nonetheless, the FBI persisted in claiming that Cuba was training American radicals for armed actions, although little evidence was ever presented to support the claims. *Granma*'s coverage of the Brigade in Cuba, which in turn was monitored by the CIA and U.S. Information Agency, had included numerous statements from the Americans speaking in solidarity with the Vietnamese resistance, condemning U.S. aggression in Indochina and, beginning in 1970, joining Cubans in commemorations of the anniversary of Hồ Chí Minh's death.[92]

In 1976, the FBI released a 400-page report, entitled *Foreign Influence — Weather Underground Organization*, that was subsequently covered in the *New York Times*. The report alleged that Cuban government personnel had aided the Weather Underground Organization, which had achieved notoriety for a series of political bombings. The group's targets were frequently associated with the U.S. war effort in Vietnam, and although the bombings were designed to avoid human injury, they were calculated for maximum symbolic effect. The group placed a bomb inside the U.S. Capitol building in late February 1971 in retaliation for the U.S. invasion of Laos twenty days earlier. The following May, the group detonated a device in a bathroom inside the Pentagon in response to renewed U.S. bombing campaigns, and the group perpetrated a long string of similar bombings of targets symbolically or directly involved in the war effort.[93]

Several Weather activists had traveled to Cuba and held meetings with representatives of the Vietnamese liberation forces, allowing the FBI to level a circumstantial claim that the Vietnamese had instructed the Americans to carry out the attacks to advance its own military agenda in Indochina. The Weathermen organization, the FBI claimed, was therefore an accomplice to the designs of a hostile foreign power. Bureau reports noted that Diana Oughten, a Weather Underground member who died in 1970 with two other activists when they accidentally detonated a bomb they were constructing at their Greenwich Village townhouse, had traveled to Cuba two years earlier where she had participated in the meetings with North Vietnamese officials and resistance fighters.[94]

The Bureau also claimed that Cuban and Vietnamese officials had influenced Weather activists at international meetings of antiwar activists in Hungary, Czechoslovakia, and North Vietnam; that Vietnamese officials had encouraged Americans to engage in violent acts as well as nonviolent street protests in opposition to the Vietnam War; and that Cuban personnel at the Cuban Mission to the United Nations in New York and the Cuban Embassy in Canada had helped Weather activists wanted on criminal charges in the United States travel surreptitiously to Europe.[95]

Although Larry Grathwohl, the FBI informer who had infiltrated the Weather Underground Organization (WUO) and later traveled to Cuba as a member of the Brigade, claimed that the group had received military training there, the FBI did not report the revelation, even a full nine months after Grathwohl was unmasked, rendering the protection of his identity irrelevant. Only later, as the U.S. Department of Justice prepared to investigate a number of FBI agents for illegal acts committed while in pursuit of fugitive WUO members, did the FBI leak the 400-page report to the press. Interviewed on Radio Havana Cuba, *brigadistas* repeatedly denounced claims that the WUO bombings had anything to do with the Brigade or with Cuba.[96]

As one scholar has suggested, the FBI may have engineered the leak "in the hopes of demonstrating that the Weathermen were agents of a foreign power. Under the law, foreign counterintelligence investigation practices were less restrictive than those for other criminal investigations."[97] The curious lines in the opening paragraph of the FBI's report, which are oddly reminiscent of Che Guevara's exhortation to internationalism, may have been an attempt by the FBI to justify its misconduct in pursuit of the WUO by positioning the group as agents of a foreign power, for which domestic due process did not apply: "The revolutionary who has committed his destiny under the banner of Marxism-Leninism establishes his identity with a world center of revolution (in this instance Havana) ... He ceases to be merely 'domestic' when he adopts his international identity as a revolutionary."[98] Nonetheless, according to the *New York Times*, there was "no indication in the report that the bureau or other intelligence services ever established that weapons, communications equipment or espionage tools had been fed to the antiwar radicals by the Communists."[99]

The flimsiness of the FBI claims notwithstanding, history suggests that the charge that some American radicals may have attempted to acquire military training in Cuba should not be so easily dismissed. Indeed, by the late 1950s, American dissidents had participated, or attempted to participate, as fighters in several foreign theaters. Three decades before, for instance, almost 3,000 American antifascists, communists, and anarchists joined the Spanish Civil War as volunteers, fighting as an integrated multiracial force against the fascist government of Francisco Franco.[100] At least two dozen white youth joined the Cuban Revolution on the side of the *fidelistas* in the late 1950s, where they fought as guerrillas with Fidel Castro's forces.[101] Over 10,000 African Americans are estimated to have attempted to join the Ethiopian struggle against Italian invasion in 1935, although most were prevented from doing so by the U.S. State Department, which threatened the volunteers with the loss of their U.S. citizenship.[102] Dozens of African American and Latino radicals attempted to join anti-imperialist campaigns in Latin America and Africa from 1969 to 1973, some perhaps successfully.[103] It is not clear to what degree the FBI was cognizant of this history, or whether it informed policy. Nonetheless, the bureau's claims that some American radicals had sought military training abroad were congruent with a clearly defined history of U.S. left-wing internationalism.[104]

Other events similarly supported FBI claims that Americans might be trying to acquire weapons training in Cuba. Two factors in particular make the contention worth examining. First, Cuba had made little secret of its policy of aid to global leftist movements, including via the provision of military training, arms, and advisers. As late as 1974, Henry Kissinger revealed that Cuba's aid to left-wing movements in Latin America remained a core reason for Washington's intransigence toward easing hostilities with Cuba, despite the dramatically scaled-down nature of Havana's involvement in the hemisphere after Che Guevara's death in 1967.[105] As Deputy Assistant Secretary of State of Inter-American Affairs Robert A. Hurwitch saw it, Cuba's "internal interference" in the form of "support to dissident elements in various countries," including Venezuela, Bolivia, and Guatemala, was a primary concern not only to the United States, but to other nations in the hemisphere in which Cuban-trained operatives were blamed for a host of armed actions against regimes friendly to U.S. interests.[106]

And while the Cuban government's actual material aid for global revolution waned for a time after 1967, the rhetoric of armed insurgency persisted in Cuban cultural production and in the nation's media. Cuban newspapers such as *Granma* and *Juventud Rebelde* continued to promote revolution as a means of achieving Third World independence. The quarterly periodical *Tricontinental*, published by OSPAAAL, which was translated into four languages and had acquired a global readership of tens of thousands by 1969, regularly included graphics and images during the late 1960s and early 1970s promoting armed struggle as the only legitimate route to liberation from colonialism and foreign exploitation. In one glossy photograph of a still life mimicking a liquor advertisement, for instance, the ingredients for a "freedom cocktail" were gasoline, sulfuric acid, and potassium chlorate, the makings of a modified Molotov cocktail that could be detonated without an ignited wick.[107]

U.S. policy toward Cuba, of course, frequently mirrored the acts that Washington accused Havana of fomenting in Latin America. In the hindsight offered by the post-9/11 era, scholar Lars Schoultz has observed that campaigns of agricultural sabotage, assassination plots, and bombings aimed at Cuba, originating in U.S. territory following the Cuban Revolution, unambiguously compose "what we today would call state sponsored terrorism."[108] These acts of aggression continued in various forms throughout the 1960s and into the next decade. As detailed in chapter 3, ongoing acts of aggression against Cuba originating from U.S. territory, often executed by Cuban exile groups with tacit or overt CIA backing, exacerbated the diplomatic headaches of U.S. officials who were attempting to negotiate an antihijacking agreement with Cuba in the early 1970s. By imploring the Cuban government to cease and desist from harboring Americans who hijacked planes into its territory, the United States invited Cuban accusations of hypocrisy. The United States, the Cuban officials pointed out, had not only harbored Cubans who had hijacked planes to the United States, but had in fact sheltered, aided, and armed numerous individuals who had engaged in terrorist acts against Cuba.[109] Writing in 1973, the year that Havana and Washington reached an agreement to halt the hijacking epidemic, Uruguayan poet Mario Benedetti suggested that the primary peril posed by the Cuban Revolution among U.S. officialdom was not the specter of left-wing subversion in the Third World but the example of its successful resistance to U.S. global power. "The imperialists have never tired of accusing Cuba of exporting revolution. But of course the real and unforgivable export for which Cuba is responsible (just like Vietnam) is the example of a small country far from the great powers, that is capable of defeating the empire and even humiliating it in the eyes of the world."[110]

Ironically, Washington's unwillingness to take appropriate measures to curtail paramilitary attacks against Cuba was a primary reason for Castro's increasingly critical rhetoric toward the United States as early as the spring of 1959, before hostilities between the two nations appeared inevitable, and was ultimately one of the contributing factors that explains why Cuba strengthened its early protective alliance with Moscow. Although Castro's public embrace of communism and increasingly close ties to the Soviet Union signaled the final demise of cordial U.S.-Cuba relations, these tensions were also hastened by Washington's support for paramilitary aggression against the island.[111]

Cuba's support for revolutionary movements in Latin America waned after 1967, following Che Guevara's death in Bolivia while attempting to initiate a popular insurgency against the U.S.-backed government there. Cuba's efforts to foment revolution into Latin America would not rekindle until the Sandinista Revolution in Nicaragua in 1979, which received important Cuban aid. Instead, Havana's efforts would focus on the African continent.[112] Claims about North American dissidents receiving paramilitary training in Cuba, while probably known to be inaccurate by many within the U.S. security community, nevertheless occurred within a context of rising U.S. concern about Cuba's revolutionary internationalism and military aid abroad.

This projection of foreign fears onto domestic ones was likely enabled by the presence of a tiny but highly visible number of radical leftist organizations inside the United States that actively pursued quasi-military agendas. Shortly after the Brigade's formation in 1969, one such group, the Weather Underground, publicly declared its intent to engage in armed struggle within the United States, a promise that it soon fulfilled. As the FBI was well aware, several current or future Weather members had been active in the formation of the Brigade.

Revolution in Cuba and anti-imperialist insurgency in Vietnam figured prominently within the political theory of the Weather Underground. *Prairie Fire*, Weather's 1974 manifesto, contained numerous acknowledgments of Cuba's influence on their ideas, particularly their claim that armed struggle within the United States would be necessary to halt U.S. aggression in Vietnam. The Weather Underground hoped to "attack imperialism's ability to exploit and wage war against all oppressed peoples" by disrupting the state's civic and military apparatus.[113] Quoting a statement attributed to Julie Nichamin, one of the founders of the Brigade and an affiliate of the Weather organization, the FBI's 1976 report, *Foreign Influence*, attempted to highlight Cuba's role in inspiring the actions of armed insurrectionists in the United States. "The Cubans," the report noted, "understand the importance of a revolution from within the heart of imperialism: the imperialists will be destroyed by the combined revolutionary movements from within and outside. Che's call for two, three, many Viet-Nams includes a call for the creation of a Viet-Nam within the very boundaries of the imperialist Mother Country: the United States."[114]

The Weather Underground also drew upon influences closer to home. Key among them was the Black Panther Party, which also advocated armed struggle as part of a multifaceted strategy to bring about African American self-determination from internal colonialism. While not active in the Brigade's initial formation, Black Panthers and affiliates of the organization traveled to Cuba with the Brigade in the late 1960s and early 1970s. Of all the North American social movements of the 1960s era, none elicited a more ferocious campaign of state repression than did the Panthers, which J. Edgar Hoover famously singled out in 1969 as the "greatest threat to internal security of the country."[115]

Hoover's obsession with the Panthers led to FBI and police campaigns of harassment, repression, and even assassination, a crusade waged with an extraordinary intensity that was wholly out of proportion to the group's activities. "State repression of the Panthers," writes historian Robert O. Self, "along with the long FBI campaign against Martin Luther King, Jr., stands among the darkest and most cynical acts of American officialdom in the 1960s."[116] It is significant that, despite the gravity of the FBI's claims against the Brigade, the bureau's response to the group appears to have been limited to surveillance, investigation, and public slander. At no time did the FBI's campaign against the Brigade rival the ferocity of the bureau's campaign against the Panthers.

The internationalism of the Panthers, who adopted as political influences a pantheon of global revolutionaries and intellectuals of African, Asian, European, and Latin American origin, would lead many Panthers, ideologically and sometimes physically, to Cuba. In fact, Huey Newton and Bobby Seale, the organization's cofounders, had first met in 1962 at a rally opposing the U.S. embargo against Cuba at Merritt College in Oakland.[117] The Panthers developed political relationships with representatives of Algeria, China, Cuba, North Vietnam, and North Korea, allowing the group to position themselves as international spokespeople for the Black Power movement, bolstering their claims to be the vanguard of the revolutionary black movement in the United States. The Panthers had repeatedly defended the right of African Americans and other "internally colonized" groups to use political violence inside the United States in the service of both self-defense and revolution, positioning the group within a global continuum of Third World liberation and anticolonial rebellion.

The Panthers' internationalism went on full display in August 1970. As the volunteers of the third Brigade prepared to travel to Cuba and the carnage of America's war in Vietnam continued to haunt the evening news, the Panthers offered to send volunteer combatants to Vietnam to help defeat the U.S. occupation. Affirming the organization's ideology of "revolutionary intercommunalism" in solidarity with oppressed people worldwide, Party cofounder Huey Newton formally offered to send Black Panthers to work in the service of the National Liberation Front of North Vietnam and the Provisional Revolutionary Government of the Republic of South Vietnam. Conceptualizing global capitalist relations as a struggle between a super-exploited Third World "countryside" and the imperial "city" of the United States, Newton, in a letter to South Vietnamese commander of the People's Liberation Armed Forces Nguyen Thi Dinh, linked black liberation in the United States with the struggle of the North Vietnamese to repel U.S. aggression, asserting that "your struggle is also our struggle, for we recognize that our common enemy is the American imperialist."[118] Although no Panthers were ultimately sent to fight in Vietnam, the South Vietnamese forces did not reject the offer outright. Expressing "profound gratitude," Nguyen replied that, "when necessary, we shall call for your volunteers to assist us."[119]

The internationalist dreams of African American radicals, including the desire among some to participate in foreign theaters of revolutionary struggle, is a theme that surfaces throughout the history of U.S. black radical movements during the twentieth century. Indeed, black armed internationalism in North America, ranging from the desire to help defend Ethiopia from Italian invasion to the black volunteers in the antifascist Abraham Lincoln Brigade and those who later sought to participate in anticolonial movements on the African continent in the 1960s, occurred within the context of a global anticolonial era. As discussed later in this book, a number of African American activists from the United States made their way to Cuba in the 1960s, 1970s, and 1980s hoping to be trained by Cuba and sent to participate in revolutionary movements in Africa. According to Piero Gleijeses, who interviewed Cuban military commanders and consulted Cuban archives, Stokely Carmichael managed to convince Amílcar Cabral to accept "a contingent of twenty or thirty African Americans, on the condition that they be trained in another country," as fighters in Guinea-Bissau's war of independence against Portuguese colonialism.[120] Neither is the phenomenon of armed internationalism distinct to the black radical tradition. A number of white North Americans attempted to participate as fighters in the Cuban Revolution, and one, William Alexander Morgan, became a central figure in the overthrow of the Batista government.[121]

Indeed, the FBI's claims that the Black Panther Party might be seeking military training in Cuba are confirmed by Eldridge Cleaver. Cleaver's insistence on the viability of armed revolution within the United States had put him, and the New York branch of the Party that he led, at odds with Huey Newton and much of the original Oakland branch of the organization, which by 1969 was increasingly emphasizing social welfare programs such as the Free Breakfast for School Children Program and campaign bids to enter Oakland electoral politics.[122] Although both Cleaver and Newton lived for some time in Cuba as political asylees—Cleaver from 1968 to 1969, and Newton from 1974 to 1977—it was Cleaver who actively sought military aid for the Panthers from Cuba. However, in his memoir, *Soul on Fire*, Cleaver maintained that the idea for "a Black Panther training facility in Cuba" had actually come from the Cubans, and had been "proposed by Castro's people in New York—in fact, by their representative to the United Nations."[123] Such a facility would undoubtedly have been welcomed by some members of the organization. "Our highest hope," Cleaver later wrote, "was to have a center in the Caribbean that would prepare revolutionary cadres to slink back into the United States."[124]

If Cleaver is to be believed, these hopes were at least partially fulfilled. Cleaver claimed Cuban personnel provided weapons training to members of the Black Panther Party at a rural site in Canada during 1967 and 1968.[125] And although the Cuban government declined to provide the Panthers with the grenades that they had asked for—a request that Cleaver claimed was eventually fulfilled by the government of North Korea[126] — the Cubans allegedly promised the Panthers a military training site outside Havana. Interviewed extensively by scholar Ruth Reitan in the 1990s, Cleaver doubled down on his earlier claims, made during the 1970s, that the Panthers had been provided with an abandoned farm near Havana, where Panthers would be brought for military instruction.

As Reitan tells it, "on a number of occasions, the Cubans took Cleaver to the site for target practice. There he was trained with a variety of weaponry, including AK 47s, pistols, machine guns and antiaircraft weapons." However, Cleaver's primary interest was bomb-making. "Explosives training for the Panthers was already under way by Cuban military personnel in Canada," Reitan writes, "and the Panther leadership thought it easier and safer for the Cubans to teach them these techniques north of the border than for the trainees to travel all the way to Cuba and risk the FBI or CIA's discovering them."[127]

Cleaver's story has never been corroborated. Skeptics point to the unlikelihood that the Cuban government would have engaged in something so reckless, given the claims emanating from the FBI about Cuban guerrilla training for U.S. radicals. Cuban officials had repeatedly voiced their disapproval of armed struggle inside the United States, viewing it as dangerously naïve, and had tried to dissuade Americans from pursuing it. But as Cleaver saw it, the Cuban government's assurance of support for the Black Panthers was congruent with Havana's record of aid to foreign revolutionary and anticolonial movements, a point that Cleaver was highly cognizant of. In an interview with scholar Henry Louis Gates published in 1975, Cleaver insisted that the Cubans had reneged on an earlier promise of constructing "a permanent, well-organized facility" for the training of Black Panthers. "If you remember the whole spirit of the Tri-Continental Congress that was taking place there, then you will understand that this request was in accord with the atmosphere at that time. The Cubans supported liberation movements, just as Algeria did. They gave them kind of official status, they provided them with facilities, and this was what we were supposed to have."[128]

As a nation menaced by a proximate superpower, however, Cuba's principle-driven and idealistic solidarity with global left-wing movements was also pragmatic. Indeed, Havana saw aid to foreign movements as a counterweight to Washington's attempts to isolate Cuba within the world system, and a way to ensure Cuba's survival through the development of a liberated Third World that was economically independent and politically sovereign.[129]

Havana's embrace of armed struggle also arose out of its disillusionment with Moscow's Cold War doctrine of "peaceful coexistence." While ensuring the survival of the United States and the Soviet Union from nuclear

Armageddon, it had done little to shield Vietnam from a U.S. intervention of genocidal ferocity, and had not protected Latin America from U.S.-backed coups and bloody dictatorships. The CIA-sponsored overthrow of the democratically elected government of Jacobo Árbenz in Guatemala in 1954, in particular, became a cautionary tale for a young Che Guevara, who had been in the country at the time. As scholar Vijay Prashad has observed, the strategy of aiding revolutionary insurrection in the Third World was embraced "not only as a tactic of anticolonialism but significantly *as a strategy within itself*," one intended to shed the immobility that superpower détente demanded of the Third World.[130]

Cuba would now attempt to export its revolution, first into Africa and Latin America until 1967, and continuing in Africa throughout the next two decades. "Cuba defends itself by attacking its aggressor. This was our philosophy," Cuban military commander Víctor Dreke, interviewed by Piero Gleijeses, would later note. "The Yankees were attacking us from every side, so we had to challenge them everywhere. We had to divide their forces, so that they wouldn't be able to descend on us, or any other country, with all their might."[131] Indeed, as scholars William M. LeoGrande and Peter Kornbluh have noted, it was precisely the escalation of the Vietnamese conflict that compelled the CIA to pivot away from Cuba in 1967, decelerating its campaign to destabilize the nation and scaling down and then closing the CIA station in Miami, which had been the agency's largest in the world outside of Langley, Virginia.[132]

Havana's support for foreign movements included, for the most radical architects of Cuban revolutionary internationalism such as Che Guevara, the burgeoning protest movements in their northern neighbor. These aims, too, intersected with Cuba's hemispheric and global objectives. Whether or not the U.S. movement actually achieved the capacity for armed revolution was secondary to the disruption that such a movement might exert upon the imperial apparatus of the United States if Washington was unable to contain internal upheaval within its borders. This, then, was the pragmatic motivation behind Cuba's encouragement, whether material or rhetorical, of the U.S. protest movements. "One of the ways to continue to weaken the power of American imperialism," Cuban historian Tomás Fernández Robaina contends, "was to support the social fight inside the United States, just like they would support the guerrillas and partisans everywhere."[133]

At the heart of this policy was the question of not only Cuba's security, but that of Vietnam, which the Cuban leadership regarded as the era's most vital front in its global bid to confront U.S. global domination. Guevara's "Message to the Tricontinental," which was largely a plea for the world's anti-imperialist forces to support Vietnamese resistance to U.S. attack, was regarded by the U.S. Senate Internal Security Subcommittee as "probably the most powerful gathering of pro-Communist, anti-American forces in the history of the Western Hemisphere."[134] Guevara's message contained the now famous lines: "We must carry the war into every corner the enemy happens to carry it: to his home, to his centers of entertainment; a total war. It is necessary to prevent him from having a moment of peace, a quiet moment outside his barracks or even inside; we must attack him wherever he may be; make him feel like a cornered beast wherever he may move."[135]

The United States, Guevara hoped, would become bogged down with domestic concerns, hampered in its ability to maintain its military presence in Vietnam, much less launch a military assault upon Cuba. For their part, Vietnam's national liberation forces placed hope in the same strategy, founding in 1967 the South Vietnamese Peoples Committee for Solidarity with American People to facilitate alliances with the U.S. antiwar movement. The intersection of idealistic Cuban internationalism, on the one hand, with Havana's national security imperatives on the other, therefore played a role in its support for U.S. left-wing movements. Cleaver clearly regarded Cuba's aid to U.S. radicals as a matter of reciprocity between allies:

> I know that the support activity that American militants and the Left movements gave to Cuba was useful to them and it was something that went a long way in taking the heat off Cuba.... So there was a quid pro quo established for people functioning with that ideology: you scratch my back, I scratch your back. It was that kind of thing. This is what they were saying, this is what they were promising to the world, and this is what we wanted to take them up on. When we sought to take them up on it, it wasn't as though we went there begging; we went there to get what was ours. They didn't want to give it to us.[136]

As early as 1960, the Cuban leadership had regarded the African American freedom movement as the vanguard of revolutionary social transformation in America. Black Americans, conceptualized as an "internally colonized" nation, one proximate to political power due to their significant presence in urban industrial centers after World War II, were the section of the U.S. population that Cuba's revolutionaries thought most capable of igniting conditions of social upheaval within the United States. In a statement in 1967, the year that dozens of U.S. cities, including Newark and Detroit, exploded in rebellion, Cuban President Osvaldo Dorticós Torrado affirmed that racial unrest in urban centers of the United States showed the "internal contradictions that . . .

A poster produced by OSPAAAL reads: "We will destroy imperialism from the outside; they will destroy it from the inside." In the summer of 1967, as dozens of U.S. cities exploded in racial rebellion, Cuban editorials, press accounts, and cultural production increasingly reflected the policy view that the African American freedom struggle represented a potent threat to Washington's ability to govern at home and project its military power abroad. Artist unknown/OSPAAAL; courtesy of Docs Populi.

inhibit the military capacity of imperialism to combat revolutionary movements by forcing it to be concerned with its own domestic front."[137]

By 1968, Cuban officials considered the socialist Black Panther Party to be the most ideologically advanced facet of the U.S. black freedom movement, the one best positioned to lead a movement for revolutionary change, and the one whose vision of multiracial solidarity made it capable of uniting with movements in other communities of color and with white radicals. Coverage of the Panthers was featured prominently in Cuban state organs such as *Granma*, and *Tricontinental* had featured essays written by Panthers Huey P. Newton and George Murray.[138]

Yet the rise of the Black Panthers coincided fatefully with the weakening of Havana's willingness to support revolution abroad. The most obvious cause of the shift was Guevara's death two years earlier in Bolivia, where he had been captured and executed in a joint operation of the CIA and the Bolivian army. Guevara's death extinguished one of the most forceful visions of global anti-imperialist insurgency emanating from Cuba, if not the world.

However, the events that precipitated Guevara's departure from his post in the Cuban government prior to his ill-fated expedition in Bolivia were at least partly a product of Cuba's complicated relationship with the Soviet Union. Cuba's alliance with U.S. dissidents during the 1960s, especially black radical activists, would ultimately be influenced as much by Havana-Moscow relations as ideological developments within Cuba. As scholars of the Black Panther Party have noted, support for the organization from the revolutionary governments of Algeria and China similarly diminished in the early 1970s, as they reached diplomatic agreements with the United States and tensions with Washington cooled.[139]

Scholar Ruth Reitan, drawing upon interviews that she conducted with Domingo Amuchástegui, a former Cuban intelligence officer who served as a liaison with visiting American radicals, and with Eldridge Cleaver, whose time in Cuba illuminate the tensions that developed between the Cuban government and some U.S. black radicals, argues that Havana's willingness to provide material support for U.S. black radical movements was ultimately compromised by a bipartite dispute within the Cuban government regarding the most effective way to safeguard Cuba's national security aims in the face of both U.S. hostility and Cuba's political isolation within Latin America.[140] The radical foreign policy view within the Cuban government, associated with Che Guevara and others close to the physician-turned-guerrilla strategist, held that the survival of the young socialist nation could best be ensured through Cuban support for left-wing revolution elsewhere in the Third World — the "two, three, many Vietnams" that Guevara had famously called for in his "Message to the Tricontinental," written in 1966 in West Africa.[141]

The Black Panther Party elaborated a reverse reading of the Guevara doctrine. At a time when federal and National Guard troops had been used to quell urban rebellions, particularly after the assassination of Martin Luther King Jr. in April of 1968, and at a time when ascendant protest movements had become a preoccupation in Johnson's White House as the war effort floundered, the Panthers perceived that successful anti-imperialist struggle abroad had the potential to weaken the U.S. state's ability to suppress radical movements at home. In a speech to the OSPAAAL conference in Havana in August, Panther leader George Murray proclaimed that "every time a Vietnamese guerilla knocks out a U.S. soldier, that means one less aggressor against those who fight for freedom in the U.S."[142]

Although Guevara's foreign policy focused upon the prospects for revolution in the Third World, it did not entirely rule out the possibility of revolutionary transformation in North America. According to the *foco* theory of revolution formulated by French theorist Régis Debray and popularized by Guevara, mass insurrection could be ignited by a relatively small group of disciplined combatants who could inspire the masses to action through exemplary guerrilla actions, *creating* the social conditions for revolution, instead of waiting for them to materialize.[143] For Guevara, black Americans were the social class best positioned within American society to foment that rebellion, and the African American freedom movement was the formation most likely to initiate the spark that could ignite a revolutionary conflagration within the wider society.

According to Reitan, the opposing policy view was associated with the more cautious Cuban Communist Party. It held that the survival of Cuba, a small nation beset by a hostile superpower, depended upon close ties with Soviet global power, a relationship that afforded Cuba a measure of military protection and significant economic support. Moscow, however, had no intention of provoking conflict with Washington in its "backyard" after the resolution of the Cuban Missile Crisis in October of 1962. By the mid-1960s, Soviet officials were actively attempting to dissuade Cuba from pursuing armed revolution in Latin America in an effort to avoid a confrontation with Washington. The Cuban Communist Party shared this view or was at least influenced by it. And if revolution was a remote possibility in Latin America, it was unthinkable, party officials surmised, in the heart of the superpower to the north. Unlike the Guevaraist faction, the Cuban Communist Party maintained that the objective conditions for the ignition of a successful revolutionary struggle simply did not exist in the United States, no matter how bright might be the "spark" of street protest and urban unrest.

Cuban policy toward the U.S. black freedom movement therefore fluctuated depending upon which faction in Havana—communist party or Guevaraist—was most successful in influencing policy. Havana's signals to U.S. black radicals were therefore inconsistent, causing confusion, disappointment, and resentment when expected aid from Havana was not forthcoming. While the Cuban government's internationalist rhetoric, which included support for U.S. radicals, continued to be visible in political speeches, billboards, and Cuban state media well into the 1970s, Havana's actual material support for U.S. activists grew scarce lest the U.S. government use evidence of Cuba's hand in its domestic troubles to justify military action against it.[144]

Even as Havana's hopes for armed revolution in Latin America dimmed after 1967, one factor that explains the continued expectations among some American radicals for military training in Cuba, as well as the FBI's claims that such training was actually occurring, is the delay between the shift in Cuban foreign policy away from active attempts to foment revolution in the Americas and awareness of this policy shift outside Cuba. Certainly it was no secret that Cuba had trained foreign revolutionaries on the island and abroad. When it was discovered that the French theorist and writer Régis Debray had received military training in Cuba and had joined Che Guevara's guerrilla unit in Bolivia as a fighter, the revelation made international headlines. U.S. intelligence contended that up to 2,000 Latin Americans had received "either guerrilla warfare training or political indoctrination in Cuba" between 1961 and 1964.[145]

Nonetheless, most foreigners who traveled to Cuba in the late 1960s and early 1970s seeking to enlist in Cuba's revolution — or hoping to receive training to participate in movements elsewhere — appear to have done so without ever confirming that such opportunities existed in Cuba. A significant number of would-be volunteers arrived from Latin America, owing partly to Cuba's attempts to ignite left-wing revolutions there and partly to proximity. North Americans, however, were rebuffed altogether. While a number of the Americans hijacking airplanes to Cuba between 1968 and 1973 had come with the hope of becoming integrated into Cuba's revolutionary project or being sent as volunteers for anti-imperialist movements in the Third World, such requests appear to have been categorically denied.

Although Cuba appears to have evaluated Latin Americans showing up in Cuba seeking military training on a case-by-case basis, North Americans were rebuffed altogether. The risk of antagonizing the United States, coupled with the utter absence of the proper "objective conditions" for a successful revolutionary struggle in that country, was obvious from the beginning.

But there was also the Cuban perception of the utter absurdity, given present conditions, of prospects for successful armed struggle in a North American context, despite the guerrilla dreams of self-styled U.S. revolutionaries who asked the Cubans — sometimes seriously, sometimes in apparent jest — for their advice. In his memoir, Stokely Carmichael recalled "a legend among Harlem nationalists" in which some militant activists, sitting with Fidel Castro during his 1960 stay at the Hotel Theresa in Harlem, had informed the Cuban leader of their intent to foment armed struggle in America. Castro walked to the window and peered out, finally responding: "The Sierra Maestra, the mountains. I don't see any mountains out here."[146]

Such exchanges would repeat many times during the next decade. In an article published just days after Che Guevara's capture and execution in Bolivia, the *Village Voice*'s Stephanie Harrington recalled how Guevara had attended a dinner in his honor in December 1964 at a New York townhouse, on the occasion of his visit to the U.N. General Assembly, with an array of New York intellectuals and high society in attendance. An activist leader from the civil rights organization Northern Student Movement asked Guevara how U.S. students could best emulate the Cuban rebels, at which Guevara "laughed, and gently explained that the situation here was a little different and that he didn't think metropolitan America was a setting in which such tactics could succeed."[147]

"Missiles" as Spies

Distinct from the FBI's contention that *brigadistas* were propagandists and paramilitary recruits for Havana, claims that the Venceremos Brigade was a front for Cuban intelligence objectives within the United States were predicated upon the theory that the group was controlled directly by the General Directorate of Intelligence (DGI), Cuba's intelligence agency. In April 1975, Senators Richard Stone, Herman Talmadge, James Allen, and Jesse Helms, all members of the Senate Committee on Foreign Relations, submitted Resolution 131 in response to reports that Secretary of State Henry Kissinger, in his upcoming visit to the Organization of American States, planned to explore options for easing the then eleven-year-old U.S. embargo against Cuba. In the resolution, the Senators argued that Havana's intelligence penetration of the United States indicated that the Castro government constituted a continuing menace to the United States. According to the report, Cuba's primary instrument of intelligence penetration into America was the Venceremos Brigade, which it deemed "one of the most extensive and dangerous infiltration operations ever undertaken by a foreign power against the United States."[148]

The Committee's report alleged that the Brigade had been "created for the purpose of acting as a screen and tool of the Cuban intelligence apparatus."[149] According to the report's authors, the Brigade was far more than the creation of misguided American radicals. The report outlined three DGI-guided intelligence priorities for the Brigade. Cuba needed "factual and current information on every aspect of activity in the United States"; it needed to leverage to its advantage "any manifestation of dissent" within the United States by inculcating other American radicals with the ideologies of Cuban communism and other global revolutionary movements; and it desired to show solidarity toward North Vietnam by acting as a "conveyor belt for anti-war propaganda."[150]

However, the report went further, alleging that the DGI was using Brigade members as a pool of potential recruits for the establishment of a Cuban intelligence operation inside the United States, creating "a vast network for the collection of intelligence of military, political, industrial, and economic nature."[151] Brigade members were thus imagined as potential spies for Havana.

Similarly alarming was the report's speculation that the DGI might be utilizing the Brigade to situate Cuban-born spies within the United States. These "illegals," as FBI reports termed them, would be Cuban-born intelligence agents trained in Cuba and the Soviet Union and spirited into the United States. The DGI, claimed the report, was directly subservient to the KGB, which had allegedly "insisted on the priority of establishing a good network of illegals in the United States instead of confining the Directorate's interest to the activities of the anti-Castro exiles."[152] According to the report: "Soon after the Soviets made the proposal, the DGI found out that it was totally unprepared, because of a lack of the necessary data, to embark on this operation. To furnish covers for illegals entailed a monumental amount of collection and analysis of information that its agents attached to the U.N. Center in New York could not accomplish without inside assistance.... Consequently, a plan was devised and the Venceremos Brigade was brought into existence."[153]

U.S. intelligence officials had long contended that the Cuban Mission to the United Nations in New York was functioning as a hub for Cuban espionage operations inside the United States. Although J. Edgar Hoover's 1973 characterization of the Mission as the "epicenter" of Cuban intelligence activities in the United States may have been an exaggeration, Cuba's intelligence services, including the DGI, almost certainly maintained a presence at the Mission during the late 1960s, and the FBI and CIA often scrutinized personnel there.[154] In 1969, two Cuban diplomats, accused of illegal intelligence activities inside the United States, were barred from returning to their posts at the Mission. Jesus Jiménez Escobar and Chafik Saker Zenni were accused of providing aid and advice to U.S. radical groups, including the Black Panther Party.[155]

Heightening the aura of intrigue surrounding Cuba's UN Mission was the fact that it often served as a conduit between U.S. radicals and the Cuban government. The Mission received regular visits from left-wing activists, intellectuals, and journalists, and played a role in the coordination of solidarity delegations such as the Venceremos Brigade. The sensational *Long Island Press* exposé of October 1970, entitled "Cuba: School for U.S. Radicals," claimed that personnel at the Mission had advised Students for a Democratic Society (SDS) members Mark Rudd and Jeff Jones, who had both traveled to Cuba, "concerning slogans to be used by SDS in demonstrations planned for that fall."[156]

Both men denied that Cuba had provided them with any guidance concerning the protest. Nonetheless, visits to the Mission by high profile U.S. activists provided ample fodder for tabloid speculation. In January 1968, SNCC chairman H. Rap Brown and an associate, Robert Smith, visited the Mission for a meeting with José Viera, secretary of the Cuban United Nations delegation. Emerging from the building carrying a package that he had not had with him when he entered, Brown was apprehended by a police officer demanding to inspect it. Brown refused, and the officer attempted to take the two men into custody. A scuffle ensued, and Brown and his companion escaped back into the building, where they were protected by Cuban guards exercising the Mission's right of extraterritoriality. Brown maintained that the package contained Christmas gifts that had been given to him by the Cubans.[157]

Interviewed years later by Tom Hayden, diplomat Ricardo Alarcón, Cuba's longtime Representative to the United Nations, recalled that on one occasion, an anti-Castro operative knocked on the door of his Manhattan apartment to deliver a package that the man claimed contained a gift from SNCC activist Stokely Carmichael. Instead, it contained a written threat.[158] Like Cuban diplomatic missions worldwide, the Cuban U.N. Mission in New York and its staff had regularly been a target of assassination plots and bombing attacks by anti-Castro Cuban operatives, a campaign that escalated in the mid-1970s with a series bombings, including a blast in December 1979 that slightly injured two policemen.[159]

The April 1975 Congressional report provided no evidence connecting the Brigade to spying of any kind in the United States. Nonetheless, it was true that Cuba maintained a spy network inside the United States, and it appears that U.S. officials sometimes grafted their fears of the Venceremos Brigade onto the quite real presence of Cuban espionage operations. Indeed, the Cuban government maintained a keen interest in protecting itself from threats originating in the United States, ranging from the CIA's sabotage campaigns, which continued into the 1970s and, especially, the predations of Cuban American anti-Castro paramilitary organizations based in the United States, many of which operated openly and with virtual impunity from prosecution in South Florida. Cuban exile groups such as Alpha 66, Omega 7, the F4 Commandos, the Coordination of United Revolutionary Organizations and others had been linked to a long and ignominious history of bombings and murders in the United States and Cuba since the early 1960s.[160]

In response, Cuba dispatched intelligence agents into the United States to monitor them. Although little is known about the activities of such spies in the 1960s and 1970s, more recent events provide some indication of the nature of Cuban espionage in the United States. Twenty-one alleged Cuban spies were convicted in the United States between 2001 and 2006 alone in a Bush administration crackdown. Ana Belén Montes, a German-born U.S. citizen who was a respected senior analyst at the Defense Intelligence Agency and served as the U.S. intelligence community's highest-ranking Cuba expert in the 1990s, admitted in 2002 to spying for Cuba in order to protect the nation from U.S. regime-change efforts.[161] But the most high profile case had come earlier, in September 1998, when five Cuban intelligence agents were arrested in Miami after infiltrating Brothers to the Rescue, a Cuban exile group, and after collecting information on the activities of F4, Alpha 66, and the Cuban American National Foundation.[162] "The Five," as the agents came to be known in Cuba, where they were honored as national heroes, openly acknowledged their mission of infiltrating South Florida exile groups who were considered terrorists within Cuba. "They are people who've got training camps there in paramilitary organizations and they go to Cuba and commit sabotage, bombs and all kinds of aggressions," Gerardo Hernandez, one of the Five, told *BBC News* in 2007. "And they had impunity, so at a certain point Cuba decided to send some people to gather information on those groups and send it back to Cuba to prevent those actions."[163]

While the Cuban government willingly provided intelligence to the FBI to aid its investigation of Luis Posada Carriles, the Cuban-born, CIA-trained perpetrator of a string of terrorist actions including the 1976 bombing of a Cuban commercial airliner that killed all 73 people aboard, the FBI failed to pursue Carriles and other paramilitary figures, who remained largely unmolested within the United States.[164] Instead, the bureau used the intelligence that Cuba had provided to uncover the network of Cuban agents investigating suspected terrorists operating in the United States, arresting five of them.[165] Although the Venceremos Brigade was not publicly accused of aiding the Five, the activities of the Cuban agents, who were not operating alone,[166] demonstrate that earlier FBI accusations regarding Cuba's intent to implant Cuban-born intelligence agents were accurate, even if their connection to the Venceremos Brigade was spurious.

Cuba has also utilized American-born intelligence agents, usually to penetrate U.S. government agencies. In this case, the spies were Americans who were sympathetic to the Cuban Revolution. Recent events again suggest the nature of such operations. In June 2009, the U.S. Justice Department charged a husband and wife team — Kendall Myers, a retired former senior State Department intelligence analyst, and Gwendolyn S. Myers, a bank financial analyst — as agents of the Cuban government in a spy career stretching back thirty years. The investigation focused on Kendall, the holder of a Ph.D. in

European Studies from The Johns Hopkins University, who had been an instructor at the U.S. State Department's Foreign Service Institute and who had gained Top Secret security clearance at the State Department in 1985. Gwendolyn, who did not herself achieve security clearance at any U.S. government agency, had once worked as a staff member for James Abourezk, a South Dakota Senator who had worked to normalize relations with Cuba.

According to the FBI, Kendall was recruited as a spy during a 1978 trip to the island that was arranged at the invitation of an official at the Cuban Mission to the United Nations in New York. The arrest affidavit included excerpts from Kendall's diary, in which he described the 1978 trip to the island as solidifying his sympathy with Cuba:

> Going through the [Museum of the Revolution in Havana] was a sobering experience. Facing step by step the historic interventions of the U.S. into Cuban affairs, including the systematic and regular murdering of revolutionary leaders left me with a lump in my throat.... They don't need to try very hard to make the point that we have been the exploiters. Batista was only one of the long list of murderous figures that we thrust upon them in the name of stability and freedom.... There may have been some abuses under the present regime, life may be more complicated by rationing, etc., but no one can make me believe that Cuba would have been better off if we have defeated the revolution. The idea is obscene.[167]

The Myerses maintained that they were motivated solely by their opposition to U.S. policies toward the island and received no cash compensation for their service. At their sentencing hearing, the couple claimed that they had not acted "out of anger at the United States or from a feeling of anti-Americanism. Nor did we ever intend to hurt any individual Americans." Their objective, the Myerses maintained, was to "help the Cuban people defend their revolution" and "forestall conflict between the two countries."[168]

The Myerses pleaded guilty. Kendall, who also happened to be the great grandson of Alexander Graham Bell, was sentenced to life in prison; Gwendolyn was sentenced to five and a half years.[169] Gwendolyn's first call after her arrest was to her former mentor, Senator Abourezk, who had once taken a team of South Dakota college baseball players to Cuba during the Carter-era thaw in U.S.-Cuba diplomacy. "If we'd have ended the embargo years ago, there would have been no spying and none of this stuff would have happened," Abourezk later remarked. "To me, if the Cubans are spying, it would be a defensive thing. What's Cuba going to do to the U.S.? Invade? Are you kidding?"[170]

The charges against the Myerses and other Cuban agents working in the United States may have contributed to a significant and unexplained increase in FBI harassment of the Venceremos Brigade in 2009 and 2010.[171] Although not affiliated with the Brigade, the Myerses represented precisely the kind of scenario that the FBI had outlined in the 1976 report, *Foreign Influence,* issued two years before Kendall's trip to Cuba. Alleging that the DGI was responsible for setting up the Brigade's delegations, the FBI's report had warned that the Cuban intelligence agency's ultimate objective was "the recruitment of individuals who are politically oriented and who someday may obtain a position, elective or appointive, somewhere in the U.S. Government, which would provide the Cuban Government with access to political, economic and military intelligence."[172] Cuban intelligence officers, the *New York Times* reported, "were described as particularly eager to recruit Americans who had political contacts or who were related to United States government officials."[173]

Nonetheless, despite the remote possibility that the Venceremos Brigade's presence in Cuba might have provided Cuban intelligence operatives with the opportunity to recruit American radicals as spies, the FBI ultimately produced no evidence that this had in fact occurred. Furthermore, both the FBI and the Internal Security Subcommittee reports stretched credulity on a number of key points regarding the alleged recruitment of Brigade members as intelligence agents. The authors of the Senate report went as far as to claim that DGI agents in the Brigade volunteer camps routinely "used physical labor to soften resistance" and ease the process of collecting intelligence from the Americans.[174] The authors contended that "practically every Cuban national attached to the Brigade camps, right down to the food service and maintenance personnel, is a member or a co-opted member of the DGI."[175] Such high priority was placed on this function that "all other DGI operations were held to be subordinate to the collection of intelligence from the members of the Venceremos Brigade ... In fact, so many DGI personnel are needed to staff these camps that nearly all other operations must be suspended when the camps are active. Even maintenance and clerical personnel of the Directorate are pressed into service, as numerous photographs obtained by the Subcommittee indicate."[176]

While there is currently no available means of evaluating the presence of DGI agents working in the solidarity camps where the Brigade stayed, the claim that the DGI, the highly sophisticated intelligence agency charged with protecting Cuba from a complex matrix of global and domestic security threats, suspended "nearly all" of its operations so that its agents could collect information from the Americans, stretches credulity.

And what kind of intelligence might Brigade participants be able to provide? The Senate report's claim that *brigadistas* were being recruited as intelligence agents for the transmission of political and scientific secrets is dubious at best. According to the authors, a committee of Brigade members had been formed during the trip to report on the University of California at Berkeley's nuclear weapons, the University's Lawrence lab, research labs devoted to bacteria, the Los Alamos proving grounds, the missile guidance systems of U.S. Polaris submarines, NASA's Apollo program, a "moving target indicator" and "a helicopter project to be used in Vietnam."[177]

While undoubtedly valuable intelligence targets, one problem exists with the claim that Brigade participants could achieve access to such sensitive projects: Brigade returnees were under regular U.S. surveillance, and their names had been entered into a range of security databases, including, in all likelihood, the FBI's "Security Index," a list of suspected political subversives to be detained in the event of a national emergency. It is therefore unlikely that "alumni" of the Brigades would ever obtain the security clearances necessary for access to classified material. Indeed, they would almost certainly never in their lifetimes obtain U.S. government top-secret clearance. In this regard, Brigade members' participation in a high profile pro-Cuba organization most likely precluded any future hopes for effective spy work, even if they had aspired to it.

Finally, the report charged that a special Brigade subcommittee had been formed for "the collection and transmission to Cuba of telephone directories" from the United States. "A telephone directory," the report explained, "can be a simple and ready source of corroborating evidence, even in a cursory background investigation. The importance of a telephone directory in intelligence operations is such that it is a crime in Cuba to mail a telephone directory out of the country."[178]

This is a strange contention. Having already suggested, probably correctly, that the DGI operated out of the Cuban Mission to the United Nations in New York, the authors apparently overlooked the fact that telephone books were readily available at the New York Public Library. Mission employees, by virtue of diplomatic immunity, were "free to go anywhere they want in New York," as one unnamed American official had earlier lamented to the press.[179] The DGI, it can be assumed, did not have to rely on smugglers to obtain U.S. phonebooks.

DESPITE HAVANA'S consistent disavowal of armed struggle inside the United States, the Cuban government has also steadfastly refused to abandon some of those who have sought to use political violence to achieve social change in its northern neighbor. Cuba's provision, since 1961, of formal political asylum to U.S. dissidents, including those accused of participating in political violence inside the United States, demonstrates the diplomatic risks that Havana has been willing to incur in order to honor its convictions — the subject that is the focus of chapter 5.

Other acts also suggest the Cuban leadership's sympathy for U.S. dissidents who have led beleaguered lives, even if the Cuban government did not condone their aspirations for armed struggle. When Weather Underground activist John Jacobs died of cancer in 1997 after twenty-seven years living underground to avoid capture by the FBI, the Cuban government allowed some of his cremated remains to be scattered at the site of the Che Guevara Mausoleum in Santa Clara. Near Guevara's grave was placed a plaque bearing a photo of Jacobs and a short biography that read, in part:

> John Gregory Jacobs, known in the United States revolutionary movement as "J.J.," was born September 30, 1947. . . . He organized protests against the Vietnam War in many parts of the United States; and was a principal author of what became known as the "Weatherman Statement." . . . Though he never got to Cuba in [his] lifetime, the leadership of the Cuban Revolution were his models. His family and friends are extremely grateful to the Cuban government, the Central Committee of the Cuban Communist Party, and others for the honor and respect shown him by allowing some of his ashes to be spread at the monument to Che Guevara. . . . He wanted to live like Che. Let him rest with Che.[180]

Although Senator Eastland failed to substantiate his claims about the perils posed by the "missiles, in human form," Cuba's willingness to grant the benefit of the doubt to Americans who claimed to live by Cuba's revolutionary ideals surfaced in other ways. Between 1968 and 1973, some of the Cuban Revolution's most zealous American supporters would test the limits of Cuba's policy of support for radicalism in its northern neighbor by hijacking airplanes to the island.

3

Revolution in the Air
Hijacking, Political Protest, and U.S.-Cuba Relations

In that hothouse of revolution and charged hope, all kinds of people meet and form relationships that would be unlikely to occur almost anywhere else in the world.
—**Lee Lockwood,** 1970

BEGINNING IN 1968, Cuba acquired an unwelcome distinction as the world's most popular place to land a hijacked airplane. Although the perpetrators came from throughout the Americas, the majority arrived from the United States, making U.S. citizens or residents the world's most frequent air hijackers. Making over ninety attempts to reach Cuba in commercial and private aircraft between 1968 and 1973, hijackers guided more flights from U.S. skies to Cuba's airspace than all other global air hijacking destinations combined.[1]

Seeking political asylum, a haven from racism, contact with Third World revolutionary movements, escape from criminal charges, and adventure, the majority of the hijackers framed their actions in explicitly political terms by invoking left-wing tropes of social justice and political protest or claiming persecution in the United States.[2] The perpetrators included an ex–Black Panther, facing criminal charges in California, who hoped "to start a new life ... among revolutionary, socialist-minded people who wouldn't hold my past or my race against me";[3] a divorced college professor who wanted to "help the revolution of Fidel Castro";[4] a father-and-sons team who, robbing a bank to fund a "revolutionary commando organization," hijacked a plane to Cuba to escape murder charges;[5] and a man who wanted to go to Cuba because he was "tired of TV dinners and tired of seeing people starve in the world."[6]

As the phenomenon grew, air hijacking, referred to variously as "air piracy" and "skyjacking," became a fixture of American public life. Extorting tens of millions of ransom dollars from airline corporations and occasionally threatening to blow up aircraft, hijackers commanded political attention and popular fascination. Commercial airline pilots threatened to strike en masse, and emergency funding was allocated to build a nationwide airport security apparatus costing $300 million. Hijacking invaded popular culture, becoming fodder for comedic television gags as pundits debated the epidemic's connection to the era's social ferment. In a characteristic segment, *NBC News* surmised that, far from being left-wing political refugees or idealistic youth, the air pirates were psychopathic and mentally ill, "a wax museum of freaks, perverts, criminals and assorted social misfits."[7] Hijackers' fascination with the communist Caribbean nation was evidence, right-wing commentators charged, of the decadence of the era's rebellious youth and of the perilously seductive aura of Cuba's revolutionary mystique.

Yet the Cuban government was little more enthused by the arrival of self-styled American revolutionaries, some of whom appeared to be mentally unstable. "Most of the hijackers," Fidel Castro opined a year into the episode, "are not completely normal people."[8] Imprisoning many as common criminals or suspected CIA spies, Cuban officials treated hijacking as a both a nuisance and a national security problem. Nonetheless, Cuba refused to extradite its uninvited American guests. As U.S. officials fulminated over their inability to retrieve fugitives from the socialist island, Cuba afforded many of them the opportunity to make a new life for themselves as exiles beyond the reach of U.S. legality.

This chapter seeks, first, to understand the U.S.-Cuba hijacking surge of 1968–73 by exploring how the Caribbean nation functioned in the American radical imaginary at the apex of the sixties era. Constructing Cuba in idealized terms as an alternative to consumer capitalism, white domination, and U.S. global hegemony and as a portal to Third World movements within the geopolitical context of the Cold War and decolonization, left-wing U.S. hijackers sought to become global actors beyond the constraints of the U.S. imperial state. Hijackers also occasionally framed their actions in ways that suggested age-old paternalistic tropes of Cuba. Arriving without invitation and imagining the Caribbean island as a permissive space that should welcome them as revolutionary comrades, some hijackers inadvertently echoed older American fantasies of imperial entitlement, dating as far back as the late 1800s, that imagined Cuba as a space of lawlessness and personal license for foreigners.[9] These tendencies notwithstanding, the hijacking surge from the United States to Cuba in the late 1960s can be most productively understood by situating it within the larger relationship between Cuba and the U.S. protest movements of the 1960s.

The story of the 1968–1973 hijacking era, however, is also the story of U.S.-Cuba diplomacy during the Cold War. Indeed, the phenomenon marks the unlikely meeting point where the protest politics of the late sixties era collided with U.S.-Cuba foreign relations. Although the two nation-states were locked in a diplomatic impasse, hijackers forced the United States and Cuba into an unprecedented series of dialogues, culminating in a 1973 antihijacking agreement, which foreshadowed the mild thaw in relations during the coming Carter era.[10] As such, hijacking adds a crucial "nonstate" element to evaluations of Cold War diplomacy between Washington and Havana, a relationship that has most commonly been framed as a product of the workings of intransigent governments acting independently of the public generally, and social movements specifically.[11]

Similarly, the rise of American hijacking to Cuba provides an unexplored counterpoint to the peculiarities of U.S. immigration policy toward Cuba and the ways in which these policies, based in a history of unequal power relations and imperial hubris, were shaped by Washington's Cold War logic of unrelenting antagonism and destabilization toward its neighbor in the Caribbean. Indeed, Cuba's provision of asylum to beleaguered Americans closely replicated the U.S. policy of granting sanctuary, under the 1966 Cuban Refugee Adjustment Act, to all Cubans reaching U.S. soil with "dry feet," including those accused of hijacking and other serious offenses. As Cuban émigrés traveling to southern Florida formulated themselves as refugees from communist repression, U.S. hijackers traveling in the other direction understood themselves as refugees from a racist and capitalist America. The hijacking surge provided Cuba with an unwieldy but useable counterpoint to the imperial exceptionalism of U.S. policy while also exposing the ways in which Cuba's attractiveness as a legal sanctuary for American dissidents was a consequence of Washington's own policy of diplomatic acrimony, which had severed the normal channels through which the two nations might ostensibly act as equal juridical actors, in "realist" fashion, to resolve an issue such as air piracy.

The distinctive transnational nexus of social, cultural, and diplomatic histories that is visible in the 1968–73 hijacking period comes into perhaps its sharpest focus in the instance of black radical hijackers. Imagining Cuba as a haven from U.S. white supremacy that would provide an opportunity to forge political connections with African diasporic and global anticolonial movements, African American hijackers constituted a disproportionate number of Cuba's unbidden guests. Their perceptions of Cuba's racial project paralleled earlier renderings of the island by U.S. Pan-Africanists, who understood the island nation as a vital part of the African diaspora, one whose fate was bound up with that of Black Americans. The circulation of people of African descent between Cuba and the United States in the early and mid-twentieth century influenced Black racial politics in early and mid-twentieth century U.S. long before Cuba's 1959 revolution.[12] However, considerably less attention has focused on the relationship between African American activists and Cuba after 1961. Although air hijacking became a high-profile medium for African American encounters with Cuba during the Black Power era, no published work has examined these relationships through air piracy.[13]

Scholarship on hijacking has often been limited by an unwillingness to imagine hijackers as anything more than terrorists, mentally ill idealists, and common criminals. Academic treatments of hijacking have examined the 1968–73 U.S.-Cuba hijacking spate primarily through the lenses of aviation policy, security studies, and counterterrorism.[14] Two well-researched articles have defined recent scholarly treatments of air hijacking in the Americas. The first, published in the *American Journal of Sociology* in 1986, argued that hijackings were a "contagious phenomenon," in that successful hijackings often generated additional hijacking attempts. The article developed a mathematical model of the contagion thesis, applying it to hijackings occurring during the 1968–1972 surge.[15] Another, published in the journal *Criminology* in 2005, used a rational choice framework of crime analysis to evaluate the efficacy of counterhijacking measures, finding that hijackings decreased when apprehension seemed more certain or when punishments became more severe.[16] These studies built upon a wide range of earlier work. Indeed, as hijackings surged during the late 1960s, the incidents became the focus of a number of mass-market books on air piracy that attempted, with varying degrees of success, to explain the rise of the phenomenon, develop psychological and criminal profiles of the perpetrators, and examine official responses to hijacking in the United States and abroad.[17]

As a social phenomenon, however, the saga's human actors, whether hijackers or Cuban and U.S. officials, cannot so easily be reduced to the facile binaries of "political actors" and "criminals."[18] Hijacking to Cuba, like the historical era in which the trend emerged, was considerably more complex. Since the modern notion of legality is explicitly tied to nation states, many left-wing American hijackers — like Cuban refugees and *bolseros*, who are their arguable counterparts — changed legal status when they crossed national borders, transforming themselves from "outlaws" in the United States to "refugees" in Cuba. Both émigrés from Cuba and hijackers from the United States embody contested notions of legality that lie at the very heart of post-1959 U.S.-Cuba diplomatic relations. Hijackers, collectively, must be located within a larger historical continuum, not as heroes or villains, but as transnational historical actors who belong within the history of U.S.-Cuba relations precisely because they are multifaceted, complex, and contradictory subjects.

Skyjackers and the Irresistible Revolution

The hijacking surge that began in 1968 replicated, on a far larger scale, an earlier series of skyjackings from the United States to Cuba by sympathizers of Cuba's revolution. The first air hijacking in U.S. history was committed by Antulio Ramírez Ortiz, who hijacked a flight from Miami, Florida, to Cuba on May 1, 1961. Ortiz claimed that Rafael Trujillo, the dictator of the Dominican Republic and longtime abettor of U.S. interests in the region, had offered him $100,000 to assassinate Fidel Castro, and that he wanted to warn the Cuban leader. Ortiz, a Miami electrician of Puerto Rican descent, had checked in to his flight under the pseudonym "Elpirata Cofresi," an allusion to nineteenth century Puerto Rican pirate Roberto Cofresí.[19] Other hijackings to Cuba followed, and in August 1961, Ernesto "Che" Guevara expressed concern about hijackings to the United States, telling White House aide Richard Goodwin, whom he had met at the meeting of the Alliance for Progress in Uruguay, that Cuba was not responsible for the hijackings.[20] Then, after several Cuban exiles hijacked planes *back* to Cuba beginning in 1961, President Kennedy ordered that "a border patrolman" would begin riding on select flights, a predecessor to the U.S. "Sky Marshals" program.[21]

But the surge of air hijackings that began in 1968 also brought Americans into contact with Cuba in ways that echoed earlier patterns of travel to the Caribbean nation from its northern neighbor. Indeed, skyjackers were not the first Americans to imagine Cuba as a refuge from legal troubles, a scene of adventure and uninhibited license, or a haven from both racial and political persecution — representations of the island that long preceded Cuba's 1959 revolution.[22] However, the revolutionary process of the late 1980s initiated a new set of circumstances that shaped American understandings of Cuba. As historian Van Gosse has noted, perceptions of the anti-Batista insurgency among Americans, particularly young white men, were informed by early media portrayals of Fidel Castro and Che Guevara as masculine and ruggedly independent "rebels with a cause" who were endeavoring to change the island's legacy of poverty, corruption, and foreign domination.[23] A decade after the triumph of Castro's rebels, portrayals of the revolution's icons as independent, masculine, bearded outlaws continued to inform popular U.S. perceptions of the Cuban Revolution. Like the guerrillas, American hijackers, overwhelmingly young and male, often regarded themselves as outlaws with ideals, manifesting real and threatened violence to achieve ambitions that they formulated as legitimate political acts within the context of the social upheaval and radicalism of the late 1960s era.

Some of the ability of American hijackers to imagine their acts in political terms stemmed from their perception of the congruencies between the Cuban Revolution and broad left-wing ideals during the late 1960s. Institutionalizing structural changes that channeled the nation's material wealth and human capital into a socialist system, the revolutionary government had soon enshrined education, health care, and housing not as social services, but as universal human rights to which all Cubans were entitled. The nation's reputation as a relative haven from U.S.-style Jim Crow racism also solidified a durable base of African American support.[24] The perception of Cuba's racial egalitarianism, encouraged by the new government's campaign to dismantle racial segregation on the island in 1959, when the United States still adhered to the doctrine of gradualism; its official encouragement of black American tourism to a land "free of racism," a claim bolstered by the endorsement of guests such as boxing legend Joe Louis; Castro's famed stay at Harlem's Hotel Theresa in 1960, where he met with Malcolm X and Robert F. Williams, and where a generation of black New Yorkers, including Stokely Carmichael and Nehanda Abiodun, would first encounter Cuba's revolution; and the Cuban leader's strongly worded denunciations of U.S. antiblack racism contributed to the island's appeal as a Caribbean sanctuary from racial apartheid.[25]

Cuba's image as a racial sanctuary was bolstered by the Castro government's propensity to grant formal or de facto political asylum to Americans, particularly black radicals. In 1961, NAACP activists Mabel and Robert F. Williams had obtained asylum in Cuba after fleeing trumped-up kidnapping charges in North Carolina.[26] Foreigners "being persecuted by reactionaries and exploiters," Castro later affirmed, referring to Robert F. Williams, "can find asylum here. It does not matter if they speak English and [were] born in the United States."[27] While Ghana had also recently been a refuge for several black American dissidents, Kwame Nkrumah's deposing in 1966 foreclosed Ghana's further status as a haven, and although several black radicals later went to Algeria, Cuba became the primary destination for U.S. political exiles in the late 1960s.[28] So ubiquitous was Cuba's reputation as a sanctuary that rebelling Attica prisoners requested safe passage to Cuba or another "non-imperialist" nation as one of their demands in 1971.[29] Hijacking, despite its dangers, afforded American dissidents a travel route to an island haven to which no legal avenue existed as a result of the U.S. embargo.

Foreign Volunteers in Revolutionary Cuba

Hijackers were not the only Americans seeking to reach Cuba in the late 1960s. Most famously, the Venceremos Brigade, an offshoot of the New Left organization Students for a Democratic Society (SDS), began sending multiracial delegations of volunteers to Cuba in 1969, the very year U.S.-Cuba hijackings reached their peak. Cutting sugarcane and tending citrus fields while learning about Cuban socialism and interacting with members of left-wing movements from around the world, the Americans drew the ire of the FBI and the U.S. House of Representatives Committee on Internal Security, which alleged that the Americans were being trained in guerrilla warfare and indoctrinated with Soviet communism: "anarchists," not "agrarians," as senator James O. Eastland termed them. Nonetheless, although most of Cuba's foreign visitors during the late 1960s were members of sanctioned delegations, Cuba's appeal to leftists sometimes resulted in the arrival of unexpected visitors.

Indeed, Cuba's radical allure was a global affair. One such dissident enticed by Cuba's promise was Ulloa Bornemann, a young Mexican communist and a member of the Liga Comunista Espartaco who had become interested in Cuba after reading press accounts of the revolution, including U.S. journalist Herbert Matthews's widely read 1957 *New York Times* interview with Castro during the war against the Batista government. Bornemann decided to try to enlist in Cuba's revolution, although he had no connections on the island and did not have the formal backing of his organization. Flying to Cuba — as a regular ticketed passenger — on a commercial aircraft in September 1967, Bornemann insisted to Cuban officials upon arrival that he wished to assist in the sugar harvest and receive "military and political training." Although the Cuban government offered to allow him to do volunteer work and travel the island, officials treated his requests for military training with mixed amusement and suspicion. He was ultimately deported from the island as an unwelcome guest and a possible foreign agent. Cuba, the officials told Bornemann, was a frequent destination of young men arriving without invitation "from all over the world," seeking to join Cuba's revolution. Such guests created a nuisance for Havana's cash-strapped government, which would not spare scarce basic amenities, or even a job that could be filled instead by a Cuban, much less the provision of military training to an unknown and uninvited foreigner.[30]

The would-be foreign volunteers that Cuban officials referred to may have included four Colombian men and an Ecuadoran who had arrived the month before. Unlike Bornemann, they arrived as hijackers. Commandeering a

Colombian airliner to Havana with seventy-eight passengers aboard, including two vacationing Chicagoans, the pilot later identified the skyjackers as admirers of Fidel Castro. The hijackers reportedly asked to stay in Cuba, a request that was granted.[31] During the next two years, several more aircraft from Colombia, Mexico, and Venezuela were hijacked to Cuba, often by persons seeking political asylum. Early in 1969, *Time Magazine* reported that a Colombian airport guard who "idolized Che Guevara" had hijacked a Colombian airliner bound for Medellín, forcing the pilot to land in Santiago de Cuba.[32] A significant number of hijackers reached Cuba from Latin America between 1968 and 1972, demonstrating the hemispheric dimensions of Cuba's appeal as a political haven for leftists and a destination for young adventurers.[33]

The notion that one could join Cuba's revolution as a foreigner was not, however, without precedent on the island. A decade before North Americans began hijacking planes for this purpose, some two dozen U.S. citizens actually participated in the armed campaign on the side of Castro's insurgents, a history that has been documented by historian Van Gosse. The widely aired 1957 *CBS* television special entitled "Rebels of the Sierra Maestra: The Story of Cuba's Jungle Fighters," filmed on location, documented something unexpected: three young, gun-toting Americans in the midst of the guerrillas. They had deserted their posts at the U.S. military base at Guantanamo. The youngest was fifteen years old, and the oldest, at twenty-one, told journalist Robert Taber that they "came to do our part for the freedom of the world mostly. We just heard so much about... how Batista was so cruel and he was a dictatorship [sic], and how with the war in Hungary and the people fighting for freedom there, we just felt moved to come here."[34] Donald Soldini, an eighteen-year-old American from a progressive family, shared similar ideals. Making his way to Santiago de Cuba and managing to join Raúl Castro's column in the mountains, he ran guns and took part in numerous battles, at one point barely escaping execution after being captured by Batista's forces. "I was always the internationalist," he later told Gosse in an interview. "When Israel invaded Egypt, I was highly indignant and I went to the Syrian Embassy and enlisted in their army! I was looking for a cause, a good fight."[35] Soldini's internationalist fervor foreshadowed what was to come: a stream of young men from abroad, arriving in Cuba in the late 1960s and early 1970s, hoping to be trained and sent to fight in Third World liberation movements.

Take Me to Havana!

In October 1971, *Time Magazine* wrote that "strong, masculine, idealistic and politically radical" had been the usual characteristics ascribed to hijackers, who often became "folk heroes of the New Left."³⁶ The hijacking phenomenon began in 1968 almost innocuously. *The Sun* featured the year's first hijacking with a photo of a stewardess bearing the caption: "Coffee, tea, or — Castro?"³⁷ News reports were occasionally sympathetic, portraying hijackers as "unwelcome" but generally "congenial," and downplayed hijackers' threat of violence.³⁸ Cuba permitted all commercial flights hijacked into its airspace to land, and crew and passengers reported courteous treatment from Cuban airport staff and government officials, who capitalized on the incidents as opportunities for both goodwill diplomacy and compulsory tourist revenue. Stranded crew and passengers alike often received extravagant treatment: live Cuban bands, steak and shrimp dinners, or a night in one of Havana's best hotels; others were given cigars or photos of Che Guevara while they waited on the tarmac, and the Cubans sent the bill to the airlines.³⁹ A December 1968 *Time Magazine* article entitled "What to Do When the Hijacker Comes," published in the magazine's travel section, encouraged hijacked passengers to enjoy their overnight hotel stays at the Havana Libre (formerly the Hilton) or the Varadero Internacional, courtesy of the Cuban government; take advantage of shopping for cigars and rum, and to "bring your bathing suit" to enjoy Varadero Beach, a "15-mile-long-ribbon of white sand." A hijacker identified only as "José," who had commandeered a commercial flight in November 1968 reportedly chatted with passengers and handed out .32-caliber bullets as souvenirs, and at least one honeymooning couple on the flight did not seem to mind their diversion to Havana: "Cubans really are very friendly people."⁴⁰

By the decade's end, however, the sky had darkened. Media coverage of hijackings turned somber, then fearful. In his acclaimed work *Soul on Ice*, published the year the hijacking epidemic exploded but written three years earlier, Eldridge Cleaver seemed to presage the coming skyjacking era in an allegory that caustically painted U.S. officialdom, not the spectacle of sixties social unrest and cultural ferment, as a threat to humanity: "It is not an overstatement to say that the destiny of the entire human race depends on the outcome of what is going on in America today. This is a staggering reality to the rest of the world; they must feel like passengers in a supersonic jetliner who are forced to watch helplessly while a passel of drunks, hypes, freaks and madmen fight for the controls and the pilot's seat."⁴¹

The hijacking surge quickly assumed frightening dimensions. Commandeering planes to obtain political exile, escape criminal charges, and extort ransoms, hijackers frequently imagined themselves as beleaguered, driven to acts of last resort by circumstances beyond their control. For skyjackers, commandeering an aircraft full of passengers could also be imagined as an act of political protest. Appropriating private property under federal jurisdiction and holding passengers as hostages, hijackers who captured a plane could leverage significant negotiating power to achieve political ends. Circa 1970, a 747 jetliner cost approximately $20 million and could carry 400 passengers. With airport security lax, commercial airliners and their passengers were uniquely vulnerable to becoming vessels for political demands or extortion. Airborne, the plane became a formidable weapon against people and structures, a frightening specter that created national anxiety about flying that would only be eclipsed decades later by the events of September 11, 2001. Political hijackers conveyed messages that found guaranteed amplification from the resulting media coverage, and their demands were treated with the utmost seriousness in light of the potential danger to passengers and crew. Indeed, the global record of hijackings in the late 1960s and early 1970s worldwide shows that hijacking could be used as an effective lever to gain concrete political demands, particularly in Europe and the Middle East.[42]

Hijackings could also be executed in a manner that transformed them into acts of social protest. On May 5, 1972, a white youth from Fargo, North Dakota, named Michael Lynn Hansen used a pistol to take airline passengers on a compulsory detour to Cuba. His intention, he said, was to protest the ongoing U.S. air bombardment of North Vietnam, a few days after he had been inducted into the U.S. Army by a California draft board.[43] "This hijacking is only the first in a series," he wrote in a note to the pilot. "The skies of America will not be safe again until the United States Government ceases its aggression against the people of Indochina. If American bombs continue falling on Indochina by July 4, 1972, our organization will execute Mr. Nixon." The note was signed "the anti-imperialist movement."[44] Hijacking a Western Airlines flight out of Salt Lake City, Hansen and his captives touched down in San Francisco, Los Angeles, Dallas, Atlanta, and Tampa before landing in Cuba. No one was reported injured in the incident, and the plane and passengers returned unharmed to the United States.[45]

Not all hijackings were similarly bloodless. Among the most notorious airborne dramas of the era was perpetrated by a father-and-sons team dubbed the "Tuller gang." On October 29, 1972, Charles A. Tuller, a former U.S. Commerce Department executive-turned Maoist, civil rights activist, and a self-described "white middle-class revolutionary"; his sons, Bryce, age nineteen, and Jonathan, age eighteen; and an accomplice, William White Graham, attempted a bank robbery in Arlington, Virginia, to finance what they claimed was a secret "revolutionary commando organization in the United States."[46] Having taken a telephone company job as a cable splicer and then enlisting in the Army to learn about weapons, Bryce Tuller, accompanied by his younger brother Jonathan, allegedly used stolen uniforms to pose as telephone workers, cutting phone and alarm lines to the bank before walking in to offer their assistance. But when the bank manager reportedly made a sudden movement, Jonathan Tuller shot him dead. Confronted in the bank by Israel P. González, a twenty-seven-year-old policeman who happened to be Cuban-born, Jonathan Tuller fatally shot him as well. The four men fled by car, driving cross-country and arriving in Houston, Texas, on October 28, undetected by authorities.

The next day they hijacked a commercial jet to Cuba, but not before killing a third man, ticket agent Stanley Hubbard.[47] En route to Cuba, the elder Tuller lectured his captive audience of nervous passengers about the virtues of Cuban society, informing them that "Cuba was the only country where freedom is guaranteed."[48] Spending almost three years in Cuba, the Tullers returned to the United States unnoticed via Jamaica and then the Bahamas — Graham remained in Cuba — in June 1975. Within days after their return to the United States, the three Tullers attempted to rob a Kmart in Fayetteville, North Carolina, but the heist ended with Bryce's capture; the others turned themselves over to the FBI.[49]

The motley crew of hijackers with widely varying motivations created a logistical and national security nightmare for the Cuban government. Often unaware of the details of specific criminal cases in the United States involving hijacking perpetrators and lacking reliable intelligence from U.S. law enforcement agencies due to the absence of diplomatic channels between the two nations, the Cuban officials nonetheless needed to accurately differentiate between skyjackings that seemed to be crimes of criminal opportunism and those that might be justified as acts of expediency by Americans fleeing legitimate political repression in the United States.[50] Havana adamantly defended its right to grant asylum to foreigners as a matter of "sovereign prerogative," and the government's official policy was to grant asylum to persons who, "being politically persecuted had no choice but to resort to such an extreme remedy when his life was in danger."[51] As articulated, Cuba's prerogative conformed to both the language of Article 14 of the Universal Declaration of Human Rights, adopted by the General Assembly of the United Nations in 1948, which asserted that "everyone has the right to seek and enjoy in other countries asylum from persecution," and the General Assembly's Declaration of Asylum, unanimously adopted in 1967, which stated that "it shall rest with the state granting asylum to evaluate the grounds for the grant of asylum," including determining whether the asylum seeker was fleeing genuine political repression.[52]

However, by the fall of 1969, the Cuban government regarded only "a few" of the perpetrators of hijackings from the United States to Cuba as "persons in real danger as a result of their political activities." The rest, according to the authors of Cuba's antihijacking Law No. 1226 of September 1969, drafted in an attempt to deter hijackers, were carried out by "common criminals, corrupt individuals, mentally unbalanced persons and socially unadapted persons anxious to change their country of residence or prompted by strictly personal motivations, which cases cannot be considered as being of a revolutionary nature."[53] How Cuban immigration and intelligence officials interpreted the highly subjective and relative categories of "criminal" and "refugee" could determine whether hijackers ended up free on the streets of Cuba or confined, sometimes for years, in Cuban prisons. Most commonly, Cuban officials regarded hijackers as potential FBI or CIA assets seeking to infiltrate Cuba.[54]

Hijackers affiliated with U.S. black liberation organizations presented a delicate situation for the Cuban government in light of Havana's historical position of support for the African American freedom movement. Although the Cuban government remained committed to a position of support for the Black Panther Party until the group's dissolution in the mid-1970s, there was no guarantee that individual Panthers acting on their own volition would be well received by the island's immigration officials if they reached Cuba via an airline hijacking. For its part, the Black Panther Party never condoned or encouraged air hijackings — notwithstanding several hijackings that were executed by Panthers or affiliates of the organization — and members of the organization were not immune from imprisonment in Cuba.

Screenings by Cuban officials were also complicated by dynamics internal to the Black Panther Party, as the case of William Lee Brent reveals. A member of the Party's original Oakland chapter beginning in 1968, Brent rose quickly through the ranks but was indicted on charges stemming from a shoot-out with San Francisco police in 1969. Brent, high on "pills," sleep deprived, and carrying an automatic weapon in his capacity as a bodyguard to senior Panther leaders, writes that he was attempting to obtain change for a twenty-dollar bill at a San Francisco gas station when the station attendant noticed the gun in his waistband. Fearing that Brent was attempting a robbery, the attendant panicked and handed him a large number of bills from the register. Dazed, Brent claims that he did not notice the large amount of "change," and walked away with the cash.[55]

The Black Panther Party's leadership, however, summarily expelled Brent from the organization for "recklessness" and violation of the organization's policy on drug use.[56] The incident, David Hilliard later wrote, represented "another episode in the 'stupid revolution'" in which individuals impersonating the organization's members, and sometimes Panthers themselves, com-

The Cuban press's dissemination of images lionizing African American militancy and black nationalism, while congruent with the Cuban government's support of U.S. Black Power organizations, nonetheless stood in contrast with the Cuban government's discouragement of Afro-Cuban racial solidarity politics on the island. Artist unknown. *Direct from Cuba*, November 1971; author's collection.

mitted crimes that undermined the organization's public image. According to Hilliard, Brent's robbery, which received significant media attention, "confirm[ed] every charge of the media, painting us as hypocrites and opportunists, members of an outlaw organization using politics to justify petty thievery."[57]

Apprehended at the gas station by uniformed police, Brent believed that he was about to be killed and fired at the approaching officers, wounding two. Facing serious charges and now politically isolated, Brent hijacked TWA flight 154 from Oakland to Havana on June 17, 1969. In Cuba, Brent expected to be welcomed as a political refugee and granted formal asylum. Instead, he was confined in a Cuban prison for twenty-two months as a suspected spy. Brent's plight mirrored that of numerous other hijackers. To Cuban officials, Americans arriving unannounced as hijackers fit the profile of spies; to Panther leadership, Brent's gas station heist, inadvertent or not, fit the profile of a police agent provocateur attempting to smear the Party's public image.[58]

Although precise statistics are unavailable, African Americans appear to have comprised the majority of American hijackers who received formal political asylum on the island. The racial dimensions of U.S.-to-Cuba hijacking are therefore central to the phenomenon's significance, including its reverberations within the diplomatic arena. Whereas the Castro government has justifiably been portrayed as censorious to racial nationalist politics within Cuba, its support for North American black nationalist organizations, including through its provision of formal asylum to their members, complicates the notion that the regime was uniformly hostile to the politics of black racial solidarity.

The Cuban government's ambivalent relationship to black nationalism may be viewed with regard to factors both unique to Cuba's post-revolutionary period and those emerging from far older currents within the nation's history. The revolutionary regime's articulation of communist revolution in class-based terms conceptualized racism, in line with classical Marxist analysis, as primarily a function of economic forces. Racial equality could thus be achieved through the construction of a classless, economically egalitarian society. Campaigns to dismantle the vestiges of formal racial segregation left over from the Batista era during the early months of 1959, as well as the Castro government's investment in massive social programs, benefited Afro-Cubans disproportionately and achieved advances toward racial equality that were unprecedented in the nation's history. As scholar Mark Q. Sawyer contends in an often critical study of contemporary Cuban racial politics, "[t]he regime has done more than the government of any other nation, perhaps, to address the problem of racial inequality, yet it has taken some missteps."[59]

A decade after the 1959 revolution, racial inequities in many areas of Cuban society persisted; the Cuban government in turn continued to oppose race-specific solutions to resolve them. Insisting that the rising tide of socialist equality would lift all boats and that the institutional underpinnings of racial inequality had been resolved, the Cuban government foreclosed further public discussions of racial discrimination on the island, going as far as to shut down black social, religious, and political organizations.[60]

In this climate, organizing around race as a political principle was framed as unnecessary at best, and counterrevolutionary at worst. And while the Castro government justified its opposition to race-based politics by highlighting the quite real gains of the revolution in the arena of racial equality, its opposition to independent Afro-Cuban political initiatives evinced recognizable continuities with Cuban nationalist discourses dating back to the late 1800s. Formulating the Cuban nation as a "raceless" entity that subsumed racial identities within an inclusive and antiracist "nation for all," the early intellectual architects of Cuban nationalism argued that national unity depended upon black Cubans relinquishing calls for racial justice.[61] Thus, by the late 1960s, while forging a significant break with the island's segregationist past, the Castro government's explicitly antiracist nationalism was nevertheless structured by older discourses of race and nation that limited the capacity of black Cubans to autonomously address racial concerns.

Ironically, however, black nationalist ideologies provided a means of legibility between U.S. black radical hijackers and the Cuban government through the "internal colony thesis," a political idea with a long history within communist theory.[62] The notion that southern African Americans constituted a colonized black "nation" within the heart of America was articulated in audacious terms during the late 1960s by the Republic of New Afrika (RNA), a black nationalist movement that advocated the creation of an independent territorial nation for people of African descent in the U.S. South as an alternative to subject status within the American white supremacist nation-state.[63] Employing an internationalist, Pan-African "Malcolm X doctrine" that conceptualized people of African descent in America as occupying an internally colonized political subjectivity — members of a subordinate nation within the nation of the United States — the RNA formulated themselves as "New Afrikans" instead of "Americans" or "African Americans": citizens of an independent black nation who could be positioned under international law to negotiate for external protection and universally guaranteed human rights.[64] The RNA conducted themselves as members of a sovereign black nation who could negotiate with Cuba as sovereign agents, a political subjectivity that Cuba honored in the same way that it treated members of SNCC and the Black Panther Party as official representatives of African Americans.[65]

Hijack House

American hijackers arriving in Cuba, including those seeking political asylum, faced a variety of obstacles. Cuban immigration and intelligence officials tended to view hijackers with skepticism, regarding most as simple criminals, potential spies, or mentally unstable individuals.[66] Although hijackers who considered themselves revolutionaries often expected to be welcomed by Cuban authorities, many were sorely disappointed.[67] Greeted on the airport tarmac by heavily armed Cuban soldiers, hijackers who successfully reached Cuban soil were usually imprisoned in immigration jails pending evaluation and held on charges of "illegal entry." Cuban officials performed lengthy background checks on hijackers, often utilizing their U.S. movement contacts to obtain information. Eldridge Cleaver, who had obtained political asylum in

Cuba late in 1968 after arriving legally by boat, vouched for several skyjackers that he knew personally stateside, and justified Cuba's security precautions in an interview with scholar Henry Louis Gates: "You get all kinds of people who come to Cuba. You get some kooks, real kooks. It's conceivable you could get a C.I.A. agent. So this is what they do: they try to find out what you are, then they put them to a special programme [sic], which means cutting sugar cane or something like that, off in the provinces, and they keep them in prison anywhere from one month to two or three months, depending on the case."[68]

Once released onto the streets, hijackers were invariably challenged by the everyday realities of life in Cuban society. The "Tuller gang" hijackers, who had initially described themselves as revolutionaries and entertained romantic notions of an insurgent Cuban society, changed their minds after spending months in the "living hell" of a Cuban prison and laboring in sweltering sugarcane fields. Eventually they were placed in an aging hotel, paid for by the Cuban government, and issued ration cards like the ones Cubans used to secure food, basic clothing, toiletries, and other provisions guaranteed to all citizens. Bryce, once known by teachers at T. C. Williams High School in Alexandria as an activist for student rights, had become rabidly anticommunist.[69] And while little is known of the experiences of hijacker Michael Lynn Hansen — the Fargo man protesting U.S. aggression against Vietnam — while in Cuba, according to the FBI he had been jailed in Cuba for over three years before being released. Abruptly released from prison, he was arrested by U.S. sky marshals in Barbados soon after in June 1975 and was taken to New York to face air piracy charges.[70]

For some hijackers, the circumstances of the act itself influenced their reception by the Cuban government. Black Panther affiliate Anthony Bryant, who hijacked a plane from New York to Cuba on March 5, 1969, writes that he decided in mid-flight to rob the passengers, allowing "the blacks and those who had little money to keep it,"[71] but ran afoul of his Cuban interrogators in Havana when they learned of the heist. Complicating matters further, one passenger who had been carrying a substantial sum of money turned out to be an employee of the Cuban government. Bryant went on to become one of the most famously unhappy — and virulently anticommunist — American hijackers stranded in Cuba. Detained in Cuban prisons and forced to work in agricultural labor collectives for political dissidents, he eventually returned to the United States, writing a book about his experiences and becoming a key figure in the Miami-based, right-wing paramilitary anti-Castro group Comandos L.[72]

Such changes of heart occurred frequently among hijackers whose dreams of life in revolutionary Cuba were dashed by the government in Havana. The *Miami Herald* repeatedly ran articles about disillusioned American hijackers who had romanticized life in "communist Cuba" before setting foot on the island, only to become disillusioned and homesick. A June 1969 article entitled "Life Worse in Cuba, Unhappy Black Panthers Wail" detailed the travails of several Black Panthers, who said that they had been "isolated and imprisoned" after separately hijacking planes to Cuba the previous year. Raymond Johnson, a twenty-two-year-old Party member from Alexandria, Louisiana, maintained that he had been suspended from Southern University for protesting in the aftermath of Martin Luther King Jr.'s assassination and that he was facing arson charges there that he maintained were fabricated. Hijacking an aircraft from New Orleans, Johnson hoped to receive political exile in Cuba and a haven from Louisiana racism.[73] Allegedly changing into a "black leather jacket, black shirt, black trousers, and a black beret" in the airplane's restroom, Johnson emerged with a .38-caliber revolver and ordered the crew to fly to Havana. On the way, he relieved the passengers of $405 in cash, an action that destroyed his chances for a favorable reception from Cuban officials, who consistently took pains to ensure the well-being of passengers on hijacked planes and viewed robbery as an apolitical crime, not a political act. Johnson's hopes for political asylum in Cuba were dashed. Cuban authorities returned the money to the passengers, and Johnson was jailed.

Johnson later reported that he and four other Black Panthers in Cuba were forced to work in labor collectives in remote sections of the island. Quoted by a U.S. reporter, Johnson allegedly stated his wish that his plight be communicated to the Panther leadership in the United States, "so the party will know the unrevolutionary way we are being treated."[74] Charging racism, Johnson attributed the Cuban government's censure of the attempts by himself and his comrades to organize on behalf of the Black Panther Party in Cuba, encourage black Cubans to wear natural hairstyles, and promote awareness of African heritage in Cuba.[75] "We think there's racial discrimination in Cuba," Johnson told the reporter. "It's a peculiar kind of racial discrimination. In some ways it's comparable to attitudes in the United States. White Cubans have a subconscious conspiracy to maintain control of the island. We feel the Cubans have a misunderstanding of the political, cultural and revolutionary thinking of the black revolution." Johnson maintained that Cuban authorities had repeatedly jailed him and the other Panthers after they protested the conditions and expressed their desire to leave the country.[76]

Yet these press portrayals of Johnson warrant further examination. Treatments of hijacking in the *Miami Herald*, in particular, reveal the ways in which U.S. newspapers were far from neutral observers. Indeed, the newspaper's coverage of hijacking must be read against the paper's institutional investment in maligning the Cuban Revolution, an editorial position that reflected the city's growing population of Cuban exiles during the 1960s. The *Herald*'s coverage of hijacking to Cuba, which tended to portray the perpetrators universally as psychopathic criminals even when they claimed to be fleeing political repression, provided a counterpoint to the political investments of the Cuban state media, which tended to portray Cuban émigrés to the United States universally as counterrevolutionaries and criminals, even when they articulated claims of political repression against the Castro government that mirrored those leveled by U.S. hijackers against America. U.S. media coverage of hijacking ultimately provided Washington with a rare coup in its war of image with Havana on the question of racial equality.

While Cuba had prevailed handily in the battle for African American public opinion since 1959,[77] negative reports about life in Cuba from hijackers such as Johnson allowed U.S. newspapers to construct a counternarrative to Cuba's reputation for racial equality.[78] Newspapers such as the *Herald* seized upon the experiences of disgruntled black hijackers as ostensible proof of both the lie of Cuban racial equality and the poor judgment of hijackers, and American leftists more broadly, in imagining Cuba as a revolutionary paradise and a haven from white supremacy.

Hijackers' dreams of a new life in Cuba, however, were sometimes fulfilled. Most were eventually released from Cuban detention and allowed to take jobs, enroll in university classes, and even participate in political civic associations such as the Committees for the Defense of the Revolution (CDR). Initially jailed as a suspected spy, former Black Panther William Lee Brent was eventually granted the opportunity to work and live in Cuba indefinitely. After being released from prison, some hijackers were sent to "Hijack House," as Brent dubbed a converted prerevolutionary mansion in a formerly wealthy Havana neighborhood, which functioned as a kind of halfway house for American radicals who had arrived in Cuba clandestinely. At least two of its occupants were fleeing legal charges stemming from separate shoot-outs with San Francisco police. One American of Salvadorian descent had come to Cuba, according to Brent, "hoping to make connections with Salvadorian rebels [in Cuba] and be sent to El Salvador to fight for his people."[79] These foreigners staying in Cuba were housed and fed courtesy of the Cuban government, likely at considerable likely at considerable expense: lodging, food, clothing, and basic necessities were provided at no cost to the Americans of Hijack House, who were treated as political refugees and official guests of the government. Although everyday Cubans also received guarantees of provisions through the rationing system, which sought to ensure the equal distribution of goods throughout the population, especially to children, mothers, and the elderly, Cubans were required to work, attend school, or enroll in military service. Other hijackers were allowed to live rent-free in Havana hotels, the only housing available given the island's short supply of available housing.[80]

Even "Tuller gang" associate William White Graham described his stay in Cuba in favorable terms, in marked contrast to his former comrades. In a 1975 interview with the *Washington Post*, Graham confirmed that he had been imprisoned after arriving in Cuba, but said that he had also voluntarily participated in a microbrigade of Cuban workers constructing houses in the Havana suburbs. Since then he had been allowed to stay for free at a dilapidated Havana hotel and was studying Spanish, literature, and history at the University of Havana. Graham also maintained that he had broken with the elder Tuller and sons, whom he claimed had shot the bank employee and the ticket agent. "I don't want to be associated with them. See, I consider myself a kind of revolutionary and their actions have graphically demonstrated that they are nothing of the kind... Revolutionaries aren't murderers." Although stranded in Cuba for the time being, Graham claimed that he still entertained his fantasy of returning to the United States to participate in revolution there.[81]

The Cuban government ultimately proved most hospitable to hijackers who displayed a genuine desire to adapt to life in Cuba and who respected its national sovereignty. This included refraining from political organizing in Cuba, including on racial or black nationalist terms.[82] Brent, initially enduring twenty-two disillusioning months in Cuban prison, was eventually released and put up at Hijack House in Havana. Vowing never to return to prison, in Cuba or anywhere else, and interested in the political possibilities of Cuban-style socialism, Brent took significant initiative to integrate into Cuban society. He volunteered with two others from Hijack House to cut sugarcane with the Nuestra América Brigade organized by the Instituto Cubano de Amistad con los Pueblos (ICAP). Initiated in 1960, ICAP coordinated international solidarity delegations from abroad arriving to support the Cuban Revolution, often through volunteer agricultural and construction work. Brent went on to work at a pig farm and then a soap factory before earning his Bachelor of Arts in Hispanic Languages from the University of Havana. He eventually settled into life in Cuba permanently, becoming a high school English teacher in Havana, marrying U.S. writer Jane McManus, who had come to live in Cuba legally, and airing a regular music program on Radio Havana Cuba.[83]

In 1975, Brent met with Huey Newton, who had also received political asylum on the island and had reinstated Brent into the BPP on an honorary basis. Asked by Newton why some of the black Americans who had come to Cuba illegally, such as Anthony Johnson, had become disillusioned with Cuba while Brent had not, Brent attributed the difference partly to unrealistic expectations of Cuba: "Part of the problem... is they came with stars in their eyes, hoping the Cubans would train them in guerrilla warfare, arm them, and sneak them back to the States to engage in armed struggle, or help them get to Africa. It didn't happen and they're pretty pissed off about it."[84]

Charlie Hill, a hijacker who came to Cuba in 1971 as a member of the RNA with two other members, confirms Brent's summation, maintaining that many hijackers who experienced significant problems in Cuba were those who had come with "unrealistic" and "romantic" expectations of Cuba, and those who tried to organize politically within Cuba, an activity that the Cuban government regarded as an infringement upon its sovereignty.[85]

However, hijackers' ambitions to forge informal links with political movements abroad were more successful. Attracted to Cuba in part by the island's image as a confluence of global revolutionaries, black and Latino hijackers from the United States were frequently awed by Havana's wide array of radical visitors, students, and volunteers from across the decolonizing world, many of whom were receiving free education or technical instruction courtesy of the Cuban government. Years later, Hill recalled his experience of Cuba in the early 1970s as an epiphany on the potentials of global solidarity. Experiencing Havana's global radical public, he said, was "like when Malcolm went to Mecca." Outside of official channels, Charlie Hill participated in an ad hoc political study group composed of leftists, mostly young people such as himself, from Africa and Latin America.

But the Americans, however internationalist, were repeatedly turned down in their attempts to join foreign movements, by both the Cuban government and representatives of foreign movements themselves. Although Hill and a number of other black American hijackers had initially hoped to travel on to Angola or Guinea-Bissau, their attempts were foreclosed by both the Cuban government's wariness of the dire diplomatic implications, vis-à-vis Washington, of training Americans to participate in armed political movements, and by the African governments' similar wariness in accepting them as recruits.[86]

Hijacking Diplomacy

In February 1969, soon after the rate of hijackings began increasing, U.S. Secretary of State William Rogers warned that the emerging epidemic presented "an increasingly serious problem" for the American government.[87] Rogers conceded that "none of these incidents has as yet involved us in a serious international problem," adding that "the Cubans have been meticulous about returning relatively promptly hijacked aircraft, passengers and crew." However, Rogers warned that the potential risks were nonetheless significant, including an air "accident with loss of life," or a scenario in which "we are unable to obtain the return of the aircraft or the passengers and crew" if Cuba became less cooperative.[88] By 1972, with still no end to the hijackings in sight, commercial pilots exerted pressure, calling for an international strike on June 19 unless the United Nations took decisive action to halt airline hijackings occurring globally.[89]

The costs to U.S. aviation corporations were also significant. Although U.S. companies were prohibited by the terms of the U.S. embargo from doing business with Cuba, hijackings forced airlines to pay Cuba for the servicing of aircraft and the provision of food and lodging to the passengers. Hijacking, some claimed, was an economic boon for the Cuban government, which suddenly found itself in a position to do business with U.S. companies.[90]

Hijackers also made direct financial demands for ransoms and other payments, often for extravagant amounts. The *New York Times* reported in November 1972 that U.S. airlines had paid $9.3 million in just fifteen months to hijackers. The highlights included a July 1972 incident in which a team of five hijackers had obtained $1 million in cash for the release of the plane's passengers; the hijackers then forced the plane to fly to Algeria.[91] Less than a month later, a hijacker in Reno who claimed he was protesting the Vietnam War had demanded — and received part of — $2 million in cash and gold bars to be used, he said, in the treatment of wounded Vietnamese children.[92] In November, Southern Airways reported that it was in dire financial straits after paying $2 million to three Havana-bound hijackers. The year before, a man referred to as "D.B. Cooper" had famously hijacked a Northwest Airlines flight, parachuted out of it at high altitude after receiving $200,000 in cash, and then disappeared into thin air, never to be seen again.[93] Scrambling to raise large sums of money to appease hijackers or bomb-threat extortionists, airline companies went to great lengths to procure hard currency, sometimes long after bank hours, in one case sending company representatives on a nocturnal mission to a Reno, Nevada, gambling casino to locate enough cash to meet a hijacker's $250,000 demand.[94]

Although the money might eventually be returned, lenders charged a premium for such high-risk loans. "The hijacker," lamented the chairman of the Civil Aeronautics Board in November 1972, "has his gun not only against the pilot's head, but trained on the whole air transport system and its economic well-being."[95] Approximately fifteen hundred sky marshals were riding on flights by late 1971, at an annual cost of over $37 million.[96] By January 1973, the Federal Aviation Administration ordered comprehensive antihijacking measures implemented in 531 commercial airports, focusing especially on baggage searches and x-ray machines, at a cost of $46 million. Total yearly antihijacking expenditures for airlines were projected as high as $300 million.[97]

Cuba's reception of hijackers depended ultimately upon the circumstances of the act and the disposition of the perpetrator. Americans who appeared in Cuba without warning placed the Cuban government in a disadvantageous position. Unable to readily differentiate between dissidents fleeing legitimate political repression and those deemed to be opportunistic criminals on the lam, the Cuban government grew increasingly frustrated by the tide of unwanted airborne visitors. The prevalence of hijackers who appeared to be adventuristic, mentally unstable, or violent ultimately cast a shadow of suspicion over all Americans showing up at Cuban airports, including those arriving on regularly scheduled flights from third countries.

Hijackers who blurred the distinctions between political activism and criminal opportunism, however relative and contested those categories might be, ultimately created an image problem for both American leftists traveling to Cuba by conventional means and the Cuban government itself. Hijackers whose actions appeared to lack compelling political motivations contributed to the prevailing depiction of Cuba as a global haven for outlaws. Such hijackers unwittingly became fodder for media critics who portrayed all American travelers to Cuba as criminal deviants, irrespective of the actual circumstances of their travel.[98] Rejecting the nation's seemingly irresistible appeal to Americans on the lam, the Cuban government asserted that it had "absolutely no interest, nor does it desire in any way, that Cuban territory be used as a refuge by persons responsible for common criminal acts that occur in any part of the United States territory." Cuba reiterated its willingness to negotiate an antihijacking agreement with the United States.[99]

U.S. officials were well aware of Cuba's disadvantageous position. "No self-respecting nation," Deputy Assistant Secretary of State of Inter-American Affairs Robert A. Hurwitch opined, "wants to be in the international limelight as a haven for these depraved and irrational people."[100] According to scholar Jorge Domínguez, "the Cuban government may also have believed that hijacking violated its own norms: Hijacking threatened non-elite combatants and did not increase support for a revolutionary cause. Most hijackers — clearly not revolutionaries — embarrassed the Cuban government."[101]

Yet while Cuba contributed to its hijacking problem through its liberal granting of asylum — or at least refusing to immediately turn hijackers over to the Americans and instead imprisoning them on the island while their cases were evaluated — Cuba's unwanted image as a haven for outlaws was also bound up with U.S. policy. In a perceptive editorial, the *Washington Post* argued that hijacking was an outgrowth of Washington's "attempts to stigmatize Castro as an outlaw and to expel him from the inter-American system." Hijacking thus reflected as much the consequences of the United States' own hostile diplomacy as it did Cuba's decision to grant political asylum to foreign dissents:

> There can be no serious argument that it was the American policy of "isolating" Cuba which forced the Cubans into the unwanted role of being viewed by American criminals and psychopaths as a good place, the only convenient place, to hijack a plane. Such people, Havana has correctly observed, "saw our country as a site where the U.S. itself had destroyed all legal international instruments to act against them." Through 85 "successful" hijackings the United States tolerated these consequences of its isolation policy, without, of course, conceding that they were the consequences.[102]

The mutual discomfort of the U.S. and Cuban governments led to bilateral talks, brokered by the Swiss Embassy in Havana — the two nations maintained no embassies — of uncommon civility to reach a mutually beneficial pact to curb airline hijacking. Citing a general "climate of insecurity ... in air and ocean navigation" caused by rampant hijackings, the Cuban government had issued Law No. 1226 on September 16, 1969, which stipulated that hijackers would be held "criminally liable under Cuban criminal laws."[103] Hijackers would now be prosecuted in Cuba, or returned to the United States to face the legal system, and U.S. officials hoped that such a threat, if well publicized, would act as a deterrent against future hijackings.[104]

It was, however, not the first time that one of the nations had attempted to reach a mutual understanding regarding hijacking. Writing to newly inaugurated President Nixon on February 7, 1969, Henry Kissinger cautioned that:

> I think you should be aware of one historical aspect of this problem which may prove embarrassing to us. In 1961, when there were several cases of

ships and planes seized by Cubans escaping to the United States, we did not respond to a Cuban note proposing a mutual agreement to return the persons responsible for those actions to the country of registry of the ship or plane. In effect, we refused to consider essentially the same proposal we have now made to the Cubans.[105]

Indeed, Cuba had weathered a long history of air and sea hijackings, beginning shortly after the revolution's victory in 1959, to which the United States had not responded. Accusing Washington's antihijacking proposal of being over a decade late, Cuba reminded U.S. officials of over two hundred instances in which Cubans had hijacked aircrafts and boats to the United States, sometimes killing passengers or crew, before being welcomed as heroes by the Cuban exile community of South Florida and treated by the U.S. government as political refugees. A paper presented by the Cuban delegation at the 1970 meeting of the Assembly of the International Civil Aviation Organization in Montreal, Canada, charged that "the Government of the United States . . . [has] encouraged the illegal exit from our country by every possible means, with utter disregard for the life and security of persons, and especially, through the illegally occupied territory of the U.S. Naval Base in Guantánamo, which has also contributed to the aforementioned climate of insecurity."[106]

Since 1966, the Cuban Refugee Adjustment Act had stipulated that all Cubans reaching U.S. soil, including through the hijacking of boats and airplanes, would be accorded amnesty and a direct path to U.S. citizenship. The paper presented by the Cuban delegation paraphrased sections of the text of Cuba's antihijacking Law No. 1226 of 1969, which accused the United States of using hijacking as one more political weapon in the arsenal that it had deployed against Havana:

> The Government of the United States and lackey Latin American governments, as a part of the policy of blockade and aggression against Cuba, have fostered and encouraged the hijacking and sequestration of Cuban ships and planes, receiving common murderers as heroes, and, on occasion, taking possession of the ships and planes. . . . This activity in connection with Cuban planes and ships and other acts and violations of international law and principles, provoked by imperialism in its policy against the Cuban Revolution, have created a climate of illegality conducive to the proliferation of these new phenomena of violence. . . . The Government of the United States and lackey governments of Latin America have maliciously attempted through their press organs and international news agencies to

evade their responsibility for the origin and execution of these acts, now that the consequences of such acts are affecting the countries whose governments have irresponsibly encouraged them to be carried out against Cuba.... The Cuban Revolutionary Government is unwilling to respect multilateral agreements adopted by international organizations, such as the OAS, an organization stripped of its prestige and with no moral authority, which has been an accomplice in the policy of economic blockade and imperialist aggression against our country and is responsible, along with the Government of the United States, for the fact that Cuba has often been the victim of pirate hijackings of its planes and ships; nor will it respect agreements on this matter adopted by the UN, which did nothing in the face of such acts against Cuba.[107]

Cuba had, in 1961, managed to negotiate the return of twenty-four hijacked ships and planes that the United States had initially refused to return.[108] Yet in the overwhelming majority of cases, Cuba paid the highest price for hijackings as a result of hostile noncooperation from Washington. According to Jorge Domínguez, Cuba "lost 264 planes and boats, which had not been returned, through hijacking to the United States between 1960 and 1970."[109] By the late 1960s, Cuba's record of returning hijacked planes and ships was so much better than that of the United States that Henry Kissinger, contrasting Cuba's response to hijacking with Syria, Lebanon, and Jordan, conceded that "Cuba has now become one the best-behaved of the hijacking states, since it immediately allows the planes and passengers to return and often jails the hijackers."[110]

Kissinger's inadvertant admission that America's response to hijacking was less "behaved" than Cuba's, since the United States had generally *not* returned planes and hijacking perpetrators to Cuba in cases of hijackings originating in that country, revealed another facet of Washington's insistence on diplomatic exceptionalism. The choice of the word "behaved" invoked the structure of feeling of a century of U.S. policy toward Cuba, in which the resolve of Cuba's bigger and stronger northern neighbor to dictate its will in the Caribbean found expression in a range of racial and gendered metaphors, visible in both official rhetoric and popular culture, that depicted Cuba as infantile and rebellious — misbehaved — in need of paternalistic guidance and benevolent control. As scholars such as Louis A. Pérez and Lars Schoultz have demonstrated, these expressions of dominance rooted in symbolism have displayed remarkable continuities over time.[111] The Cuban government's insistence on demanding "strict reciprocity" from the United States with regard to hijacking was thus situated self-consciously within a long history of unequal diplomatic power and imperial arrogance, a history that Havana had no intention of repeating.

Similarly, Washington's double standards with regard to hijacking mirrored aspects of U.S.-Cuba immigration policy, in which official U.S. policy classified U.S. citizens commandeering airplanes to Cuba as criminals, and Cuban citizens commandeering airplanes and water craft to South Florida, under almost identical circumstances, as political refugees. Indeed, as Kissinger's memo acknowledged, in addition to jailing hijackers and allowing hijacked planes and their passengers to return to the United States, Cuba had also "offered to return all hijackers provided we would do the same (a commitment we cannot make because of the political asylum aspect)."[112] In spite of its poor record of reciprocity with regard to Cuban hijackers, the U.S. delegation at the Montreal meeting of aviators proposed, without apparent irony, that nations taking no action against hijackers should be subject to an international air boycott.[113]

In October 1972, the "Tuller gang" murder-hijacking, together with a successful $2-million ransom-motivated hijacking of a Southern Airways flight to Cuba the next month — the 100th and 101st hijacking attempts to Cuba, respectively — switched negotiations between the two countries into high gear. However, Cuba continued to press for diplomatic reciprocity, insisting that the United States agree to crack down on violent paramilitary anti-Castro groups, composed of Cuban exiles, operating with relative impunity in South Florida. The evolving diplomatic language of mutuality — nothing had yet been agreed — was tested on December 6, 1972, when three armed Cubans forced a Cuban fishing vessel to take them to Key West in a bid to reach the political sanctuary that U.S. law extended to Cubans under the 1966 Cuban Adjustment Act.

Reciprocity prevailed, the Cubans were arrested, and for the first time since 1959, Cubans who had reached the United States seeking sanctuary were ordered to return to Cuba. To some, however, the breaching of the long-standing U.S. policy was unacceptable. "If the price of a skyjacking accord with Castro is the deportation of three trusting men," said one State Department official, "then the price is too great." The three Cubans appealed the deportation order and were eventually released in Florida on bond.[114]

Cuba and the United States signed the Cuba–United States Memorandum of Understanding on Hijacking of Aircraft and Vessels and Other Offenses on February 15, 1973. It was the first accord of any kind between the two nations since Castro took power in 1959. As a five-year agreement, both parties agreed

"OUR MAN IN HAVANA?"
—Shanks in "Buffalo Evening News"

A December 1972 cartoon in the *Buffalo Evening News* suggests that the skyjacking epidemic had been a boon for Fidel Castro. Airline hijackings by Americans seeking to reach Cuba forced Washington to abandon its diplomatic intransigence and accede to negotiations with Havana, talks in which the Cuban government successfully leveraged the crisis to demand diplomatic reciprocity. Courtesy of the *Buffalo News*.

to prosecute hijackers to the fullest extent, ensure the protection of passengers and planes, and give serious consideration to the extradition of hijackers to their country of origin.[115] As a "memorandum of agreement," however, the accord was distinct from a treaty, as the U.S. government did not formally recognize the government of Cuba. As such, the agreement was not legally binding. Rather, it would be adhered to in good faith. It was also not retroactive, did not apply to previous hijackings, nor, at least in theory, did it affect the status of those Americans who were already in Cuba, whether in prison or free. Significantly, the accord also provided both nations with a loophole for persons seeking political asylum:

> The party in whose territory the perpetrators of the acts described in Article First arrive may take into consideration any extenuating or mitigating circumstances in those cases in which the persons responsible for the acts were being sought for strictly political reasons and were in real and imminent danger of death without a viable alternative for leaving the

country, provided there was no financial extortion or physical injury to the members of the crew, passengers, or other persons in connection with the hijacking.[116]

This was an exceedingly narrow set of criteria. Speaking to the U.S. House of Representatives Subcommittee on Inter-American Affairs during a special session devoted to the hijacking agreement, Robert A. Hurwitch voiced his confidence that the terminology would not be applicable to future U.S. hijackers: "We cannot visualize any such instance happening in our country, where a person is imminently in danger of death and is forced to hijack to escape."[117] Some American radicals who had sought asylum in Cuba — or would seek it in the future — would likely have disagreed. Nonetheless, air hijackings from the United States to Cuba declined dramatically after the Memorandum of Understanding in February 1973.

Only two successful hijackings of aircraft from the United States to Cuba occurred during the remainder of the decade. The 1968–1973 hijacking epidemic provoked a shallow crack in the diplomatic stalemate between the United States and Cuba, and the 1973 agreement is often regarded as one of the early signs of the modest improvement in relations between the two nations that occurred under the Nixon and Ford administrations.[118] But while mutual cooperation to respond to hijacking preceded the more significant Carter-era thaw in U.S.-Cuba relations, hijacking did not itself cause the thaw, nor did the episode ultimately represent a watershed in foreign relations between the two nations.[119] Indeed, even as it announced the accord, the Nixon administration took pains to dispel any suggestion that the agreement signaled "a change of policies" or the beginning of a diplomatic rapprochement.[120] Further, Cuba nullified the antihijacking agreement in 1976, after the bombing of Cubana de Aviación flight 455 over Barbados by CIA-linked operatives, an act of terrorism that killed all 73 people aboard, although Cuba continued to honor the agreement in practice.[121]

Rather, the historical significance of the hijacking phenomenon lies in the way in which it marked the unlikely meeting point where the era's radical political protest movements, the Cuban Revolution, and U.S.-Cuba foreign relations collided in the late 1960s. Although the U.S. government had, since the early 1960s, recognized Cubans who hijacked sea and air vessels to the United States as Cold War refugees from communism, its unwillingness to regard American hijackers to Cuba as anything other than common criminals revealed the paternalistic contradictions of America's Cold War policies toward Cuba. This contradiction, one rooted in a history of uneven diplomatic relations between the two nations long preceding Cuba's 1959 revolution and the nation's entry onto the fraught terrain of the global Cold War, shows the continuities between Cuba's past and present relations with its larger northern neighbor. The durability of these dynamics of unequal power, relations that ultimately find their origins in the island's history of colonization and foreign possession, reveal the limits as well as the continuities of the Cold War as a frame to examine U.S.-Cuba relations during the post-1959 revolutionary era.

America's air pirates of the Caribbean also illustrate some of the limitations of viewing history's "outlaws" within the narrow frameworks of criminality or terrorism. As historian Marcus Rediker has argued with regard to eighteenth-century sea piracy, a phenomenon that is not dissimilar from its later airborne counterpart in the Caribbean, the "villains" of any era occupy a moral and legal status that is highly relative, shifting in relation to the parameters of nation states and political discourses.[122] Whether their bids for political asylum in Cuba were successful or resulted in lengthy stays in Cuban prisons, U.S. skyjackers seeking political asylum attempted to formulate themselves as independent agents within the transnational spaces afforded by international air travel, negotiating the legalities of multiple nation-states as sovereign agents. Some hijackers, who leveraged political demands or imagined themselves as outlaws with ideals, may fall within historian Eric Hobsbawm's framework of "social banditry."[123] Other hijackers might more meaningfully be regarded as a kind of transnational lumpenproletariat, especially in the way that Frantz Fanon rehabilitated Marx's concept to uncover the latent revolutionary potential of a society's "hooligans," "petty criminals," and "hopeless dregs," a reading of Fanon's influential work *The Wretched of the Earth* that found special resonance among former members or self-styled affiliates of the Black Panther Party, several of whom hijacked planes to Cuba.[124]

Whatever they may be, hijackers as a group must be understood as historical actors who played an audacious role in U.S.-Cuba relations. Americans who hijacked planes to Cuba in the late 1960s overwhelmingly articulated their actions within prevailing tropes of social protest and left-wing political activism of the era, a politics that they imagined, sometimes accurately and sometimes wishfully, was congruent with the Cuban Revolution and the policy aims of Havana. Whether they imagined Cuba as an "outlaw nation" beyond the reach of the U.S. imperial apparatus, a sanctuary from criminal charges, a haven from American racism and political repression, or a portal to revolutionary movements abroad, American hijackers constructed Cuba in ways that paralleled long-standing American imaginings of the island.

4

Joven Cuba inside the Colossus
The Antonio Maceo Brigade and the
Making of a Cuban American Left

Viví en el monstruo, y le conozco las entrañas; —y mi honda es la de David
(I have lived inside the monster, and I know its entrails; —my sling is David's).
—José Martí

ANY EXAMINATION OF Cuba's influence on U.S. radicalism, and the ties that North Americans forged with the post-1959 revolutionary nation, must contend with the buried history of Cuban American leftism.[1] In the mid-1970s, a loose movement of young Cuban émigrés in the United States and Puerto Rico, many of them exiled from the island as children, began seeking renewed ties to the land of their birth. Politicized by their involvement in the protest movements of the late 1960s, particularly the black civil rights movement, opposition to the Vietnam War, and participation in the movement for the independence of Puerto Rico, these émigré youth began openly defying the anti-Castro leadership of exilic Cuban communities to seek reconciliation with the Cuban government and the normalization of U.S.-Cuba diplomatic relations.

Among the most radical formations of this changing face of Cuban America was the Brigada Antonio Maceo — the Antonio Maceo Brigade. Formed in 1977 by exilic Cuban students, young professionals, and activists, many of them associated with the literary and political magazine *Areíto*,[2] the Antonio Maceo Brigade organized delegations to travel to Cuba to reunite with family, tour the island, and evaluate the Cuban Revolution for themselves, free from the filter of the anti-Castro media in Miami. Modeled loosely upon the Venceremos Brigades, Maceo Brigade delegations also participated in construction projects and visited factories, schools, and hospitals to witness the impact of the revolution's social programs.

Welcomed in Cuba as the returned children of the diaspora and covered heavily in the Cuban media, the arrival of the first group of fifty-five young

Cuban émigrés in Havana in December 1977 challenged Cuban popular perceptions — shaped by both the recent history of right-wing Cuban exile terrorism against the island, and by the Cuban government's universal labeling of all émigrés as traitors to the nation — of Cubans abroad as counterrevolutionaries bent on destroying the gains of the revolution.

The Maceo Brigade's encounters with Cuba in 1977 helped lay the foundation for a series of meetings between progressive Cuban exile leaders and members of the Cuban government, principally Fidel Castro, in Havana in November and December of 1978. No U.S. officials participated. Known as "the dialogue," the meetings contributed to a historically significant shift in the Cuban government's strained relationship with the island's diaspora. Castro agreed to open legal routes of travel to the island for émigrés, which had been closed by both the U.S. and Cuban governments, and to allow families torn apart by migration to reunite on the island. Aided by the brief warming of U.S.-Cuba relations under the administration of President Jimmy Carter, visits to Cuba by progressive Cuban Americans resulted in a significant shift in the Cuban government's relations with its diaspora, initiating an early precursor to the growing contemporary openness among Cuban Americans toward reconciliation with the Cuban government and the full normalization of U.S.-Cuba relations.

The Maceo Brigade's activism generated a firestorm of opposition from exile hardliners, who denounced its members as traitors, communist sympathizers, and "agents of Castro." Like the Venceremos Brigade, with which it often collaborated, the Maceo Brigade also became the target of an investigation by the FBI, whose reports claimed that the group was "organized and is controlled by the Cuban government for propaganda/intelligence."[3] But while the Venceremos Brigade endured defamation and charges of collusion with a foreign power, its Cuban émigré counterpart additionally experienced ostracism within their communities and palpable physical danger from Cuban émigrés who opposed dialogue with Castro.

These domestic Cold War politics reached a boiling point in Miami, Union City, New Jersey, and New York in the mid-1970s, amidst a wave of bombings and political violence as right-wing Cuban exile groups sought to intimidate anyone who supported reconciliation with the communist government in Havana. Violence also occurred in Puerto Rico, and in April 1978, Maceo Brigade cofounder Carlos Muñiz Varela was assassinated in Guaynabo as the Brigade's second contingent was preparing to visit Cuba. A year later, the paramilitary group Omega 7 claimed responsibility for the murder of Eulalio José Negrín, a prodialogue community leader and Cuban immigrant, in Union City.[4]

Despite the intimidation campaign, the Maceo Brigade soon established itself in half a dozen U.S. cities, with a significant presence also in Puerto Rico. Satellite chapters operated in Spain and Venezuela. As a political formation growing out of the nexus between the Cuban exile experience in the United States and the multifaceted political protest movements of the 1960s era, the Maceo Brigade succeeded in creating an unprecedented political space for Cuban American leftism. Shattering public perceptions, in both Cuba and the United States, of right-leaning political homogeneity in the émigré community while also challenging the attitudes of some among the non-Cuban U.S. Left who assumed that none of the island's émigrés were among those who defended the revolution's right to exist, the Maceo Brigade challenged and redefined the parameters of Cuban American politics.

The Maceo Brigade's trajectory complicates persistent scholarly and popular narratives that continue, despite much evidence to the contrary, to emphasize Cuban American right-wing political homogeneity and anti-Castro intransigence. These Miami-centric narratives, informed by the pronounced rightward tilt of the city's Cuban community after 1959, nevertheless obscure the political diversity that has always characterized the island's wider postrevolutionary diaspora, including within some anticommunist but otherwise heterodox constituencies.[5] The exile media, which in Miami has historically been controlled by anti-Castro hardliners, has proven especially invested in amplifying the mythology of right-wing and anticommunist uniformity. Nonetheless, this façade began to crack in the mid-1970s as political differences within Cuban communities in the United States and Puerto Rico emerged along clearly demarcated and intensely polarized lines. As a growing segment of the community grew to favor dialogue with the Cuban government and reconnection with the island's people, the Maceo Brigade emerged as its most radical expression, one that not only advocated for the normalization of U.S.-Cuba relations, but supported the social gains of the Cuban Revolution outright. The Maceo Brigade was an early pioneer in the *exilio* community's continuing shift toward favoring normalized relations with Cuba in the contemporary period.

Despite its importance, the Maceo Brigade has been condemned to relative obscurity. Summaries of the group exist in a number of essays and books on Cuban American politics, and brief reflections on the Brigade are included in several memoirs written by former participants. Yet the group has seldom received the sustained treatment that it deserves.[6] Scholars generally agree that the Brigade's activism marked a turning point in the history of Cuban exile politics in the United States. According to María de los Ángeles Torres, the group's trips to Cuba in the late 1970s "paved the way for future relations between the Cuban government and Cuban communities abroad. Both in Cuba and in the United States the myth of a monolithic Cuban community had been shattered."[7] The Maceo Brigade also receives scant mention in examinations of the U.S.-Cuba diplomatic rapprochement of the late 1970s and plays only a minor role in treatments of the high-profile "dialogue" that occurred in the fall of 1978 in Havana between Fidel Castro and members of the Cuban diaspora.[8]

This chapter examines how the Brigade's activism both influenced and responded to the larger context of U.S.-Cuba diplomatic relations. The history of the Maceo Brigade provides new insights into the relationship between Cuba and its post-1959 diaspora, the immigration and ethnic history of Cuban Americans in relation to the Cold War, and the ways in which Cuban émigré politics shaped U.S.-Cuba diplomatic relations, from the modest Cold War détente of the Carter years through the hardening of anticommunist doctrine during the Reagan Revolution of the 1980s.

The Maceo Brigade has also remained marginal to studies of the U.S. Left. This chapter reframes of the Maceo Brigade's history and significance, locating its complex relationship with the Cuban Revolution within the broader context of the era's political protest. I contend that the story of the Maceo Brigade, and the concurrent rise of progressive exilic Cuban politics which it helped shape in the United States and Puerto Rico, is as much a part of the history of social upheaval and political protest during the "long" 1960s and 1970s as it is a part of the singular history of the Cuban diaspora. As immigrants whose radicalization was shaped in pivotal ways by the domestic forces of the black civil rights and the anti–Vietnam War movements, as well as the global impact of the Cuban Revolution and the transnational struggle for an independent Puerto Rico, the Maceo Brigade exists within the constellation of activist currents within U.S. communities of color that scholar Cynthia A. Young has termed a "U.S. Third World Left."[9] Looking abroad to the decolonizing world and to Third World revolutionary movements for inspiration and ideology, many activists within these movements came to see their global political position not as marginalized "minorities" within North America, but as members of a global majority of Third World people resisting oppression and envisioning, as scholar Sohail Daulatzai has put it, "freedom beyond America."[10]

These global political imaginaries also provided an important means of legibility between U.S.-based political movements and the Cuban revolutionaries that they engaged with on the island and off. As the editors of the Cuban periodical *Tricontinental* wrote in an introduction to a 1970 interview with

Chicano activist Corky González, a member of the organization Crusade for Justice, and Puerto Rican activist Cha Cha Jiménez of the Young Lords Party, these communities of color in the United States, including African Americans, Puerto Ricans, and "Mexican–North Americans" constituted a "segment of the Third World imbedded in the United States."[11] The Maceo Brigade, and the multifaceted Cuban diasporic left that it grew out of, is both part of this history of U.S. movements who sought to understand their domestic subject position by framing it in relation to the Third World, yet also unique unto itself. As the other chapters of this book argue, the Cuban Revolution has been a more persistent presence within the multifaceted U.S. Left than any other foreign revolutionary nation-building project of the twentieth century. Illuminating the role of the diasporic Cuban left provides a critical bridge between these two political projects.

RENDERING A RIGOROUS PORTRAIT of the Maceo Brigade is a uniquely daunting task. The field of Cuban Studies continues to be characterized by political and personal minefields borne of the trauma of separation from the island and the protracted political battles that continue to be waged over the future of the nation and the historical memory of the 1959 revolution. Scholar Marifeli Pérez-Stable, who was active in the Maceo Brigade during its early years, has observed that discussions of the Cuban Revolution and its aftermath have frequently reduced it to a series of binaries—"paradise or hell, progress or ruin, democracy or tyranny"—that foreclose more nuanced understandings. "Intellectual discourse on Cuba," Pérez-Stable writes, "is rarely just about scholarship. Instead, its analysis is colored by notions of the good society, human rights, and individual ethics. Choices are clear, indictments scathing, praises unbounded—prime examples of all-or-nothing thinking."[12] More than two decades later, the field of Cuban Studies continues to reflect the tensions embedded within it.

Outside of academe, similar tensions prevail. One Cuban American scholar and activist describes his involvement in "progressive solidarity work with Cuba" as akin to negotiating a "political minefield" in which the subject is caught between "the fervent anti-communist cant of my Cuban relatives and neighbors, the U.S. pro-Cuba left's sometimes insufficiently critical, single-minded defense of the revolution, and the frequently impenetrable 'party line' positions of many revolutionaries."[13] The historical importance of the Maceo Brigade lies, therefore, in the group's challenge to these binaries, particularly within the fraught context of 1970s Miami, an environment that tolerated little interpretive nuance on the question of Cuba. Given the prominence of a number of the Maceo Brigade's past members within scholarship on the Cuban diaspora and within the Cuban American Left itself, the portrait of the group contained within this chapter incorporates their perspectives as both agents and interpreters of the history that they helped shape.

Young Cuban America Turns Left

Exilic Cuban leftism is not as anomalous as has often been supposed. The diaspora of Cubans residing in the United States, from Little Havana in Miami to "Havana on the Hudson" in Union City, New Jersey, was never a political monolith. This pluralization became accentuated in the 1970s, when the exile community began to reflect two often diametric political camps: those who remained preoccupied with fomenting the overthrow of socialism on the island and the return to Cuba of those exiled by the revolution, and those who became focused on the well-being of the Cuban immigrant community in the United States.[14] Emphasizing social service provision, education, and anti-Latino/a discrimination, the latter camp created space for a new Cuban political agenda by refocusing attention away from the external goal of overthrowing Castro, an arena dominated by right-wing hardliners.

Within this shifting reality, a number of Cuban émigré formations emerged that undermined the hegemony of the community's self-appointed hardline stewards. One of the first organized challenges to the hardline agenda came from within academic circles, which created pluralistic intellectual forums for the study of the Cuban nation and its diaspora from a range of perspectives. According to scholar María de los Ángeles Torres, the Miami-based Instituto de Estudios Cubanos, which first met in 1969, "encouraged a less antagonistic approach to the Cuban government."[15] The journal *Cuban Studies/Estudios Cubanos*, sponsored by the University of Pittsburgh, published a wide range of scholarship on Cuba.[16] Although contact between Cuban and U.S. academics remained limited for much of the era, collaboration across the Florida Straits continued through what Cuban scholar Milagros Martínez calls "irregular means," and exchanges between scholars from the two countries increased during the mid-1970s.[17]

By mid-decade, a range of Cuban American community and civic groups had emerged representing a broader range of viewpoints than had ever been in evidence before. While not universally supporting outright normalization of U.S.-Cuba diplomatic relations, many nevertheless sought to forge closer ties between exiles and the homeland. Religious organizations, such as Christians for Justice and Freedom, also played a significant role. The largest, the

Hialeah-based Christian Evangelical Reformed Church headed by Reverend Manuel Espinosa, maintained branches in Los Angeles, Miami, and Key West.[18] Known collectively as "*dialogueros*," a term that was often used pejoratively by critics to their right, these moderate activists, public figures, and newspaper editors favored communication with the Cuban government on a limited range of issues ranging from political prisoners to the right of exiles to travel to Cuba. By creating alternative political currents within the Cuban community in the mid-1970s, *dialogueros* challenged the hegemony of the right-wing leadership and helped set the stage for the emergence of a Cuban American Left at the end of the decade.

One of the most potent forces contributing to the emergence of leftism among U.S. Cubans in the 1970s was driven by demographics. Young émigrés, particularly those who had departed from the island as children, were far more likely than members of their parents' generation to favor the normalization of U.S. diplomatic ties with the island.[19] Exilic Cubans active in efforts to forge ties between the island and its diaspora frequently wrote of the pain of being torn from the geography of their birth. Rootlessness and the anguish of lost heritage constituted recurrent themes in the reflections of young exiles. Sociologist and poet Lourdes Casal, a key figure in early efforts to build bridges between the diaspora and the nation and a cofounder of the Maceo Brigade, captured these feelings poignantly in verse:

> Exile
> is living where no house
> holds the memories
> of our childhood
> and where we cannot visit
> our grandmother's grave[20]

Some young émigrés poured their energy into literary endeavors. In 1974, a collective of young Cubans founded the magazine *Joven Cuba*—Young Cuba—in New York. The publication created a textual space for the search for a new Cuban identity in the United States. Emerging at the juncture between their experiences as Cuban émigrés, on the one hand, and as youth coming of age during the tumult of the social and political upheaval of the 1960s in the other, the *Joven Cuba* collective emphasized the racial minority status of Cubans in the United States and encouraged politicized émigré youth to seek ties with other U.S. Latinos/as, including Chicanos/as, Puerto Ricans, and Dominicans. "Young Cuba," as the magazine's first editorial explained in a reflection on their experiences as a racialized immigrant group in a foreign nation, "is the disappointment that we suffer when we believe we are Americans, and they remind us that, in fact, we are not... And so our own consciences ask us: what are we?"[21]

For these Cuban youth of the early 1970s, the evolution of their subjectivity as Latinos/as in America was inseparable from their experiences within the social justice movements of the sixties era. Writing in the first issue of *Joven Cuba*, the collective explained their search for political identity: "*Joven Cuba* is the generation of the '70s. We were born in the midst of a changing society, and we grew up in a society in crisis. Our childhood memories of Cuba have been influenced by the 1960s, in the midst of the assassination of [Martin Luther] King, the protest of Black America, the war in Vietnam, and the demonstrations in the universities. Are we part of a historical continuity, or do we live in the past?"[22]

Like the members of *Joven Cuba* collective, a significant number of young Cubans who returned to the island in the late 1970s with the Maceo Brigade had been radicalized by the rising tide of social upheaval and political protest of the previous decade. An article in *The Guardian* concerning three Cuban Americans visiting Havana as tourists in 1979 reported that the visitors, who identified as politically left-leaning, shared "a common heritage" of formative experiences, including "discrimination against Spanish speakers and blacks, the turbulence of the 'sixties, and American policy in Vietnam [that] made them examine the conventional wisdom they were taught at home." One of the travelers, Rafael Betancourt, who had previously traveled to Cuba as a member of the Maceo Brigade, told the reporter that although his family had emigrated from Cuba to the United States after the revolution because of their "sense of justice and decency," upon moving to New Orleans he was "hit in the face by the realities of racism."[23]

In 1973, Lourdes Casal became one of the first young Cubans in the United States to return to the island. A black-identified mix-raced Cuban who had arrived in the United States at a time when most Cuban émigrés were light-skinned or white, Casal was compelled to reevaluate her ideological position toward the Cuban Revolution in part due to her experiences as a black woman within the alien social terrain of the United States. Of African, Chinese, and Spanish descent and the daughter of a school teacher and a doctor, Casal had attended private schools in a prerevolutionary Havana where, she later wrote, "the children of the bourgeoisie (and the middle sectors which could afford them) were educated with little contact with the black masses and other oppressed sectors of the population."[24] As she was growing up, the island's racial legacy haunted her:

I still remember how I listened, wide-eyed and nauseated, to the stories — always whispered, always told as when one is revealing unspeakable secrets — about the horrors committed against my family and other blacks during the racial war of 1912.... The stories terrified me, not only because of their violence, but because my history books said nothing about these incidents. The racial war of 1912, in which thousands of blacks lost their lives was, at best, a line or a footnote in the books.... I could not understand. It seemed aberrant to me, that memories which were still alive in participants and witnesses, even in victims and relatives of victims, could have been so completely obliterated from the collective consciousness, so completely erased from everyday discourse and from history books. This puzzlement led to an early obsession with the issue of race relations in Cuba; an obsession which was not then academic or scholarly, but a burning set of questions deeply related to my own identity.[25]

After the victory against the Batista dictatorship in 1959, Casal soon became disillusioned with the direction of the rapidly radicalizing revolution. Emigrating from the island three years later at the age of twenty-three, she became active in the resurrected Directorio Revolucionario Estudiantil (DRE) — the Student Revolutionary Directorate — which had played an important role in the clandestine struggle against the Batista government in Cuba but had now become an anti-Castro movement based in the United States and financed by the CIA. Although DRE executed several successful attacks on post-revolutionary Cuba, including the August 1962 shelling of the Sierra Maestra Hotel and nearby Blanquita Theater in Miramar from a speedboat, an action that garnered the group significant publicity, the group devoted most of its resources to the soft power of public relations.[26] In this capacity, Casal traveled around the United States and globally as a DRE representative on the CIA's payroll, speaking to college students and foreign representatives about the struggle against the Castro government.

Living in New York in the mid-1960s, however, Casal was soon forced to confront America's own racial legacy. Her political leanings shifted while living in Harlem, and she became active in the African American civil rights movement and then in campaigns against U.S. involvement in Vietnam. Viewed at a distance through the twin prisms of antiracism and anti-imperialism, Cuba's revolution now assumed a different appearance. Thus, paradoxically, it was Casal's experience of exile that would compel her to reevaluate, and ultimately come to support, the revolution from which she had earlier fled — a personal transformation that paralleled that of several other members of the

Maceo Brigade.[27] Returning to Cuba in 1973 in a trip arranged by the Instituto Cubano de Amistad con los Pueblos (ICAP), Casal soon became committed to effecting reconciliation between the island and its diaspora of exiles, ultimately becoming one of Cuba's staunchest supporters within the U.S. émigré community. She earned her doctorate in social psychology at the New School for Social Research in 1976, with a dissertation titled "Images of Cuban Society among Pre- and Post-Revolutionary Novelists," and took a teaching post at Rutgers University.

Marifeli Pérez-Stable, whose family was upper-middle class and of principally European heritage, later came to reevaluate the racial dynamics of her Cuban childhood through her immersion within civil rights and antiwar protest during the late 1960s:

> Well before I understood the full gamut of its ignominy, segregation had shocked me. True, my shock stemmed from the realization that Tata — the Jamaican woman who had cared for me in Cuba — couldn't have sat next to me on a bus in many parts of the United States. Thus, the Civil Rights Movement and, later, the Vietnam War defined my political coming of age. While in college, I wrote my first paper critical of the U.S. embargo on Cuba. The Sixties had awakened in me a commitment to social justice that led me to see Cuba in a different light. Like Vietnam's, the revolution's defiance of the United States won me over. I came to see the victory at Playa Girón — as the failure of Bay of Pigs is known in Cuba — as a long-postponed affirmation of national sovereignty.[28]

Out of this range of experiences emerged a number of progressive Cuban American organizations and collectives in the mid-1970s, many with their own literary endeavors. A group of young Cubans associated with the left-leaning magazine collective *Areíto*, whose contributors composed many of the Maceo Brigade's founders, linked their "political radicalization" to a set of shared experiences emerging out of their participation in the social protest movements and cultural experimentation of the sixties. In a collection of personal reflections that was published by a Mexican press as *Contra Viento y Marea* — Against Wind and Tide — the activists echoed the routes to personal politicization of other North American youth of the era, particularly youth of color, whose radicalization was often linked to their experiences in racially marginalized communities, their contact with social protest movements, and the influence of historical events.

According to the members of *Areíto*, their radicalization was born of their "direct involvement in struggles for civil rights and justice for minority groups in the United States," their "identification with the struggle of the Puerto Rican community" in the United States and, like so many other youth during the era, to the "war in Vietnam and activism against the U.S. intervention" in Indochina, and the U.S. "invasion of Cambodia and the shootings at Kent State, the death of Che in Bolivia, the 1968 Democratic Convention, and the assassinations of Robert Kennedy and Martin Luther King."[29] These experiences, the activists wrote, encouraged their politicization as "new men and women,"[30] a phraseology that the activists borrowed directly from Cuban revolutionary ideology, popularized be Che Guevara, of the "New Man." The *Areíto* collective members thus located themselves within the era's context of social ferment and political protest, linking their political evolution to that of the larger multiethnic U.S. Left even as they drew parallels between their new political selves and the Cuban revolutionary project.

Scholars of the "long" 1960s era have argued that the multifaceted struggle for African American rights, citizenship, and freedom, which became known as the civil rights movement and its later incarnation, the Black Power movement, functioned as one of the era's primary "engines" of social change. The social forces released by black liberation struggle helped set in motion a constellation of other latent tensions in American society that became expressed in a range of other social-justice movements that sought, in different ways, to challenge the established political order of racial, sexual, gender, class, and cultural relations. Some of these diverse forces coalesced in the late 1960s around the anti–Vietnam War movement, which concentrated a broad array of often disparate movements in opposition to the war.[31] Left-wing Americans during the "long" 1960s era, including Cuban émigrés, often traced their personal process of radicalization to their involvement in these two movements.

Yet the radicalization of Cubans associated with *Areíto*, influenced so strongly by their immersion within the protest currents of the era, was also specific to their experiences as racialized immigrants. The turn toward leftism among young Cubans in the United States, and in particular their reevaluation of the larger exile community's hostility toward the Cuban Revolution, was also shaped by the context of the social protest and rebellion. One young exile who protested the Vietnam War as a teenager — who would later travel back to Cuba in 1982 — traced his political break with his family to May 1970, after the shooting of Kent State students by the Ohio National Guard. His family's response to the tragedy — "four less communists"— compelled him to "question all of their political positions, including those on Cuba."[32] Writing in *Contra Viento y Marea*, the *Areíto* activists identified domestic political upheavals as key forces that influenced their adoption of a more sympathetic

The cover of the spring 1978 issue of *Areíto*, which was dedicated to coverage of the AMB, features a rendering of legendary Afro-Cuban Cuban revolutionary leader and military strategist Antonio Maceo on the centennial anniversary of the Protest of Baraguá. Author's collection.

view of the Cuban Revolution and a more critical perspective of U.S. policy toward the island:

> In general, the revaluation process usually commenced far from Cuba. Through the struggle for civil rights or against the U.S. intervention in Vietnam, we discovered that we could not identify with a conservative vision of the world. Our "progressive" principles excluded Cuba. It was a very painful area that we dared not face. But the inconsistencies between adopting progressive positions and practices, and to be, at the same time, Cuban exiles, were too flagrant. Little by little, we began reconsidering our position with respect to Cuba. It was a process of years.[33]

The leftward radicalization of Cuban youth, however, was sometimes at odds with that of other American supporters of Cuba, who did not have personal and familial links to the island, did not have the same stake in its future, and had not run the same risks of community ostracism for advocating U.S.-Cuba reconciliation. Due to the political makeup of the Cuban émigré community in the 1960s, which was composed overwhelmingly of Cubans who fled the Cuban Revolution or had come to oppose it after its triumph, the great majority of the revolution's defenders in North America had initially been non-Cubans. Organizations such as the Fair Play for Cuba Committee in the early part of the decade and the Venceremos Brigade at the end of the 1960s and throughout the next decade had become the primary political voices of opposition to Washington's policy of diplomatic, economic, and military antagonism toward the revolution. Some young Cuban émigrés felt shut out of this process by non-Cuban U.S. leftists who assumed that all Cuban Americans were right-wing.[34]

Others, while supporting the normalization of U.S. relations with Cuba and approving of many of its social gains, remained troubled by Marxism and the revolution's turn toward communism. Marifeli Pérez-Stable noted that for émigré youth, the formation of the Antonio Maceo Brigade was "the end of a road that began in the sixties," in which Cuban youth had come into contact with the political protest of the era. "In those movements there were people who sympathized with Cuba, including the Venceremos Brigade. And they would say to us, 'And you?...What do you think of Cuba?' 'No. Not Cuba, because they are communists,' we would reply."[35]

Ambivalence dogged some Maceo Brigade participants even as they prepared to embark for the island. "While the leftists recited the wonders of Castro's Cuba," wrote María Nodarse-Pérez about her days as a student activist at Columbia University, "my Cuban friends and relatives dredged up tales of horror. Even at the airport I still felt divided: I was intellectually loyal to the left and emotionally loyal to the right."[36]

"Dialogueros" and U.S.-Cuba Relations

The increasing political pluralism of Cuban America in the late 1970s coincided with a broader climate of diplomatic rapprochement between the United States and Cuba. While state relations between Cuba and its diaspora had been a secondary concern to both Havana and Washington in the earlier part of the decade, the 1978 dialogue between members of the Cuban diaspora and representatives of the Cuban government occurred against a diplomatic backdrop that created a context in which the Cuban government was motivated to embrace exile leaders for reasons of both principle and pragmatism. As U.S.-Cuba relations cooled again in 1977 and 1978, the talks with exile leaders provided the Cuban government with a means to simultaneously improve relations with the island's diaspora, whose progressive currents Havana increasingly recognized, while also meeting one of Washington's demands for improved diplomatic relations: the release of political prisoners in Cuban jails. The Maceo Brigade's radical vision, which combined unequivocal support for Cuban national self-determination with calls for the greater recognition of the island's diaspora, therefore sought to capitalize on political changes in both the exile community and within U.S.-Cuba relations.

Although publicly the Nixon and Ford administrations adhered to a policy of unrelenting hostility toward the Cuban Revolution, communication between Washington and Havana, often conducted in secret, occurred on a wide range of issues.[37] Occasionally, high-level talks occurred through official channels. Negotiations in the early 1970s to curb air hijacking to Cuba from the United States, culminating in the 1973 antihijacking agreement, signaled that both governments were willing to engage in dialogue on concerns of mutual interest. Indeed, although the Nixon administration denied that the 1973 antihijacking agreement signaled a thaw in U.S.-Cuba relations, the event foreshadowed the rapprochement that would occur under the Carter administration a few years later.[38] Secret talks commenced in New York between envoys of both governments in 1975, and in March of that year, Henry Kissinger declared publicly that the U.S. government now saw "no virtue in perpetual antagonism" with its communist neighbor.[39]

However, the watershed in U.S.-Cuba relations — and with it, the opening of a political opportunity for Cuban Americans who had been working for reconciliation — came in 1976 with the election of Jimmy Carter, who initiated a significant thaw in Washington's position on reconciliation with Havana. The objective, Carter said, was to "set in motion a process which will lead to the reestablishment of diplomatic relations."[40] Of course, the United States had demands. Among other things, Cuba would have to end its support of left-wing movements in the Third World. During his confirmation hearings before the Senate, appointed Secretary of State Cyrus Vance told the Senate, "If Cuba is willing to live within the international system, then we ought to seek ways to find whether we can eliminate the impediments which exist between us and try to move toward normalization."[41] Here, "international system" implied a global system dominated by the United States. Nonetheless, it was a palpable shift in Washington's tone. In response, Fidel Castro cautiously characterized Carter as the "first president in more than 16 years who hasn't committed himself to a policy of hostility against Cuba."[42]

Sure enough, one of Carter's first acts was to lift the Kennedy-era ban on travel to Cuba for American citizens, allowing charter flights to commence directly from Miami to Havana. In April, liberal South Dakota Senator George McGovern, visiting Cuba with a college basketball team and carrying a personal message from Carter to Castro, called for the creation of athletic and cultural college-exchange programs between the two nations.[43] In August, U.S. Senator Frank Church, who had led the high-profile congressional investigation of secret CIA, FBI, and NSA spy campaigns on both U.S. dissidents and foreign nations such as Cuba, visited the island to discuss U.S. policy. The senator tried to convince a skeptical but polite Castro that the CIA would no longer try to overthrow the Cuban Revolution, and he pushed for the release of seven American citizens held in Cuban jails.[44] "Interest Sections," which assumed some of the functions of the embassies that had been shuttered in 1961, were established in each other's capitals in September 1977, and negotiations commenced over Cuba's fishing rights in the Florida Straits and for greater cooperation between the U.S. Coast Guard and the Cuban Border Guard.[45]

In November, for the first time since the severing of diplomatic relations, seven Cuban university professors traveled to the United States to join a group of American academics for an unpublicized conference in association with Yale University — the conference was kept secret as a precaution against violence from right-wing Cuban exile groups — before attending the National Latin American Studies Association meeting in Houston.[46] Tourist reports of Havana, written by American travelers eager to experience the "new Cuba," began to trickle in to U.S. newspapers in 1978, as the island hurriedly built tourist infrastructure to soak up the influx of foreign currency.[47] Cubans living in the United States and Puerto Rico also began visiting Cuba, and a plethora of travel agencies run by Cuban émigrés sprang up virtually overnight to arrange the trips. In July, Fidel Castro showed up to present a birthday cake to a U.S. man who was about to attempt a ninety-mile "swim for peace" from Cuba to Florida.[48]

As the end of the embargo appeared increasingly imminent, hundreds of U.S. companies sent representatives to Havana to explore the possibilities for trade. Fidel Castro personally led many of the tours, charming top American capitalists in rum-fueled social events and engaging in marathon conversations about the possibilities for trade in the event that the United States lifted the embargo.[49] Speaking at a ceremony marking the mutual opening of the Interest Sections, head of the Cuban mission Rámon Sánchez Parodi emphasized Cuba's willingness to treat U.S. concerns "with a constructive spirit," reminding the U.S. reporters in attendance that although the initiative to open the interest sections had come from the U.S. side, "on our side, Cuba has always been open to establishing normal relations between the two countries."[50]

But normalization was not to be. At issue was Washington's growing concern over Cuba's independent foreign policy. Although Havana had provided material support to anticolonial and left-wing political movements across the Third World since the early months of the 1959 revolution, Cuba's foreign policy had its most dramatic impact in the mid-1970s in Africa. "Cuba is a small country," scholar Jorge Domínguez wrote in *Foreign Affairs* in the fall of 1978 amid growing international attention to Cuba's military and humanitarian presence on the continent, "but it has a big country's foreign policy."[51] The United States had long voiced its annoyance with Cuba's backing of left-wing movements and governments, especially in the Americas. Havana's historical aid to the Puerto Rican independence movement, including its armed wing, and its hosting of the Conference of Solidarity with the Independence of Puerto Rico in 1975, were but recent examples, and the U.S. Senate Internal Security Subcommittee had devoted hearings on armed independence activities, orchestrated by groups such as the Fuerzas Armadas de Liberación Nacional (FALN) and Los Macheteros, in the United States and Puerto Rico.[52] Cuba had provided aid and political sanctuary to several members of the island's armed *independentista* groups, which considered Puerto Rico to be a colony of the U.S., and Havana raised the issue of the island's status repeatedly with U.S. officials.

However, by the mid-1970s, Cuba's significant presence in central and southern Africa had become a far deeper concern for U.S. officials, owing to the region's strategic importance and because of the Soviet presence there. Whereas U.S. policy in southern Africa in the 1970s favored white minority and neocolonial governments, Cuba had lent substantial support to left-wing, anticolonial, and antiracist movements. The latest flashpoint was Angola, and Havana's massive aid to the Popular Movement for the Liberation of Angola (MPLA), culminating in the deployment of over 30,000 of Cuba's most elite troops, had proven decisive in routing a military invasion by South Africa. In 1975, President Ford declared that prospects for improved relations had been "destroy[ed]" by Cuba's operations in Africa.[53]

Cuba's foreign policy on the continent continued during the Carter years, including in the strategically vital region of the Horn of Africa. In 1977, Havana dispatched troops to aid an ostensibly left-wing government in Ethiopia, which had become allied with the Soviet Union, to repel an invasion by Somalia, which was now allied with the United States. Cuba's Africa policy, combined with Havana's refusal to cease its support for Puerto Rican independence, eventually strained the U.S.-Cuba rapprochement under the Carter administration beyond repair, contributing to a perception that the administration was helpless to contain Cuba's political ambitions in the Third World.[54] Charging that Cuba's meddling in Africa and the Middle East had nullified prospects for normalized relations, Carter accused Cuba of "acting under the domination of the Soviets" to disrupt prospects for harmony in the region.[55]

Meanwhile, Havana had its own requirements for the normalization of relations: the lifting of the U.S. embargo, and reining in anti-Castro paramilitary groups operating with virtual impunity in South Florida. Although the famed CIA station on the campus of the University of Miami — code-named JMWAVE, which between 1961 and 1967 became the largest CIA base in the world outside of its Virginia headquarters — had been formally closed down, the CIA maintained an active anti-Castro agenda. Having unilaterally canceled its 1973 hijacking agreement with the United States after the bombing of Cubana de Aviación flight 455, the latest in a string of deadly actions perpetrated by U.S.-trained anti-Castro operatives, Castro maintained that a halt to "the campaign of terrorism against Cuba" remained a requirement for the renegotiation of the pact.[56] Lambasting Washington's requests for Cuba to remove its military forces from Africa as "imperial arrogance," Castro observed wryly that it was "all right for the imperialists to have troops and advisers everywhere in the world, but we can't have them anywhere."[57] Ever keen to accuse the United States of hypocrisy over its claims to support democratic movements abroad, Castro asked rhetorically: "Why doesn't the United States blockade South Africa, a racist, fascist country whose troops are committing crimes in Africa and whose minority is oppressing 20 million blacks?"[58]

Reconciliation, of course, had limits on the Cuban side as well. Although Castro used the occasion to discuss Cuba's willingness to begin releasing political prisoners held on the island, an issue that had been a source of international criticism,[59] no full normalization of relations could occur, Castro maintained, as long as the blockade — a "knife in the chest of Cuba" — remained in place. "How can people talk about human rights," the cuban leader asked, "while medicine cannot be sold in Cuba?"[60]

Carter, having made rhetoric about human rights a pillar of his administration's foreign policy, had repeatedly called for the release of political prisoners in Cuba as one of the preconditions for the normalization of full diplomatic relations. Although the presence of political prisoners in Cuban prisons had been condemned by organizations such as Amnesty International, Castro brushed aside Washington's use of the prisoners as leverage for diplomatic negotiation by drawing attention to contradictions within America's own internal human rights record. The United States, Castro pointed out, had also come under international criticism recently with regard to its prison population, which was made up disproportionately of poor people and people of color. "They like to tell us that we must release Cuban counterrevolutionary prisoners," Castro told a Havana audience in 1977. But first, Castro declared, Washington would have to free "an equal number of U.S. blacks who had to go to jail because of the regime of exploitation, the hunger, the poverty, the discrimination and the unemployment that the United States reserves for a large part of the black population."[61]

Editorial attacks upon the perceived double standards of U.S. discourses of human rights were regular fare in the Cuban press. The English language edition of *Granma International*, a weekly version of Cuba's primary state-run newspaper, ran a series of articles and editorials identifying the contradictions within America's global claims to promote social equality and human rights. "There are over ten million unemployed people in the United States today," a July 1977 editorial pointed out. "No article of the Constitution of that country guarantees the right to work. Twenty million children, that is, a third of the total number of children, grow up without adequate medical and social care."[62] And the United States, some in Cuba charged, had waged its own campaign of repression against domestic dissent, one that had produced its own cohort of political prisoners. "Protests against U.S. aggression in Vietnam and the mass movement demanding civil rights for black people and other minorities," *Granma* editorialized in December 1978 in an article that cited a 1973 book by an American author on U.S. political prisoners, "have led to the imprisonment of thousands of dissenting citizens."[63]

Yet despite these impediments to the normalization of relations, the Carter administration's initial overtures toward peace briefly opened new opportunities for negotiation. The fall 1978 "dialogue" that occurred between U.S. Cuban exiles, including members of the Maceo Brigade, and the Cuban government in Havana thus occurred within a larger political climate of diplomatic rapprochement between the United States and Cuba. Castro announced that Cuba's new readiness to engage in dialogue with Cuban exiles — without the direct participation of U.S. officialdom — was premised upon several factors, and the modest change in Washington's diplomatic stance was only one of them. According to Castro, the increasingly visible political plurality of the Cuban American population, a slim majority of which now favored dialogue with Havana despite the ferocious opposition of anti-Castro stalwarts, had made Cuban officials reconsider their assumption of the political homogeneity of the U.S. exile community.

But Cuba, Castro emphasized, also had less to lose. The Cuban Revolution, which was now twenty years old, had consolidated its power internally and was less vulnerable to both U.S. meddling and the predations of Cuban opponents outside the island. "It is irreversible," Castro emphasized; "I think Cubans abroad have realized this."[64] Two months later, Ramón Sánchez Parodi, head of the Cuban Interests Section in Washington, reaffirmed Castro's call for dialogue with Cuban Americans, naming the Antonio Maceo Brigade as one of the primary organizations representing the bloc of Cubans in the United States who favored negotiation.[65]

The Maceo Brigade in Havana

The favored position of the Maceo Brigade in the eyes of the Cuban government was due in no small part to the group's conspicuous radicalism. The group represented the most left-leaning formation of the budding Cuban émigré progressive movement, and many of its members had come to support not only the Cuban Revolution's right to exist, but admired its social gains. The idea to organize a delegation of Cuban émigrés to visit the island was first raised at a meeting of the Instituto de Estudios Cubanos in 1974. By some accounts, it was Casal who first suggested the formation of a Cuban American delegation, drawing upon her experience returning to the island the previous year. Yet in additional to Casal, several representatives from *Joven Cuba* and the newly formed *Areíto* collective had also been invited to Cuba by the government, spending two weeks on the island, during which they had reunited with family members and met with Cuban officials.[66] The *Areíto* collective subsequently proposed a larger delegation to the Cuban government, although the group had not yet been named for Antonio Maceo.

There are conflicting accounts regarding the origins of the group's name. One version holds that the suggestion to name the group after the legendary Afro-Cuban military commander of the island's wars of independence from Spanish domination in the late 1800s came from Casal.[67] Others remember a different origin story. When the group of fifty-five arrived in Cuba in 1977 they had not formally chosen a name, although they had designed shirts bearing the words "Encuentro de Jóvenes cubanos"—the encounter of young Cubans—to commemorate the trip. Upon arriving at the Julio Antonio Mella camp outside Havana, however, the Cuban ICAP representatives informed them that the delegation had been named the Brigada Antonio Maceo, and presented members of the contingent with t-shirts bearing the name.[68]

Precise origins of the name notwithstanding, the Maceo Brigade's namesake is significant, invoking both Cuba's historical impetus for self-determination and independence from foreign rule and the island's embedded and unfinished struggle for racial equality, a struggle that had been cut short by both internal and external forces.⁶⁹ Both themes would play a significant role in influencing Cuba's nationalist imaginary after 1959. The brigade's journal, *Baraguá*, drew its name from Antonio Maceo's 1878 "Protest of Baraguá," in which the legendary Afro-Cuban leader had refused to recognize Spain's terms of peace to end the Ten Years War, which had failed to abolish slavery on the island and grant full Cuban independence. The FBI, which would soon launch an investigation into the Maceo Brigade, concluded that the group's name "represents the Brigade's protest against the United States blockade imposed upon the Government of Cuba."⁷⁰

The other part of the group's name was also indicative. "Brigade" implicitly signified their support of the current Cuban government, one that had welcomed, since the early 1960s, solidarity delegations of sympathizers from around the globe. Many of these had similarly used — or were given — the warlike designation, which conceptualized political solidarity within the wider battle for Cuban self-determination, while also gesturing toward a global tradition of left-wing and communist solidarity travel, from the Abraham Lincoln Brigade of the Spanish Civil War to the Cuban and international labor brigades that had taken part in the Cuba's 1970 sugarcane harvest.

Yet to some Maceo Brigade participants, their status as an invited delegation compromised their independence. "The 'brigade' motif," one member later wrote, was characteristic of "politically sympathetic and controlled groups visiting a socialist land. We gladly accepted it in exchange for the chance to set foot on the forbidden space that Cuba had become for us."⁷¹ The Brigade's ideological orientation thus represented an amalgamation of themes from the emerging Cuban American progressive movement, the broader U.S. New Left and U.S. Third World Left, as well as older currents of Cuban nationalism. In a 1978 issue of *Areíto* that was composed entirely of articles and reflections on the Maceo Brigade, the collective omitted the significance of Maceo's blackness, situating the leader's legacy instead within long-standing Cuban nationalist discourses, popularized by José Martí, that emphasized national unity and social equality through the positing of a raceless Cuban national identity. In a column entitled "Por Qué Antonio Maceo?," the collective wrote that the naming of the Brigade after the general christened in Cuban history as the "Bronze Titan" grew from

> Our desire to maintain a continuity with the history of our homeland, with its historical figures, with its revolutionary heroes; Our rebellion against the foreign decisions and historical circumstances that uprooted us from our homeland; Our protest against the blockade which impedes us from knowing the true Cuban reality; Our respect and admiration for Antonio

Maceo, with whom we identify not only for his patriotic and warrior values, but for the quality and depth of his revolutionary thought, particularly in its international dimensions and with regard to the Caribbean; Our commemoration of the Protest of Baraguá, whose centennial we celebrate this year of 1978.[72]

Conceived as a way for young Cuban exiles to witness what they called "the Cuban reality" with their own eyes, the delegation endeavored to help émigrés end their estrangement from their homeland and, simultaneously, to end the island's isolation from its diaspora. The group maintained that members of the post-1959 Cuban diaspora had a right to visit Cuba in order to reconnect with their community's history and to gain firsthand knowledge of daily life there as an alternative to the uniformly hostile renderings of the island prevalent within the U.S. exile press in Miami.

Nonetheless, the group made clear in their recruitment materials that their desire to witness Cuba for themselves, and to counteract what they perceived as the biases of the anti-Castro exile leadership stateside, did not equate to a position of unequivocal support for socialism or for the Castro government. Rather, the trips would be an opportunity for participants to witness the revolution's "errors" as well as its "achievements," and to draw their own conclusions. All Cubans in the United States, the Brigade maintained, had a right to "define their own relationship with their homeland."[73] Arising out of a normative political environment that demanded absolute political conformity from Cubans in the United States, the Maceo Brigade hoped to offer a radical alternative to the prevailing conservative forces dominating the diaspora's relationship to the island.

The group's commitment to political plurality notwithstanding, several criteria, requested by the Cuban government, were applied to those who wanted to join the Brigade's trips to ensure that members of the delegation were supporters of the Cuban Revolution. In order to participate, applicants must have left Cuba involuntarily as youth, at the decision of their parents; they must not have participated in violent "counter-revolutionary activities" while in the United States nor "maintain an attitude of violence against the revolution"; and they must oppose the U.S. embargo and be in favor of the normalization of relations between the two nations.[74] Participants had to be approved by the Maceo Brigade's organizing committee, and the list also had to be approved by Cuba's Ministry of the Interior, which wanted to ascertain that the applicants were not CIA agents or right-wing infiltrators. The Maceo Brigade conducted their organizing and recruitment for the trip in secret for fear of reprisals from right-wing exile groups.[75]

The first brigade in December 1977 numbered fifty-five — the number of visas granted by the Cuban government. It was the first time since 1959 that a group of émigrés had been invited to Cuba. Ricardo Escartín, an official in the Cuban Interests Section in Washington, called the Maceo Brigade's delegations symbolic of a mutual "maturation" of relations between the nations. He hinted at one of Havana's criteria for agreeing to allow the visit: "After all, their leaving wasn't their fault. It was the decision of their parents."[76]

The Maceo Brigade's experiences in Cuba paralleled those of other international solidarity brigades, including previous groups from the United States, such as the Venceremos Brigade. Arriving in Havana's airport on the night of December 22, 1977, the group was greeted to cheers from an assembled crowd of Cubans and a round of daiquiris. Boarding Japanese-made buses, the group was taken to the Julio Antonio Mella International Camp outside Havana that was run by Cuba's bureau for foreign solidarity, the Instituto Cubano de Amistad con los Pueblos — the Cuban Institute for Friendship Between Peoples (ICAP), where the group would be based. Like the Venceremos Brigades, the Maceo Brigade's itinerary included both volunteer labor and tours of the island's social programs and development projects. Setting out on the first day at 6 A.M., the group left a wreath of flowers on the tomb of Antonio Maceo before arriving at a Havana psychiatric hospital to observe as patients sang, danced, and participated in work projects as part of their rehabilitation program. The hospital included a photo display showing the stark images of the hospital before the revolution: patients poorly fed and dirty, virtually naked, standing or stooping in groups in a yard.

By the third day, the Brigade was already hard at work helping to construct sections of a giant concrete housing project to be occupied by Cuban textile workers, a labor that would continue nearly every morning for the remainder of their stay. Afternoons were spent touring the region: the giant dairy farm at Valle de Picadura, whose genetically modified herd was overseen by Fidel Castro's older brother, Ramón; new housing construction in the outlying Havana district of Alamar; the brand new tourist hotel Mar Azul; and the beaches east of Havana as far as Guanabo. Other afternoons were allotted as free time, and the *brigadistas* took the opportunity to walk the streets of Havana and converse with residents. At night, entertained by Cuban musicians and performers, they drank and danced until the small hours of the morning.[77]

The brigade would stay in Cuba for two weeks, traveling the length of the island from Havana to Santiago de Cuba, where they visited the mausoleum of José Martí. In Holguín, a freshly painted billboard bearing an image of Antonio Maceo welcomed the group to the city. A film crew from the Instituto

Cubano del Arte e Industria Cinematográficos (ICAIC) trailed the group throughout their stay, resulting in the film *55 Hermanos*, released in theaters in Cuba in 1978 and eliciting enormous public interest on the island. The film intersperses footage of the group reuniting with family members and neighbors, participating in a construction project, and visiting historic sites with lengthy interviews with *brigadistas*. The film's nuanced treatment of the experiences of Cuban émigrés in the United States and Puerto Rico, including discussions of class differences and diverging political orientations among Cuban Americans, as well as anti-Cuban discrimination and persistent unemployment within the Cuban immigrant population in the United States, represented a notable departure from more heterogeneous depictions of the Cuban diaspora within the Cuban media up to that point.

Traveling the island, the *brigadistas* had plenty of time to contemplate the changes that had occurred in the place they had once called home. "The country we found on our return," wrote brigade participant Manolo Gómez in a personal reflection printed in the *New York Amsterdam News*, "was not the Cuba we had left behind. Gone are the abandoned beggar children in rags who roamed the streets of Havana in the 1950s as they still do in all Latin American capitals today. Gone, in fact, are all the brutal images of hopeless poverty associated with underdeveloped nations and once true of Cuba as well."[78]

Although organized by ICAP as a typical solidarity delegation composed of volunteer work, tours of social programs, and meetings with Cuban workers, civil organizations, and government officials, the Maceo Brigade was different from all other foreign delegations in that its participants were Cuban. Virtually all of the *brigadistas* still had family on the island, and some felt constrained by the itinerary of the trip, which was determined by the Cuban government and emphasized showcasing the revolution's social gains over the opportunity for participants to reunite with family. Some visited the homes where they had been born, many of them now dilapidated — the country's resources were being used to develop the provinces, often at the expense of maintaining infrastructure and buildings in Havana — only to be overwhelmed by grief upon finding that, inevitably, another Cuban family now lived in their house. Some *brigadistas* whose families had been wealthy tried to visit their old mansions, finding them now occupied by foreign embassies or government offices, or divided up into apartments now occupied by families. One participant in a delegation in 1979, moved by the performance put on by the patients at the psychiatric center, nonetheless mourned the sense of loss invoked by witnessing the distinctly Cuban music and dance: "all that — our music, our culture, our people, our language — had been robbed from us."[79]

The Maceo Brigade's stature grew in 1978 as a second, much larger delegation was planned from the group's national office in Medford, New Jersey. Branches of the group appeared in a dozen U.S. cities, as well as in Spain, Venezuela, and Mexico. Numbering approximately 178 participants from throughout the country, the second contingent would also be more ideologically diverse than the first. According to the FBI's prolific reproductions of the group's recruitment materials, the selection process for this trip would accept not only applicants who supported the Cuban Revolution, but those with much more ambivalent views. Nonetheless, *brigadistas* on the second trip had to agree to the group's points of unity, which included support for the normalization of U.S.-Cuba relations, including an end to the U.S. embargo, and a "rejection of the hostile acts against Cuba" perpetrated by the U.S. government and militant right-wing Cuban exile groups.[80] For many of the new participants, the trip offered an opportunity to make up their own minds about a place they felt conflicted about. "My own attitude," recalls one participant in the second brigade, "... can best be described as feeling caught between a rock and a hard place — between the political division in my immediate family and the romantic attitude toward Cuba in American universities. Hence, I simply needed to see Cuba with my own eyes."[81]

The Cuba that the émigrés encountered frequently suggested more questions than answers. Accustomed to being racialized as "Latino/a" or "Hispanic" within the United States and cast as racial minorities, Cubans returning to the island with the Maceo Brigade were sometimes surprised to find that Cuba's racial logic had shifted in their absence. Like most Cubans in the United States at that historical moment, the members of the Maceo Brigade were overwhelmingly light-skinned and of middle class origin, a profile that was now more distinctly out of sync with the majority of the island's population than at any other time in its recent history. This dissonance is captured by scholar Flavio Risech, who reflected on his 1982 return to the island through an intersectional gaze borne of his growing awareness of his gay identity as well as his newfound understanding of his racial position within the Cuban diaspora:

> Those like myself who are light-skinned bear a particular burden, as we return to our *patria* to find that we are perceived not only as not fully Cuban but as whites in a society now over half composed of darker-skinned people. In a sense I and others like me change race when we cross this border: only a profoundly coded *cambio del piel* — a kind of cross dressing involving shifting between two very different social constructs of race — could make it possible for me to be a *blanquito* there and a latino and therefore something of a "person of color" here.[82]

Indeed, the demographics of race and class on the island were still shifting in the 1970s. Owing to the heavily *blanco* and middle-class composition of the waves of emigration out of Cuba in the 1960s, the nation's population had become phenotypically darker and socioeconomically more working class. These characteristics of the Cuban outmigration would hold until the Mariel emigration crisis of 1980 — known in U.S. parlance as the "Mariel boatlift"— the first major wave of emigration that included large numbers of working-class and Afro-Cubans. By the mid-1970s, too, new discourses of race were also becoming prominent on the island. As Cuba's military and humanitarian involvement in Africa deepened, recognition of the island's connection to the continent, historically, genetically, and politically, became more widespread. Amid Cuba's tide-turning aid to Angola in its battle against South African and U.S.-backed forces, Castro notably declared in the mid-1970s that Cuba was a "Latin African" nation that was linked to the continent both genealogically, through the history of slavery, and politically, through Cuba's aid to anticolonial movements after 1959. Although the upper levels of the Cuban government remained disproportionately composed of nonblack Cubans in the 1970s, members of the Maceo Brigade returned to an island that had changed in both the phenotypic composition of its population and the racial imaginary of the nation.

The Maceo Brigade's presence in Cuba was front-page news on the island in 1978 and 1979, as the group's contingents enthusiastically threw themselves into labor projects, listened to talks by Cuban officials, development engineers, and health workers, and toured the island. *Prensa Latina* described the Brigade as "the most important youth organization of the Cuban community abroad,"[83] while *Granma International* noted that "[t]hey have sought and found abroad the roots of their nationality thus binding them to the Cuban Revolution."[84]

For many Cubans, the arrival of the Maceo Brigade came with little warning. Accustomed to thinking of émigrés as Florida-based terrorists or as departed family and loved ones who never returned, the arrival of the young Cubans from the United States and Puerto Rico challenged their assumptions about the Cuban diaspora. "Their arrival came as a big surprise," admitted one ICAP officer who worked closely with the Brigade. "These were Cuban[s] who came back. And we admired them, we were grateful to them, although we did not know how they would react to the new Cuba."[85] The shifting views on the island toward émigrés were reflected in new colloquialisms. Instead of *gusanos* — counterrevolutionary "worms"— Cubans had begun playfully referring to the "transformed" visitors as *mariposas*: butterflies.

That year, a contingent of fifteen children of Cuban émigrés living in the

Antonio Maceo Brigade members visit the José Martí Mausoleum, one of Cuba's most politically significant sites, in Santiago de Cuba, 1978. Courtesy of Raúl Alzaga.

Members of the Antonio Maceo Brigade with Ramón Castro, the brother of Fidel and Raúl. Yohel Camayd-Freixas Papers, courtesy of the University Archives & Special Collections Department, Joseph P. Healey Library, University of Massachusetts Boston.

The Antonio Maceo Brigade and the Making of a Cuban American Left 179

Antonio Maceo Brigade members with Fidel Castro after a meeting with the Cuban leader and other government officials, 1978. Courtesy of Raúl Alzaga.

United States and Puerto Rico made a parallel voyage to Cuba, traveling as a delegation dubbed the "*Maceítos.*" Traveling unescorted by their parents, the *Maceítos* stayed at a camp with hundreds of other visiting children from over thirty countries. Encouraged to communicate through art, they composed drawings bearing handwritten captions. "We, the *Maceítos*, are the children of Cubans who left Cuba after the triumph of the Revolution," read one. "Our parents were young and didn't know what they were doing."[86] Although the delegation recalled an earlier youth group from the United States — a recent children's contingent of the Venceremos Brigade which had traveled as the "*Venceremitos*"— the *Maceítos* also symbolically reversed the legacy of Operation Pedro Pan. Instead of fearful Cuban parents sending their children away from the imagined perils of communism, Cuban émigré parents, hopeful about the prospects for personal and national reconciliation, now sent their children to (re)experience the new revolutionary nation.[87]

That year, Cuba's premier cultural organization, Casa de las Américas, awarded its highest literary prize to the *Areíto* collective's book, *Contra Viento y Marea*. The jury, which included eminent Nicaraguan poet Ernesto Cardenal, selected the book for "its great human qualities" and "its literary qualities," as well as "its evident political importance, especially for young revolutionaries throughout the world."⁸⁸ That same year, *Casa de las Américas* published a special edition of the book. The *Areíto* members decided to donate the cash prize back to Casa de las Américas to help fund the upcoming 11th World Festival of Youth and Students, to be held in Cuba in the summer.⁸⁹

The Dialogue

The Maceo Brigade's delegations to Cuba "paved the way," in the words of the FBI, for a series of direct talks in 1978 between the Cuban government and representatives of émigré communities abroad during two sessions held in Havana during November and December of 1978.⁹⁰ The meetings, known as "the dialogue," convened representatives of exile communities — 75 delegates during the November meeting, 140 during the December — to discuss the release of Cuban political prisoners, the reunification of families separated by migration, and the right of U.S. émigrés to visit the island.

Fidel Castro personally invited members of the *Areíto* collective, as well as the Maceo Brigade, the New York–based Casa de las Américas — a U.S. counterpart to its Havana namesake — Manuel Espinosa, and Jorge Roblejo Loríe, the head of a Miami group working to obtain the release of Cuban prisoners.⁹¹ In a post-midnight press conference at the Palace of the Revolution in Havana on December 10, Castro announced that the Cuban government would initially release 400 prisoners, and free 3,200 more within the next six or seven months. The exile delegates, some of them ex-prisoners themselves or veterans of the Bay of Pigs invasion, greeted Castro's announcement with jubilation and, in a testament to the meeting's cathartic tone, attendees rose to their feet and sang the Cuban national anthem as Castro stood onstage with bowed head.⁹²

During the talks, the Maceo Brigade presented a ten-point program outlining their demands of the Cuban government. The audacious program advocated nothing less than the reunification of the Cuban diaspora and the full participation of émigrés in the social and political life of the island:

1. Return of Cuban citizenship: We request that the Cuban Revolutionary Government pass a law that will allow Cubans living abroad to regain their Cuban citizenship, if they so wish.
2. Cultural, Scientific and Sports Exchange: We propose further conversations to discuss these exchanges between Cubans living on the island and Cubans abroad.

3. Educational Exchange: We request that the Cuban Revolutionary Government investigate the possibility of study in Cuba for young Cubans living abroad.
4. Special Activities: We request participation, as observers, of young Cubans living abroad in special activities of the State, the Party and mass organizations, as well as in scientific and professional events of special interests.
5. Participation in the Socialist Democracy: We request that the Cuban Revolutionary Government study the possibility of Cubans living abroad participating in the election of Representatives to the organs of people's power at all levels.
6. Permanent Return: We request that the Cuban Revolutionary Government begin to lay the legal and material groundwork for the permanent return to Cuba of those who wish to return.
7. On the Political Prisoners: We request that the Cuban Revolutionary Government free the largest possible number of people who remain in prison due to counter-revolutionary offenses. We are submitting a list of prisoners and former prisoners compiled through members and supporters of the Brigade.
8. Visits of Relatives: We request that the Cuban Revolutionary Government facilitate visits to the island of those Cubans abroad who wish to see their families.
9. Leaving Cuba for family reasons: We request that the Cuban Revolutionary Government study the possibility of establishing a program through which Cubans living on the island may visit their family abroad.
10. Reunification of the family: We urge the Cuban Revolutionary Government to grant permanent exit from the country to immediate family members (parents, siblings, and spouses) who have been separated.[93]

Yet while the Maceo Brigade had helped create the context of diasporic rapprochement in which the talks occurred, the group ultimately played a relatively minor role in them. The first inroads between Havana and Washington on the issue of political prisoners had actually been initiated in secret by Cuban intelligence agents who had contacted Bernardo Benes, a former anti-Batista fighter turned Miami banker and civic leader, who had become known for his efforts to integrate Cubans into the city's Anglo-dominated political and business world. Benes's negotiations with the Cuban government would lead to the release of thousands of Cuban prisoners who had been convicted of counterrevolutionary activity. The meetings were kept secret. Spending approximately 150 hours talking with Fidel Castro and thousands more with senior Cuban officials over several years, Benes became the primary, if covert, intermediary between the Cuban and U.S. governments, allowing the estranged parties to negotiate despite the severance of formal diplomacy. Benes's advocacy, which emphasized the release of Cuban political prisoners and the reunification of families separated by migration, laid the crucial foundation for the 1978 dialogue.[94] Although the Maceo Brigade's agenda overlapped significantly with that of Benes, the latter's agenda ultimately took precedence. The issue of political prisoners offered the Cuban government a viable avenue through which it could simultaneously improve relations with the exile community abroad while also meeting one of Washington's demands for improved diplomatic relations. The Maceo Brigade's more radical agenda, on the other hand, included demands that appealed to a much smaller cross section of the exile community. Most Cuban Americans, who were still strongly opposed to the Cuban communist system, had no interest in reinstating their citizenship or returning to the island permanently as long as Fidel Castro was in power, nor did they want to participate in the political life of the socialist system.

Nonetheless, these events were unprecedented in the history of post-1959 Cuba's relations with its diaspora. Prior to the Maceo Brigade's trip to the island, Cubans who left had been universally branded traitors and counterrevolutionary *gusanos* by the Cuban government and much of the populace. A lingering climate of fear, originating in the threat of sabotage and armed attacks against the island perpetrated by exiles living in the United States, encouraged many on the island to view Cubans abroad, particularly those living in the United States, with suspicion. The majority of the fall 1978 dialogue's participants came from the United States, but delegates also arrived from Spain, Canada, Costa Rica, the Dominican Republic, Venezuela, Mexico, Puerto Rico, Panama, and Jamaica. While the Maceo Brigade had explicitly forbade participation by exiles who had engaged in paramilitary actions against Cuba, the dialogue had no such prohibition. Indeed, the talks were extraordinary in that they included a number of Cuban American veterans of the Bay of Pigs invasion, including some who had been captured and imprisoned in Cuba.[95] Fidel Castro also invited a number of delegates from Venezuela who had been officials within the Batista government, a move that allowed Castro, as Holly Ackerman has observed, to "test the political waters with all segments of the community in the exterior."[96] In this sense, the dialogue marked a watershed moment in the history of Cuba's relations with its diaspora and was a significant breakthrough in the stalemate of mutual animus.

Upon their return to the United States, participants from the first meeting formed a group dubbed the "Committee of 75" that continued to lobby the U.S. government to secure passage for released Cuban prisoners. However, as the prisoners began to be scheduled for release in batches, their emigration to the United States encountered problems. The U.S. government had failed to grant all of them visas, citing worries that some might be criminals or planted Cuban intelligence agents. The Carter administration was now in an awkward position. Now that the United States was faced with the proposition of accepting the prisoners, it seemed to be echoing the Cuban government's own claims that some of the prisoners were indeed individuals who had been convicted of apolitical crimes, not political activities. Moreover, having condemned the presence of political prisoners on the island as a violation of human rights, it was now unwilling to match Cuba's gesture by granting them sanctuary in a timely fashion. Arguing that it was "the United States that led them into counter-revolutionary activity here," Castro argued that the United States had a "moral obligation" to accept the Cuban prisoners, many of whom had family and friends in South Florida.[97]

Bernardo Benes continued to advocate on their behalf. Writing to Carter in September 1979 to urge the administration to provide 5,000 visas for released prisoners in Cuba, Benes protested that, "the ex-political prisoners have been badly ignored," leading to "a very deep feeling of 'Anti-American' sentiment... developing in Cuba amongst the ex-prisoners populace who feel 'betrayed' by the United States." Echoing Castro, with whom he had negotiated the prisoner release on behalf of the United States, Benes contended that "there is a moral responsibility in our part (U.S. Government) not to forget this people [sic] because the majority of them served long jail sentences as a result of their involvement in anti-Castro operations sponsored by United States Intelligence Agencies in the 1960s."[98] Benes also spoke out of a personal sense of obligation. According to historian Robert Levine, the Miami banker had raised the funds for a 1966 armed raid into Cuba by Tony Cuesta, the leader of the Miami-based paramilitary group "Comandos L" which had conducted dozens of raids into Cuba, on one occasion managing to sink a Russian freighter in the port of Caibarién. Wounded and captured during the raid that Benes had funded, Cuesta was imprisoned in Cuba, and Benes made sure that he was among the first group of released political prisoners in 1978.[99]

The dialogue was ultimately a public relations coup for Fidel Castro. Although the presence of political prisoners in Cuba had long been a source of international criticism, the Cuban leader's offer to release a substantial number — minus those who had committed what he called "extremely serious offenses" such as terrorism or crimes linked to the Batista's dictatorial government — placed the onus upon the United States to grant them immediate sanctuary.[100] "At a stroke," a reporter for *The Guardian* opined, "Castro got himself off the human rights hook."[101] The talks allowed the Cuban government to shift the narrative of its relations with its diaspora by highlighting the intransigence of both the right-wing stalwarts of the Cuban American community and the cold warriors within the Carter administration such as Zbigniew Brzezinski, the President's hawkish National Security Adviser, instead of Cuba's imprisonment of counterrevolutionaries. Identifying émigrés willing to negotiate with the Cuban government not as treasonous *gusanos* but as the "true representatives" of Cuban communities abroad, Castro praised their "courage and valor in defying the threats ... of terrorist elements in the United States opposed to the dialogue,"[102] legitimizing the growing openness among exiles for relations with the island while highlighting the hardening ideological lines within Cuban communities in the United States that had become increasingly polarized by reconciliation politics.

Right-wing Cuban exile leaders, in turn, accused Castro of cynically trying to divide the exile community. As *dialogueros* became increasingly vocal in their advocacy for the normalization of U.S.-Cuba relations, the Cuban government gained a crucial ally constituency inside the United States that supported Havana's single greatest diplomatic hope: the lifting of the U.S. embargo. As the Cuban government began allowing prisoners and ex-prisoners to leave the island in November, 1978, some of the formerly imprisoned added to the calls for a halt to open hostilities. Cuesta, arriving in Miami with the first group of forty-six released prisoners, explained to reporters that he and others opposed to Castro now had "no alternative but to silence the guns and open up to other paths."[103]

Not surprisingly, Castro's legendary charisma and outsized persona influenced the tone of the talks. Maceo Brigade member Mariano Díaz-Miranda, a doctoral student in Latin American history at the University of Texas who traveled to Cuba with his two sisters, also members of the Brigade, described the Cuban leader as "very magnetic, very charming."[104] Although some of the delegates regarded Castro as their lifelong nemesis, the Cuban leader's participation in the marathon meetings, which lasted for many hours, sometimes helped shift their perceptions of both Castro and the revolutionary system that he was so closely associated with. One of the delegates was Fernando Mena, a man who had fought in the revolution against Batista but came to oppose the new regime headed by Castro. He was eventually sentenced to a six-year prison term in Cuba on charges of counterrevolutionary activity. But Mena, explaining that he was "neither Castroite nor Communist," acknowledged the impact of the dialogue with the Cuban leader: "Castro made us do something the Revolution considers revolutionary. And he made us feel good about it." Other participants, anxious for the opportunity to negotiate with the Cuban government for the release of loved ones in prison and the right to visit family members but still deeply distrustful of Castro, participated in the talks more warily. Miguel González-Pando, also a Bay of Pigs veteran, found the Cuban leader friendly and "disarming," despite his misgivings, when he met the man he had once tried to overthrow. Reinol González, a delegate who had spent sixteen years in a Cuban prison after being convicted of plotting to assassinate Castro, admitted that he was surprised when his former adversary embraced him upon arriving in Havana.[105] Castro also made offers to individual delegates to free family members as an apparent gesture of goodwill. Salvador Madruga, a Miami businessman and a veteran of the Bay of Pigs, was promised the release of his father from a Cuban prison.[106] While these events did not signal the end of mutual distrust, they represented a significant shift in the tenor of relations between the post-1959 diaspora and the island. For these émigrés, the Cuban Revolution was now a fact of life, its government a legitimate entity to negotiate with, not overthrow.

Yet for all the impact of the Maceo Brigade and other émigrés in Havana, the inner workings of the dialogue were orchestrated through the traditional channels of insider diplomacy. Delegates to the Havana dialogue had been given the impression by the Cuban government that the issue of political prisoners was open for direct negotiation, when in reality the technicalities of the prisoner release had already been secured in secret through the negotiations of Benes. With Cuba's presence in Africa off the table — the Castro government had repeatedly made it clear that its involvement on the African continent was nonnegotiable, even if it meant that the U.S. embargo remained in place — the issue of Cuban political prisoners offered both sides an avenue for diplomatic reciprocity. Nonetheless, Carter's mounting irritation in 1978 over Cuba's presence in Africa, which now included aid to Ethiopia, compelled him to insist that the negotiations be kept secret so as to preserve Washington's public position of condemnation, and he requested that the State Department not participate in an announcement of the prisoner agreement.[107] Castro therefore announced the prisoner release unilaterally, during the Havana dialogue in November. The prisoner issue now became an opportunity for Cuba to again achieve two goals simultaneously: the improvement of U.S.-Cuba relations, and the improvement of relations with the island's diaspora.

With Cuba now releasing prisoners, Castro took the opportunity to request some diplomatic reciprocity of his own: the release of four Puerto Rican nationalists imprisoned in the United States. The four activists, Oscar Collazo, Rafael Cancel Miranda, Irving Flores Rodríguez, and Lolita Lebrón, had been convicted of a gun attack inside the U.S. House of Representatives in 1954 in a protest against the island's colonial status under the United States. Five lawmakers were wounded in the incident. The anticolonial *independentistas* were hailed in Cuba as symbols of the Puerto Rican independence movement and became a global cause célèbre, and Fidel Castro had for years campaigned for their release from prison. This time, the Carter administration was ready to listen. In 1979, Carter agreed to a deal in which the United States would free the Puerto Rican prisoners in return for four U.S. citizens held in Cuban prisons on espionage and sabotage charges, three of whom had worked under the direction of the CIA.[108] Deeming that the Puerto Ricans' prison terms had stretched far longer "than the terms normally served by those convicted of equally or even more heinous offenses," the Carter administration, which had made "human rights" a pillar of its international policy, explained that their release "would be a significant humanitarian gesture and would be viewed as such by much of the international community."[109] The 1978 dialogue thus allowed Havana to score a victory in its long-standing support of the Puerto Rican movement against colonization.

The 1978 dialogue signaled a major shift in relations between Cuba and its post-revolutionary diaspora. True, most details of the actual prisoner release were negotiated in private by Benes and Cuban officials and, as scholar Robert Levine points out, the face-to-face discussions between émigrés and Cuban officials in Havana resulted in few concrete negotiations because most of the substantive decisions had been worked out in advance. Indeed, State Department official Peter Tarnoff had made it clear that the Cuban American attendees "may negotiate nothing, absolutely nothing, in the name of the United States."[110] However, Levine's characterization of the dialogue as "largely for show" overlooks the enormous symbolic importance of the talks for the Cuban émigrés who participated, many of whom experienced the occasion as a long-awaited moment of catharsis.[111] "The dialogue" was a cordial encounter between the Cuban revolutionary government, including Fidel Castro, and those who had fled the revolution.[112]

Like the Venceremos and Maceo Brigades, whose actual material contribution to Cuba through their volunteer labor was relatively small, the importance of the 1978 dialogue lay largely in its personal impact on the participants, and the ways in which their experiences in Cuba shaped their future work and political outlook. The encounters were also criticized for others reasons. The insider nature of the prisoner deal fueled allegations that Fidel Castro had cynically given exile participants the impression that they had wielded influence during the Havana dialogue, when in reality the most substantive negotiations had been proceeding through closed channels.[113] Other problems arose during the prisoner release. As agreed, the Cuban government began freeing prisoners in January 1979, and these, together with their family members who wished to emigrate, were eventually granted visas by the U.S. government. However, the United States balked at granting visas to *former* Cuban prisoners who were also requesting haven in the United States for themselves and their families. Although the Cuban government was now allowing these former prisoners to leave the island, upon requesting U.S. visas they were informed that they had to apply through the regular immigration channels, a proposition that often resulted in a delay of several years.[114]

The dialogue was also marred by allegations that the Cuban government had rigged the travel arrangements in order to profit financially from the arrival of the exiles, who began traveling to Cuba by the tens of thousands after the Cuban government lifted the entrance restrictions for Cubans living abroad. Cuba classified visiting exiles as "tourists," just like all foreign visitors who were not part of a formal solidarity delegation. Flights and hotel arrangements — in some cases even if the visitors had family to stay with in Cuba — had to be booked through agencies operated by the Cuban tourist bureau, which sometimes charged inflated prices or sold only expensive package deals. The members of the Maceo Brigade on the other hand, as official guests of the Cuban government who had been selected for the solidarity delegation as a result of their support for the principles of the Cuban Revolution, paid significantly lower prices: a few hundred dollars for an entire month on the island.[115] Cuba also prohibited the sending of packages from the United States to Cuba for fear that they might contain bombs. As a result, Cuban émigrés had no way to send goods to their families on the island. Thousands of exiles arrived in Havana only to pay exorbitant prices for consumer goods, bought as gifts for relatives on the island, in specially opened Cuban "dollar" stores which sold goods at marked-up prices.[116] The differences in treatment only exacerbated resentment toward the Maceo Brigade among other Cubans émigrés. In an essay published in the *Miami Herald*, one brigade member rationalized the group's privileged treatment this way: "A few people in our group felt terribly guilty as they watched the other Cubans hugging and kissing their relatives goodbye. But the truth was that the intransigence of *la comunidad* in its right-wing political views had led to the formation of the Antonio Maceo Brigade. The brigade was a welcome alternative for those of us who . . . wanted to understand — not destroy — the revolution."[117]

The Backlash

News of the dialogue broke in the U.S. press in November of 1978.[118] Opposition from anti-Castro hardliners was swift and ferocious. Those perceived as deviating from the narrow line of anticommunism and unrelenting antipathy toward the Cuban revolutionary project had faced marginalization throughout the 1970s, accused of being communist sympathizers and "agents of Castro." Hardliners considered themselves to be in a state of war, and those U.S.-residing Cubans who suggested negotiation with Havana were accused of treason. As calls for dialogue with Cuba gained momentum mid-decade, right-wing Cuban militants, many of them ex-CIA operatives, increasingly deployed violence to intimidate anyone — community leaders, newspaper editors, musicians, religious leaders, professors — perceived as challenging the community's supposedly uniform antipathy to the communist government in Havana. Even past members of Brigade 2506, veterans of the Bay of Pigs invasion, found themselves suddenly turned upon. Salvador Madruga, who had participated in the 1978 dialogue with the hope of obtaining the release of his imprisoned father, was unceremoniously expelled from the Bay of Pigs veterans association in Miami for participating in the talks, and a number of other veterans met a similar fate.[119]

In reality, intransigent anti-Castroism was not as uniform in Miami as it appeared. According to one poll, conducted by Florida International University at the time of the dialogue, 85 percent of Hispanic-surnamed Miamians supported continued negotiations with Cuba.[120] These views, however, were seldom expressed publicly. A cloud of fear hovered over the city, punctuated by intermittent violence, which encouraged significant political conformity. As Robert Levine puts it, dissenters within Miami's Cuban community constituted a "silenced majority."[121]

Even Benes was ostracized and began to fear for his life. Picketed by protestors outside his office and threatened at his home, he wore a bullet proof vest for a year. "I went from being a business and community leader to a social leper," he later recalled.[122] In 1983, long after the dialogue, a bomb destroyed Benes's bank offices. Newspapers were targeted for running opinion pieces supporting negotiation with Havana or failing to be sufficiently anti-Castro in editorial tone. When the New York offices of *El Diario–La Prensa* were bombed in 1978 after the newspaper ran an editorial endorsing travel to Cuba, Benes opined that, "no one is interested in free speech in Dade County — only in Havana."[123]

Anti-Castro operatives also targeted a number of non-Cuban activists and organizations. In March 1973, Cuba solidarity activist Sandra Levinson miraculously escaped serious injury when a bomb destroyed the offices of the Center for Cuban Studies in New York as she was sitting inside.[124] Levinson, the Center's director, was also affiliated with the Venceremos Brigade and had been helping to organize an event called Expo Cuba which was to showcase Cuban art and film, and would feature sympathetic educational events about the Cuban Revolution. The exposition was scheduled to begin on July 26, the twentieth anniversary of the failed attack on the Moncada Barracks, the event that signaled the beginning of the insurgency against Batista. Another bomb destroyed part of the Martin Luther King Labor Center where the event was to open, injuring a janitor inside and four police officers who were showered with falling debris on the street below.[125] Three people were stabbed during protests outside the event and, amid more bomb threats, Expo Cuba was finally cancelled two days after opening.[126] Violence by anti-Castro militants occurred in at least sixteen nations, targeting Cuban embassies, economic interests, and personnel around the world.

The great majority of Cuba-related political violence in the 1970s, however, was directed against Cubans living in South Florida. By 1977, the epidemic of bombings, numbering over 100 in the Miami area alone since 1970, compelled the *New York Times* — the writer's mislabeling of a key ingredient of Caribbean cuisine notwithstanding — to opine that "political violence has become as much a part of life in Miami's Little Havana as fried bananas and black beans."[127] Miami now had among the highest rates of political bombings of any city in the world. Omega 7 and Comando Cero were the most powerful Cuban American terrorist associations, the primary arms of a web of paramilitary groups that had been consolidated under Orlando Bosch, a Cuban exile with whom the CIA had maintained contact with in the early 1960s.[128] Omega 7 took credit for dozens of attacks in Florida, New Jersey, and New York, targeting any individual or entity perceived as supporting, collaborating with, or doing business with Cuba.

Neutrality was no guarantee of safety. Those "who are not a part of the struggle against communism," Omega 7 warned, could also be targeted.[129] In March, 1979, Omega 7 claimed responsibility for three bombings in New York and New Jersey which targeted entities said to be conducting business with Cuba — which the groups anonymously accused of being "the Fifth Column created by Castro in the United States to satisfy his need for American dollars." One bomb detonated in a suitcase that was about to be loaded onto a TWA flight to Los Angeles with 101 passengers; another exploded outside a Union City building housing a firm selling pharmaceutical drugs to Cuba; yet another was detonated outside a Weehawken building housing the New Jersey Cuban Refugee Program.[130]

In New York, the Cuban Mission to the United Nations was targeted, and assassinations planned against its personnel. In October 1979, Omega 7 took credit for bombing Cuba's U.N. Mission, slightly injuring three people. The Mission had also been bombed at its previous location in New York in 1976, and again in 1978.[131] Omega 7 narrowly missed assassinating Cuban Ambassador Raúl Roa García and his driver with a car bomb in March 1980. Then on September 11, 1980, Omega 7 militants gunned down an attaché to the Cuban Mission to the United Nations, Félix García Rodríguez, as he drove in his car.

Counterrevolutionary violence had targeted Cuban interests throughout the Caribbean, Latin America, and Canada since the early 1960s, as anti-Castro operatives carried out assassinations, kidnappings, and bombings against Cuban government personnel and interests. However, the diplomatic events of the mid-1970s provoked a fresh wave of violence, as anti-Castro forces sought to sabotage prospects for the normalization of relations.

The uptick in violence in 1976 reached a tragic climax on October 6, when Cubana de Aviación flight 455, carrying seventy-three passengers and crew, including the entire Cuban Olympic fencing team, was blown out of the sky near Barbados, killing all aboard in the most deadly act of aviation terrorism in the western hemisphere prior to September 11, 2001. CIA intelligence reports indicated that Orlando Bosch and Luis Posada Carriles, the latter a former CIA operative who had worked as a training instructor for the agency's anti-Castro operations, had planned the bombing in Caracas.[132] A month earlier, exiled Chilean economist Orlando Letelier, who had also served as the Chilean ambassador to the United States under the government of Salvador Allende, was assassinated in a car bomb attack in the Embassy Row neighborhood of Washington, D.C., less than a mile from the White House. The attack was traced to operatives of the organization run by Carriles and Bosch, Coordination of United Revolutionary Organizations, who had been recruited by agents of the government of Augusto Pinochet. Ronni Moffitt, Letelier's twenty-five-year-old U.S. assistant and coworker at the Institute for Policy Studies, was also killed.[133]

For the Maceo Brigade, the violence hit especially close to home. In January 1978, a bomb exploded outside Viajes Varadero Travel Agency in San Juan, Puerto Rico, which was run by Maceo Brigade member Carlos Muñiz Varela.

On April 28, as the Brigade planned their second contingent to Cuba, assassins shot the twenty-six-year-old Muñiz Varela to death near his mother's home in San Juan. Phoning in to a Miami radio station, a member of Omega 7 claimed responsibility for Muñiz Varela's killing in a communiqué: "This despicable fellow named Carlos Muñiz is the first one to fall in this Fidel-American plot," it read in part, "but he will not be the only one."[134] Less than one year earlier, the film *55 Hermanos* had included footage of Muñiz Varela condemning the bombing of Cubana de Aviación flight 455 as a "massacre" perpetrated by "counterrevolutionaries" as the Maceo Brigade visited a memorial dedicated to the victims to lay a large wreath of flowers.[135] Arriving in Havana soon after Muñiz Varela's assassination, the Maceo Brigade's second contingent was named in his honor. Nonetheless, the violence continued, with Omega 7 vowing to "consider any Cuban or Puerto Rican or American who travels to Cuba, no matter what his purpose, as our enemy."[136] Two more bombs exploded outside Viajes Varadero, now run by Varela's friend and Maceo Brigade member Raúl Álzaga, during the following two years, and Brigade members repeatedly received death threats. In Puerto Rico, the campaign of terror against progressive Cubans paralleled the repression against the island's independence movement, which similarly experienced targeted bombings and political assassinations orchestrated by armed rightwing formations, often with the knowledge of the FBI and the island's police.[137]

Terrorist groups repeatedly made good on Omega 7's promise to target any entity associated with the Cuban government, as well as any Cubans in the United States who advocated dialogue with Havana. In 1975, dialogue advocate Luciano Nieves was shot to death in the parking lot of a hospital where he had gone to visit his son. According to media reports, a group taking responsibility for the murder had attempted to kidnap Nieves in a bid to exchange him for political prisoners in Cuba.[138]

After anonymous callers threatened to blow up a school housed in the Holy Family Church in Union City because the church's leader had participated in the 1978 Havana dialogue, the church's replacement leader, Reverend Eduardo de Zayas, remarked that "terrorism here is worse than in the era of McCarthy. The accusation of communism comes against anyone who moves toward peace."[139]

The violence continued. On November 25, 1979, Omega 7 assassins targeted Union City community leader Eulalio José Negrín, a member of the "Committee of 75" who had participated in the 1978 Havana negotiations with Castro and had recently run for State Senate as a Republican, shooting him in front of his thirteen-year-old son. Colleagues of Negrín called for a federal investigation into the "systematic campaign of terror" against them, charging that previous requests to law enforcement had been ignored.[140]

Some perpetrators were tried and convicted. After Orlando Bosch fired upon a Polish freighter docked in Miami with an improvised bazooka, he was sentenced to ten years in prison in 1968. Paroled in 1972, he fled the United States, enabling his role in the deadly bombing of Cubana de Aviación flight 455 in collaboration with Luis Posada Carriles in Venezuela, as well as a string of bombings of Cuban embassies in Latin America. Carriles, the mastermind behind the bombing of flight 455 who had once been trained in demolition techniques by the CIA, was never convicted of the crime, and the United States rejected repeated extradition requests from Cuba and Venezuela after he settled in Miami.[141] In 1979, Valentín Hernández was convicted of the murder of Luciano Nieves and remained in prison until his parole in 2004. Hernández's suspected accomplice in the assassination, Jesús Lazo, was never apprehended. Eduardo Arocena, accused of ordering the assassination of Félix García Rodríguez, and of making an attempt on the life of Cuban diplomat Raúl Roa García, was sentenced to life in prison in 1984.[142] Then in 1991, Cuban exiles Virgilio Paz Romero and José Dionisio Suárez Esquivel were each sentenced to twelve years in prison for their part in the assassination of Orlando Letelier.[143] Two other men, Guillermo Novo Sampol and Alvin Ross Díaz, were later acquitted.[144]

Following Negrín's assassination, dialogue activists in Boston appealed to the FBI for protection. But while the bureau had closely monitored the violence, its investigative gaze also fell upon the victims. Indeed, appeals to the FBI for protection sometimes ended up in the bureau's voluminous surveillance files on the Maceo Brigade. According to one file notation, a member of the group filed a request through her lawyer because she had received a threat in the mail. A clipping from a newspaper in Miami that included a photograph of Maceo Brigade members, including herself, standing with Fidel Castro in Havana in 1978, had been mailed to her. Around the photograph were written words in Spanish that translated as: "The blood has not spilled in vain. To us who are suffering, you will pay." With the clipping was included an envelope bearing her mother's home address in Miami Springs, Florida.[145]

The FBI and the Maceo Brigade

The Maceo Brigade's alignment with the U.S. Left, together with its sympathetic assessment of the Cuban Revolution and its willingness to embrace

Marxist analysis, left the group vulnerable to accusations of Cuban control. Although other Cuban American organizations had received FBI attention, the Maceo Brigade's radicalism singled it out for special scrutiny.[146]

Nonetheless, like the bureau's investigation of the Venceremos Brigade, its files on the Maceo Brigade also contain much material that demonstrates the veracity of the group's claim's to be performing humanitarian work — namely, the reunification of the Cuban diaspora — and political advocacy for the normalization of U.S.-Cuba relations. The bureau's habit of making faithful representations of the group's aims but then attaching unsubstantiated claims of outside Cuban intelligence control remain a hallmark of its investigations of both the Venceremos and Maceo Brigades. One report alleged that the Maceo Brigade

> is an organization of young Cubans who have not participated in counter-revolutionary activities or were either born outside of Cuba of Cuban parents or born in Cuba but left at an early age. They believe in the lifting of the Cuban blockade, normalization of relations between the U.S. and Cuba, and the ending of "hostile actions toward Cuba by the U.S. and of terrorist groups in the Cuban community in the exterior." The AMB was organized and is controlled by the Cuban government for propaganda/intelligence.[147]

Claims of Cuban intelligence control of the Maceo Brigade were certainly enabled by the fact that the group's organizers planned their delegations in close association with the Cuban government, whose representatives had invited the group to visit the island and provided visas. The conduit through which all foreign delegations interacted with the Cuban government was ICAP, as well as the Cuban Mission to the United Nations in New York. Although the delegations were organized by the Maceo Brigade, the Cuban government exerted important influence, going as far as to screen applicants in an effort to detect CIA assets or right-wing infiltrators and saboteurs.

The FBI reports on the Maceo Brigade were based upon surveillance of the group, assessment of print materials such as *Baraguá*, and the testimony of informers within the Maceo Brigade. Using these sources, the bureau compiled detailed reports on the group. One, produced in 1984, alleged that the Dirección General de Inteligencia (DGI), Cuba's foreign intelligence agency with a function similar to that of the CIA, regarded the Brigade as "the most outstanding of all the political action organizations in the United States," one which "produces better leaders than the other organizations and actually generates leaders for other Cuban exile organizations."[148] However, the report goes further, claiming that the Maceo Brigade was "organized and controlled" by the Cuban government,[149] which allegedly used the group solely as a means through which to control the progressive Cuban émigré movement in the United States. The report also alleged that two of the Brigade's members had been recruited as intelligence agents, claiming that

> some of these Antonio Maceo Brigade leaders have received training in the training sub-section of the terrorist section of the Cuban Exiles Political Action Activities Department, a sub-directorate of the DGI. This training has been in the areas of ideology, psychology, organizing and propaganda techniques, interviewing techniques, and methods for collecting intelligence of value to the Cuban Intelligence Service. Two Brigade members who have received this basis [sic] intelligence training, _____ (redacted) and _____ (redacted) have been declared by the San Juan Office of the Federal Bureau of Investigation (FBI) as Intelligence Officers of the Government of Cuba and the Cuban Intelligence Service.[150]

Nothing came of these claims, however, and no Brigade members were ever arrested as foreign agents. Other claims within the 1984 FBI report are contradictory. For instance, the report notes that Cuba "does not currently furnish the Brigade with direct financial assistance,"[151] but goes on to state: "it is ... felt that the Brigade, as well as the VB, is partially financed by money obtained by the Government of Cuba from its narcotics activities abroad,"[152] a reference to prevailing claims that the Cuban government was actively involved in the Latin American drug trade. The same report does maintain that the Cuban government had funded both the Maceo Brigade and the Venceremos Brigade in the *past*. Based upon the claims of an informer within the Center for Cuban Studies in New York, the report states that "ICAP spends one million two hundred thousand Cuban pesos (approximately one million twenty thousand American dollars at the January, 1984 exchange rate) per year on the Antonio Maceo Brigade and the VB.... The Cuban government was financially subsidizing the Antonio Maceo Brigade for propaganda and other work in the American-Cuban exile community."[153]

However, the report provided no further information or documentation. Such figures might indeed be accurate if they referred to funds that Cuba expended housing, feeding, and transporting their U.S. visitors, which was the Cuban government's practice for almost all foreign solidarity delegations. The report, however, leaves the impression that the Cuban government was continuing to funnel money to the Maceo Brigade and the Venceremos Brigade to finance their political activities in the United States, activities that the FBI believed were dictated by ICAP on behalf of the Cuban intelligence agency. "It has been learned through sources," the report states, "that the DGI directs the Antonio Maceo Brigade to engage in active campaigns against United States policies on behalf of the Government of Cuba."[154]

No one from either the Maceo Brigade nor the Venceremos Brigade was ever arrested or charged in connection with these claims, most likely because they were never substantiated. It is unlikely that the FBI, having proof that a hostile foreign power was funding subversive political activity in the United States, and during the Cold War climate of the Reagan years for that matter, would elect not to prosecute.

In other cases the FBI's reports appear to reflect a lack of dissemination of intelligence data within the bureau, or simply subpar research. In a heavily redacted list of Maceo Brigade members and affiliates sent from the bureau's Washington Field Office to the Intelligence Division for background investigation, the summary of the activities of one member of the Brigade — the identity of the person is redacted — speculates that the subject traveled to Havana in 1978, "probably to attend a 'dialogue' with Castro." According to the report, "topics *supposedly* discussed were release of Cuban political prisoners, repatriation of U.S. citizens in Cuba, and Cuban Americans returning to Cuba to visit their families."[155] However, there was no need for the FBI to guess. The nature of the 1978 dialogue was well known by the FBI, because Benes debriefed the bureau's agents after each and every meeting with Cuban officials.[156]

Neither the FBI nor any other entity ever publicly produced any evidence that the Maceo Brigade was under the control of Cuban intelligence, nor that it received direct financial support from Havana. Although the Cuban government undoubtedly had a keen interest in cultivating supporters within Cuban communities abroad, the claim that the Maceo Brigade was merely a puppet of the Cuban government is simply not congruent with the group's organizational history or the available evidence.

Nonetheless, despite denials by the group's members, accusations that the Maceo Brigade was composed of "Castro agents" persisted for years. In 1993, cofounder Andrés Gómez defended the Maceo Brigade's now long-standing relationship with the Cuban government. "There is no question," Gomez admitted, "that the Antonio Maceo Brigade is a leftist organization that coincides with the goals and aspirations of the Cuban revolution. But sympathy and solidarity with the Cuban revolution do not mean being an agent. We receive no payments or instructions from Cuba."[157]

Like the FBI's allegations that members of the Venceremos Brigade were engaged in espionage activities for Cuba, similar allegations against the Maceo

Brigade are highly unlikely. In the case of the Venceremos Brigade, its members, who had been placed under FBI and CIA surveillance and likely had files associated with their names, were highly unlikely to ever receive high-level security clearance from the U.S. government, where they would be in a position to pass government secrets to Cuba. The Maceo Brigade's intelligence target, on the other hand, was assumed to be the rightwing Cuban political and paramilitary entities, but here the same problem applies. Members of the group, well known to the right-wing Cuban community because their names and photos appeared in a variety of tabloids, would be unlikely to ever successfully infiltrate anti-Castro groups. In this light, the FBI's assertions during the early 1980s that Maceo Brigade members were being recruited for intelligence work are dubious at best.

Epilogue

The Cold War returned to Washington with full force amid the dawning of the Reagan Revolution in 1980. Hope for a U.S.-Cuba reconciliation faded. Forced from the mainstream by Republican electoral victories, progressive politics retreated to the grassroots. They did not disappear, however, and the Maceo Brigade joined a host of other left-wing formations during the era that rejected Reagan's vision of "Morning in America." As historian Bradford Martin notes, progressive activists in the 1980s successfully dampened the most bellicose of the Reagan administration's foreign policy aims, particularly in Central America, where progressive advocacy in the United States likely averted a U.S. war in Nicaragua.[158] The Maceo Brigade continued to organize delegations to Cuba, and became a vehicle through which Cuban American leftists participated in a variety of progressive movements, particularly on the issue of U.S. foreign policy in Latin America.[159]

The Maceo Brigade helped create an unprecedented political space for Cuban American leftism, leading the radical edge of an emerging Cuban émigré progressive movement in the United States. Its impact was transnational and far-reaching. In Cuba, the Maceo Brigade played a key role in initiating a shift in Havana's policy toward Cuban emigrants, becoming the catalyst for a series of events that forever altered the relationship between the island and its diaspora. In the United States, the Maceo Brigade, composed overwhelmingly of young people and students, became an early precursor to the growing contemporary openness among Cuban American youth toward reconciliation with the Cuban government. Indeed, while the Cuban American voting bloc in South Florida remained a dependable constituency of the Republican Party for almost four decades, the Democratic Party's performance among Cuban American voters in the presidential elections of 2008, 2012, and 2016 suggests a sea change.[160] The continuing trend among Cubans in the state to favor the normalization of U.S. relations with Cuba represents a growing challenge to Washington's fading but still potent hostility toward the Cuban political system.

A number of the Maceo Brigade's early members remain critical defenders of the Cuban Revolution. Raúl Alzaga, writing in 2009, contended that *Areíto* magazine, the Maceo Brigade, and the Havana dialogue "represented the first major crack in the monolithic image of a rabidly counter-revolutionary Cuban community abroad. They represented a new option within an exile community that until then had been controlled by far-right violent groups."[161] Almost a dozen of the Maceo Brigade's "alumni" went on to pursue successful careers in academia, where many have produced scholarship related to Cuba and its diaspora.

Reflections on the Maceo Brigade's significance sometimes recall Carlos Muñiz Varela, who was assassinated just as the group took its full shape. In Cuba, Varela is remembered as part of the brief reunification that occurred within the Cuban diaspora at the end of the 1970s. Honored in Cuba with an elementary school and an orthopedic rehabilitation center both bearing his name, a plaque adorns the house where Varela was born in Colón, identifying it as a historical site. A monument in the town is dedicated to all Cuban victims of terrorism, with Varela's name appearing at the top of the list.[162] Years after Varela's assassination, Andrés Gómez, a participant in the Brigade's first contingent who would remain a leader within the Brigade in the 1990s and 2000s, would recall:

> Carlos contributed to [...] one of the Brigade's greatest accomplishments — the development in Miami and Puerto Rico of a more pluralistic and participative political climate on topics related to Cuba. The Brigade allowed Cubans abroad to reinsert themselves in their country's patriotic legacy, with the honor and privilege of having defended, against wind and tide, the sovereignty, freedoms and revolutionary process of the Cuban people from the same places dominated by their enemies.[163]

5

Assata Is Welcome Here

Black Radicalism, Political Asylum, and
the Diplomacy of Exile and Freedom

Ten million people had stood up to the monster. Ten million people only
ninety miles away. We were here together in their land, my little family,
holding each other after so long.
—**Assata Shakur,** closing lines, *Assata*

Through the "clutch of circumstance," I found myself in Cuba. I have
been away from my people for a quarter of a century. Much has changed.
The flight I commandeered all those years ago is still not over. It is a
flight without end.
—**William Lee Brent,** closing lines, *Long Time Gone*

ON NOVEMBER 3, 1979, headlines announced the prison break of JoAnne Chesimard,[1] a former Black Panther and a member of the organization's clandestine offshoot, the Black Liberation Army (BLA). As the *New York Times* reported it: "three black men who had come to visit Miss Chesimard, drew .45-caliber automatic pistols, seized two guards as hostages and commandeered a prison van.... The three men and the 32-year-old Miss Chesimard, who was serving a life term plus 65 years for murder and assault, were joined by a fifth confederate, tentatively described by authorities as a white woman. They fled in two cars ... the guards were released unharmed."[2]

Convicted in 1977 by an all-white jury of murdering a New Jersey State trooper, although no physical evidence indicated that she had been the shooter,[3] Chesimard's trial had been widely covered in the African American and left-wing press as a symbol FBI efforts to suppress black radical movements. One of New York's oldest black newspapers, the *New York Amsterdam News*, referring to Chesimard by the Yoruba and Muslim names that she had taken years earlier, did not conceal its jubilation at the news of the jail break. "[T]hey say three brave brothers and a sister went to fetch Assata Shakur from the cold confines of steel and stone where she had been held fast against her will. Who the four were, I know not. But, every Black person knows them and have met them in the collective unconscious mind of the race."[4]

Ascending to the top of the FBI's Most Wanted list amid a massive search, Shakur assumed the status of a folk hero. Supporters in New York and Los Angeles likened her to an escaped slave, posting their own notices in the windows of their homes: "Assata Shakur is welcome here."[5] But the woman dubbed the "soul of the Black Liberation Army"[6] by law enforcement officials and a "fanatical black Joan of Arc"[7] in lurid tabloid reports had vanished. Five years passed. And then, in an October 1987 report from Cuba, *Newsday* revealed that Shakur was living in Havana, where she had been granted formal political asylum by the government of Fidel Castro.

Shakur's sanctuary in Cuba recalled earlier episodes in which African American activists facing legal charges had found asylum there. Several dozen had taken refuge on the island since the early 1960s, a number that included members of the National Association for the Advancement of Colored People (NAACP), the Black Panther Party (BPP), and the Republic of New Afrika (RNA). The presence of U.S. asylees in Cuba during the late 1960s had rankled U.S. authorities, drawing media attention to the ties between Cuba's communist government and the U.S. radical Left and triggering calls for tougher sanctions against Havana.[8]

Coming amid the renewed Cold War acrimony of the Reagan era, however, Shakur's sanctuary would be different. For her U.S. supporters, Shakur's presence on the island symbolized the convergence of state repression against U.S. black radical movements, on the one hand, and Washington's indefatigable efforts to destroy the Cuban Revolution on the other. For the Cuban state, the provision of asylum for Shakur allowed it to extend concrete support to the remnants of the Black Panthers, the U.S. black freedom organization with which Cuba had forged its strongest ties historically. For U.S. officialdom, Shakur's sanctuary signaled Cuba's continuing ability to flout U.S. power in the hemisphere.

Yet Cuba's willingness to defy Washington through the provision of asylum to U.S. dissidents outlasted the Cold War. By the mid-1990s, as Cuba sank deeper into the malaise of economic collapse following the dissolution of its Soviet benefactor, the United States redoubled its efforts to apprehend Shakur. Although Washington and Havana maintained no active extradition treaty, the United States added the return of Shakur to its list of formal conditions for the normalization of diplomatic relations with Havana, wedding the fate of Shakur and other U.S. political asylees on the island to U.S.-Cuba relations. Both the Cuban government and Shakur hardened their resolve. When New Jersey's governor announced a $100,000 reward for Shakur's apprehension in 1998, Cuba's Foreign Ministry spokesman, citing his nation's "sovereign right" to grant political sanctuary to foreigners, countered that Shakur was not a criminal but a "well-known civil rights activist" who had fled from state repression.[9] As the FBI continued efforts to apprehend her, Shakur defiantly characterized herself as a "a 20th century escaped slave," and described Cuba, which had provided haven to thousands of war refugees and left-wing dissidents from across the Third World, as "one of the largest, most resistant and most courageous palenques that has ever existed on the face of this planet."[10]

Shakur's portrayal of post-1959 Cuba to a palenque,[11] the clandestine communities of escaped enslaved Africans and indigenous people that existed in the Caribbean during the era of slavery, provides an entry point through which to evaluate the complex politics of solidarity between revolutionary Cuba and the African American freedom struggle, a relationship that has increasingly been the focus of scholarship.[12] In particular, Shakur's political asylum on the island is a key part of the nexus between Cuba's project of revolutionary internationalism, which sought to forge strategic ties between Havana and left-wing allies across the Third World, and the global dimensions of U.S. black radicalism, which has sought to connect the freedom dreams of the black radical imagination to the wider African diaspora and to liberatory traditions worldwide.[13]

These linkages are illuminated in vivid terms within Shakur's own public statements and writings from exile. In characterizing Cuba as a "palenque," Shakur simultaneously signaled the island's extant status as a haven for oppressed people from across the decolonizing world, a political geography that included, in Marxist fashion, "internally colonized" African Americans and others whose political location inside the empire to the north had been forged by the historical and geopolitical forces of slavery and imperialism. As Trinidadian historian and social theorist C. L. R. James noted, Cuba's trajectory from slave colony to U.S.-dominated neocolony to independent nation existed within a peculiar Caribbean context, a region whose modern identity had been shaped in its most fundamental terms by plantation slavery. Cuba's revolution, according to James, embodied not only the singularly Cuban aspirations of its architects, but the revolutionary tradition of the wider black Caribbean, including that of the Haitian slave revolution. "What took place in French San Domingo in 1792–1804," James wrote, "reappeared in Cuba in

1958.... Whatever its ultimate fate, the Cuban revolution marks the ultimate stage of a Caribbean quest for identity."[14]

Shakur's asylum in Cuba remains one of the most historically important episodes within the complex relationship between post-1959 Cuba and the African American freedom struggle. At the apex of the civil rights and Black Power movements during the "long" 1960s era, Cuba provided formal political sanctuary to a small but influential group of U.S. black activists, making the African American freedom struggle an integral part of the island's relationship with both grassroots social justice movements in its northern neighbor and the nation's struggle against the power of Washington. For African American activists, asylum in Cuba provided not only legal refuge but also global political legitimacy.

Although black radicals facing charges were often vilified in the U.S. media as little more than common criminals, the Cuban government's provision of formal asylum imparted a powerful confirmation of their claims to be political refugees fleeing state-sanctioned persecution. Robert F. Williams, an NAACP member and advocate of black self-defense, was granted formal political asylum in Cuba in 1961. Student Nonviolent Coordinating Committee (SNCC) leader Stokely Carmichael toured the island in 1967, engaging in public displays of solidarity with Fidel Castro. The BPP sent an official delegation to the island in 1968, and Panther leaders Eldridge Cleaver and Huey Newton later obtained formal political asylum there. A number of members, former members, or self-styled affiliates of the BPP and the RNA hijacked airplanes to reach the island beginning in 1968, with several becoming long-term residents of Havana. Angela Davis visited the island following her release from prison in 1972 to recognize the Cuban government's role in the global campaign for her freedom while she was imprisoned.

Thirty years later, Shakur's metaphorical likening of Cuba to a "palenque" suggested the longevity of Cuba's place within the U.S. black radical imaginary, both as a potential site of sanctuary from U.S.-style racism and anti-left political repression, and as a more abstract terrain of liberatory possibility. This chapter examines Cuba's provision of political asylum[15] to Americans to illuminate the role that asylum and exile have played in the history of engagements between the Cuban Revolution and U.S. left-wing social movements, and to understand how these relationships have intersected with U.S.-Cuba diplomatic relations. The chapter focuses upon the experiences of African American asylees, who comprised the majority of long-term U.S.-affiliated political exiles on the island, and whose presence there ultimately proved the most influential to both left-wing social movements and to U.S.-Cuba relations.[16]

Political sanctuary became an avenue through which Havana extended tangible aid to the burgeoning black freedom movement to its north while simultaneously advancing its project of anti-imperialism vis-à-vis Washington. Capitalizing upon institutional racism and anti-left state repression in the United States, Cuba's provision of sanctuary to African American political asylees allowed the Cuban government to deploy a scathing critique of U.S. power, one that disputed Washington's claims to moral superiority in the arena of human rights. Positioning itself as a vanguard of Third World self-determination and facing a neighboring hostile superpower, Cuba's alliances with U.S. black radicals became intertwined with Havana's Cold War national security aims, which sought allies abroad and the undermining of Washington's capacity to isolate Cuba diplomatically and assault it militarily. Arriving in Cuba in 1984, over a decade after the Cuban government had classified her as a U.S. "political prisoner" during her incarceration in New Jersey, Shakur's presence on the island was a direct outgrowth of the historical ties between the African American freedom struggle and the Cuban Revolution.

As scholars such as Piero Gleijeses and Isaac Saney have demonstrated, the Cuban internationalist imaginary, while looking out most intently toward Africa during the 1970s and 1980s, when Cuba sent tens of thousands of soldiers and advisers to aid in anticolonial and left-wing movements, also embodied the aspirations of the larger Third World for independence and dignity.[17] Embodied in the slogan *"Patria Es Humanidad"*— Homeland is Humanity — words that later appeared in giant letters on a terminal of Havana's José Martí International Airport, Cuban revolutionary internationalism proposed that Cubans had a patriotic duty to stand in solidarity with all of the world's people, making the island the symbolic home of all global anticolonial freedom fighters.[18] Thus African American and other U.S. exiles arriving in Cuba from the early 1960s through the 1980s encountered not only Cubans, but also political refugees from throughout the decolonizing world, including wounded soldiers from Vietnam, orphans and wounded children from independence movements in Algeria, Ethiopia, Guinea-Bissau, Angola, and Namibia, and asylum-seekers from left-wing movements throughout Latin America who had come to Cuba for medical treatment, education, and technical training. Whereas Cuba's policy of foreign aid was primarily aimed at cultivating diplomatic goodwill and fomenting left-wing revolution in the Third World, Havana's bold provision of asylum to dissidents from its powerful northern neighbor adds an overlooked element to our understanding of the scope of Cuban foreign policy toward the United States.

Cuba's provision of asylum to Shakur and other U.S. dissidents also deepens our understanding of U.S.-Cuba state relations, widening the traditional Cold War framing of this conflict. Indeed, following the September 11, 2001, terrorist attacks, the specter of American radical exiles in Cuba helped fill the discursive void left by the decline of the Cold War, allowing Washington to update its 1982 designation of Cuba as a "state sponsor of terrorism" by highlighting the Cuban government's sheltering of Americans accused of terrorism, air hijacking, and murder. In the peculiar afterlife of the Cold War evident within the prosecution of the Bush administration's War on Terror, the United States now deployed the rhetoric of "antiterrorism" to bolster its attempts to marginalize Cuba within the world political system while demonizing the surviving legacies of black radicalism descended from the 1960s.

Havana's willingness to support radical left-wing movements in its northern neighbor, including through the provision of political asylum to embattled figures such as Shakur, constitutes an underexamined element of Washington's antagonism of post-1959 Cuba. Indeed, even as the Cold War recedes further into the past, Washington's ire over the presence of U.S. asylees in Cuba appears to be increasing. With the FBI's May 2013 addition of Shakur to its "most wanted terrorists" list and the increase of the reward for her apprehension to an extraordinary $2 million, the "bounty" for Shakur was now among the highest for any fugitive in the world. Shakur's status as a protected guest of the Cuban government provided the U.S. with one of its last remaining pretexts for its insistence that the aging communist regime poses a threat to American interests.

Curiously, despite her visibility as a historical figure, one who has become both iconic as a symbol of black resistance and notorious as the target of the FBI, Shakur has received far less scholarly attention than might be expected.[19] This is especially significant given the power of her iconography within the multiethnic U.S. Left, where she has been variously embraced as a folk hero of the receding Black Power era, a symbol of revolutionary black feminist agency, and a living embodiment of successful resistance to antiblack state power, one who is recognizable even within mainstream popular culture, first as the godmother of slain hip-hop legend Tupac Shakur and now as a canonized historical figure to the modern Black Lives Matter movement. As scholar Dylan Rodríguez contends, Shakur has represented "a venerated (if sometimes fetishized) signification of liberatory desire and possibility for many U.S. radicals and revolutionaries."[20]

Despite the lacuna in published scholarship, Shakur is salient to both the history of the African American freedom struggle and to U.S. relations with

Cuba, a nation that has sometimes been characterized as a U.S. neocolony that, like Shakur, "got away." As scholar Joy James notes, "Assata Shakur became a fugitive in the only communist country in the hemisphere. Cuba thus shares an 'outlaw' status with the black female fugitive it harbors."[21] The status of Shakur and other exiled U.S. radicals on the island, whose fate is now bound up with shifting tides of U.S.-Cuba diplomacy and unprecedented transformations within Cuba itself, may hold one key to understanding the future of relations between the United States and its Caribbean neighbor.

The Socialist *Palenque*

The fraught politics of asylum became a source of U.S.-Cuba diplomatic tensions almost immediately following the 1959 revolution. Several dozen members of the overthrown government of Fulgencio Batista, including some accused of torture and wartime atrocities, sought refuge in the United States, which subsequently refused to return them to Cuba to face trial. When some of the émigrés arrived in South Florida on hijacked airplanes and boats, the craft were not returned to Cuba. The unwillingness of U.S. authorities to return the hijacked property to the island contributed significantly to the increase in tensions between the two nations throughout the year of the revolution. Washington's refusal to return Cubans accused of crimes on the island would be a thorn in Havana's side throughout the next four decades, contributing to the perception among Cuba's leadership that the United States was not interested in diplomatic reciprocity with Cuba's new government.[22]

Havana, however, would soon engage in its own politics of sanctuary. The Cuban government's willingness to grant political asylum to Americans first burst into headlines in 1961, when Havana granted sanctuary to Mabel and Robert F. Williams. Leaders of the National Association for the Advancement of Colored People (NAACP) in Monroe, North Carolina, who had formed a black gun club to help local residents defend themselves against racial violence from white vigilantes and the Ku Klux Klan, the Williamses soon found themselves sought by the FBI on trumped-up kidnapping charges.[23] Making their way surreptitiously to Cuba, they received a heroes' welcome. Received by Fidel Castro himself, they were accorded a status akin to foreign diplomats and accompanied by the Cuban leader in public events. Speaking at Havana's Chaplin Theater in October 1965, Castro juxtaposed Cuba's status as a haven for global left-wing political refugees with the continuing emigration of Cubans to the United States seeking sanctuary from the upheaval wrought by the revolution against Batista. "Although it is true that certain citizens who have been brought up in accord with the ideas of the past prefer to leave for the United States," Castro argued, "it is also true that this country has become the sanctuary for the revolutionaries of this hemisphere."[24]

By invoking Cuba's newfound status as a global haven for persecuted leftists, Castro sought to both mitigate Cuban émigrés' charges of political repression in Cuba under the new revolutionary regime, and to position Cuba as an ally of anti-imperialist movements worldwide. Claiming that the Williamses had been "pursued by bloody and imperialist oligarchies," Castro argued that their political sanctuary in Cuba was justified by imminent need:

> This is not only a land for Cubans. It is a land for revolutionaries, and the revolutionaries of this hemisphere, including U.S. revolutionaries, have the right to consider themselves our brothers. Some leaders, like Robert Williams, who was brutally persecuted there, found asylum in this land. And like Williams, all those who are persecuted by the reactionaries and exploiters over there can find asylum here. It doesn't matter that he speaks English and was born in the United States. This is the homeland for the revolutionaries of this hemisphere.[25]

The legal framework for Cuba's provision of political asylum to foreigners was based, like all sovereign nations, in Article 14 of the Universal Declaration of Human Rights. Adopted by the General Assembly of the United Nations in 1948, the article asserted the right of all people of the world "to seek and enjoy in other countries asylum from persecution," albeit with a condition: "This right may not be invoked in the case of prosecutions genuinely arising from non-political crimes or from acts contrary to the purposes and principles of the United Nations."[26] Thus arose both the modern legal basis for Cuba's ability to grant formal asylum to foreign dissidents, and the right of their home countries to dispute the veracity of dissidents' claims to political persecution. The basis for Cuba's provision of asylum to U.S. citizens was further bolstered in December 1967, when the U.N. General Assembly adopted the Declaration on Territorial Asylum. Affirming that asylum granted by a nation, "in the exercise of its sovereignty," including to "persons struggling against colonialism, shall be respected by all other States," the language of the Declaration reinforced the inalienable right of nations to determine their own criteria for defining what, exactly, constituted legitimate political repression, asserting: "It shall rest with the State granting asylum to evaluate the grounds for the grant of asylum."[27]

Both the United States and Cuba would henceforth deploy this language to defend their provision of asylum to foreigners. The United States claimed that its Cuban asylees were refugees from communism and political repression, and Cuba claimed that American asylees were refugees from capitalist inequality, racism, and political persecution, the latter category also including potential defectors from the U.S. military during the Vietnam War.[28] The Declaration on Territorial Asylum coincided almost perfectly with the onset of the airline hijacking outbreak from the United States to Cuba in January 1968. Using the United Nations' framework for defining and assessing asylum, Cuban officials defended their provision of political sanctuary to U.S. air hijackers as a matter of "sovereign prerogative." When the Cuban government passed an antihijacking law the next year, at the height of the hijacking outbreak, the law, while condemning air piracy, nonetheless defended Cuba's right to determine the fate of all hijackers entering its territory. "The Cuban State, in exercise of its sovereignty, reserves the right to grant asylum whenever it deems it justified," Cuba's 1969 Law No. 1226 maintained, "to those persons who, because of political reasons, arrive in our country, having found themselves in the need of making use of this extreme resource to escape a real danger of death or grave repression."

Although air hijacking forced Cuban officials to differentiate between hijackers who appeared to be common criminals and those who appeared to be fleeing genuine political repression, virtually all Americans entering the country illegally, including those who claimed to be victims of political persecution, received at least temporary sanctuary. American political exiles in Cuba became the unwitting beneficiaries of Cuba's attempts to curtail the exceptionalism of the U.S. policy on sanctuary, which awarded Cubans reaching U.S. territory the status of political refugees while failing to recognize Cuba's legal right to accord Americans the same status in Cuba.

Sanctuary and the Cuban Press

U.S. black activists with some familiarity with Cuban cultural production and the island's press were not unjustified in assuming that Cuba's leaders, and indeed the Cuban public itself, might be sympathetic to their claims of political persecution. Cuban media coverage of the United States had painted a uniformly bleak portrait of life in *"el imperio,"* throughout the 1960s, particularly for African Americans and other people of color, for poor people, and for left-wing political dissidents. Cuban newspapers and periodicals such as *Granma* and *Tricontinental,* both of which had English editions and were widely read in the leftist circles in the United States, had provided detailed coverage of repression faced by the U.S. black freedom movement. In editorials and news coverage, Cuban journalists lambasted the horror of U.S. racial segregation and the televised brutality meted out to nonviolent demonstrators as proof of the poverty of America's Cold War claims to moral authority in the arena of political freedom.

Cuban press coverage of U.S. social movements was not confined to the English editions of the Cuban press intended primarily for North American audiences. Typical news briefs in *Bohemia*, Cuba's oldest magazine, in 1965 included, for instance, an article entitled "Racistas contra la Religión," about the arrest of Southern Christian Leadership Conference leader James Bevel, and one entitled "La Policía me Hirió" describing the death of Jimmie Lee Jackson, a civil rights activist shot by an Alabama state trooper.[29] *Verde Olivo*, the organ of the Cuban revolutionary armed forces, repeatedly detailed instances of U.S. police violence and corruption, and in 1969 covered the Camp Lejeune incidents, in which violence broke out between black and white Marines at a base in North Carolina.[30] John Clytus, an African American man from California who had come to Cuba in 1964 in search of a haven from U.S. Jim Crow racism but soon grew bitterly disillusioned with communism, later described the tone of the Cuban press coverage: "Newspaper headlines screamed about the racial unrest in the States. In every article, the 'Negroes' in the States were portrayed as being at the mercy of the Ku Klux Klan, the police, and police dogs."[31]

The abuse of prisoners in the United States had also attracted significant coverage in the Cuban press since the mid-1960s. In particular, Cuban journalists sought to illuminate the racial and economic dimensions of criminal sentencing, characterizing imprisonment as a political weapon deployed disproportionately against the poor. One article in *Verde Olivo* entitled, significantly, "La vida de un hombre vale un dollar"—"the life of a man is worth a dollar"—examined the practice of medical experimentation on U.S. prisoners, sponsored by pharmaceutical corporations and other moneyed interests in collaboration with doctors, comparing the ignominious practice to medical experimentation in Nazi Germany.[32] Coverage of the U.S. carceral state thus allowed Cuba to dispute the exceptionalism and selective memory of Washington's narrative of human rights, which condemned political incarceration in Cuba and other "unfriendly" nations, but failed to acknowledge the raced and classed politics of incarceration in the United States.

Lurid depictions of U.S. racial capitalism in the Cuban press had been supplemented, however, by consistent attention to the civil rights movement. By the late 1960s, Cuban media coverage also focused upon the anti–Vietnam War movement and the emergence of Black Power, foreign coverage that garnered notice in radical circles stateside. *Granma*, including its weekly English edition, repeatedly commemorated the August 1965 Watts rebellions and other urban conflagrations as evidence of the persistence of racism in U.S. society, while noting the conspicuous absence in Cuba of racial violence and urban unrest.[33]

State repression against the Black Panther Party was also regular fare in the Cuban media. When Chicago police assassinated Panther member Mark Clark, along with the chairman of the Illinois chapter of the party, Fred Hampton, as the latter slept in his bed in the predawn of December 4, 1969, *Granma* ran a photo of Panthers and community members filing past Hampton's open casket on its front page, beside an article about the LAPD's four-hour, military-style assault upon the Los Angeles headquarters of the Southern California chapter of the organization five days later.[34] William Lee Brent, a former Black Panther seeking to flee to Cuba in 1969 to avoid criminal charges stemming from a shootout with San Francisco police, cited the Cuban media's positive press coverage of the Black Panther Party as one of the factors leading him to believe that he might be welcomed there as a political asylee. "Shortly after I joined the Panthers I'd heard that revolutionaries who needed political asylum could get it in Cuba with no problem," Brent later wrote. "I considered myself a revolutionary and I certainly needed asylum."[35]

Solidarity with U.S. dissidents also surfaced as a regular theme in Cuban cultural production. When Angela Davis, a black radical professor and communist activist then teaching at the University of California, Los Angeles, was charged in connection to a deadly courtroom shootout in Marin County, California, in August 1970 and subsequently went into hiding to avoid capture, although she maintained her innocence, the Cuban government and its associated political and cultural ministries joined an international movement that rose in her defense. Cuban artists produced several iconic posters that would soon be reproduced around the world. In one, a stylized image of Davis's silhouette is emblazed with the words "libertad para Angela Davis"—freedom for Angela Davis—while another image shows Davis accompanied by the words "Los pueblos unidos jamas seran vencidos"—the people united will never be defeated.[36] Cuban singer and songwriter Pablo Milanés composed a song entitled "Canción para Ángela Davis" in 1971, with a later version recorded by legendary Cuban singer Silvio Rodríguez that is still widely remembered by Cubans who grew up during the era.

Cuba's rhetorical solidarity with the U.S. black freedom struggle was rendered in vivid hues by the Organization of Solidarity with the People of Asia, Africa, and Latin America (OSPAAAL), which produced a series of iconic posters, most of them multilingual, proclaiming the island's support for the

African American freedom struggle. On August 18, 1968, OSPAAAL sponsored a Day of Solidarity with the Struggle of Afro-Americans as a "tribute to the uprising of the black population of Watts" three years earlier, the events that became known as the Watts Riots.[37] Journalist and SNCC organizer Elizabeth Sutherland Martínez, traveling in Cuba to gather material for a book about Cuban society after the revolution, noted that "some sixty thousand Cubans showed up on two or three days' notice" to attend demonstrations staged for the Day of Solidarity.[38] OSPAAAL's poster commemorating the day, designed in collaboration with artist Emory Douglas, the Black Panther Party's Minister of Culture, combined black ink with bright shades of orange, purple, and blue and depicted Panthers, armed with rifles and wearing the group's signature berets, below the words "Solidarity with the African American People" followed by translations in French, Spanish, and Arabic. Another poster portrayed the death of George Jackson, a Black Panther gunned down by guards at San Quentin State Prison in August 1971 in an alleged escape attempt, showing the prostrate form of a black man with blood streaming out of bullet wounds pooling into a red, white, and blue puddle in the likeness of an American flag. The caption read: "Power to the People, George."

Other posters featured imagery and slogans justifying political violence in the service of black liberation. In one, a snarling panther, with bared fangs and red eyes and the words "Black Power" appearing in its snarling mouth, included below it the words "Retaliation to Crime: Revolutionary Violence" with translations appearing in smaller letters. With OSPAAAL's designation of August 18, 1970, as the "Day of international solidarity with the African American people," the organization produced a commemorative poster depicting a stylized image of an African American man holding a rifle inside an outlined shape of America, with the large words "we will destroy imperialism from the outside; they will destroy it from the inside."[39]

OSPAAAL's journal, *Tricontinental*, with an English edition circulated globally, had featured regular analysis of the waning civil rights movement and accelerating Black Power movement since August 1966. Like the Cuban periodical *Pensamiento Crítico*, which dedicated an entire issue to examining the Black Power movement in 1968 but was not translated into English, *Tricontinental*'s coverage of the African American freedom movement emphasized those aspects that evinced critiques of capitalism, linked the U.S. black struggle to global movements, and embraced the doctrine of self-defense and armed struggle as a means of achieving liberation.[40] Cuban periodicals had regularly amplified the voices of African American radicals within their pages.

Robert F. Williams edited a special issue of the literary supplement *Lunes de Revolución* in 1960, and essays by and interviews with activists such as SNCC leader Stokely Carmichael, Panthers Huey P. Newton and George Murray, and Venceremos Brigade activist Phil Hutchings filled *Tricontinental*'s pages later in the decade alongside coverage of ongoing anticolonial movements in the Congo and Guinea-Bissau, situating the African American freedom movement within a larger global context that included continental African anticolonial struggles.[41] In the magazine's inaugural issue in the summer of 1967, for instance, an essay by Carmichael entitled "The Third World: Our World" preceded one by Frantz Fanon analyzing the assassination of the Congo's Patrice Lumumba, and an article on the post-Lumumba guerrilla movement in that country.[42] Siding with the internationalism of the BPP and Carmichael over the gradualist integrationist vision of the Congress of Racial Equality and Martin Luther King Jr., Havana effectively chose sides within stateside debates about the direction of the African American freedom struggle. In the pages of *Tricontinental* and through high-quality cultural production, OSPAAAL signaled Cuba's support for black radicals in ways that located their movements within a global context of anti-imperial and antiracist struggle, raising Cuba's status within the U.S. black radical imagination as a diasporic ally and a potential sanctuary for those who claimed the mantle of political refugees.[43]

As pressure mounted from Washington and international human rights organizations during the mid-1970s over the presence of political prisoners in Cuba's own jails, the island's media again sought to deflect these accusations by running coverage that highlighted the links between incarceration and political repression in the United States. One *Granma* article in March 1977 entitled "Human rights in U.S. prisons?" cited a recent report by the American Medical Association documenting widespread medical neglect in the American prison system, including the finding that 15 percent of prisoners surveyed in thirty prisons suffered from a form of tuberculosis. The article went on to condemn incidents of medical testing conducted on U.S. prisoners, including the infamous Tuskegee syphilis experiments conducted on African American prisoners, a story that had broken in the U.S. media in 1972.[44] "Discrimination and racism continue to be basic elements of U.S. society," contended a May 1977 *Granma* article that contained a profile of Ella Mae Ellison, a young black woman and a mother of four who had been falsely accused of bank robbery and murder, and sentenced to life in prison.[45]

Framing the United States as a violator of its own people's rights, the Cuban media attempted to dispute the human rights narratives of the Ford

Cuba's recognition of the existence of political prisoners in the United States, particularly those from the African American freedom movement, had first gained visibility within Cuban cultural production in 1968 amid the "Free Huey" campaign in response to the jailing of Black Panther Party leader Huey P. Newton, and again in 1971 with the arrest and imprisonment of radical intellectual and communist activist Angela Y. Davis. Rafael Morante/OSPAAAL, 1971; courtesy of Docs Populi.

OSPAAAL poster publicizing the case of the "Wilmington 10" prisoners, a group of young African American activists wrongfully convicted of arson after a racially charged 1971 riot in Wilmington, North Carolina. The case, which became an international cause célèbre, allowed Havana to dispute the exceptionalism of Washington's narrative of U.S. democracy and human rights in the mid-1970s amid international pressure on Cuba to release its own political prisoners. Rolando Córdoba/OSPAAAL, 1979; image courtesy of Docs Populi.

Black Radicalism, Political Asylum, and the Diplomacy of Exile and Freedom   213

George Jackson, a prisoner who had became internationally renowned as a writer and a member of the Black Panther Party while incarcerated, was shot to death by prison guards in August 1971 during a rebellion at San Quentin State Prison. Although Jackson never visited Cuba, his writings and legal case had been publicized by the Cuban media, due in part to advocacy by Angela Davis. Rafael Morante/OSPAAAL, 1971; image courtesy of Docs Populi.

and Carter administrations, which asserted that U.S.-style liberal democracy was a bulwark in defense of universal freedoms. News coverage of the United States in *Granma International* went to lengths to point out the mendacity of Washington's claims to moral superiority, creating a tabloid of horrors with headlines such as "U.S. Official Agency Admits to Having Considered Putting Fungicides in Foodstuffs for Mexicans to See if Cancer Resulted" and "Constitutional Amendment on Equal Rights for Women Rejected in Florida."[46] When the U.S.-based National Conference of Black Lawyers and other racial justice organizations submitted a petition to the U.N. Commission on Human Rights in December 1978 calling attention to widespread violations of the rights of people of color in the United States, including the presence of a number of jailed activists that the report identified as political prisoners,[47] *Granma* seized upon the story, publishing an article lambasting what it called the "imperialist fabrication" of U.S. claims to be a global beacon of political freedom. Including a photo of Assata Shakur, who *Granma* identified as a "poetess and historian ... a courageous activist in the black civil rights movement" and a political prisoner, the article's cataloguing of violations of political freedom in the United States was typical of the state-run newspaper's coverage of U.S. affairs during the 1970s:

> Political repression in the United States takes the form of street arrests of demonstrators; intimidation of trade union and student organizations; the keeping of police files on hundreds of thousands of people who oppose the imperialist political system; the tapping of telephones and the opening of mail on a large scale; the infiltration of progressive organization [sic] by agents, informers, and provocateurs; and the fabrication of charges backed by false testimonies so that the "troublemakers" can be put away in one of the 400 federal prisons. Among these thousands of political prisoners, isolated and hidden away by the authorities, are Indians imprisoned after the protest at Wounded Knee in 1970; black citizens imprisoned for their civil rights activities; and Chicanos and Puerto Ricans. It is often sufficient that social activists rank among the dispossessed for them to find themselves political prisoners, labeled by a web of falsehoods as "common criminals."[48]

Featured in major publications such as *Granma*, the central organ of the Central Committee of Cuba's Communist Party and the island's most ubiquitous newspaper, and *Bohemia*, the nation's most venerable periodical, Cuban media coverage in the late 1970s also contained another subtext. It confirmed that the Cuban government remained sympathetic to left-wing social justice movements in the United States, and that Havana recognized state repression as an important obstacle confronting progressive social movements there. Coming after Cuba had provided formal political asylum or temporary protection to several dozen American dissidents, including both little-known air hijackers and high-profile figures such as Huey Newton and Eldridge Cleaver, and during a time when the U.S. government was increasing its pressure on Havana to extradite U.S. political asylees and fugitives on the island, the press coverage in *Granma* signaled that Havana intended to stand firm in its commitment to provide aid to U.S. asylum seekers. The article's contention that the term "common criminals" had been falsely attached to legitimate political dissidents in the United States must be read in light of the Cuban government's granting of asylum to Americans accused of criminal acts, including armed actions such as bank robberies and bombings, that U.S. authorities maintained had no political import. Havana's willingness to challenge Washington's efforts to define the parameters of legitimate political struggle for

African Americans lies at the very heart of Cuba's provision of asylum to Assata Shakur and other U.S. black radical activists.

Revolution in America

When Robert F. Williams's self-defense cadre, the Black Armed Guard, repelled a Ku Klux Klan legion that was attempting to block an integration campaign in Monroe, North Carolina, in 1957, they acted within a longer arc of armed black resistance to white supremacist terrorism and vigilante violence stretching from Reconstruction through the civil rights era.[49] Long obscured within historiography, including the emergent civil rights scholarship of the 1960s, the history of armed black self-defense adds an important dimension to modern understandings of the post-Emancipation African American freedom struggle, one which has increasingly received significant scholarly attention.[50]

Yet if African American self-defense and armed political struggle was a buried history in the 1960s popular imagination of the United States, the same was not true in Cuba. Although the island's revolutionary leadership and state press supported Martin Luther King Jr. and the integrationist demands of the civil rights movement, it was the personas of radical figures such as Robert F. Williams, Malcolm X, Stokely Carmichael, Angela Davis, and Huey P. Newton who electrified the imaginations of Cubans during the 1960s. According to LeRoi Jones, Cubans had cheered Williams on the street "everywhere he went" as he strolled around wearing a pistol during his visit to the island in 1960, owing to the Cuban media's publicizing of his confrontations with white supremacists. When Williams received word in Havana that the Klan had threatened to bomb his family's house in North Carolina, Williams, still armed, marched into the United States Embassy, with a reluctant Jones in tow, and threatened to shoot the U.S. ambassador if he failed to contact North Carolina officials to arrange protection for his family.[51] The Williamses advocacy of armed defense in the face of white vigilante intimidation contributed to the hero's welcome that he received in Cuba upon arriving there as a political refugee in 1961 — an early indication of Havana's willingness to contest Washington's criminalization of African American armed political action.[52]

For Cuba's revolutionaries, armed struggle, not pacifist protest, would become the legitimate methodology of black freedom on U.S. soil. Commemorating the August 1965 Watts rebellion in the pages of *Tricontinental*, OSPAAAL proclaimed that "Black Americans took up arms to fight against 400 years of fascism," a struggle whose aims, OSPAAAL contended, included "the destruction of the economic, political, and social system prevailing today in the United States."[53] With the ascendance of a militant and internationalist wing of SNCC, associated with figures such as Carmichael and H. Rap Brown, followed by the meteoric rise of the Black Panther Party to global attention in 1968, Cuba's leadership and the island's media effectively chose sides within the African American freedom movement, vigorously promoting the doctrine of armed struggle as the only viable means to achieve black liberation. By collapsing spontaneous and often unfocused urban rebellions such as Watts, Newark, and Detroit within the formal political aims of the Black Power movement, Cuban editors and political theorists drew from the boiling rhetoric of the movement to produce an optimistic but oversimplified assessment of U.S. black radical politics.

Rhetoric was one thing; armed revolution was a different matter entirely. Despite the Cuban media's flamboyant public stance in support of the right of African Americans to overthrow a system that oppressed them, privately the Cuban government was more cautious. Cuban leaders, many of whom were veterans of the armed guerrilla struggle against Batista, appear to have issued unequivocal statements to visiting American radicals in the late 1960s who sought guidance from their Cuban hosts. Popular revolution, most Cuban officials believed, was not feasible in the U.S. because the "objective conditions" required to support a successful revolution within the wider society simply did not exist.[54] Antiracist armed struggle in the heart of the United States might be a just war, but it was not a winnable one.

The assessment of the Cubans, of course, was not novel. Martin Luther King Jr. had articulated a similar concern in a 1959 essay on nonviolence, written in response to Robert F. Williams, whose right to deploy the tactics of armed self-defense in North Carolina King had supported. Although King opposed "violence as a tool of advancement" for moral reasons, the sacrifice of human life that would inevitably follow it being chief among them, there were also strategic ones that paralleled the reservations of the Cuban government. The use of offensive political violence, King argued, placed its wielders in "a position where they confront a far larger adversary than it is possible to defeat in this form of combat."[55] King's critique of political violence was therefore tactical as well as moral. As seen in chapter 2, Cuban officials repeatedly insisted to zealous American radicals, including from the Weather Underground and the Black Panther Party, that they would be better served by directing their energies into building mass-based popular movements to fight for social justice in the heart of the empire.

Nonetheless, Havana did not dismiss outright the violent revolutionary dreams of some Americans. While the Cuban media had provided sympathetic coverage of urban rebellions throughout the mid- and late 1960s, with *Granma* repeatedly defending the right of African Americans to "shake the foundations of the power structure," it was black radicals' ability to situate the African American freedom struggle within an international context that resonated most strongly with the Cuban and Third World revolutionaries whom they encountered on the island.[56] Panther activists visiting Cuba found receptive ears when they positioned the African American freedom struggle within the global continuum of colonization and decolonization, a transformation that was being wrought by both peaceful and violent means. Panther leader George Murray, speaking at the OSPAAAL conference in Havana in August 1968, vowed that the struggle of African Americans, waged with rocks, guns, and Molotov cocktails as urban rebellions had flared after the April assassination of Martin Luther King Jr., was part of a global uprising of the colonized, one that reached even into the heart of North America. "We recognize," Murray proclaimed, "that we are a colony within the imperialist domains of North America and that it is the historic duty of black people in the United States to bring about the complete, absolute, and unconditional end of racism and neocolonialism by smashing, shattering, and destroying the imperialist domains of North America. In order to bring humanity to a higher level, we will follow the example of Che Guevara, the Cuban people, the Vietnamese people."[57]

Privately too, Cuban officials intimated that they recognized African Americans' right to wage their struggle by any means necessary. Charlie Hill, a member of the Republic of New Afrika who arrived in Cuba in 1971 on an airplane that he had hijacked with two comrades, all of whom hoped to travel on to Africa to fight in Cuban-supported anticolonial movements, maintains that some of the Cuban officials that they interfaced with supported armed struggle in the United States "morally," but made it clear that Cuba would not support it materially — that is, through the provision of military training, funding, or logistical support.[58] Nehanda Abiodun, a former member of the Black Liberation Army who arrived in Cuba as a political asylee in 1990, also insists that while the Cubans acknowledged that African Americans had a "right" to resist oppression through armed struggle, they viewed such efforts as irresponsible at best, and suicidal at worst. "What was said to me was that you cannot wage armed struggle without mass support," Abiodun later recalled.[59] "Until you have a mass organization that can support those who are doing armed struggle, all is for naught."[60] Hill's and Abiodun's claims about

Cuba's position on armed revolution in North America are echoed by numerous other American radicals who tried to acquire military training in Cuba,[61] and is confirmed by a former Cuban intelligence officer who was responsible for screening a number of arriving American leftists, including Eldridge Cleaver.[62]

Understanding Havana's position on clandestine political action in the United States is important for contextualizing Cuba's provision of formal asylum to American dissidents accused of engaging in acts of political violence. The Cuban government's intermittent discouragement of armed action inside the United States was tempered by an apparent hesitance to condemn it outright. This was likely due to several factors. First, Cuban officials were acutely aware of the improbable odds that had been arrayed against their own revolutionary victory in 1959, an event that had inspired leftists worldwide in part because it suggested that a small group of determined rebels, employing the classic tactics of guerrilla warfare, could overthrow a modern government and seize political power. As some American radicals arriving in Cuba had reminded their hosts, the initial force of rebels that had sailed from their clandestine staging area in Mexico and landed in eastern Cuba with Fidel Castro in December 1956 numbered barely eighty people. Within a few days, only a dozen remained alive, but the small guerrilla cell slowly grew, owing to popular support in the Cuban countryside. On the eve of the *fidelistas'* final march into Havana on New Year's Day 1959, the regular fighting force numbered barely three thousand men and women. The guerrilla groups operating in the urban theater of the war were similarly modest. While Cuban leaders maintained that conditions in late-1950s Cuba were starkly different from those in 1960s North America, it also remained true that the Cuban Revolution had triumphed in the face of seemingly insurmountable odds.[63]

Looking to Third World revolutionary movements for inspiration and validation, clandestine U.S. formations attempted to deploy scaled-down versions of Third World guerrilla tactics inside U.S. cities. Chief among these groups were the Black Liberation Army (BLA), itself an outgrowth of the Black Panthers; the Weather Underground Organization (WUO), an offshoot of Students for a Democratic Society (SDS); and the Puerto Rican Fuerzas Armadas de Liberación Nacional (FALN) and the Macheteros, both of which grew out of a dramatic upsurge in Puerto Rican independence activity. All of these organizations forged relationships of some kind with Cuba. Departing from the doctrine of self-defense, all three groups advocated armed actions directed against the U.S. government and its proxies. As the Vietnam War raged on in the early 1970s, the WUO hoped to strike back at the U.S. military apparatus from within, "bringing the war home" and "avenging" the bombs dropped on Indochina, which had not been halted by the conventional antiwar movement, with revolutionary violence aimed at U.S. government and military installations.[64] The FALN is alleged to have carried out a string of bank heists and a campaign of over 100 bombings on U.S. soil in what they conceptualized as an anticolonial war for the independence of Puerto Rico, with at least symbolic Cuban support. Two New York–born Puerto Rican nationalists — William Morales and Víctor Manuel Gerena, pursued on charges of murder, terrorism, and bank robbery — retreated to Cuba in the 1980s, where they remain under formal political asylum. The BLA is alleged to have carried out a string of clandestine actions, ranging from bank robberies staged to finance their operations and fund community programs, intimidation and robbery of local drug dealers, and is accused of the assassinating over a dozen police officers in retaliation for police killings of African Americans.[65] "Revolutionary violence," BLA members wrote, "is . . . a strategy designed to drive the capitalist system further into crisis."[66]

Recognizing the likely outcome of their efforts, the BLA appears to have foreseen precisely the type of scenario that ultimately led one of their most high-profile members, Assata Shakur, to appeal for foreign sanctuary after escaping from prison in 1979. In a communiqué two years prior, the BLA had noted that U.S. government repression in response to the group's activities made necessary "the establishment of principles of political sanctuary beyond the shores of the imperialist U.S.," including locations for political asylum.[67]

Nonetheless, Shakur eventually distanced herself from armed struggle as a feasible strategy for effecting political transformation in North America. In her autobiography, Shakur explained the pitfalls of what she called "substitut[ing] military for political struggle":

> Some of the groups thought they could just pick up arms and struggle and that, somehow, people would see what they were doing and begin to struggle themselves. They wanted to engage in a do-or-die battle with the power structure in amerika, even though they were weak and ill prepared for such a fight. But the most important factor is that armed struggle, by itself, can never bring about a revolution. Revolutionary war is a people's war. And no people's war can be won without the support of the masses of people. . . . It was inconceivable that we could survive, much less win anything, without their support.[68]

It is beyond the scope of this book to evaluate either the veracity of U.S. law enforcement claims regarding individual actions attributed to the BLA and

220 Black Radicalism, Political Asylum, and the Diplomacy of Exile and Freedom

Appropriating a well-known image created by Emory Douglas, the famed Black Panther Party artist who was also the group's minister of culture, Cuban artist Lázaro Abreu depicts armed Panthers as signifiers of African American militancy and a representation of Havana's recognition of the group as the highest expression of the U.S. black freedom struggle. Lázaro Abreu/OSPAAAL, 1968; image courtesy of Docs Populi.

other armed groups, or to provide a more nuanced examination of left-wing paramilitary activities in the United States. However, given that a significant number of the Americans who were granted sanctuary in Cuba had either participated in armed actions in the United States, had been falsely accused of participation by U.S. officials, or had traveled to Cuba in hopes of continuing on to Africa or Latin America to join armed movements there, the history of left-wing revolutionary violence in America during the 1960s and 1970s remains an important area of inquiry for understanding Cuba's provision of political asylum to American radicals.[69]

Profiles of Exile

The experiences of Americans who became long-term political asylees in Cuba varied widely according to their individual circumstances. Assata

Shakur and Nehanda Abiodun, whose legal cases were known in Cuba before either arrived seeking asylum, received a high level of government patronage and access to resources. Eldridge Cleaver, who arrived on the island with the aid of Cuban military personnel, was similarly provided with a high degree of assistance once on the island, although Cleaver's time on the island would eventually become tainted by conflict with Cuban authorities. Others, including William Lee Brent, Michael Finney, and Charlie Hill, who arrived as airline hijackers in 1969 and 1971 and are additionally examined in chapter 3, were subsequently screened and detained in Cuban prisons pending approval of their asylum and experienced a more complex transition to life on the island as a result of entering the country illegally and without prior contact. Although all three were subsequently granted asylum and eventually made successful lives for themselves in Cuba, they did so with less direct assistance from the Cuban government. The following portraits of U.S. exiles in Cuba, constructed from available sources and oral history,[70] provide a window into their lives and the political condition of exile in Cuba.

ELDRIDGE CLEAVER

The Minister of Information for the Black Panther Party whose memoir, *Soul on Ice*, had become a bestseller and defined its author as one of the era's prominent organic radical intellectuals, Cleaver arrived in Cuba on Christmas Day, 1968.[71] Known for his oratorical ability, fiery rhetoric, and advocacy of armed revolution, Cleaver sought legal sanctuary in Cuba as a result of charges stemming from a shoot-out with Oakland police. On April 6, 1968, as urban uprisings engulfed cities across the nation following the assassination of Martin Luther King Jr., Cleaver had led a dozen Panthers in an ambush attack on Oakland police officers, wounding two. Pursued, Cleaver and another Panther, seventeen-year-old Bobby Hutton, engaged the police in a ninety-minute gunfight before being cornered and forced to surrender. Police took Cleaver into custody but murdered the unarmed Hutton, although the teenage Panther had surrendered.[72] Cleaver and the Panther leadership claimed that police had initiated the attack. However, in 1980, Cleaver publicly admitted what others had long alleged: that he and a renegade group of Panthers, acting in defiance of Huey Newton's directives against spontaneous violence in the wake of King's assassination, had taken to the Oakland streets in cars looking for police officers to shoot in retaliation to brutal police responses to the urban rebellions unfolding in cities nationwide.[73] "I will tell anybody that that was the first experience of freedom that I had," Cleaver remarked in an interview years later. "I was free for an hour and a half because during that time the repressive forces couldn't put their hand on me because we were shooting it out with them."[74] Nonetheless, when the Cuban government accepted Cleaver's request for legal sanctuary, Havana had almost certainly received the Panthers' official version of the shoot-out, which conformed to the narrative of ruthless police repression that would have elicited sympathy from the Cubans.

Cleaver's task now was to reach Cuba. He briefly considered hijacking an airliner, but discarded the plan due to the fact that he was under heavy police surveillance. In his 1978 sequel memoir, *Soul on Fire*, Cleaver recounted the mad rush by his supporters to secure a viable route to the Caribbean: "A couple of white sympathizers offered to hijack a jet (with hand grenades) and whisk me off to the islands."[75] In the end, Cleaver slipped out of Berkeley disguised as an elderly man with glasses and unkempt hair — members of the San Francisco Mime Troupe had helped arrange his "costume"[76] — and flew to New York, then Montreal. Escorted by uniformed Cuban personnel aboard a Cuban freighter departing from Canada, Cleaver was instructed to hide in a small cabin on the ship, and sometimes within its closet, for the duration of the two-week voyage to avoid being recognized by the ship's civilian passengers, in case any might be U.S. government informants.[77] The Cuban government thus intended Cleaver's passage to the island, and presence once there, to be entirely covert.

With Huey Newton in prison and Chief of Staff David Hilliard now facing legal charges of his own, Cleaver's Cuban exile was intended to preserve the Panthers' leadership structure.[78] But Cleaver had additional plans. In Cuba, he hoped to commence operations at a secret facility where the Cubans had ostensibly promised to provide guerrilla training for members of the Party. Cleaver had already seen the site on a previous visit to the island and later claimed to have received weapons training there.[79] Cleaver also hoped that the Cuban government would provide the Panthers with a radio program akin to Robert F. Williams's program several years earlier, *Radio Free Dixie*, which had broadcast on Radio Havana Cuba, and to facilitate the production of print propaganda.[80] While Radio Havana Cuba had regularly broadcast interviews with Panther leaders and continued to do so while Cleaver was on the island, no dedicated program was forthcoming. Cleaver would later become bitterly disappointed by the Cuban government's failure to support these plans. But in the fall of 1968, with Cleaver in dire need of a foreign sanctuary, the Caribbean nation appeared to be an ideal refuge. "Cuba was our first choice," Cleaver later wrote. "We did not suspect that the Cubans were playing a double game, that the rules had changed; and the opportunities in the Castro island seemed ideal in many ways. They were Communists, blacks had a share in the power, and they were close enough to America for a return of guerrilla forces."[81]

Cleaver was installed in a commodious apartment in a high-rise on Calle L in the heart of Havana's Vedado district. He was assigned two officers from the Ministry of the Interior — one black, one white — whether for his protection or to watch over him, he was not sure. According to journalist Lee Lockwood, "Cleaver's Cuban hosts had made it clear that he was a welcome guest as long as he chose to remain, but that he must keep his presence quiet and refrain from overt political activity for the time being."[82] Cleaver was taken on a tour of the island, during which time one of the Ministry of the Interior officers checked out two AK-47 rifles so that he and Cleaver might go hunting.[83] But upon returning to Havana, Cleaver's impressions of Cuba soured. It soon became clear that no Black Panther training facility would be made available, nor was a radio program forthcoming. Although several other Panthers, including Alprentice "Bunchy" Carter of the party's Los Angeles chapter and Bobby Seale, were reportedly waiting for the word to rendezvous with Cleaver in Havana, the Cuban government, perhaps having second thoughts about a Panther training base on the island, appears to have deliberately stalled their arrival until after Cleaver left Cuba for Algeria.[84] As detailed in chapter 2, the Cuban government's unwillingness to arm and train Black Panthers for guerrilla warfare in the United States, which the Cubans considered a reckless and foolhardy proposition, was a major factor in Cleaver's disillusionment with his Cuban hosts.

But the Panther leader soon developed other reservations. Adding to his uneasiness was the realization that Cuba's claims to racial democracy appeared to have been exaggerated. While Cuba's revolutionary process had sought to redistribute the nation's wealth and had ameliorated many significant markers of racial inequality, the Cuban government appeared to be making little effort to remedy one conspicuous feature of the new government's leadership, one that had also troubled Stokely Carmichael the year before: its continued composition largely of white or light-skinned Cubans in the upper echelons. Other discoveries about Cuba's racial climate disquieted Cleaver. The government, he claimed, appeared to be trying to discourage Afro-Cubans from embracing "natural" hairstyles and African clothing. "Their analysis," Cleaver later theorized, "was that . . . cultural-nationalism leads to Black Power."[85] For Cleaver, the perceived threat of Afro-Cuban political power to Cuban revolutionary regime was symbolized most poignantly by the contrast between the nationalist martyrs Antonio Maceo and José Martí in Cuba's historical memory and contemporary cultural imaginary. While José Martí's image was ubiquitous in Havana, Maceo was considerably less visible. And while the writings of Martí, formulated as the intellectual father of modern Cuban nationalism, were widely available, Cleaver had difficulty procuring writings about Maceo.

Hoping to learn more about the legendary military strategist, Cleaver eventually visited the "National Library,"[86] only to be told that the leader's writings were in a restricted archive.[87] Read through Cleaver's longtime support for interracial coalition politics between radical black and white activists in the United States, Cleaver's critical perception of Cuban racial politics is significant. For whereas his belief in the sincerity of white radical supporters of the Black Panthers[88] was predicated, however, upon the preservation of an autonomous black leadership, the Cuban situation appeared exactly the opposite to his North American eyes: an apparently nonblack regime requesting the allegiance of a multiracial society that included several million Afro-Cubans.

Cleaver's perceptions of Cuba were also influenced by the timing of his arrival, which coincided with the peak of the outbreak of air hijacking from the United States to Cuba. Some American hijackers had become disillusioned with Cuba as a result of the typical Cuban regimen for foreign hijackers, which included incarceration, lengthy background checks, and often "volunteer" stints cutting sugarcane in Camagüey, a province in central Cuba. Despite his growing misgivings about the Cuban government, however, Cleaver shared Cuban officials' perceptions of some of the U.S. hijackers as mentally unstable individuals or opportunist criminals, and was sympathetic to the Cubans' concern that some might be U.S. spies. Cuba's imprisonment and scrutiny of hijackers entering the country, Cleaver maintained later, was necessary for reasons of "security."[89] Nonetheless, some of the hijackers had been Black Panthers or affiliates of the organization, and Cleaver soon established contact with them in Havana. Upon learning that one hijacker in the city had been the first black hijacker from the United States to reach Cuba, Cleaver invited the man to meet him, but was taken aback by the hijacker's summation of life in Cuba: "he was so cynical about Cuba, that it was impossible to talk to him. He was totally, completely negative."[90] But if Cleaver was not at first sympathetic to the claims of some hijackers, he soon came to share with them a certain camaraderie borne of mutual disillusionment. "We [all] kind of went there, very naïve — open-minded and idolizing Cubans."[91] Cleaver's Vedado apartment soon became a hangout for dispirited black U.S. hijackers and a group of young Afro-Cubans.

Cleaver soon began to organize his guests, among them a hijacker from Louisiana named Raymond Johnson,[92] into a Cuban section of the Black Panther Party. Cubans in the area reportedly began referring to the apartment as the *casa de las panteras*.[93] Although Cleaver likely did not regard himself as a permanent resident of Cuba and may not have intended the group of new Panther recruits, numbering approximately nine U.S. recruits and an unknown number of Cubans, to be a formal chapter of the organization (unlike the International Section that he would soon establish in Algeria, whose membership similarly included several American air hijackers[94]), Cleaver's actions were met with disapproval from his Cuban hosts. Although willing to provide political asylum to Americans, the Cubans' request for Cleaver to maintain a low profile likely grew from Havana's perception that openly harboring Cleaver, wanted in the United States for his role in ambushing the police officers, could provoke U.S. retribution. Cuban officials also likely viewed the organizing of a wing of a foreign-based political group, particularly one from the United States, as an infringement upon Cuba's sovereignty. Nonetheless, Cuban officials' response to the group's formation must also be viewed alongside the Cuban government's tendency to stifle expressions of black "race-based" political initiatives on the island during the period.[95] While calls for Afro-Cuban racial solidarity had long existed on the island, the arrival of a distinctly U.S. variant, one influenced by both the black internationalism of the Black Panthers and the black cultural nationalism that was increasingly gaining currency in the United States, was viewed by some as a North American racial logic ill-suited to Cuba and by others as a threat to the island's racial status quo.

Cleaver's relations with his Cuban hosts soured further after Cuban officials announced that some of the disgruntled U.S. hijackers, some of whom had refused to either work or enter university studies, as was required of Cubans, would have to leave Cuba. Cleaver and the group of newly anointed American and Cuban Panthers decided to resist the deportation, sheltering the hijackers inside the large apartment. Cleaver then rashly informed the Cubans that they had weapons in the apartment, including the two AK-47s, which had apparently been left in the apartment and were now in Cleaver's possession.[96] As tensions escalated, Cleaver's presence in Havana was betrayed to a *Reuters* reporter in the city; the Cubans in turn accused Cleaver of blowing his own cover to encourage foreign media coverage of the situation. News of Cleaver's presence in Cuba was immediately front-page news in the United States. The Cuban government, now under U.S. government pressure and seeking to defuse the problem of the *casa de las panteras*, agreed to provide Cleaver with safe passage to Algeria.[97] There, Cleaver was joined by other Panthers, including several air hijackers, establishing an International Section of the Black Panther Party. The U.S. government did its best to make life difficult, declaring Cleaver a Cuban national, thereby preventing him from collecting royalties from *Soul on Ice*, upon which he had depended for income.[98]

Cleaver would remain disillusioned with Cuba for years. Motivated by his growing anticommunism and political turn to the Right, as well as his residual resentment of his experience in Havana, Cleaver continued to fire off invectives against the Cuban government in interviews. In his 1978 memoir *Soul on Fire*, which chronicles his transformation from radical left-wing firebrand to born-again Christian and an admirer of his former archnemesis, Ronald Reagan, Cleaver referred to Cuba as "Castroland," and characterized his exile on the island as "six months in a wretched and restless existence — sort of a San Quentin with palm trees, an Alcatraz with sugar cane."[99] As for Fidel Castro, Cleaver had harsh words. "The white racist Castro dictatorship is more insidious and dangerous for black people than is the white regime of South Africa, because no black person has illusions about the intentions of the Afrikaners, but many black people consider Fidel Castro to be a right-on white brother. Nothing could be further from the truth."[100] Viewing Cuba's revolution now through the prism of both his experiences on the island and his newfound right-wing worldview, Cleaver charged that although "it's true that people were eating better than under Batista, that they held jobs and enjoyed improved housing," the island was now ruled by another "dictatorship."[101]

WILLIAM LEE BRENT

When Brent hijacked a plane from Oakland, California, to Cuba in June 1969, he was an ex-member of the Black Panther Party, within which he had risen to the rank of a captain and a bodyguard to Panther leaders such as Bobby Seale. Ejected from the Party after wounding three San Francisco police officers in a gunfight stemming from an apparent robbery of a gas station,[102] Brent found himself isolated — Panther leadership had branded him a police provocateur after the incident — and facing serious legal charges. Abandoned by the Panthers, Brent's $50,000 bail was ultimately posted by white radicals and university students in Berkeley. Fearing a lifetime in prison, Brent resolved to hop bail and reach Cuba by the shortest and quickest route available: a hijacked airliner. "I knew nothing about Cuba or what living under a socialist government would be like," he later admitted in his memoirs, "but I did know U.S. laws had no force in Cuba."[103]

The Cuban government, Brent also surmised, might be sympathetic to his plight. "The Panthers were known and respected there," Brent wrote. "The Cuban media had given the Party lots of publicity through interviews with several top Panther leaders, including Huey."[104] Cuba's state-run media had embraced the movement to free Newton from prison, and when Panther leaders George Murray and David Hilliard attended the OSPAAAL conference in August 1968, during which the organization's Executive Secretariat had proclaimed Cuba's solidarity with the movement to free Huey Newton from prison, the *Black Panther* newspaper printed a transcript of the statement.[105] Other U.S. black activists, Brent knew, had also obtained asylum there, including Eldridge Cleaver.

Described in an FBI report of his airplane hijacking as "very well educated" and "extremely polite," according to interviewed crew members, but carrying a pistol,[106] Brent apparently hinted at his motivations to the airplane's crew. "This man was not irrational," the plane's captain had told reporters. "He told me that he was a desperate man and had to leave the country."[107]

Like most American hijackers, Brent first experienced Cuba from the inside of a prison cell, where he would remain for twenty-two months. Cuban immigration officials, he later learned, had suspected him of being a spy, and likely viewed his ousting from the Panthers, an organization that was highly respected in Cuba, as suspicious. When Cuban intelligence officers were finally satisfied that he had no sinister intent in Cuba, Brent emerged from prison determined to prove his ability to adapt to Cuban society.

Housed at the Cuban government's expense in a room in a spacious converted mansion in Havana — "Hijack House," as its American occupants had christened it — with over a dozen others who had come to Cuba illegally, Brent came to know something of the American exiles in Cuba beyond his own experience. Volunteering to cut sugarcane with a brigade of international volunteers, Brent spent eight months working in the cane fields, where he met volunteers and political asylees from throughout Latin America. Upon his return, Brent became active in La Reunion de Residentes Norteamericanos, an informal association of U.S. residents living in Havana. Although he initially struggled with Spanish, Brent later enrolled at the University of Havana, eventually graduating with a bachelor's degree in Hispanic Languages in November 1981.

Brent worked as a high school English teacher at several schools in Havana, including at the prestigious Vladimir Ilich Lenin Vocational School, taught occasional classes at the University of Havana, and worked as a broadcaster for Radio Havana Cuba. He married American writer Jane McManus, herself a voluntary expatriate living in Cuba who had arrived in the mid-1960s, one of several dozen American leftists living and working in Cuba as journalists and technicians.[108] The two enjoyed a relatively comfortable life by Cuban standards, enjoying a spacious apartment in the Miramar district of Havana and driving an aging Volkswagen Beetle, thanks in part to the income that McManus received from publishing travel books on Cuba in association with the government's tourism bureau.

FBI reports provide a glimpse into the bureau's efforts to gather information about American exiles in Cuba. The FBI, of course, had compiled a dossier on Brent long before his hijacking. Brent's file classified the Panthers as "a black extremist organization ... [that] advocates the use of guns and guerrilla tactics to bring about the overthrow of the United States Government."[109] Although FBI briefs noted Brent's hijacking immediately after the event, one of the bureau's first investigative actions in order to determine Brent's status in Cuba was to contact law enforcement sources who were "familiar with black militant activities" in the San Francisco Bay Area, and to send agents to visit individuals who had known Brent personally. The FBI also sought to determine information about Brent's presence in Cuba on at least one occasion through a request to the U.S. Interests Section in Havana, but to no avail: the Cuban government reportedly made no response.[110] Lacking the ability to apprehend Brent in Cuba, the FBI relied instead on intelligence provided by informants.

Unsurprisingly, many of the most willing informants were hijackers and other fugitives in Cuba who had become disillusioned with life there and hoped to receive reduced jail sentences upon return to the United States. As Brent reveals in his memoirs, some of the American exiles that he met, particularly the hijackers, were quite keen on leaving Cuba. One, a black teenager whom Brent identifies as "Diana," reportedly disliked the accommodations at Hijack House and regretted her decision to come to Cuba. As Brent recounts her summation of life as an exiled hijacker: "It's the same old thing, day in day out: Sit around drinking rum, go to the beach or take in a movie in Havana, and back to this damned house again."[111]

Brent appears to be describing Diane McKinney, a seventeen-year-old girl who had helped her eighteen-year-old boyfriend hijack a single-engine airplane from Gastonia, North Carolina, to Havana in April 1970. According to newspaper accounts, the couple wanted to come to Cuba to escape the bitter racism of the American South. In a letter that she managed to send to her aunt, McKinney related that she had been living at a residence that she referred to as "Hijackers Hotel" in Havana. "The food is bad, the people are crazy, and the whole place is just out of this world," the teenager wrote, adding that, "I am very sorry that I left home."[112] McKinney's boyfriend, Ira Meeks, returned to the United States in 1975, and was promptly arrested on hijacking charges. Meeks soon began cooperating with the FBI, supplying them with dubious intelligence. According to Brent's FBI file, Meeks claimed that he had known Brent in Havana's Cabana Prison as "Chico," a man who he said "used a lot of drugs."[113]

Testimony from other informants further clouded the FBI's portrait of Brent's life in Cuba. As early as March 1970, an agent at the FBI's Las Vegas field office filed a report claiming that an American hijacker who had returned to the United States and had been indicted in Miami had identified a photograph of Brent as "a fellow Negro who had come to Cuba in 1969 as an aircraft hijacker." According to the report, the informant claimed that, "Brent had used an African name which he could not recall and had been living in comfortable quarters at the Havana Lebra [sic] Hotel. He understood Brent to be sympathetic to the Black Panthers who had been hoping to go to Africa.... Brent was not happy in Cuba because of the Cuban attitude against Negroes and Black Panthers."[114] Notwithstanding the fact that Brent never reported staying at the Havana Libre, nor did he ever publicly report, for his part, a Cuban bias against Black Panthers, there is one other problem with the veracity of this report: at the time of its filing Brent was still in prison, where he would remain for approximately another year. With as many as two dozen American hijackers in Cuban jails during 1969 and 1970, the FBI's reports on Brent are a garble of questionable sources and unsubstantiated conjecture, a problem that inhibited the bureau's efforts to determine details of his life in Cuba.

Nonetheless, FBI agents continued to compile information about Brent. One informant, interviewed by the bureau's agents in West Palm Beach, Florida, in 1974, stated that he had recently returned from Cuba, where he claimed to have met Brent, a man that he described as "a black militant who expounds his militancy at every opportunity [and] currently resides in the hijacking community in Havana."[115] In 1983, an informant who had traveled to Cuba with the Venceremos Brigade reported to the FBI that Brent had come to give a talk to some of the *brigadistas*. The informant related that Brent was employed at the "Lenin School" and passed along Brent's home address in Havana. "Although Brent indicated that he would like to return to the United States," the report stated, apparently paraphrasing the informant, "[Brent] feels that the New Left movement in the United States is dead... He remains dedicated to communist revolution around the world."[116]

Although much of this information was likely of little use to the FBI's efforts to have Brent extradited, the reports contain occasional claims about Brent's life that do not appear in his autobiography, *Long Time Gone*, including a few tantalizing clues about his activities. A July 1984 report drawing upon the testimony of an informant who had posed as a member of the U.S.-based Cuba Coordinating Committee (CCC), an organization working in solidarity with Cuba in the United States, who had met Brent and McManus in Cuba, contended that Brent had participated in the Cuban government's foreign solidarity activities outside the island. According to the report, "Brent, in the past two years, has traveled to Central American countries as a good will ambassador for the Cubans. He is utilized by the Cubans to contact the leadership of countries where his black race is an advantage."[117]

If Brent did travel to Central America, it is likely that he accompanied a Cuban solidarity delegation, possibly to El Salvador, Grenada, or Nicaragua, countries in which the scale of Cuba's humanitarian and political involvement in the early 1980s was second only to its involvement on the African continent. Indeed, although Brent makes no mention of travels away from Cuba in his memoirs, a photograph of him in *Long Time Gone* does show him in Grenada in the early 1980s.[118] If the Cuban government had, in fact, facilitated Brent's travels in a humanitarian or diplomatic capacity, the omission of them in his memoir is understandable, as they might have been viewed as compromising to the Cuban government. News that the Cuban government had utilized an American fugitive, even in a low-level capacity, in its foreign diplomatic activities during the early 1980s would undoubtedly have risked negative diplomatic consequences. Indeed, the Reagan administration's designation of Cuba as a "state sponsor of terrorism" in 1982 focused upon Cuba's involvement in Latin America and Africa, the two issues that most consistently strained its relations with the United States during the 1980s.[119] As U.S. political asylees in Cuba repeatedly observed, Cuban officials viewed the direct involvement of Americans in its military or foreign campaigns as a potential provocation of Washington, a risk that Havana was unwilling to take.

Brent died of pneumonia in a Havana hospital on November 4, 2006, at the age of seventy-five. He never returned to the United States, and although he lived in Cuba for the remainder of his life, he never became a Cuban citizen. Brent's 1996 memoir, entitled *Long Time Gone: A Black Panther's True-Life Story of His Hijacking and Twenty-Five Years in Cuba*, offers one of the only published first-person accounts of the American political exile experience in Cuba. Completed amid the implosion of the Cuban economy during the Special Period of the 1990s, *Long Time Gone* reveals Brent's search for solace and redemption in Cuba, with Brent eventually admitting his "great disappointment with the course the Cuban revolution has taken,"[120] a disillusionment borne of the government's failure to fully deliver on its promises of universal prosperity. Speaking to a reporter in 1996, Brent echoed a common refrain among a younger generation of Cubans in Havana: "The youth of Cuba support the revolution, but they want change. There are too many old men at the top and young people at the bottom."[121] Near the end of his life, Brent came to believe that Cuba's revolution had become an "illusion," one that had not lived up to the expectations of the countless Cubans who had sacrificed so much in support of it.[122]

MICHAEL FINNEY AND CHARLIE HILL

Arriving in Cuba in 1971 and extending through four decades, Finney and Hill provide among the most complete portraits of American exile in Cuba.[123] The origins of their asylum on the island lie in the U.S. black liberation movements of the 1960s. Finney, a nineteen-year-old San Francisco native, a political science student at the University of California, Berkeley, and the son of San Francisco's first black policeman, and Hill, a Vietnam veteran and father of two who had returned from the war in 1969, were members of the Republic of New Afrika (RNA), a black nationalist movement founded in 1968 by former associates of the martyred Malcolm X.

Formed in the wake of the assassination of Martin Luther King Jr.'s dream of racial integration, the RNA advocated the creation of an independent territorial nation for people of African descent in the United States, carved from the territory of the former slavocracy of the U.S. South, and the long overdue payment of reparations to the descendants of African slaves in America. Members of the RNA renounced their U.S. citizenship and conceptualized themselves instead as "New Afrikans": members of a colonized black nation inside America that they contended had a right, under international law, to political self-determination and territorial independence. Although their roles in the organization were largely honorific, the group's voted leadership was composed of a pantheon of luminaries from across the U.S. black freedom movement. Robert F. Williams, who had earlier taken refuge in Cuba, became the first President of the group's "provisional government"; Betty Shabazz, widow of Malcolm X, served as the group's vice president; Queen Mother Moore was the Minister of Health and Welfare; and H. "Rap" Brown was the Minister of Defense. Amiri Baraka, who credited his 1960 trip to Cuba as crystallizing his political radicalization, and Maulana Karenga, the leader of the US organization who later founded the Kwanzaa holiday in 1966, served as coministers of culture.[124]

Regarded by law enforcement as a "black extremist" organization, the RNA maintained a self-defense militia to protect itself from white vigilantes and police repression. The group was soon involved in violent confrontations with law enforcement. A police raid on an RNA conference at a Detroit church in 1969 resulted in the death of an officer; another officer was killed in a police raid on an RNA farmhouse in Jackson, Mississippi, in 1971.[125] Requested by the RNA's leadership to transport guns and dynamite from the Bay Area to

Jackson to fortify their compound against police attack, the two young men and a third RNA member, Ralph Lawrence Goodwin, the son of a lawyer who, at twenty-four years old, had just graduated from Berkeley with a degree in physics, agreed. Driving through the desert just outside Albuquerque — coincidentally, the city where Hill's mother lived — with "three huge Afros,"[126] out of state plates, and a trunk full of weapons on November 8, the three were stopped by a white New Mexico State police officer who demanded to search the car. Minutes later, the officer had been shot dead.[127]

Despite the largest police dragnet in New Mexico history, the three eluded capture, aided by Hill's knowledge of the area, his military experience in Vietnam, and the RNA paramilitary drills that Finney had undergone in the hills outside Oakland. Hiding first in the desert — at one point burying themselves in the sand during the daylight hours with only their faces exposed for several days — the three men then hid in the houses of sympathetic local residents, including an airport employee who was later sentenced to five years in prison for aiding the fugitives.[128] After nineteen days on the lam, the three men kidnapped a tow-truck driver, forcing him to crash his truck through the fenced perimeter of the Albuquerque airport. Brandishing weapons, they commandeered TWA flight 106 as surprised passengers boarded it on the tarmac, directing the pilot to fly to Cuba.[129]

Uncertain about what would await them in Cuba, the three nonetheless chose the communist Caribbean nation largely because of its reputation for providing political asylum for U.S. black radicals on the lam, and because of its relative proximity to the United States. Robert F. Williams's radio program, *Radio Free Dixie*, which the North Carolina native recorded in exile in Havana and beamed into the southern United States on the powerful signal of Radio Havana Cuba, was an RNA legend.[130] The men also admired Cuba's developing military and humanitarian presence in Africa, which was becoming widely recognized within African American political and intellectual circles. The three comrades regarded Cuba as a multiracial society with a strong black presence, one that had both aided liberation movements in Africa and provided asylum to U.S. black radicals, including those who arrived in hijacked airplanes. "We understood as freedom fighters that if anything ever happened in the U.S. and we had to leave [the U.S.]," Hill later explained, "the best thing was to come to Cuba."[131]

Upon arrival in Cuba, Hill and his comrades were held for security clearance in a detention facility for approximately ten weeks. Cuban intelligence officers routinely compiled detailed dossiers on the private and political lives of those entering the country illegally, especially those seeking political asylum, and the three RNA members were subjected to lengthy background investigations. According to Hill, they were treated well, "with respect and dignity."[132] Released to a halfway house for U.S. and foreign exiles in Havana, the three were then relocated to dilapidating hotels around the city, former tourist havens in which the Cuban government had been housing Cubans who had no homes. Like other U.S. exiles, the Cuban government placed no restrictions on Hill's associations with Cubans.[133]

From his early days in Havana, the city's atmosphere of internationalism deeply moved Hill. Forming a political study group with other exiles and temporary residents from the United States, they cut sugarcane with the Nuestra América Brigade, which included volunteers from all over Latin America. "I met guys that were not at the halfway house, and that were members of armed movements," Hill later recalled. "I met Brazilian guys, Colombian, guys who had been in the struggle. They were guerrillas, man. People from all over the world struggling for freedom and democracy, freeing themselves from colonialism and racism."[134]

Goodwin, however, never lived to realize his ambitions of reaching Africa, a sojourn that his father had made shortly before his son's fateful car trip to Mississippi with Finney and Hill. Goodwin's exile in Cuba would be cut short by tragedy. In 1973, he drowned at a Havana beach, reportedly while attempting to aid a girl who was drowning.

Hill, like all residents of Hijack House,[135] initially had no formal work obligations. Classified by the Cuban government as a political refugee, he was assigned to a Cuban *responsable* — an official in charge — from the Instituto Cubano de Amistad con los Pueblos (ICAP) who was tasked with addressing the concerns and requests of the exiles. Issued a ration card, Hill's rent, food, and basic amenities were provided by the Cuban government. However, he soon transitioned into an existence similar to that of most Cubans, moving in the early 1980s from a room in a hotel in Havana, paid for by the Cuban government, to an apartment in the Havana district of Playa. He studied for free at the Universidad de La Habana, first in electrical engineering, then in history. Taking a series of jobs, including at a Havana clothing store, Hill paid his own rent and, like all Cubans, received free health care and a ration card for obtaining his allotment of foodstuffs, fresh produce, and basic necessities.

With his Spanish rapidly improving, Hill also began working as a translator and guide, approaching English-speaking tourists at the downtown Parque Central and along the city's seaside Malecón, and teaching English to Cubans. Hill, who began to also go by the name Fela Olatunji, became formally initiated into Regla de Ochá, part of the African syncretic spiritual practice more commonly known outside Cuba as Santería, which had experienced a revival in Cuba during the early 1990s Special Period, as Cubans sought to cope with the hard times wrought by the economic collapse following the disintegration of the Soviet Union. Hill's time in Cuba was not without legal trouble: he was imprisoned at least twice, including on charges of falsifying a currency document.

In October 1980, when thirty-three American prisoners in Cuba, accused primarily of drug trafficking and hijacking, were pardoned by Fidel Castro and flown to Miami aboard an airliner chartered by the U.S. Justice Department, Finney and Hill were included on the U.S. list, although they were not imprisoned in Cuba. Nonetheless, they had no intention of returning to the United States. Several U.S. hijackers from the 1968–1973 era had decided to return to the United States, including self-styled Black Panther affiliate Anthony Bryant, who had become a staunch anticommunist while in Cuba and was subsequently acquitted of all charges stemming from the hijacking by a Miami jury.[136] But the three RNA hijackers were not anticommunists, nor did they feel confident of prevailing against the murder charges awaiting them in New Mexico. Although their names were included on a U.S. State Department list of jailed Americans that Cuba was scheduled to release in 1980, their inclusion appears to have been a result of a U.S. request for their extradition, not the Cuban government's desire to be rid of them. Quoted in the *Los Angeles Times*, the assistant district attorney of Bernalillo County, New Mexico, commented that his office had been "informed their names had been withdrawn from the list because they asked not to be returned," adding that he was "surprised they were able to negotiate their remaining in Cuba when others were being sent out."[137]

However, in 1983, with no desire to return to the United States but anxious to leave Cuba, Finney and Hill did attempt to emigrate from the island. "Most of the time I spent here was on trying to leave," Finney admitted to a reporter in 1985.[138] This time, they hoped to reach Africa—the destination that they had originally asked to be flown to, according to media reports of the hijacking[139]—either to Tanzania or Guinea-Bissau. But although the Cuban government had given them $300 and put them on a flight to Jamaica, Cuban officials informed them that no assistance in securing political connections or further travel arrangements would be provided. Finney and Hill's stay in Jamaica ultimately lasted a matter of minutes. The two were sent back to Cuba after unamused Jamaican customs officials failed to believe the story that they had concocted that they were American tourists who had lost their passports.[140] The two men had previously tried to volunteer to serve in Cuba's armed forces in Angola, where they hoped to participate in Cuba's ongoing military campaign there against the forces of the apartheid government of South Africa and their proxies. However, Cuban officials informed them that they would be permitted to join the Angolan anticolonial struggle only if they did so on their own — and at the invitation of the Angolans — and without direct Cuban involvement. Angolan representatives in Havana declined their overtures.

Both men slowly came to accept that they were likely in Cuba for good. When the Special Period arrived in the early 1990s as a result of the collapse of the Soviet Union, Hill experienced the same privation as ordinary Cubans, as consumer goods disappeared from store shelves, food and basic necessities dwindled to alarmingly low levels, and evidence of malnutrition appeared in parts of the island for the first time in decades. Amid the economic cataclysm in Cuba, Hill again considered leaving the island but again elected to stay, lacking viable options for political asylum elsewhere. Although the Cuban government appears to have offered both men the opportunity to become Cuban citizens, neither ever accepted it. Hill maintains that his decision stemmed from his desire to keep his political autonomy and maintain his uniquely U.S. perspective on race and politics, including his identification as a black nationalist and Pan-African internationalist.[141]

Due to Havana's housing shortage, Finney lived in hotels in the city for almost a decade after arriving in Cuba before being given an apartment by the Cuban government. Earning a degree in history from the University of Havana and working for over two decades as a respected broadcaster for Radio Havana Cuba under the deejay name "Langston Wright," a nod to his two most beloved writers from home, Finney's radio broadcasts in English and flawless Spanish could be heard on the AM dial throughout the United States. Of all of the U.S. asylees arriving in Cuba during the hijacking era, Finney was among the most successful in adapting to life in Cuba, developing a stable professional career and achieving accolades within government and professional circles. Like many exiles, however, Finney's time in Cuba was marked by the pain of separation from homeland, community, and loved ones. Although married at the time of the 1971 hijacking and the father of a one-year-old girl, he and his wife, unable to see each other, divorced in 1976. Finney eventually married again, this time to a Cuban gynecologist, with whom he had a daughter. "Exile," Finney told a reporter in 1980, "is probably one of the most difficult human conditions that exists. You're always homeless. You're always in a place that's not yours."[142] In 2005, Finney died of throat cancer at a hospital in Havana.[143]

Charlie Hill, who hijacked a commercial airliner to Cuba in 1971 as a member of the Republic of New Afrika, in Old Havana in August 2015. As of this writing, Hill's political exile in Cuba, spanning over four decades, is the longest of any American. Photo by the author.

ASSATA SHAKUR

More than any other U.S. political exile in Cuba, Shakur grew to symbolize Cuba's provision of sanctuary to American dissidents, embodying both the FBI's campaign to retrieve fugitives from the island and the Castro government's commitment to provide sanctuary, even in the face of strong diplomatic pressure, for those it considered political refugees. Arriving in Cuba during the summer of 1984, possibly via the Bahamas[144] and, according to her account, without advance contact with the Cuban government,[145] Shakur was nevertheless immediately granted the status of a political refugee by the Cuban government, which had classified her as a political prisoner during her incarceration in New Jersey.[146] She was provided with an apartment in Havana and a living stipend, and was reunited with her daughter, Kakuya, who had been both conceived and born behind bars in 1973.[147]

Upon escaping from prison in 1979, Shakur had immediately regarded Cuba as an obvious destination for political asylum. A longtime admirer of the Cuban Revolution, Shakur also favored the geographic proximity of the island to the U.S. mainland which, despite Washington's travel ban, would allow her family to visit her surreptitiously.[148] Most importantly, she said, the Caribbean nation had "a long history of supporting victims of political repression... not only of people in the United States, like Huey Newton, Robert Williams, Eldridge Cleaver... but also people who were victims of political repression in other places, like Chile, the apartheid government of South Africa, Namibia. I felt this was a place that held the principle of international[ism] very close to heart."[149] For a time, Shakur lived quietly, undiscovered by the U.S. media. Despite several quiet visits to Cuba by members of Shakur's family, the FBI did not publicly reveal knowledge of her presence there.[150] The Cuban media likewise made no mention of her.

Shakur's low profile on the island would be short lived. In the fall of 1987, as Lawrence Hill Books[151] prepared to release her memoirs as *Assata: An Autobiography*, Shakur's presence in Cuba was exposed. On October 11, *Newsday* reporter Ron Howell published the first interview with Shakur since her arrival on the island, confirming her presence and providing the first public glimpse into her life there. Shakur, Howell reported, was receiving her living expenses, including rent, from the Cuban government, which had assigned her a government *responsable* to assist her with her transition, as well as family counseling for Shakur and her daughter to help them adjust to life in Cuba.[152] Although most American exiles studied at the University of Havana, the article reported the unusual claim that Shakur was studying politics, sociology, and philosophy at the Escuela Superior del Partido, a system of colleges run directly by the Cuban Communist Party and populated by its members.[153] "She is clearly trusted by the Cubans," wrote Howell, an observation that would prove prescient of the coming years as Shakur worked closely with the Cuban Communist Party as a translator and an intermediary between the government and visiting American delegations.

Released in December 1987, *Assata*, originally subtitled *The Autobiography of a Revolutionary*,[154] traced Shakur's life from childhood in North Carolina to adulthood in New York City, lingering upon her activist years and her subsequent trials as a member of the BLA. However, the narrative ends shortly after her arrival in Cuba, omitting most of Shakur's Cuban experience.[155]

Like other American exiles, Shakur's early impressions of Cuba were powerfully informed by her perceptions of the nation's ethos of revolutionary internationalism. She arrived in Cuba during the nation's military involvement in Angola and its support for the anti-apartheid movement in South Africa, and Cuba's highly publicized involvement in postcolonial Africa, beginning in the early 1960s but accelerating in the mid-1970s, was a significant source of her admiration for the nation's internationalism. This involvement, in turn, created new streams of political asylees arriving in Cuba during the 1980s. Shakur's interviews and writings during the early years of her exile repeatedly reveal that she was deeply affected by her encounters with other political exiles and war refugees who had come for sanctuary or medical treatment, often from countries directly affected by U.S. power: "I'm being introduced at a party. The hostess tells me that the man is from El Salvador. I hold out my hand to shake his. A few seconds too late, i realize he is missing an arm. I'm so upset and ashamed i'm almost shaking.... In Cuba i could see the results of u.s. foreign policy: torture victims on crutches who came from other countries to Cuba for treatment, including Namibian children who had survived massacres, and evidence of the vicious aggression the u.s. government had committed against Cuba."[156]

Now fluent in Spanish and highly respected by Cuban officials, Shakur's close association with the Comité Central, the Central Committee of the Communist Party of Cuba, allowed her to function as an adviser to the Cuban Government on matters of race in the United States, the status of African Americans, and the nature of the U.S. black freedom struggle. Working directly with the Comité Central, Shakur assumed the role of an official intermediary between the Cuban government and U.S. black activists, maintaining a level of access to government officials that no other U.S. political exiles enjoyed. As Nehanda Abiodun later observed, "that's Assata's unique contribution — working with the Cuban leadership to help them understand our struggle."[157]

By the early 1990s, Shakur had become well known in Havana's cultural and political circles. Working as an English-language editor for Radio Havana Cuba and becoming a familiar face at public events sponsored by Cuban organizations such as the Instituto Cubano de Amistad con los Pueblos (ICAP) and Casa de las Américas, Shakur met hundreds of visiting Americans and solidarity delegations, including the Venceremos Brigade, which met with Shakur as a group on several occasions in the 1990s. Shakur's engagements with U.S. delegations occurred unofficially, to protect the travel licenses of the groups, and to avoid the possibility of legal charges of aiding and abetting a fugitive.[158]

Academic and literary delegations, too, regularly met with Shakur. In March 1989, filmmaker and writer Toni Cade Bambara met Shakur and her daughter while on her third trip to Cuba, this time as part of a group sponsored by the Writers Guild of America, East. Shakur asked Bambara to pass along greetings to several other artists in the United States, including the poet Sonia Sanchez. Given scarcities on the island, visitors to Cuba would often bring supplies and consumer goods for friends. When Bambara asked Shakur what she needed, Shakur replied: "spices.... I need everything of course but I'd appreciate some spices... and lots of hugs.... I don't need anything... just tell them to get here."[159] Historian Manning Marable, traveling to Cuba in 1997 with a delegation from Columbia University's African American Studies program, recounted his meetings with Shakur in an essay entitled "The Color Line: Black Political Prisoners: The Case of Assata Shakur."[160] Interacting with non-U.S. foreign political and academic delegations, Shakur sought in particular to publicize to the world the existence of human rights violations against communities of color and poor people inside the United States.[161]

Shakur's exile in Cuba intensified, rather than diminished, her visibility as an icon of the contemporary black radical imagination. By the mid-1990s, Shakur's autobiography had begun appearing on the syllabi of dozens of college courses in the United States, alongside classic works of autobiography in the African American literary tradition. Like Elaine Brown's 1992 autobiography *A Taste of Power*, Shakur's writing and interviews contributed to a growing activist and academic commitment to recovering the centrality of the experiences and contributions of black women in the Black Power era.[162] Writing in the Nation of Islam's newspaper *The Final Call* in 2002, reporter Nisa Islam Muhammad summed up Shakur's iconography of black revolutionary femininity: "Assata Shakur is a Black American folk hero. She is a freedom fighter that escaped the chains of oppression. She made it to the other side. She is a sister that defied the definitions of expected behavior by a Black woman."[163] With the release of Cuban filmmaker Gloria Rolando's film *Eyes of the Rainbow* in 1997, which features extended interviews with Shakur in Havana, U.S. audiences saw Shakur speaking in her own words from exile for the first time.[164] Shakur's association with the Black August Collective in 1998 which, with the Malcolm X Grassroots Movement (MXGM), sponsored a series of high profile hip hop concerts and political encounters in Havana and New York, drawing artists such as Common, Mos Def, and the Roots, further solidified Shakur's resonance within the contemporary black radical imagination.[165] Shakur, who also happened to be the godmother of slain hip-hop icon Tupac Amaru Shakur,[166] eventually achieved a visibility within the lyrics of hip-hop artists that, for African American women historical figures, is surpassed only by Harriet Tubman.[167] As scholar Joy James contends, "Shakur is singular because she is a recognizable female revolutionary, one not bound to a male persona."[168]

While Chicago hip-hop artist Common's 2001 tribute "A Song for Assata" is the best known, other artists invoked Shakur in ways that linked her exile with the politics of U.S.-Cuba relations. In a 2000 song entitled "The Bullet," the Bronx-based group the Welfare Poets situates Shakur's prison escape and Cuban sanctuary within a larger continuum of resistance within communities of color to racism and colonial legacies in the United States and its territories, notably Puerto Rico. Invoking Malcolm X's influential 1964 speech, "The Ballot or the Bullet," the song implicitly sanctions resistance "by any means" as permissible in the face of systems of oppression that are involuntary and gratuitous, and therefore not ameliorable through electoral mechanisms:

> We didn't vote for the demonic blockade on Cuba
> We didn't vote for the false trumped-up charges on Assata
> Got these crackers so mad
> Only ninety miles from America
> And they still can't fuckin' touch her
> Now you tell me who's freer
> Now that's black power.[169]

Shakur's characterization of herself as an "escaped slave" taking refuge in the twentieth-century internationalist "palenque" of Cuban exile underscores both the durability of the memory of slavery within the African American political imaginary and the intersections between the U.S. black freedom struggle and Cuba's project of revolutionary internationalism, itself rooted in an explicitly antiracist and anticolonial imaginary. Understanding contemporary antiblack racism in the United States as a political condition rooted in the haunted historical terrain of America's unresolved legacy of slavery, African American activists such as Shakur drew vivid metaphors likening the persecution of contemporary black freedom fighters with that of their ancestors who endured and resisted enslavement.

The metaphor of Shakur as a runaway slave resonated powerfully with her supporters. Writing in *Essence* shortly after the release of *Assata*, one writer observed that Shakur's prison escape, executed in a manner reminiscent of "our enslaved ancestors," had made Shakur a modern-day folk legend.[170] The echoes of slavery in Shakur's persecution, incarceration, and escape to Cuba also reverberated, consciously or otherwise, in the statements of police and political officials. When the State of New Jersey announced its $1 million bounty in 2005, for instance, New Jersey State Police Superintendent Rick Fuentes revealingly declared, "She is now 120 pounds of money."[171]

Assata Shakur in Havana, 1998. More than any other American political asylee in Cuba, Shakur's presence would come to symbolize Havana's willingness to provide formal sanctuary to those it considered refugees from political repression in the United States, a position that the Cuban government maintained even in the face of significant U.S. pressure. SHOBHA/Contrasto/Redux.

Shakur's repeated invocations of slavery's legacy to articulate both her political condition as an exile in Cuba, as well as the subject status of people of African descent in the United States, particularly those caught in the webs of the criminal-justice system, suggests that for Shakur, slavery continues to haunt modernity. Shakur's continual deployment of ideas about slavery and freedom to explain her subjectivity — first as a "New Afrikan" neo-slave held hostage within the carceral plantation of the U.S. prison system, then as a prison fugitive and an "escaped slave" harbored within the urban black and multiracial "underground railroad" of radical multiracial activist communities that had sheltered her while she was on the lam, and finally, as a modern "maroon" in exile in Cuba, an island refuge that had provided her with liberation from the neo-enslavement of prison but not yet true freedom, due to both repeated U.S. attempts to engineer her return to the "plantation" of mass incarceration and the continuance of forms of antiblack racism in Cuba itself — offers a view into both the limits of Cuba as a sanctuary for African American radicals and the limits of black freedom in a white supremacist world.

Indeed, Shakur has repeatedly maintained that her own freedom, and that of people of African descent, has not yet been attained anywhere on the globe, including in post-1959 Cuba, a nation whose efforts to bring about racial equality she has repeatedly praised. Although Shakur acknowledged that the Cuban government's efforts to eradicate racism had come further than any other country in the hemisphere, true racial equality in Cuba, she contended, had not yet been achieved. Racism in Cuba "had grown out of slavery and exploitation," she explained to visiting Americans from the humanitarian group Pastors for Peace in 2000, "and was very hard to eradicate quickly and completely."[172]

Shakur's concern for the lingering shadow of slavery, however, is subsumed within a far more prominent vision of liberation rooted in revolutionary optimism. Shakur's political ideology may be characterized as profoundly hopeful about the possibilities for social justice and, in particular, the potentials for the emancipation of the African diaspora from antiblack racism and neocolonialism. Shakur's deliberate optimism, rooted in the political ideology of the Black Panther Party, which contended that black liberation in America was attainable through revolutionary struggle, had now also become influenced by Cuban revolutionary theory, which advocated the creation of a new society through collective multiracial struggle and socialist redistribution — articulated by Che Guevara in racially universalist terms as the "New Man." Cuba's long-standing nationalist discourses celebrated the island's historical struggles for national self-determination against foreign dominion, first by the Spanish, then by the United States. Consolidated by the post-1959 revolutionary regime, which had successfully resisted U.S. efforts to destroy it, these nationalist discourses became the fertile ground for a new political optimism regarding the possibilities for national liberation worldwide through anti-imperialist struggle. "Optimism . . . has been one of the psychic vitamins that has fed me since I've been here," Shakur told one interviewer in 2000. "I've seen that internalized by people in such a way that people feel empowered to build this planet and to change it."[173]

NEHANDA ABIODUN

When Nehanda Isoke Abiodun arrived in Cuba in 1990 as a political exile, her asylum had already been approved by the government's high echelon, apparently by Fidel Castro himself. A member of the BLA, RNA, the Harlem-based Revolutionary Armed Task Force, and the New Afrikan People's Organization (NAPO), Abiodun had been a close associate of Afeni Shakur, whose son, Tupac Amaru Shakur, who she knew as a child, would later inspire a generation of Cuban hip-hop artists. By the time Abiodun arrived in Cuba, she had been underground in the United States for eight years, after the FBI alleged her involvement in the 1979 prison escape of Assata Shakur, and then a deadly robbery of a Brinks armored truck in Nanuet, New York, in 1981, in which a security guard and two police officers were killed.[174] Abiodun's engagement with Cuban youth and the island's burgeoning hip-hop movement, work that continually drew from the intersectional radicalism of both black internationalist traditions and her own feminist praxis, would eventually provide a key bridge between Cuban activists and artists and the African American freedom struggle amid the shifting realities of 1990s and 2000s Havana.[175]

Born Cheri Laverne Dalton in New York in 1950, Abiodun's first encounter with Cuba's revolution came as a young girl in Harlem. When the insurgency against Fulgencio Batista gained international attention in 1957, her father, who was an admirer of Marcus Garvey and later Malcolm X, had hoped to join the guerrilla movement, as several New Yorkers had recently done. It was not to be. "My mother said, if you go to Cuba, I will divorce you!"[176] Instead, Abiodun's father took her to the Hotel Theresa in September of 1960, joining a thousand or more Harlemites outside Fidel Castro's chosen residence for the U.N. General Assembly meetings. Abiodun's community organizing began around the same time. With neighborhood friends, she protested the expansion of a controversial university gymnasium into Morningside Park, and later worked as an organizer for low-income tenants.

Graduating from Columbia University in 1972, she became increasingly radicalized as a result of her work in community drug rehabilitation clinics, including the Lincoln Detox Center, a clinic located in a South Bronx hospital that had been founded by former members of the Black Panther Party and the Young Lords Party and utilized conventional therapies together with acupuncture and political education to successfully treat drug addiction. "I came to realize that addiction, poverty, and racism are linked," she later recalled.[177] Throughout her early life in New York and the beginning of her political trajectory, Abiodun regarded Cuba's efforts to combat racial, economic, gender, and health inequality with admiration. "I supported the Cuban Revolution in a concrete way for most of my adult life."[178]

Arriving in Havana as a political asylee, Abiodun was installed for a time in Havana's best hotels — partly to make her comfortable, and partly for her security. Provided with a cash living stipend, she was also assigned an English-speaking *responsable* who was charged with ensuring her well-being and facilitating her transition to life on the island.[179] Abiodun enrolled in six months of Spanish language classes, and began to enjoy the first respite from danger and anxiety that she had known in years. Abiodun quickly acclimated to life in Cuba, thanks in part to the mentorship of new Cuban friends, including a group of principal dancers from El Conjunto Folklórico Nacional de Cuba — National Folkloric Company of Cuba — an ensemble emphasizing Afro-Cuban dance and music.

Abiodun's security was deemed an early priority. For the first two years of her exile, Abiodun was instructed by her Cuban hosts to maintain a low profile, to refrain from making statements to the international media, and limit communication with U.S. political groups. Asked to jettison her chosen name, the Cubans also gave Abiodun a pseudonym to use in Cuba. But anonymity proved untenable. When the mandatory low-profile period expired, Abiodun was determined to reengage with political struggle. Abiodun's welfare in Cuba would now fall under the supervision of ICAP which, as a government-sponsored organization that facilitated ties between Cuba and its supporters abroad, would allow her more latitude in her political activities as a foreigner.[180] Requesting an apartment, she eventually settled in a high-rise in the Reparto Bahía section of Habana del Este. By the late 1990s, her full name, telephone number, and address appeared in Havana's phonebook.[181]

Yet despite her growing ties to Cuba's official sector, Abiodun stridently guarded her independence. Offered the opportunity to work under the Comité Central, which Assata Shakur had collaborated closely with, Abiodun declined, "not because I didn't trust them, but because I needed to be me. That would have been too much control."[182] Abiodun also declined the Cuban government's offer to update her status to that of "permanent resident," again citing her desire to preserve her independence. "I knew within my heart," Abiodun would recall, "that once I accepted being a permanent resident here that I am saying that the U.S. government has won."[183]

Like Shakur and Brent, Abiodun was soon regularly serving as a liaison to political solidarity delegations, and speaking informally to groups of visiting foreigners, often in collaboration with ICAP, and sometimes the University of Havana. However, owing apparently to her relative independence from the Cuban state, Abiodun's engagements with U.S. delegations occurred largely in an unofficial capacity, in marked contrast to Assata Shakur, who had frequently operated on behalf of the Cuban government. On the U.S. side, unofficial meetings helped protect the travel licenses of the groups and shield them from institutional scrutiny.[184] However, the unofficial nature of the meetings between Abiodun and visiting delegations appears to have been insisted upon by the Cuban government.[185]

Like other U.S. political exiles, Abiodun's early experiences in Cuba sometimes betrayed tensions between expectations and reality. The disjuncture between Cuban and U.S. understandings of race, in particular, repeatedly accosted Abiodun's sense of belonging. Sometimes it was derived from the perils of translating lived experience across linguistic and historical gulfs. Young Cubans, attempting to decipher U.S. racial discourses in English through the decontextualized audio prism of U.S. hip-hop, for instance, sometimes misunderstood what they heard. Taken on a tour of Havana by her Cuban *responsable* the day after she arrived in Cuba, Abiodun could scarcely believe her ears when the man referred to Afro-Cuban boys as "niggers," believing that it was the appropriate term.[186] Several years later, sitting among visiting African American academics and activists from the United States, the group was startled to hear a Cuban rap emcee address members of the audience using a variation of the term.[187]

For Abiodun, such linguistic stumbles could be addressed and corrected. However, the persistence of antiblack attitudes in Cuba continually revealed the distance between the Cuba of the U.S. radical imaginary, which sometimes idealized Cuba's racial climate, and the lived reality on the island, a disjuncture that all U.S. political exiles in Cuba confronted in different ways. As Abiodun would later recall:

> I think that to a certain extent, all of us were unrealistic about what Cuba was. We thought that racism, and the question of women's equality, had been resolved, only to come here and find out it wasn't. I was confronted by police when I first got here, solely because I was a black woman. I was crossing the street to go into the Havana Libre [hotel] to buy cigarettes — this was less than a year after I arrived — and two police officers were behind me, and one said to another, "she's a prostitute, let's stop her." And I had on, like, an African dress that you couldn't see nothing through. The police stopped me and asked me for my ID, and the only thing that saved me is that I didn't speak Spanish.... I asked them why they stopped us, and the police said that they didn't know I was a foreigner. And finally the officer said, 'well, you look like someone who might have problems with the law.' These kinds of things that happened to me during the first year that I was here made me realize that the idealism that I had about Cuba was not accurate. I didn't come here thinking that Cuba was a utopia of course, but I didn't think that I was going to go through the same things that I went through back home. My first year here was a conflicted one.[188]

Abiodun's arrival in Cuba at the dawn of the Special Period coincided with an acceleration of latent institutional racism, as black and darker-skinned Cubans, less likely to benefit from remittances from family abroad, given the still majority nonblack composition of Cuban émigrés, and less likely to own cash-generating property such as cars and less likely to be hired by foreign

246 Black Radicalism, Political Asylum, and the Diplomacy of Exile and Freedom

Nehanda Abiodun in Havana, 2006. Affectionately referred to as the "godmother of Cuban rap," Abiodun's political mentoring of Cuban youth, together with her interaction with global social justice movements and the singular role that she played within the birth of the island's hip-hop movement of the 1990s, allowed her to remain politically active in exile. Jose Goitia/the *New York Times*/Redux

and Cuban operators in the only vibrant economy — tourism — black Cubans were more easily marginalized in the island's shifting economic landscape. More likely to be shut out of the legal economy, some black Cubans turned to underground ones. Yet despite the signs of resurgent inequality, Cuban society was woefully unprepared to address it. Cuba's long-standing discourse of raceless nationalism, and later claims by the post-1959 revolutionary leadership to have solved the issue of racism by addressing material inequality, foreclosed open discussion of persisting racist practices such as police racial profiling. As Abiodun observed, "When you speak about the problem publicly, people would say, no, there is no racism in Cuba. Which indicated something else — that there was not a space to address the issue."[189] Although Fidel Castro had formed in 1960 the Federación de Mujeres Cubanas (FMC) — the Federation of Cuban Women, headed by former guerrilla Vilma Espín — to institutionalize initiatives for women's equality, no comparable national organization devoted to ensuring racial equality was ever formed. The FMC became, for a time, a conduit through which Abiodun and Shakur together forged links between the Cuban government and black left-wing organizations in the United States, and an avenue through which to identify ways to address Cuban racial inequality.[190]

Unlike Assata Shakur, whose close association with faculty at the University of Havana and cultural and intellectual institutes throughout the city allowed her to work with members of the Cuban Government to examine matters of race in Cuba, Abiodun's more independent status left fewer channels through which to address social issues. Modes of political contestation taken for granted in the United States, including organized social movements and public demonstrations, were not feasible in Cuba. Amid the continual threat of political destabilization from the United States, including substantial U.S. funding of opposition and U.S.-aligned Cuban organizations through the U.S. Agency for International Development and the National Endowment for Democracy, the Cuban government tolerated no organized protest movements. "You have this low intensity war against Cuba, and Cuba closes its ranks and says, there are certain things we can deal with, and certain things we can't," Abiodun contends. One of those things was homegrown racism. "I'm not in agreement with that. As an African descent woman, I experience racism wherever it is."[191]

Unable to utilize the avenues of political contestation that she had embraced in the United States, including street protest and agitation, Abiodun chose politics by other means. "I had to figure out how I could continue my contribution to the struggle in a way that would be acceptable here in Cuba," she later recalled. "I could not have a protest in the street because there was some sort of manifestation of racism. Instead, I tried to figure out how I could change things one person at a time."[192]

Thus for Abiodun, practicing politics in Cuba often required utilizing informal networks. For several years, Abiodun hosted living-room gatherings for Cubans, many of them black and darker-skinned youth, which she called "open spaces."[193] Originating out of requests from local hip-hop artists for historical information concerning the African American freedom struggle, particularly the figure of Malcolm X, the gatherings often involved a semi-structured political education curriculum—Abiodun often referred to the sessions as "classes"—as well as ciphers for informal debate and self-reflection.

While originating out of the desire for young Cubans to understand the history of U.S. struggles for racial and economic justice, the gatherings also became forums for communication on other social issues in Cuba, particularly gender and sexuality. In a Cuban context in which undiluted discussion of racism and sexual identity had not always flourished in official spheres, informal spaces such as these provided ready alternatives. "The first six people that came to the meetings, I think the first three were gay — two men and a lesbian woman — and the other three were like hardcore emcees who literally sat on the other side of the room at first. But in the course of dialogue and conversation, at the end of two years, they were all sisters and brothers."[194] Drawing a range of Cuban attendees from Abiodun's neighborhood and metro Havana, as well as visiting U.S., Latin American, and European students, the gatherings became uniquely transnational, youth-centered political spaces.

But the open spaces, at least in their formal iteration, did not last. The Cuban government, for reasons that were never revealed explicitly, eventually requested that Abiodun discontinue them. The Cuban government's intervention suggests some of the limits of political discourse in 2000s Cuba, in which the state sought to shape the contours of political discourse by sanctioning some forums for discussion of political issues, but discouraging others. Nonetheless, the curtailment of Abiodun's open spaces, but not other similar forums in Havana, suggests that other factors besides the political content of the sessions may have caused the state's unease. Indeed, noted Cuban scholar Tomás Fernández Robaina, whose research focuses on Afro-Cuban history, conducted a similar series of classes during the same period focusing on both Afro-Cuban history and the U.S. black freedom struggle. The classes, which also drew a range of Afro-Cuban youth, including several prominent hip hop artists, were held in a conspicuous location: the Biblioteca Nacional de José Martí, Cuba's most prominent library, situated adjacent to the Plaza de la Revolución.[195] Despite their similar focus and attendance, these classes were not interfered with. Indeed, forums for discussion of issues related to race and racism in Cuba were also regularly held during this period at Casa de las Américas, and the Unión de Escritores y Artistas de Cuba (UNEAC), prestigious institutions with ties to Cuba's elite intellectual circles. The Cuban government's intervention into Abiodun's living-room classes may have been due to her status as a non-Cuban and a political exile, as well as her relative independence from most state-affiliated Cuban institutions.[196]

Abiodun's mentoring of Cuban youth and hip-hop artists, rooted in her recognition of the singular role played by youth as agents of social change, sometimes assumed more personal dimensions, with young comrades and mentees alike referencing Abiodun in terms that suggest a surrogate mother figure. This affectionate designation from both Cuban and foreign youth resonated unexpectedly with Abiodun's own painful experiences of motherhood in exile. "When I first went underground I had to leave my children. Those first months I almost lost my mind. I would look at a child and almost break down.

Comrades that I had who had children would bring their children around so that I could become an aunt. Then I get to Cuba, and I get all of these young people in my life, to point where I was like, I don't need any more children!"[197] Abiodun's status as a political mentor has also been embraced by numerous visiting U.S. activists, students, and academics, with whom she has formed close friendships. Scholar Jafari Allen's perceptive work ¡Venceremos? The Erotics of Black Self-Making in Cuba is dedicated to Abiodun.[198] Beginning in 2000, Abiodun also began working closely with U.S. medical students studying tuition-free at the Latin American School of Medicine (ELAM), some of whom have recalled Abiodun's mentorship in similarly maternal terms.[199]

Abiodun's unique influence in Cuba is also apparent within the island's hip-hop movement. Although the late 1990s found Abiodun disillusioned with U.S. hip-hop, which she regarded as hopelessly mired in commercialization and misogyny, she would eventually be dubbed the "godmother of Cuban rap," playing a key role in the emergence of hip-hop in Havana and becoming a frequent source for foreign journalists.[200] Along with Assata Shakur, Abiodun played a key role in the development of an early strand of Cuban hip-hop culture that displayed a pronounced problack and pro-African racial consciousness, a strand that often used the African American freedom struggle as a reference point, and which became arguably the dominant iteration of hip-hop throughout the island during the late 1990s and early 2000s and the version that received the most government patronage.[201] Although the Cuban government initially regarded hip-hop with trepidation, the movement eventually secured financial sponsorship from the state, with most support going to artists and collectives that were overtly political yet conspicuously situated their critiques of Cuban society "within the revolution."[202] Arriving in Cuba just as hip-hop culture began to take root on the island, Abiodun's mentoring exerted a lasting impact on pivotal groups such as Obsesión, with one member of the duo, Alexey Rodríguez, naming his daughter after Abiodun.

Abiodun's involvement in Cuban hip-hop, together with her efforts to build bridges between Cubans and U.S. activists and artists, led Abiodun, the Cuban hip-hop producer and linguistics professor Pablo Herrera, and others to initiate the Black August Collective (BAC) in 1998 in collaboration with the Black August initiative of the Malcolm X Grassroots Coalition (MXGM). A New York–based, youth-led black radical organization with intergenerational ties to the RNA, MXGM sought to raise public awareness about U.S. political prisoners such as Mumia Abu-Jamal and Mutulu Shakur.[203] As a transnational initiative invoking ties between Cuban and U.S. hip-hop artists and activists,

BAC secured notable support from the Cuban government, with key roles performed by Herrera and Ariel Fernández Díaz, a music promoter, DJ, and journalist who held a post within the Ministry of Culture.

The Black August hip-hop festivals held in Havana and its vicinities in 1998, 1999, 2000, and 2003 brought U.S. artists such as Talib Kweli, Mos Def, dead prez, and Tony Touch, and performance and visual artists with prior Cuba connections, such as Danny Hoch and Fab 5 Freddy, to Havana to participate in large hip-hop festivals with Cuban artists. U.S. hip-hop artists also sent musical and recording equipment to Cuba.[204] For many U.S. hip-hop artists, their time in Cuba was significant in part because of the opportunity it afforded to dialogue with both Cubans and Assata Shakur and Nehanda Abiodun, figures that were increasingly linked together in the U.S. radical imagination.[205]

Abiodun's most significant contribution to liberation politics from exile has been her role as a bridge, for more than two decades, between Cuba and the broad multiethnic U.S. Left generally, and the black radical Left specifically. Abiodun, who has not published a memoir, is less well known than her friend and comrade, Assata Shakur, yet her impact in Cuba has been far-reaching and significant. Recently, her impact upon the trajectory of Cuban hip-hop, and upon the politics of racial and gender identity and subjectivity among youth in Havana, has been a component of several important academic studies.[206]

Over time in Cuba, Abiodun's conceptualization of the struggle for black liberation, always informed by Malcolm X's expansive vision of "human rights," and by the Black Panther Party's internationalist gaze, has merged with other intersectional radicalisms, particularly support for the rights of sexual minorities, a movement that has taken root in Cuba, eventually with high-level backing from the Cuban government.[207] "Even though I started out fighting for the liberation of my people, that is, African people, I hope that I have developed to the point where I fight for human rights, the ending of all injustices, regardless of where they exist, or how they exist."[208] Abiodun's support for Cuba's movement by and for LGBT and gender nonconforming people, rooted in her commitment to a broadly defined vision of human rights, has also intersected at times with her personal life. Abiodun, whose long-term romantic partnerships in Cuba have not been limited to men, maintains that these aspects of her private life have been accepted by her Cuban community in Raparto Bahía, her political comrades in the United States, and her contacts in the Cuban government.[209]

Abiodun continues to be supported by the Cuban government both politically and materially, including through the provision of food rations and a modest cash living stipend, as well as the use of an apartment.[210] Although security remains a perpetual concern for Abiodun, she is able, as of 2017, to continue her transnational political work. Although the Cuban government has steadfastly refused to negotiate with the United States on the matter of U.S. political asylees in Cuba, the future of Abiodun's status on the island, like that of all the U.S. asylees there, is now dependent upon the shifting tides of U.S.-Cuba relations. As she recalled in 2013: "I know that if I go back to the U.S., I will be arrested and spend the rest of my life in jail. But I don't want to die alone in Cuba. If you've ever been away from your country, even a country that you are at odds with, you know it's still what you know and what you love.... Your country is your country."[211]

Exiles and U.S.-Cuba Relations in the Age of Counterterrorism

The Reagan administration's 1982 designation of Cuba as a "State Sponsor of Terrorism" initially had little to do with the Caribbean nation's harboring of U.S. political asylees. Although administration officials made no immediate comment explaining the addition of Cuba to the list, the designation was congruent with long-standing ire in the State Department regarding Cuba's aid to Third World revolutionary movements.[212] Cuba's military presence in Africa, particularly its support for anticolonial movements in Angola and Namibia, as well as its involvement in the Ethiopia-Somali conflict, had bedeviled the Ford and Carter administrations in the mid- and late 1970s.

However, the election of Ronald Reagan in 1980 signaled a dramatic reinvigoration of Cold War politics. This time, Washington's displeasure with Cuban foreign policy focused on Havana's role in the Americas as well as Africa. As a June 1981 CIA report, entitled *Patterns of International Terrorism 1980*, stated: "Havana openly advocates armed revolution as the only means for leftist forces to gain power in Latin America, and the Cubans have played an important role in facilitating the movement of men and weapons into the region."[213]

Although the Agency's report overstated Cuba's success in the region, it was otherwise an accurate representation of Cuba's foreign-policy objectives in the Americas.[214] In Nicaragua, for instance, Cuba had been an early supporter of the Sandinista Front for National Liberation (FSLN) which had overthrown the family dynasty of Anastasio Somoza in July 1979. Havana sent medical personnel and emergency aid to Nicaragua almost immediately.[215] The United States did not at first express concern. However, as the Sandinista government veered leftward, Washington's fears of a new socialist government in the Americas alarmed the State Department. Rising concern in Washington over

Cuba's foreign policy in the hemisphere provided the larger context in which the issue of U.S. exiles in Cuba reentered Washington's diplomatic field of vision in the mid-1980s through the case of Assata Shakur.

When *Newsday* broke the story about Shakur's presence in Havana in October 1987, FBI and New Jersey State Police officials, who had previously formed a Joint Terrorist Task Force to apprehend her, issued a statement admitting that the reports "confirmed previously known task force intelligence," although it could not be verified, "due to the current relationship between the United States and Cuba."[216] But as Shakur's autobiography arrived in U.S. bookstores and the former Black Panther began to grant interviews to foreign reporters, there could be no more doubt.

Other events contributed to the increased media interest in American fugitives in Cuba. In March 1984, a New York man named William Potts hijacked a Miami-bound commercial flight out of New York, diverting the plane to Havana. Potts, who was not fleeing from criminal charges, had hoped that the Cuban government would provide him with military training and send him to South Africa to join the anti-apartheid struggle. Unaware that Cuba had flatly refused to provide similar aid to previous self-styled American revolutionaries, however, and unaware that Cuba had, since 1973, promised to impose lengthy prison sentences on hijackers entering its territory in an effort at deterrence, Potts spent the next thirteen years imprisoned in Cuba.[217] Then on New Years Eve 1984, St. Croix–born Ishmael LaBeet hijacked a commercial flight from St. Croix, U.S. Virgin Islands, to New York. Convicted of participating in the 1972 murder of eight tourists and employees of a St. Croix golf course in an incident dubbed the Fountain Valley Massacre, Labeet was being transported to prison when he used a gun that had been concealed in the restroom to disarm his guards and commandeer the plane. However, LaBeet, who later changed his name to Ishmael Muslim Ali, claimed innocence in the St. Croix killings. Led by civil rights attorney William Kunstler, LaBeet's defense maintained during the trial that LaBeet and his codefendants were tortured into providing a confession. Like Potts, LaBeet was imprisoned in Cuba for the hijacking.[218]

The increased attention to American political asylees in Cuba during the late 1980s coincided with a pivotal global development — the breakup of the Soviet Union — that would influence the fate of exiles living on the island. Unbowed in its commitment to providing asylum, the Cuban government nevertheless sought to mitigate its vulnerability by limiting the visibility of the exiles in the nation's media and public discourse. Although the Cuban government does not appear to have on any occasion denied the presence of specific political asylees residing in the country, it rarely cooperated with U.S. requests for specific information.

Cuban officials also took pains not to publicize the presence of exiles on the island through news coverage or public praise, an action that U.S. officials might view as a provocation. U.S. journalists seeking to incorporate comments from Cuban officials into their articles were usually unsuccessful, as is evident in the *Newsday* article: "Cuban officials interviewed last week refused to speak on the record about Shakur's presence in their country. They said publication of a newspaper story about her refugee status could anger the United States. And they said that while they would not interfere with attempts to interview her, they did not want to aggravate relations even further by praising Shakur as a black revolutionary."[219]

As Cuba's economy continued to languish in the mid-1990s, Washington quickened its efforts to engineer regime change. In March 1996, the U.S. Congress passed the Cuban Liberty and Democratic Solidarity (Libertad) Act, tabled since 1995, in retaliation for Cuba's lethal shoot-down of two Cessna aircraft operated by the Miami-based Cuban exile group Brothers to the Rescue, which had repeatedly violated Cuban airspace in the prior months to drop antigovernment leaflets on Havana and the countryside, despite warnings from Cuba of severe retaliatory action.[220] Popularly known as the Helms-Burton Act, the legislation aimed to "assist the Cuban people in regaining their freedom and prosperity, as well as in joining the community of democratic countries that are flourishing in the Western Hemisphere."[221] Greatly strengthening the U.S. embargo against Cuba and deploying a list of strict preconditions for Cuba to fulfill in order to achieve normal diplomatic relations with the United States, the Helms-Burton Act, passed within months of the release of William Lee Brent's autobiography, *Long Time Gone*, included "the expulsion of criminals from Cuba" as one such requirement for the normalization of U.S.-Cuba relations. "The President," Section 113 of the Act read, "shall instruct all United States Government officials who engage in official contacts with the Cuban Government to raise on a regular basis the extradition of or rendering to the United States all persons residing in Cuba who are sought by the United States Department of Justice for crimes committed in the United States."[222] The issue of U.S. exiles was now fully imbricated within U.S. foreign policy toward the island.

Lacking an extradition treaty with Cuba, however, New Jersey law-enforcement officials had to conduct their campaign to extract U.S. asylees through other channels. Late in 1997, in anticipation of Pope John Paul II's scheduled visit to Cuba in January, New Jersey Police Superintendent Carl Williams wrote to the pope to ask whether he would raise the topic of Shakur's extradition with President Fidel Castro.[223] It is not known whether John Paul II broached the topic with the Cuban leader during their private meetings. However, a New York television reporter named Ralph Penza was more fortunate. Locating Shakur in Havana in late January and videotaping an interview with her that was subsequently broadcast on WNBC-TV in New York, the segment adhered closely to the police version of events regarding the 1973 turnpike shooting, juxtaposing images of Shakur, looking healthy and relaxed in Havana as she vigorously proclaimed her innocence, with footage of the slain officer's tearful widow. Although Shakur later explained that she had agreed to the interview with Penza to "tell my side of the story, which most people have never been allowed to hear,"[224] she later published a rebuttal characterizing the segment as a "staged media event in three parts, full of distortions, inaccuracies, and outright lies."[225]

The NBC segment set off a chain of events that culminated in a significant acceleration of the U.S. government's efforts to extradite U.S. asylees in Cuba, and with it, the further integration of this effort into the fabric of U.S. foreign policy. Characterizing Shakur's televised appearance as "an affront," an outraged New Jersey Governor Christine Todd Whitman promptly wrote to Secretary of State Madeleine K. Albright asking the Clinton administration to pressure the Cuban government to extradite Shakur. Albright obliged, and the U.S. State Department later sent a formal request to Havana requesting the return of ninety-one American fugitives alleged to be residing in Cuba.[226]

In March 1998, New Jersey Congressman Robert Franks sponsored a Congressional Resolution calling on the Cuban government to extradite Shakur. Condemning the interviews with Shakur that had shown her "living freely in Cuba, portraying herself as the victim," the resolution concluded with a statement urging that the United States "should not ease any restrictions currently in place with respect to Cuba before Ms. Chesimard is extradited to the United States."[227] When the bill was introduced as House Congressional Resolution 254 on March 30, the opening text had been adjusted to call for the extradition of not only Shakur, but of "all other individuals who have fled the United States to avoid prosecution or confinement for criminal offenses and who are currently living freely in Cuba."[228]

The bill cited an FBI report alleging that Cuba was providing sanctuary to ninety-one Americans fleeing criminal prosecution in the U.S., a number that was downgraded to seventy-seven when the bill was passed in September.[229] During the bill's hearing before the House Subcommittee on the Western Hemisphere, New Jersey representative Robert Menendez juxtaposed Cuba's provision of asylum to Americans who, he argued, "live relatively well," with the communist government's treatment of its own prisoners, imprisoned by "Castro . . . for much lesser crimes, like distribution of enemy propaganda or undermining the revolution."[230] All versions of the bill argued that the improvement of U.S. diplomatic relations with Cuba should be contingent upon Havana's cooperation on the issue of U.S. asylees.

Cuban officials, however, refused to concede Havana's right to grant asylum, and reminded U.S. officials of the absence of an active extradition treaty. Cuban Foreign Ministry spokesman Alejandro González characterized Shakur as a "well-known civil-rights activist," and explained Havana's rationale for declining Whitman's request: "The [Cuban] government has reasons to disagree with the accusations made against her and fears she may be the object of unfair charges."[231]

Cuba also took exception to the broader terrain of Washington's efforts to extradite Americans from Cuba, which U.S. officials had leveled at Havana without any indication that Washington was willing to reciprocate by returning Cuban exiles residing in the United States who were wanted for extradition by Havana on similar criminal charges, including terrorism and murder. Indeed, the text of the proposed Resolution 254 had argued, in language that invoked the full hubris of U.S. exceptionalism, that nations "should respect each other's justice systems and not provide safe-harbor to individuals who have been indicted or convicted of criminal offenses."[232]

In a letter addressed to several members of the House regarding Resolution 254, Center for Constitutional Rights attorney Michael Ratner criticized the bill as "hypocritical," citing convicted or accused terrorists and human rights violators who had secured asylum in the United States, including the Cuban-born, CIA-trained Orlando Bosch, suspected of orchestrating the bombing of the civilian airliner Cubana de Aviación flight 455 in 1976, now living in Miami; and Haitian death-squad leader Emmanuel Constant, whom the Clinton administration had declined to extradite to Haiti to face trial.[233]

Members of the U.S. Congressional Black Caucus, who had voted in favor of Resolution 254, now staged their own protest through the bloc's chair, Maxine Waters. Claiming that the caucus had not realized that the congressional bill pertained to Shakur because the text referred to one "JoAnne Chesimard," not "Assata Shakur," Waters penned a letter to Fidel Castro to apologize for the vote, affirming her support of "the right of all nations to grant political asylum to individuals fleeing political persecution," including "the sovereign nation of Cuba."[234]

Amid the sudden flurry of international scrutiny, Shakur penned a message of her own to the pope. As an open letter, Shakur hoped to offer a public counternarrative to the accusations of the state of New Jersey, while also questioning Washington's exceptionalist rhetoric of human rights and anticommunism, with which it had long framed its opposition to the Castro government. Imploring the pope to "speak out against human rights violations" against African Americans and dissidents occurring in the United States, Shakur offered a personal window into her own spirituality and ambivalent relationship with Catholicism. Wrote Shakur: "It was in the dungeons of prison that I felt the presence of God up close.... I believe that Jesus was a political prisoner who was executed because he fought against the evils of the Roman Empire. ... As a true child of God, Jesus spoke up for the poor, the meek, the sick, and the oppressed."[235]

The text of the letter, which assumes a respectful and reverential tone, also suggests that Shakur viewed the pope as a potentially sympathetic actor in the convoluted saga of U.S.-Cuba relations, one who was not solely beholden to the interests of Washington. Indeed, the pope's visit to Cuba, which had transpired with the blessing of Fidel Castro, had unexpectedly catalyzed a national discussion in Cuba about religious and political freedom. Criticizing the Cuban government for its imprisonment of political dissidents and its marginalization of Christianity, the pope also condemned U.S. efforts to isolate Cuba in the international system, and leveled a particularly pointed indictment of the growing hegemony of transnational corporations.

Conducting Holy Mass in José Martí Plaza on January 25, 1998, as Castro sat in the audience next to his long-time friend, Colombian writer Gabriel García Márquez, the pope criticized the Cuban government's marginalization of religion, contending that "a modern State cannot make atheism or religion one of its political ordinances," but also implicitly endorsed the intent behind Cuba's socialist efforts to elevate human well-being above capitalist profit motives. "Various places are witnessing the resurgence of a certain capitalist neoliberalism," the pope observed, "which subordinates the human person to blind market forces and conditions the development of peoples on those forces."[236]

Speculation about the possibility for improved U.S.-Cuba relations in 1999 during the twilight of the Clinton administration led to renewed media interest in the fate of the American exiles. With tourism to the island increasing—a result of the Cuban government's bid to lure foreign capital into the country—Cuba's community of U.S. exiles increasingly feared bounty hunters.²³⁷ Then, in June 2001, the U.S. Congress passed an amendment to the Helms-Burton act known as the "No Safe Haven in Cuba Act," which classified the extradition of American fugitives as one of the criteria by which Cuba must prove that it was a democracy. "Respect for the rule of law," the bill read, "is a primary condition for the establishment of any legitimate democratic government." According to the text of the act, its purpose was "to require that, in order to determine that a democratically elected government in Cuba exists, the government extradite to the United States convicted felon Joanne Chesimard and all other individuals who are living in Cuba in order to escape prosecution or confinement for criminal offenses committed in the United States."²³⁸

With the inauguration of George W. Bush, the stakes of Washington's designation of Cuba as a "State Sponsor of Terrorism" increased exponentially. Ironically, the nexus between the 9/11 era, U.S.-Cuba diplomacy, and American dissidents in Cuba briefly gained national media attention on the eve of the September 11, 2001, hijacking attacks in the United States with the improbable capture of a long forgotten member of the RNA who had fled to Cuba thirty years earlier. On the day after Christmas in 1971, Patrick Critton, a New York high-school teacher and respected community leader, had hijacked a commercial airliner departing from Thunder Bay, Ontario. Wanted in connection with a bank robbery in New York, Critton hoped to secure political asylum in Cuba, as his RNA comrades Finney, Goodwin, and Hill had done earlier that year. Letting eighty unsuspecting passengers off at the flight's next stop in Toronto — they learned they had been hijacked only later — Critton directed aircraft and crew to Havana.

Initially imprisoned for eight months in Cuba pending his security clearance, Critton lived on the island for two years after his release before departing for Africa, ultimately spending two decades in Tanzania. Returning discreetly to the United States in 1994, Critton quietly rededicated himself to teaching and community work. Characterized as a "model citizen"²³⁹ by neighbors in Mount Vernon, New York, Critton taught history at a Brooklyn high school, ran a program for troubled urban youth, fundraised for United Way, and counted the police chief among his personal friends.²⁴⁰ But in 2001, Critton's luck ran out: he was captured by Canadian authorities on September 10, 2001.²⁴¹ Critton's case was national news in the United States for a few hours the next day before vanishing from the networks as Al-Qaida hijackers crashed commercial airliners into the World Trade Center and the Pentagon.²⁴² As U.S. policy toward Cuba became increasingly framed by the national security and foreign policy objectives that grew out of the 9/11 attacks, pressure on Havana to extradite U.S. asylees was influenced by the political discourses and imperial logic of George W. Bush's "War on Terror." Nonetheless, many exiles remained confident in the continuing support of their benefactor. Former RNA member Michael Finney remained cautiously optimistic, telling a visiting reporter that despite the pressure on Cuba, "I feel safe here. I am convinced the Cuban government considers me a political fighter... I have fought for the freedom of African-Americans."[243]

In 2004, amid the full force of the War on Terror, whose rhetoric now eclipsed anticommunism as the primary discourse used to frame U.S.-Cuba relations, the U.S. Department of State's *Country Reports on Terrorism 2004* named Cuba as one of the world's four "State Sponsors of Terrorism," together with Iran, North Korea, and Syria. Notably absent was Iraq, whose designation had been rescinded in October 2004, a year after being invaded by U.S.-led forces. As the report explained, without apparent irony: "Iraq, as it transitioned to democracy, ceased to support terrorism."[244]

The report listed three reasons for Cuba's inclusion on the state sponsors of terrorism list: "Cuba [has] continued to actively oppose the US-led coalition prosecuting the global war on terrorism," and has "continued to provide limited support to designated Foreign Terrorist Organizations, as well as safe haven for terrorists" such as Spain's Basque Fatherland and Liberty (ETA), and Colombia's Revolutionary Armed Forces of Colombia (FARC) and National Liberation Army (ELN).[245] The report's discussion of Shakur and other U.S. exiles who had been granted "safe haven" in Cuba situated their alleged crimes within prevailing definitions of terrorism:

> Many of the over seventy fugitives from US justice that have taken refuge on the island are accused of committing violent acts in the United States that *targeted innocents in order to advance political causes*. They include Joanne Chesimard, who is wanted for the murder of a New Jersey State Trooper in 1973. On a few rare occasions the Cuban government has transferred fugitives to the United States, although it maintains that fugitives would not receive a fair trial in the United States.[246]

But U.S. efforts to extradite Shakur were just beginning to gain traction within the rhetorical framework and punitive state apparatus enabled by the War on Terror. As a 2005 report by the Congressional Research Service, issued coincidentally on the twentieth anniversary of a deadly bombing, by police helicopter, of the headquarters of the black radical group Move in Philadelphia on May 13, 1985,[247] observed:

Supporters of keeping Cuba on the terrorist list point to the more than 70 fugitives from U.S. justice residing in Cuba. These include such fugitives as: Joanne Chesimard, who was convicted for the killing of a New Jersey state trooper in 1973; Charles Hill and Michael Finney, wanted for the killing of a state trooper in new Mexico in 1971; Victor Manuel Gerena, member of a militant Puerto Rican separatist group, wanted for carrying out the robbery of a Wells Fargo armored car in Connecticut in 1983; and Guillermo Morales, another member of a Puerto Rican militant group, who was convicted of illegal possession of firearms in New York in the 1970s.[248]

The designation of Cuba as a terrorist state was now firmly bound up with Havana's provision of sanctuary for U.S. radicals. That same year, the State of New Jersey announced a $1 million bounty, up from $150,000, for information leading to Shakur's apprehension. The FBI's "wanted" poster characterized the BLA as a "revolutionary activist organization" and noted that Shakur, known to "wear her hair in a variety of styles and dress in African tribal clothing," was wanted for a litany of charges, including "Act of Terrorism, Domestic Terrorism, Unlawful Flight to Avoid Confinement, [and] Murder."[249] In Havana, rumors circulated that foreign bounty hunters had arrived, asking questions about Shakur.[250]

Cuba's most famous American asylee, who had recently been a fixture at events sponsored by ICAP for visiting Americans and whose phone number had once been listed in the Havana phonebook, dropped out of sight as her FBI poster reappeared bearing the new reward — an astronomical sum of money on the island — inside the U.S. Interests Section in the Vedado district of Havana. Living at undisclosed locations and reportedly moving every few months, Shakur was now effectively living "underground" on the island, allegedly protected directly by the Cuban intelligence service.[251] A *Sun Sentinel* reporter who visited Shakur's former address in Havana found that she no longer lived there. "A neighbor, asked whether he knew where she had gone, simply laughed and said it was 'a war secret.'"[252]

Protected by the Cuban government, Shakur's safety was treated as a matter of Cuban state security. Castro himself now publicly entered the fray, rejecting calls for her extradition in a televised address and excoriating U.S. officials for characterizing Cuba as a sponsor of terrorism for harboring Shakur while simultaneously allowing Luis Posada Carriles, another mastermind of the 1976 Cubana de Aviación airline bombing, to reside unmolested in Florida. Although Castro did not refer to Shakur by name, there could be no doubt about who the aging Cuban leader was referring to. Defending Cuba's provision of political asylum to an unnamed fugitive accused of shooting a New Jersey police officer, Castro characterized her as a victim of "the fierce repression against the black movement in the United States" and "a true political prisoner" who had sought protection against persecution. "They wanted to portray her as a terrorist," Castro charged, "something that was an injustice, a brutality, an infamous lie."[253]

Responses to the $1 million bounty within left-wing circles in the United States came swiftly. As "hands off Assata" committees formed in several U.S. cities, activists highlighted the historical and conceptual links between U.S. imperial antagonism toward Cuba and the U.S. government's historical repression of black radical activists. Kathleen Cleaver, who had been a Black Panther leader when her husband, Eldridge Cleaver, had sought political asylum in Cuba in 1968, condemned the new bounty for Shakur as "lynch-mob diplomacy."[254] Hip-hop artist Mos Def (now Yasiin Bey) defended Cuba's provision of asylum in an essay entitled, "The government's terrorist is our community's heroine," writing that Cuba was "exercising its political sovereignty" in sheltering her.[255]

In New York, a pitched battle ensued at City College in fall 2006 after a police association learned that students there had named a clubroom in the student center after Shakur and William Guillermo Morales, a member of the Fuerzas Armadas de Liberación Nacional Puertorriqueña, linked to a series of bombings in the United States, who had received asylum in Cuba after escaping from the prison ward of Bellevue Hospital in 1979. Although the College's administration had initially supported the students, the Chancellor of the City University of New York ultimately ordered the names removed from the clubroom's entrance.[256] The New Jersey State Assembly then filed a resolution, referencing Shakur's 2005 inclusion on the FBI's domestic terrorist list, supporting the Chancellor.[257]

Speculation about the fate of Cuba's U.S. exiles was also increasingly tied to the fate of Fidel Castro himself. In July 2006, after the Cuban government revealed that Castro had been hospitalized, leading the Cuban leader to cede authority to his younger brother, Raúl Castro, U.S. media attention again focused on the likelihood that a transition of power on the island might alter Havana's commitment to sheltering foreign exiles.[258]

Members of visiting U.S. solidarity and educational delegations, who might in previous years have held meetings with Shakur or encountered her at public events, now heard only rumors of her. Scholar and poet Ben V. Olguín, who first traveled to Cuba with the Venceremos Brigade the year after the $1 million bounty, captured the sentiments of some U.S. leftists visiting the island:

Assata. Warrior
woman we miss you,
we need you now
more than ever.
But the brigade's lesson
has always been emulación.
So we have followed you
to the same fields
slaves were once forced
to work.²⁵⁹

The dawning of the Obama era was marked by a mild thaw in U.S.-Cuba hostilities, and with it, continued media speculation about the fate of the island's American exiles.²⁶⁰ New Jersey lawmakers lost little time in making their demands known. In April 2009, New Jersey Senator Sean T. Kean wrote to President Obama urging him to "delay normalizing relations with Cuba unless they agree to extradite convicted cop killer JoAnne Chesimard."²⁶¹

In May 2011, Shakur's presence in Cuba reentered public consciousness in an unexpected way. When hip-hop artist Common was invited to the Obama White House to perform during a poetry event, right-wing pundits and police organizations protested the invitation, citing the lyrics of a song, entitled "A Song For Assata," whose title was reminiscent of Cuban singer Pablo Milanés's 1971 "Canción para Ángela Davis"— a song for Angela Davis. "She's a domestic terrorist," an official for the New Jersey State Police complained, "who wrapped her criminality and her abhorrent anti social behavior in a cause to try to disguise her disgust for America in this make believe 1960s radicalism."²⁶² New Jersey Representative Scott Garrett wrote to President Obama to urge him to make Shakur's extradition "one of the prerequisites for achieving normal diplomatic relations with Cuba."²⁶³

Then on May 2, 2013, the fortieth anniversary of the turnpike killing of officer Werner Foerster and just two weeks after the terrorist bombings at the Boston Marathon, the FBI named Shakur to its "Most Wanted Terrorists" list, making her the first woman to attain the dubious distinction and, according to the Bureau's press release, "only the second domestic terrorist" to make the list. The FBI announced its own reward of $1 million for information leading to Shakur's capture. Combined with the State of New Jersey's 2005 reward, the total reward was now an extraordinary $2 million.²⁶⁴ The FBI's press release charged that Shakur "attends government functions and her standard of living is higher than most Cubans."²⁶⁵

262 Black Radicalism, Political Asylum, and the Diplomacy of Exile and Freedom

The joint FBI and New Jersey State Police poster for Assata Shakur issued on May 2, 2013, on the fortieth anniversary of her arrest. The FBI also added Shakur to its Most Wanted Terrorist List, making her the first woman to be placed on it. Author's collection.

Law enforcement efforts to apprehend Shakur were now embedded, both discursively and materially, within the apparatus of Washington's bid to maintain global dominance, legitimized through the War on Terror and prosecuted now by the administration of Barack Obama. In Cuba, Shakur remained under the watchful eye of the Cuban security state, living at a safe house and protected by government bodyguards. Cut off from even her close friends and unable to participate in Havana's public life, from which she had derived so much satisfaction and solace, Shakur descended into the isolation of an exile within an exile. "One of the things that I am most proud of is Cuba's protection of Assata Shakur," Cuban historian Tomás Fernández Robaina stated in June 2013. "But now she is like a great mystery in Cuba. We know that she is here and that she is okay, but not for how long."[266]

UNCERTAINTY ABOUT Shakur's fate rose back into news headlines in December 2014 with joint public announcements by the governments of Cuba and the United States that a process of diplomatic normalization had begun. As global attention focused on the historic event, which seemed to herald the beginning of the end of half a century of hostility, opponents of Shakur, including Senators Ted Cruz of Texas and Marco Rubio of Florida, and Bob Menendez of New Jersey, called on President Obama to make Shakur's extradition a condition for normalization. In a letter, New Jersey Governor Chris Christie called upon the President to "demand the immediate return of Chesimard before any further consideration of restoration of diplomatic relations with the Cuban government."[267] But Cuban officials flatly refused. Interviewed by *Yahoo News*, Gustavo Machín, deputy director for American affairs at the Cuban Ministry of Foreign Affairs, told the reporter that Shakur's extradition was "off the table" because she had been granted political asylum. "There are very serious doubts about that case.... We consider that a politically motivated case against that lady."[268]

The fate of U.S. exiles in Cuba, like the fate of much in Cuba, now rests with the future of the Cuban Revolution in an uncertain post-revolutionary world. Nonetheless, although relations between Cuba and U.S. leftists have changed over time, Havana's willingness to provide sanctuary to those whom it has considered political refugees from the capitalist superpower north of the Florida Straits has remained remarkably durable. More than virtually any other aspect of Cuba's engagement with American leftists, Havana's provision of asylum to U.S. dissidents has had significant diplomatic consequences for Cuba, a point that attests to the great idealistic and strategic importance of Cuba's ties to the American radical Left in general, and to the African American freedom movement in particular. U.S. political exiles in Cuba exemplify a volatile nexus between the historical forces of Cuba's revolution, U.S. imperial power, and the broad currents of U.S. radicalism that have brought these historical forces repeatedly into engagement and confrontation since 1959.

Epilogue
Unfinished Revolutions

Tell no lies ... claim no easy victories.
—Amílcar Cabral

CUBA'S ENDURANCE within the U.S. radical imaginary has been derived, in part, from hope. For some, it has been the hope that the structural violence and organized abandonment of poverty, hunger, lack of education, and medical neglect is not foreordained, despite the persistence of Randian ideals of human nature and the hegemony of market capitalism and ascendant neoliberalism. Cuba's achievements in health care, education, and the privileging of its youth, the elderly, and the sick, despite limited resources, are admired throughout the world. In the United States, many continue to see the Cuban Revolution's humanistic ethos as one model through which to imagine new futures that prioritize human well-being and environmental integrity ahead of the health of the market, or what Martin Luther King Jr. called "machines and computers, profit motives and property rights."[1]

Most Cubans on the island continue to believe in the core ideals of the nation's revolutionary project, even if there is significant disagreement about the degree to which it has been fulfilled. Concepts such as democracy and human rights, many Cubans still argue, must be measured in part by the ability of a society to guarantee freedom from the preventable unfreedoms of poverty's consequences, including lack of access to health care and education, and by its commitment to the well-being of its most vulnerable. Freedom, they may insist, cannot be measured *solely* by the metrics of individual liberty, freedom of expression, property rights, free enterprise, and free markets to which U.S. notions of liberal democracy are tied, and the freedom of global capital overall, which threatens to consume every acre of the earth. Despite growing inequality on the island and the erosion of the social services that lie at the heart of the revolutionary project, Cuba still appears to be the most equal nation in the western hemisphere. The streets of Cuban cities are remarkably safe by global standards, and the nation continues to have far lower levels of violent crime and drug addiction than its neighbors, including the United States. For others in the United States, the hope embodied in Cuba's revolutionary process is tied to concerns regarding gender, racial, and sexual equality — concerns that are neither reducible to economic class nor separable from them. These have been Cuba's unfinished revolutions, ongoing battles waged "within the Revolution," and in these the nation's record has been more mixed, more contested. As scholars such as Alejandro de la Fuente and Devyn Spence Benson have demonstrated, the Cuban Revolution has represented both the severing and recuperation of preexisting Cuban racial ideologies, resulting in significant racial progress even as forms of racism have persisted.[2] Racial disparities in Cuba, including in the key indices of health, life expectancy, and educational attainment, still appear to be the lowest of any nation in the Americas. Nonetheless, full equality has not been achieved. While cities such as Havana and Santiago de Cuba have no racial ghettoes characterized by anything even remotely approaching the levels of segregation one can easily witness in U.S. cities such as Philadelphia or Chicago, black Cubans are nonetheless overrepresented among Cuba's poorest neighborhoods, are more likely to be harassed by the police, and are by all accounts overrepresented among the prison population.

Gender and sexual equality in Cuba have also been key terrains of hope for U.S. leftists, and in these too Cuba's record has been both significant and incomplete. That Cuban women are heavily represented in government and professional sectors, in numbers well above most Caribbean and Latin American nations, does not mean that gendered barriers have been removed, nor that Cuban society has become a gender-egalitarian utopia.[3] Persecution of gay, lesbian, and gender-nonconforming Cubans, reaching a height with the UMAPs in the mid-1960s but persisting informally throughout the next decade, are difficult to reconcile with any barometer of human freedom. Thus the current broadening of sexual rights and attitudes in Cuba, paralleling comparable shifts in the United States and throughout the Americas, is noteworthy. Granted institutional legitimacy by Cuba's Centro Nacional de Educación Sexual (CENESEX) — the National Center for Sex Education that is directed by Mariela Castro Espín, a daughter of Cuban president Raúl Castro — high-level support for gay rights in Cuba represents a dramatic transformation.[4]

Cuba's unfinished revolutions will likely play a significant determining role in the future of socialism on the island — and of perceptions of it within the

U.S. Left. Revolution, Cuba's remaining revolutionaries sometimes remind foreign critics, is a process, not a destination. Embodied in the Cuban slogan, *¡Venceremos!*, meaning "we will win," or "we will overcome," the Cuban Revolution fifty years later is an idea, a utopian dream, imperfect and contingent, one conditioned by the tenacity of everyday Cubans, a great many of whom have internalized the revolution's ideals of solidarity, internationalism, and equality, and are deeply proud of the nation's accomplishments. Nonetheless, the gulf between soaring revolutionary rhetoric, on the one hand, and the lived realities of material scarcity and limits on political freedom, on the other, constitute a paradox. As scholar Jafari S. Allen observes:

> In practice ¡Venceremos! is less an objective declaration of unqualified victory than a prophetic hope for the future. And while it is debatable to what degree Cubans believe in slogans like ¡Venceremos! that proclaim the eventual victory of the downtrodden brave enough to resist, it is clear that this seemingly quixotic rhetoric and the political education it represents has conditioned subjectivities of 'entitlement.' Cubans feel that it is their birthright to enjoy human security (e.g., free healthcare, education, and subsidized food and housing), as well as to express themselves freely as human beings, even if material realities and political exigencies find them merely subsisting in spaces of lack and uncertainty.[5]

The literature of hope mixed with ambivalence among U.S. left-wing travelers to Cuba is long. The earlier period, from the 1960s through the 1990s, is examined in this book. The more recent period parallels it, however, suggesting that the same enigmas remain. Scholar Farah Jasmine Griffin, for instance, assesses her relationship with Cuba as a "love affair," a term that will be instantly familiar to many in the United States who have engaged with the island from the standpoint of commitments to social justice. Nevertheless, as Griffin writes, "this was no idealistic, romantic love. It was difficult, challenging, questioning." In an essay entitled "Para las chicas Cubanas," Griffin suggests that the revolution's mystique had been conveyed by the power of the writings of those who had described the transformative power of their encounters with the island:

> Tales of [Fidel Castro] having opened luxury hotel pools to Cuba's poor children and his legendary stay at Harlem's Hotel Teresa [*sic*] helped to create a larger than life image of the man and the Revolution. When I was a young adult, Black intellectuals such as Amiri Baraka and Toni Cade

Bambara helped to define Cuba as space and place. The promise of a land of racial equality and the possibilities offered by Socialism made Cuba a dreamscape.[6]

This exposure, Griffin writes, left her ill-prepared to grasp Cuba's complex realities when she visited the island for the first time long after the revolution's heyday. "The Cuba I visited in the spring of 2001 is not the Cuba Bambara visited in 1973; nor is it the Cuba of her second trip in 1986."[7] For Griffin, these realities were embodied in the realization that Cuba had not fully realized its ideals of racial and gender equality, concerns that intersected for her in the visible resurgence of the underground sex economy in Cuba in the aftermath of the Special Period as growing economic scarcity impacted the island. Although sex work as a strategy to cope with economic marginalization is not unique to Cuba, many, though not all, of the sex workers that Griffin observed were young, women, and black:

> Some are with black foreign men but the overwhelming majority are white. It is a scene as common as the huge colorful murals with socialist slogans painted on them. It is a scene that breaks my heart, as I find myself falling deeper and deeper in love with this nation and with its lovely, smart and generous people. It breaks my heart because I am a black woman who wants to believe that somewhere on earth black women are free.[8]

As this book demonstrates, the U.S. Left's engagement with the Cuban Revolution has continually reflected this ambivalence of hope and disappointment. Now, as then, public discourse about Cuba in the United States has a tendency to devolve into a series of binaries. Cuba is heaven or hell, socialist paradise or floating prison, but rarely is it something more complex. In the political calculus of cold war, revolution, and counterrevolution, the idea of Cuba remains a polarizing battlefield. To see Cuba in the United States, Jafari Allen observes, "is in large part to see it through the very particularly conditioned perspectives of Cuban-American 'exiles,'" who "blame 'Castro' for the island's ills even as they continue to use powerful lobbying organizations to advocate U.S. policies toward Cuba that make life extremely difficult for Cubans, who are largely of color." However, this dichotomy has also been produced frequently by the non-Cuban multiracial American left: "The other side of this polarized discourse is characterized by turning a blind eye to the errors of the revolutionary government and attributing difficulties solely to U.S. imperialism."[9] Originating in the tumult and possibility of the 1960s era, the American Left's engagement with the Cuban Revolution, now spanning more than half a century, remains one of the most enigmatic facets of the "ties of singular intimacy" that have linked the histories of Cuba and the United States.[10] Americans and Cubans repeatedly built bridges to each other across gulfs of ideology and history, but not always in the ways that they intended. Although working as nonstate actors, American radicals repeatedly influenced U.S.-Cuba relations, becoming unlikely historical agents in a Cold War saga dominated in the public imaginary by diplomats and politicians. While the efforts of the writers, intellectuals, political activists, air hijackers, fugitives, artists, and political asylum seekers examined in this book were never the primary force animating state diplomacy between the two nations, Havana and Washington were repeatedly forced to contend with attempts by left-wing Americans to shape the foreign polices of both nations and seek personal transformation and legal sanctuary on the island.

Engagements between Cuba and the inchoate American Left continue in a variety of forms. As in its earlier incarnations, this relationship has included the political advocacy of Cuba solidarity activists, who have continued to call for an end to the U.S. economic embargo, which remains largely intact as of this writing despite the efforts of the administration of President Barack Obama to lift it. Activists have also attempted to blunt some of the more bellicose of Washington's efforts to foment regime change, which continue through a host of euphemistically named "democracy promotion" initiatives funded by the U.S. Congress.

Several organizations formed by Americans during the late 1960s and 1970s continue to maintain relationships with the island. The Venceremos Brigade, as already seen, continues to send delegations to Cuba every summer. The New York–based Center for Cuban Studies, founded in 1972 by activists, scholars, and writers to support the normalization of U.S.-Cuba relations, sponsors educational and artistic programs about Cuba to counter the effects of the U.S. embargo which, the Center's website contends, has functioned as "a de facto embargo on information about Cuba."[11] The Antonio Maceo Brigade persists as a loose association of Cuban American activists and intellectuals. Progressive think tanks and advocacy groups in Washington such as the Institute for Policy Studies and the Center for Democracy in the Americas continue to produce research on Cuba and advocate the full normalization of U.S.-Cuba relations.

Newer expressions of engagement between progressive Americans and Cuba also intersect with Havana's foreign policy aims. As scholars and Cuba observers have long noted, Cuba's medical diplomacy, through which Cuba sends thousands of medical personnel to nations around the world, has allowed Havana to continue its ideology of internationalism while also cultivating goodwill across the Global South and beyond.[12] Thus it is significant that one of the Cuban government's most high-profile engagements with the U.S. Left in the post–Special Period era has occurred in the realm of health. Cuba's medical education program for Americans, conducted at Havana's esteemed Escuela Latinoamericana de Medicina (ELAM), provides free medical education to Americans from poor and medically underserved communities in the United States, the majority of them African Americans, Latinos/as, and Native Americans. Amidst the crisis of American medical inequality, characterized by massively unequal access to health care and treatment relative to economic class and race, the successes of Cuba's health system, which has been credited with providing "First World numbers" emerging from "Third World conditions," has received significant attention for providing remarkably high health outcomes on a small fraction of the resources available in the First World.[13]

Nonetheless, the Cuban Revolution's significance within left-wing American politics has declined in some respects since the 1990s. To post–Cold War U.S. eyes, Cuba sometimes appears as a relic of a bygone era of idealism and political upheaval, a still-socialist island floating in a rising sea of neoliberalism. As the global 1960s era of decolonization, revolution, and anti-imperialist struggle slowly fades from popular memory, Cuba's prominence within the American radical imaginary has receded into the distance, becoming a more remote source of usable history. The decline of Cuba's influence in U.S. left-wing politics is also due to the increasingly visible nature of the economic and political crisis within Cuba itself. While the Cuban government has not suffered a disintegration on the order of the Soviet Union, the Havana government has made some signs of retreating from its revolutionary social contract, announcing the layoff of a half million government-employed workers in 2010 to stave off financial insolvency and diluting the quality and availability of key social services.[14] Although current economic reforms have brought increased opportunities for some Cubans to participate in newly legalized quasicapitalist economies, including private business, the new market economy has also directly accelerated prior inequities. The ability to access foreign investment capital, for instance, which often must be secured from relatives living abroad, strongly correlates to race, as black and *mulato/a* Cubans on the island are still less likely to have relatives living in the United States and overseas. Disillusionment and political alienation among Cubans, particularly acute among young people, now constitutes as formidable a threat to the future of Cuba's revolutionary project as any external one from the United States. In an increasingly stratified economy relying upon access to tourist dollars and foreign remittances, Cuba now appears to be marching not toward a more perfect socialism, but toward a period of greater inequality.

Rising inequality during the Special Period and its aftermath has also coincided with the Internet age. Evidence of the struggles of daily life in Cuba, ranging from material scarcity to crumbling buildings and strained infrastructure, is more easily disseminated abroad, as is critical commentary about it. Organized political dissidents on the island, while small in number, have similarly been able to amplify their message for a global audience more effectively in the age of social media, and the Cuban government has been less successful in maintaining the image of the revolution's successes abroad. So too, the decline of Cuba's influence within the U.S. Left is also due to the static nature of Cuban electoral politics, which continue to be populated at the upper levels by the old guard of revolutionaries from the 1960s era, a generational status quo that is perceived as concurrently less justifiable among the U.S. Left with each passing year. Social issues within Cuba have also received new attention within U.S. leftist circles, as U.S. social justice movements have increasingly reflected concerns related to identity, culture, and representation. As the recognition of LGBT rights in the United States achieves significant victories and enters mainstream political culture, Cuba's onetime suppression of the rights of its gender-nonconforming citizens continues to cast a shadow upon some of Cuba's social gains, despite the Cuban government's notably progressive stances on the issue since the 1990s, some of which surpass those in the United States in affirming the self-determination of transgender people.[15]

If Cuba is to retain the support of broad sectors of the U.S. Left, it will have to continue to reconcile the promises of its bold liberatory aspirations with the lived realities of material scarcity on the island. Chief among them is evidence that inequality in Cuba is rising in tandem with market reforms, despite efforts to mitigate disparities with socialist redistribution. Intersecting with these inequalities, but not always reducible to them, is growing racial inequality, and the increasing marginalization of women in Cuba's economy, as significant gains made in the representation of women in the state-run professional sectors are undermined by the increased prominence of the tourist sector and service industries. And while Cuba has steadfastly protected its U.S. political asylees, any retreat from it, particularly in the case of Assata Shakur, who occupies a profoundly significant status in the U.S. radical imaginary, will spell irreparable disaster for Cuba's credibility within the U.S. Left generally, and the African American and multiracial Left specifically, which has historically been Cuba's strongest base of U.S. support.

It remains to be seen how the arc of relations between the U.S. Left and Cuba will now unfold. Events on the not-so-distant horizon suggest that elements of the "long" Cuban Revolution and what grew out of it — new political and economic theories, a bold ethos of internationalism and mutual solidarity, the global reach of its iconography, its cultural cachet and contagious idealism in the face of great odds, and the survival of the revolution itself for over half a century despite the hostility of a neighboring superpower — could be rediscovered by new incarnations of the broad U.S. Left and make their presence felt in unforeseen ways. In the twenty-first century, as the United States experiences widening levels of economic inequality, disparities in access to health care, deepening racial segregation and emboldened right-wing, racist, and fascist social movements, the consequences of this era's massive transfer of wealth into the hands of a tiny economic elite raises the possibility that new political movements will develop in the future seeking to build new models of social justice informed by critiques of capitalism and empire. If that occurs, left-wing social movements may again look to Cuba's revolutionary history for usable models of socialism, internationalism, and solidarity.

Notes

Abbreviations

LAT Los Angeles Times
MH   Miami Herald
NYT New York Times
WP   Washington Post

Introduction

1. Carmichael, *Black Power and the Third World*.
2. "Black Power," *Tricontinental* 2 (September-October 1967): 172.
3. Carmichael, *Black Power and the Third World*.
4. "U.S. to Lift Passport of Stokely Carmichael," *LAT*, July 27, 1967, 11.
5. Castro, reprinted in *International Socialist Review*, 11–32.
6. Stokely Carmichael, February 17, 1968, Oakland Auditorium, The Pacifica Radio/UC Berkeley Social Activism Sound Recording Project, The Black Panther Party: http://www.lib.berkeley.edu/MRC/carmichael.html.
7. Carmichael and Thelwell, *Ready for Revolution*, 584. Italics in the original. The most complete accounting of Carmichael's relationship with Cuba is Seidman, "Tricontinental Routes of Solidarity." See also Joseph, *Stokely*, 202–10; Sutherland Martínez, *Youngest Revolution*, 154–55.
8. The use of the term "American" to signify people from the United States is rife with controversy. America (*América*) is a continent, not a country, and so the propensity of the United States to claim the term implies, for many Latin Americans, a certain superpower hubris. Nonetheless, the English-language alternatives are also imperfect. "North American" can refer to Canadians, members of Indigenous nations, and Mexicans. In much of Spanish-speaking Latin America, *estadounidense*, meaning someone from the United States, is the most commonly used term. Most Cubans refer to people from the United States as *américana/os*, *norteaméricana/os, estadounidense*, or even *yanquís* or its more affectionate counterpart, *yumas*. To facilitate ease of reading for an English-speaking audience, however, I employ both "Americans" and "North American" in this book, despite the limitations of these terms, to indicate the national origin of someone who is a U.S. citizen or resident.
9. See Lillian Guerra, *Visions of Power in Cuba*.
10. See, for instance, Bornemann, *Surviving Mexico's Dirty War*; Cardenal, *En Cuba*; and Reckord, *Does Fidel Eat More Than Your Father?*.
11. Sutherland Martinez, *The Youngest Revolution*.
12. Gott, *Cuba*, 178.
13. See, for instance, Randall, *To Change the World*.
14. See Pérez, *Cuba in the American Imagination*.

15. Martinez, "The Venceremos Brigade Still Means 'We Shall Overcome'"
16. FBI, "Foreign Influence," i, 80.
17. See Gosse, *Rethinking the New Left*.
18. David Farber, *The Age of Great Dreams*, 34.
19. Gosse, *Where the Boys Are*, especially 1–10.
20. See, for instance, Jameson, "Periodizing the 60s."
21. Rojas, *Fighting over Fidel*.
22. For instance, Huberman and Sweezy, *Cuba*; Huberman and Sweezy, *Socialism in Cuba*.
23. Mills, *Listen, Yankee*; Scheer and Zeitlin, *Cuba*.
24. Gosse, *Where the Boys Are*; Gronbeck-Tedesco, *Cuba, the United States, and Cultures of the Transnational Left*; Rojas, *Fighting over Fidel*; Tietchen, *Cubalogues*.
25. Jameson, "Periodizing the 60s," 182.
26. Gus Hall, "Letter to Castro," undated. Tamiment Library, CPUSA Papers, box 196.
27. Sale, *SDS*, 355.
28. Martínez, *Youngest Revolution*.
29. Young, *Soul Power*, 19–20.
30. For another rendering of these transnational radical identities, see Sohail Daulatzai's formulation of a "Muslim International" in Daulatzai, *Black Star, Crescent Moon*.
31. Gaines, *American Africans in Ghana*, 141.
32. In Marable, "Race and Revolution in Cuba," in Marable, ed., *Dispatches from the Ebony Tower*, 99.
33. The most complete assessment is Marable, *Malcolm X*.
34. See Prashad, *Darker Nations*. Malcolm X first presented his conception of "the ballot or the bullet" on April 3, 1964, as a speech at Cory Methodist Church in Cleveland, Ohio.
35. In his study of Cuba's influence on black and white Beat writers in the early 1960s, Todd F. Tietchen argues that Cuba functioned for a brief few years after the 1959 revolution as a "transnational counterpublic" where intellectuals and artists mingled amid the upsurge in cultural production. See Tietchen, *Cubalogues*, 113.
36. See Guridy, *Forging Diaspora*; Brock and Castañeda Fuertes, eds., *Between Race and Empire*; Greenbaum, *More Than Black*; Gronbeck-Tedesco, *Cuba, the United States, and Cultures of the Transnational Left*; and James, *Holding Aloft the Banner of Ethiopia*
37. See Benson, "Cuba Calls"; Gosse, *Where the Boys Are*; and Young, *Soul Power*. Kepa Artaraz includes some consideration to Cuba's theoretical influence on both the New Left and Black Liberation Movements; see Artaraz, *Cuba and Western Intellectuals*. Tietchen traces Cuba's influence on black and white U.S. writers in the early 1960s in great detail; see Tietchen, *Cubalogues*.
38. Jones, "Cuba Libre."
39. Baraka, *Autobiography of LeRoi Jones*, 243.
40. Dickson and Roberts, *Negroes with Guns*.
41. *Crusader*, August 13, 1960; April 29, 1961. Useful examinations of the relationship between African Americans and the Cuban Revolution are provided in Benson, "Cuba Calls"; Gosse, *Where the Boys Are*; Moore, *Castro, the Blacks, and Africa*; Tyson, *Radio Free Dixie*; and Young, *Soul Power*.
42. Griffin, "Para las Chicas Cubanas," 76.
43. Walker, "My Father's Country Is the Poor," *NYT*, March 21, 1977.
44. See Gosse, *Where the Boys Are*, 1–10.
45. Herbert Matthews, "Cuban Rebel Is Visited in Hideout," *NYT*, February 24, 1957.
46. Hayden, *Listen, Yankee!*

47. Gitlin, *Sixties*, 2.
48. For a discussion of the political formation of SDS, particularly the radicalization and internationalization that characterized the group's later years, see Berger, *Outlaws of America*.
49. See Guevara, *Motorcycle Diaries*; and Anderson, *Che Guevara*.
50. Fair Play for Cuba Committee, *Hearings before the Subcommittee to Investigate the Administration of the Internal Security Act and Other Internal Security Laws*.
51. Gosse, *Where the Boys Are*, 244–45.
52. See Berger, *Captive Nation*.
53. Bloom and Martin, *Black against Empire*, 31.
54. See, for instance, Klimke, *Other Alliance*.
55. See Mills, *Empire Within*; Wu, *Radicals on the Road*; Young, *Soul Power*; Elbaum, *Revolution in the Air*; Katsiaficas, *Imagination of the New Left*; and Westad, *Global Cold War*.
56. See especially Artaraz, *Cuba and Western Intellectuals*; and Rojas, *Fighting over Fidel*.
57. See Gosse, *Where the Boys Are*. Important discussion of this relationship is also provided in Benson, *Antiracism in Cuba*; de la Fuente, *Nation for All*; and Sawyer, *Racial Politics in Post-Revolutionary Cuba*.
58. Ruth Reitan's *Rise and Decline of an Alliance* provides the most thorough analysis of the encounter between Cuba and the African American freedom struggle in the late 1960s in a monographic work. For the broad New Left and African American freedom movement, see *Fighting Over Fidel*, and Artaraz, *Cuba and Western Intellectuals*. Several articles have also provided important analysis of this period, notably Lekus, "Queer Harvests"; Malloy, "Uptight in Babylon"; and Seidman, "Tricontinental Routes of Solidarity."
59. See, for example, Morley, *Imperial State and Revolution*; Pérez, *Cuba and the United States*; and Schoultz, *That Infernal Little Cuban Republic*. See Suri, *Power and Protest*, for an analysis of the influence of global social movements on state diplomacy during the 1960s.
60. See Anderson, *Eyes off the Prize*; Von Eschen, *Race against Empire*; Von Eschen, *Satchmo Blows Up the World*; Plummer, *Rising Wind*; and Plummer, *In Search of Power*.
61. Future scholars may well produce studies that more thoroughly explore the relationship between Cuba and the Puerto Rican independence movement, for instance, which is not examined in this book, and U.S.-based Puerto Rican organizations such as the Young Lords Party. Other studies might also give a more thorough historical accounting of the Cuban revolution's reception among various U.S.-based communist and socialist organizations such as the Socialist Workers Party and Communist Party USA, and of Cuba's influence within Chicano/a movements of the U.S. West.

Chapter 1

1. *Ramparts*, August 1970.
2. Juana Carrasco, "Arribaron a Cuba 216 jovenes norteamericanos que estaran 2 meses en la zafra," *Granma*, December 9, 1969, 1. A bulletin in the newspaper announced a televised interview with members of the Brigade, to be aired that night on national television. "Jóvenes norteamericanos, de la brigada 'Venceremos,' comparecerián hoy por TV," *Granma*, December 9, 1969, 1.
3. CIA, "Situation Information Report, Venceremos Brigade Update," December 31, 1969, 2. FOIA request by the author, 2009.
4. The most complete history of U.S. policy toward the Cuban revolution is provided in Schoultz, *That Infernal Little Cuban Republic*.
5. LeoGrande and Kornbluh, *Back Channel to Cuba*, 104.

6. UN General Assembly, *Universal Declaration of Human Rights*, 10 December 1948, 217 A (III).
7. "Solidarity with Cuba Through Socialist Construction," Venceremos Brigade pamphlet, 1972.
8. "The Venceremos Brigade, 1974: Four Years Building Solidarity with Cuba," *Cuba Va*, Venceremos Brigade, 1974, 2.
9. Westad, *Global Cold War*, 105–6.
10. Fidel Castro, speech, Plaza de la Revolución, Havana, January 2, 1969.
11. Pérez, *Between Reform and Revolution*, 258–60.
12. For one firsthand account, see Gitlin, *Sixties*.
13. An alternative origin story of the brigades is posited by Tom Hayden, who writes that he and SDS activist Carl Davidson discussed the proposition of "bringing thousands of Americans to visit, work, and live in Cuba for months at a time" with Fidel Castro during their visit in January 1968. Hayden, *Listen, Yankee!*, 103.
14. Oglesby, *Ravens in the Storm*, 231–32.
15. Ibid., 256–61. Oglesby's account in his autobiography appears to be his first public statement about his role in the creation of the Brigade. Oglesby is not mentioned in Carol Brightman and Sandra Levinson's 1971 collection *The Venceremos Brigade*, nor in Ian Lekus's 2004 article "Queer Harvests." However, longtime Cuba solidarity activist Karen Lee Wald, who was part of the January 1969 delegation associated with SDS in Havana, confirms that Oglesby originated the idea for the Brigade. See Wald, "Carl Oglesby, 1935–2011," *ZMagazine* online, November 1, 2011. https://zcomm.org/zmagazine/carl-oglesby-1935-2011-by-karen-lee-wald/.
16. Venceremos Brigade, "Cuba: 1969–1970 Venceremos Brigade," application form, 1969.
17. See Brightman and Levinson, *Venceremos Brigade*, 54.
18. "Policy Paper," National Committee, Venceremos Brigade, 1972, 1.
19. House Committee on Internal Security, "Theory and Practice of Communism, Venceremos Brigade," 7824–825.
20. *Cuba Internacional*, November 1969, 6–15.
21. Brightman and Levinson, *Venceremos Brigade*, 19.
22. Chris Camarano, "A Letter from Camp Venceremos," *Ramparts*, August 1970, 11–12.
23. Joel Britton, "Cuba today — how it looked to visiting Young Socialists," *Militant*, February 14, 1969, 6; "Young socialist reports on Cuba in Southern tour," *Militant*, March 7, 1969, 10.
24. For a discussion of SWP within the milieu of the era's left-wing movements, see Elbaum, *Revolution in the Air*, 51–53.
25. See Gosse, *Where the Boys Are*.
26. See "Huey Newton Talks to *The Movement* about the Black Panther Party, Cultural Nationalism, SNCC, Liberals and White Revolutionaries," *Movement*, ca. 1969. Republished in Foner, *Black Panthers Speak*.
27. Carmichael, *Stokely Speaks*, 104.
28. As of 2014, Yedra's celebrity is still intact in Cuba's state media. José Miguel Solís Díaz, "Fui un guajiro cimarrón y nací para trabajar," *Radio Rebelde*, May 2, 2014.
29. Juana Carrasco, "For the first time: Sugarcane . . . machetes . . . water jugs," *Granma*, English edition, January 18, 1970, 4.
30. Juana Carrasco, "For the first time: Sugarcane . . . machetes . . . water jugs," *Granma*, English edition, January 18, 1970, 4.
31. Brightman and Levinson, *Venceremos Brigade*, 14.
32. "Brigada Venceremos: Abajo Imperialismo!," Venceremos Brigade, Newsletter, no. 1, 1971, 1.

33. See Gosse, *Where the Boys Are*.
34. For a discussion of Cuba's socialist labor system and national economy in the late 1960s and early 1970s, see Karl, "Work Incentives in Cuba," 21–41.
35. Pérez, *Between Reform and Revolution*, 259.
36. Guevara, "On Revolutionary Medicine," in Gerassi, ed., *Venceremos!*, 113.
37. Francisco Suárez, "A Settlement of North Americans in the Cuban Canefields," *Prensa Latina*, English feature, 1970, 3. Like hundreds of other foreigners, Bunke came to Cuba as a volunteer after the revolution, impressed with the new nation's idealism and humanistic social gains.
38. Cuban press coverage of foreign solidarity delegations was continual in 1969 and 1970. See, for instance, "Entregan bandera a la brigada 'Guerrilleros de Bolivia,' primera millionaria de La Habana," *Granma*, December 12, 1969, 3; "Arrival of 79 young Koreans who will cut cane until the end of the 10-million ton sugar harvest," *Granma*, English edition, January 18, 1970; Brightman and Levinson, *Venceremos Brigade*, 102.
39. See, for instance, *Granma*'s coverage of a meeting between the Venceremos Brigade and a Cuban sports delegation next to an article entitled "Bulgarian youths awarded Heroes of Moncada banner," *Granma*, English edition, April 19, 1970, 3. In May, a statement from the Brigade was featured on the same page as articles entitled "Japanese young people arrive to work in sugar harvest," and "19 Dominican revolutionaries arrive in Cuba." *Granma*, English edition, May 10, 1970, 4.
40. Tony Fernández, "Thousands of workers and housewives in year-end agricultural session in the Havana green belt," *Granma*, English edition, January 11, 1970, 5.
41. Dunbar-Ortiz, *Outlaw Woman*, 274–75.
42. See, for instance, "La zafra de los 10 millones se ha convertido en algo asi como un simbolo de internacionalismo," *Verde Olivo* 10, no. 52, December 28, 1969, 6–7; Jesús González, "In the Canefields," *Granma*, English edition, January 18, 1970, 12, featuring photos of Raúl Castro, Vilma Espín, and Arnaldo Ochoa.
43. For more on socialist emulation and the Cuban labor system, see Bernardo, "Moral Stimulation as a Nonmarket Mode of Labor Allocation in Cuba"; and Mesa-Lago, *Labor Sector and Socialist Distribution in Cuba*.
44. Brightman and Levinson, *Venceremos Brigade*, 113.
45. Author's interview with Louis Segal, April 2007; Brightman and Levinson, *Venceremos Brigade*, 113.
46. Randall, *To Change the World*, 54.
47. Brightman and Levinson, *Venceremos Brigade*, 99–100, 301.
48. Marta Perez, "My Labor Wasn't Going to Enrich Some Capitalist," *Claridad*, July 15, 1973.
49. See, for instance, Oswaldo Salas Escobar, "Cosecha la Brigada Venceremos, en Isla de Pinos, unos 5 mil quintales de limon y fertiliza mas de 200 mil matas de citricos," *Granma*, September 8, 1970.
50. NARA, Records of CIA, Audio Recordings of Monitored Broadcasts from Havana and Port-au-Prince, 1968–1973. Havana International Service in English, "Statement by Venceremos Brigade Member Patricia McGaully," 263-CB-125. Radio Havana Cuba's broadcasts concerning the Brigade were monitored by the CIA and are housed at NARA in College Park, Md. For an assessment of the use of radio in U.S.-Cuba relations, see Walsh, *An Air War with Cuba*.
51. "Venceremos Brigade Presented with Millionaire Canecutters Banner," *Granma*, English edition, January 18, 1970, 1.

52. Juana Carrasco, "'The fact that young people from the United States, Vietnam, and Cuba are making a joint effort to reach a goal has profound revolutionary significance,' said Jaime Crombet," *Granma*, English edition, January 18, 1970, 5.
53. Fidel Castro, speech, Plaza de la Revolución, Havana, September 29, 1970. LLILAS Benson Digital Collections.
54. Fidel Castro, speech, Plaza de la Revolución, Havana, September 29, 1970. LLILAS Benson Digital Collections.
55. Author's interview with Orlaida Cabrera, Havana, Cuba, November 17, 2015.
56. Ibid.
57. See Tina Bristol, "Indianapolis Radicals Says: 'Venceremos Brigade in Cuba Means Hard Work and Discipline,'" *Participant*, January 1970, 4–5. Fidel Castro also alluded to other potentials of the harvest: "what this will mean from a political, moral and revolutionary point of view is undoubtedly worth much more than ten million tonnes of sugar itself."
58. Fidel Castro, speech, Plaza de la Revolución, Havana, September 29, 1970. LLILAS Benson Digital Collections.
59. Fidel Castro, speech, May 20, 1970, LLILAS Benson Digital Collections.
60. "Brigada Venceremos: Abajo Imperialismo!," Venceremos Brigade, Newsletter, no. 1, 1971, 1.
61. See, for instance, "Tour of plans in Ciego de Ávila area," *Granma*, February 1, 1970, 3.
62. Dunbar-Ortiz, *Outlaw Woman*, 281.
63. John F. Kennedy, quoted in LeoGrande and Kornbluh, *Back Channel to Cuba*, 104.
64. LeoGrande and Kornbluh, *Back Channel to Cuba*, 99–100.
65. Author's interview with Hugo Govín, Havana, Cuba, November 16, 2015. An ICAP officer, Govín was responsible for coordinating the group's travel arrangements.
66. Cluster, "Venceremos Brigade"; Dunbar-Ortiz, *Outlaw Woman*, 269; Davis, *Angela Davis*, 200.
67. Brightman and Levinson, *Venceremos Brigade*, 61.
68. "So How Was the Skiing in Cuba?," *Chicago Tribune*, April 25, 1970, 8.
69. Some of the FBI's scrutiny of the Brigade is visible in the bureau's extensive surveillance files and reports on the organization, which are obtainable under the Freedom of Information Act.
70. Jones, "Cuba Libre." Jones wrote of being "jumped on with both feet" and accused of being a "cowardly bourgeois individualist" for his disinclination to use his poetry in the service of social change.
71. Baraka, *Autobiography of LeRoi Jones*, 246.
72. Carmichael, *Ready for Revolution*, 584.
73. Davis, *Angela Davis*, 216. Davis first encountered Cuban revolutionaries in 1962 in Helsinki at the World Festival of Peace and Friendship.
74. "Solidarity with Cuba through Socialist Construction," Venceremos Brigade recruitment brochure, 1972.
75. Moses J. Newton, "Talking with the Brigadistas: U.S. and Cuban Volunteers Share their Thoughts," *Baltimore Afro-American*, May 28, 1977.
76. Miriam Ching Louie, "Triple Jeopardy and the Struggle," *Against the Current* 134 (2008), online edition.
77. For a detailed treatment of Cuban internationalism, see Dominguez, *To Make a World Safe for Revolution*.
78. *Participant*, January 1970, 4.
79. For instance, two days after the first contingent of the Brigade arrived, the front page of

Juventud Rebelde, the newspaper sponsored by the Unión de Jóvenes Comunistas, featured a cover story about the U.S. Army massacre of Vietnamese civilians at the hamlets of Sơn Mỹ, the incident that came to be known as the My Lai Massacre. *Verde Olivo* followed with an article eleven days later, which described the massacre as an act exemplifying the "genocidal fury of the Yankee army." "Son My," *Juventud Rebelde*, December 10, 1969; "Son My," *Verde Olivo* 10, no. 51, December 21, 1969.

80. Álvarez, *79 primaveras*. For discussions of *79 Primaveras* and other films by Álvarez, see Chanan, *Cuban Cinema*; and Malitsky, *Post-Revolution Nonfiction Film*.

81. Author's interview with Louis Segal, April 2007.

82. Peter Arnett, "Major Describes Move," *NYT*, February 8, 1968.

83. Gleijeses, "Cuba's First Venture in Africa," 159–95.

84. Brightman and Levinson, *Venceremos Brigade*, 349.

85. Kozol, *Children of the Revolution*, 171.

86. Davis, *Angela Davis*, 203.

87. Chris Camarano, "A Letter from Camp Venceremos," *Ramparts*, August 1970, 11.

88. Ibid.

89. *Tricontinental* 2, September-October 1967.

90. *Tricontinental* 7, July-August 1968.

91. *Tricontinental* 8, September-October 1968.

92. As quoted by Klein, "In Cuba with the Second Venceremos Brigade," 28.

93. As recalled in Dunbar-Ortiz, *Outlaw Woman*, 277.

94. Elizabeth Martinez, "The Venceremos Brigade Still Means, 'We Shall Overcome,'" *Z Magazine*, July/August 1999.

95. Brightman and Levinson, *Venceremos Brigade*, 342–43.

96. This is a pseudonym. He assumed a false identity to protect his family in South Vietnam.

97. Diary entry, quoted in Brightman and Levinson, *Venceremos Brigade*, 336.

98. Martinez, "The Venceremos Brigade Still Means, 'We Shall Overcome.'"

99. See, for instance, "Encuentro franternal en el campamento Cañero," *Verde Olivo* 10, no. 51, December 21, 1969, 7–11; "Venceremos Brigade members see off representatives of the Indo-Chinese peoples who worked on the Isle of Pines," *Granma*, English edition, September 27, 1970, 3.

100. William McKinley, State of the Union Message, December 5, 1899. Quoted in Pérez, *Cuba and the United States*, ix.

101. Susan Sontag, "Some Thoughts on the Right Way (for us) to Love the Cuban Revolution," *Ramparts*, 1969, 10.

102. Gitlin, *Sixties*, 278.

103. See Wu, *Radicals on the Road*.

104. Juana Carrasco, Alberto Landa, "Another 492 U.S. citizens making up second group of Venceremos Brigade en route to Cuba," *Granma*, English edition, February 22, 1970, 8.

105. Héctor Hernández Pardo, "U.S. young people from Venceremos Brigade installed in their canecutter's camp," *Granma*, English edition, March 1, 1970, 6.

106. "Venceremos Brigade awarded Bronze Titan banner; communiqué read," *Granma*, English edition, April 12, 1970, 3.

107. Camarano, "A Letter from Camp Venceremos," 1970; Klein, "In Cuba With the Second Venceremos Brigade," 1970; Brightman and Levinson, *Venceremos Brigade*; Dunbar-Ortiz, *Outlaw Woman*.

108. Author's interview with Tony Ryan, a member of the 1969 Venceremos Brigade, October 9, 2007.

109. Dunbar-Ortiz, *Outlaw Woman*, 272.

110. Harry Maurer, "Is it the Future? Will It Work? With the Venceremos in Cuba," *The Nation*, July 2, 1977, 8.

111. Adler, *Heretic's Heart*, 264.

112. Author's interview with Hugo Govín, Havana, Cuba, November 16, 2015.

113. Ibid.; author's interview with Orlaida Cabrera, Havana, Cuba, November 17, 2015.

114. "Bay Area Regional Response to CN Policy Paper," Venceremos Brigade, September 28, 1972, 8.

115. The first brigade, however, was roughly 80 percent white in composition.

116. Brightman and Levinson, *Venceremos Brigade*; Dunbar-Ortiz, *Outlaw Woman*.

117. Brightman and Levinson, *Venceremos Brigade*, 197–98.

118. Dunbar-Ortiz, *Outlaw Woman*, 279.

119. For an examination of FBI and local police infiltration of the Brigade, see chapter 2.

120. Dunbar-Ortiz, *Outlaw Woman*, 279.

121. Lekus, "Queer Harvests," 67.

122. Author's interview with Orlaida Cabrera, Havana, Cuba, November 17, 2015.

123. Author's interview with Hugo Govín, Havana, Cuba, November 16, 2015.

124. The former *brigadista* who informed the author of his suspicions about the presence of FBI agents on the 1969 Brigade wishes to remain anonymous. For more on the Brigade's divisions in the early years, particularly around the issue of gay and lesbian issues, see Lekus, "Queer Harvests."

125. Todd Gitlin and Laura Pulido offer contrasting and thus complimentary portraits of the ways in which Asian, black, Latino/a and white activists respectively came to radical political consciousness during the 1960's/'70's. See Pulido's *Black, Brown, Yellow, and Left* and Gitlin's *The Sixties*.

126. Brightman and Levinson, *Venceremos Brigade*, 241.

127. See, for instance, Osvaldo Salas Escobar, "Third Contingent of Venceremos Brigade Given Enthusiastic Welcome," *Granma*, English edition, September 6, 1970, 1.

128. Osvaldo Salas Escobar, "Exemplary work attitude displayed by brigaders on Isle of Youth," *Granma*, English edition, September 18, 1970, 4.

129. Author's interview with Orlaida Cabrera, Havana, Cuba, November 17, 2015.

130. Brightman and Levinson, *Venceremos Brigade*; Dunbar-Ortiz, *Outlaw Woman*.

131. Author's interview with Hugo Govín, Havana, Cuba, November 16, 2015.

132. Brightman and Levinson, *Venceremos Brigade*, 203.

133. Randall, *Women in Cuba*, 55.

134. The dimensions of Cuba's racial politics, including the Cuban government's relationship with U.S. black radicals, is examined in greater detail in chapters 3 and 5. For a detailed analysis of the relationship between race and revolution in post-1959 Cuba, see de la Fuente, *Nation for All*. Mark Sawyer offers a somewhat contrasting view of the politics of race and blackness in post-1959 Cuba, including the Cuban government's relations with African American activists. See Sawyer, *Racial Politics in Post-Revolutionary Cuba*. Finally, Reitan's *The Rise and Decline of an Alliance* offers a detailed analysis of the relationship between Black liberation movements and the Cuban revolution during the period in which the Brigade was formed. Carlos Moore offers a far more critical view of the Cuban leadership's commitment to antiracism in *Castro, the Blacks, and Africa* and Moore's memoir, *Pichón*.

135. Brightman and Levinson, *Venceremos Brigade*, 287.

136. "Brigada Venceremos: Abajo Imperialismo!," Venceremos Brigade, Newsletter, no. 1, 1971, 3.

137. Brightman and Levinson, *Venceremos Brigade*, 1971.
138. Ibid., 260.
139. Juana Carrasco, "For the first time: Sugarcane... machetes... water jugs," *Granma*, English edition, January 18, 1970, 4.
140. Ibid.
141. Ana Ramos, *Cuba Resource Center Newsletter* II, no. 2, March 1972.
142. de la Fuente, "Race and Inequality in Cuba."
143. For an overview of women and gender in Cuba during the early revolutionary period, see Chase, *Revolution within the Revolution*. For the period after 1962, see, for instance, Randall, *Women in Cuba*; and Gronbeck-Tedesco, *Cuba, the United States, and Cultures of the Transnational Left*, 235–73.
144. Brightman and Levinson, *Venceremos Brigade*, 249.
145. Randall, *Women in Cuba*, 89.
146. Ibid., 89–90.
147. Brightman and Levinson, *Venceremos Brigade*, 258.
148. "Gay Recruitment Policy of V.B. Central Committee," republished by *Berkeley Tribe* magazine, ca. 1971. Issue/volume unavailable.
149. See Lekus, "Queer Harvests."
150. Author's interview with Hugo Govín, Havana, Cuba, November 16, 2015.
151. See, for example, Gitlin, *Sixties*, 277, 279; Guerra, *Visions of Power in Cuba*, 227–30. See also Bejel, *Gay Cuban Nation*, 25. Susan Sontag also acknowledged that gay Cuban men were sent to camps, but assured readers that "they have long since been sent home." In actuality, the last UMAPs closed only one year prior. Sontag, "Some Thoughts on the Right Way (for us) to Love the Cuban Revolution," *Ramparts*, 1969, 14.
152. See Ginsberg, *Spontaneous Mind*, 327–33.
153. See Young, *Gays Under the Cuban Revolution*. For a more recent assessment, see Allen, *¡Venceremos?*
154. See Rojas, *Fighting over Fidel*; and Guerra, *Visions of Power in Cuba*.
155. See Rojas, *Fighting over Fidel*, 161.
156. *Tricontinental* 26, September-October 1971, 116.
157. "Fidel Castro takes blame for persecution of Cuban gays," BBC, August 31, 2010. http://www.bbc.com/news/world-latin-america-11147157. As of 2012, Cuba's official stance toward homosexuality, articulated most visibly by Raúl Castro's daughter, Mariela Castro, is among the most progressive in Latin America.
158. See Gosse, *Rethinking the New Left*, 159.
159. Brightman and Levinson, *Venceremos Brigade*, 16.
160. Sale, *SDS*, 355.
161. "Policy Paper," National Committee, Venceremos Brigade, 1972, 3.
162. Venceremos Brigade, "Brigada Venceremos: Abajo Imperialismo!," *Turquino*, no. 1, 1971, 9.
163. "Policy Paper," National Committee, Venceremos Brigade, 1972, 1.
164. Carol Brightman and Sandra Levinson, "Solidarity," *Tricontinental* 26 (September-October 1971): 104–19.
165. "The Venceremos Brigade, 1974: Four Years Building Solidarity with Cuba," *Cuba Va*, 1974, 1.
166. Brightman and Levinson, *Venceremos Brigade*, 31–32.
167. *Only the People Can Perform Miracles: Health Care in Cuba*, pamphlet, Venceremos Brigade Educational Commission, 1975, 2.

168. *Cuba: 'We Stand With the People of Africa — December, 1975*, pamphlet, Venceremos Brigade Educational Commission, 1975, 24 pp.

169. *Angola: African Girón (Bay of Pigs) — April 1976*, pamphlet, Venceremos Brigade Educational Commission, ca. 1976, 12 pp.

170. Venceremos Brigade, *Democracy in Cuba*, 25, 1.

171. Terry Cannon and Johnnetta Cole, *Free and Equal: The End of Racial Discrimination in Cuba*, Venceremos Brigade, 1978, 4.

172. Cannon and Cole, *Free and Equal*, 11.

173. de la Fuente, "Race and Inequality in Cuba," 143.

174. See Gosse, "Active Engagement," 23–24.

175. Martinez, "Venceremos Brigade Still Means, 'We Shall Overcome,'" 1999. For a personal account of the Brigade's work in the 2000s, see Olguín, *At the Risk of Seeming Ridiculous*.

176. See, for example, U.S. Peace Council, *Sandy Pollack*.

177. For more discussion of the role of Third World Marxism in the legacy of the long sixties, including a brief mention of the Brigade, see Gosse, *Rethinking the New Left*, 194–95.

178. Elbaum, *Revolution in the Air*, 85.

179. See Young, *Soul Power*.

180. Lekus, "Queer Harvests, 81–82.

181. See, for instance, Springer, *Living for the Revolution*, 49.

Chapter 2

1. "The Venceremos Brigade—Agrarians or Anarchists?," U.S. Congressional Record, March 16, 1970, 7462–467; speech reported by the *New York Times*, March 17, 1970.

2. See Brightman and Levinson, *The Venceremos Brigade*.

3. See Asch, *Senator and the Sharecropper*.

4. See Kelley, *Hammer and Hoe*.

5. Jameson, "Periodizing the 60s," 182.

6. See Artaraz, *Cuba and Western Intellectuals since 1959*; Gosse, *Where the Boys Are*; Reitan, *Rise and Decline of an Alliance*; Tietchen, *Cubalogues*; and Young, *Soul Power*.

7. FBI, "Foreign Influence—Weather Underground Organization," August 20, 1976, i, 80, 82. The bureau's report also quotes journalist Allen Young, editor of *Liberation News Service*, who affirmed in 1970 that: "the thing that was exciting about the Cuban revolution was that it first made the break with the Old Left. FBI, "Foreign Influence," 51.

8. Georgie Ann Greyer and Keyes Beech, "Cuba: School for U.S. Radicals," *Long Island Press*, October 15, 1970. Syndicated by the *Chicago Daily News*. Although Greyer and Beech write in tabloid style and present some unverified claims as fact, their nine-part series is valuable as the most extensive mainstream news treatment ever written on U.S. activists traveling to Cuba.

9. CIA, "Situation Information Report, Venceremos Brigade Update," December 31, 1969, 2. Obtained via FOIA request by the author, 2009.

10. Georgie Ann Greyer and Keyes Beech, "Cuba, School for U.S. Radicals," *Long Island Press*, October 15, 1970.

11. See especially Gleijeses, *Conflicting Missions*; LeoGrande and Kornbluh, *Back Channel to Cuba*; and Schoultz, *That Infernal Little Cuban Republic*.

12. Che Guevara, "Message to the Tricontinental," first published in Spanish in *Tricontinental*, April 16, 1967.

13. Ibid.

14. This figure is as of 2009, as reported to the author by a representative of the FBI's Record/Information Dissemination Section via telephone, December 2009. This body of records is undoubtedly growing, as FBI agents increased their questioning and harassment of Brigade activists for unknown reasons during 2009 and 2010.

15. "Talking Paper prepared for President Nixon," prepared by Tom Charles Huston and used by President Richard Nixon, Oval Office, June 5, 1970, published in *Final Report of the Select Committee to Study Governmental Operations with Respect to Intelligence Activities*, 937.

16. Fair Play for Cuba Committee, *Hearings before the Subcommittee to Investigate the Administration of the Internal Security Act and Other Internal Security Laws*, April 29, May 5, October 10, 1960; January 10, 1961.

17. See, for instance, Irwin Silber, "U.S.A.: The Alienation of Culture: Destructive and Revolutionary Art," *Tricontinental* 10, January-February 1969, 112–20.

18. *El Caimán Barbudo*, 1969, 13.

19. "Four students killed by National Guard in Kent, Ohio, USA, in attack on demonstration against Yankee invasion of Cambodia," *Granma*, English edition, May 10, 1970, 11.

20. *Granma*, English edition, May 17, 1970, 7.

21. See, for instance, "Fifth anniversary of the black rebellion in Watts," *Granma*, English edition, August 28, 1970, 11.

22. Fidel Castro, speech reprinted in *Granma*, English edition, May 31, 1970, 3.

23. Seymour Hersh, "Huge CIA Operation Reported in U.S. Against Antiwar Forces, Other Dissidents in Nixon Years," *NYT*, December 22, 1974, 1.

24. Ibid., 26.

25. CIA, "International Connections of US Peace Groups," Memorandum, November 15, 1967. The agency's study was "based in part on material supplied by the National Security Agency, the Federal Bureau of Investigation, the intelligence services of the US Army, Navy, and Air Forces, and other offices of CIA's Directorates of Intelligence" (1).

26. CIA, Office of Current Intelligence, "International Connections of US Peace Groups," Memorandum, November 15, 1967, 32.

27. Ibid., 33.

28. Ibid., 34.

29. Ibid., 36.

30. Ibid., 37.

31. Ibid., 35.

32. Ibid., 38.

33. Ibid., 39.

34. CIA, Office of Current Intelligence, "Situation Information Report, Venceremos Brigade Update," Memorandum, December 31, 1969, 2. The two-page report constitutes the bulk of the CIA's released declassified text files on the Venceremos Brigade as of March 2009. While more reports almost certainly exist, the CIA's records division has not acknowledged them to the author. The author's February 2009 FOIA to the CIA regarding the Brigade yielded a release of 24 pages, some of which appear to be a portion of a larger investigation into American citizens crossing into Canada to participate in the second Venceremos Brigade delegation, which departed for Cuba by ship from Saint John, New Brunswick, in February 1970.

35. FBI, "Venceremos Brigade (BRIGADE) aka American Brigade, C and C Associates, Brigada Venceremos," file no. HQ 105-195696, September 28, 1973, cover pages A, B. Obtained via FOIA by the author, April 2008.

36. "Worthy Surrenders on Illegal Entry," *Atlanta Daily World*, April 29, 1962, 1. See also Gosse, *Where the Boys Are*.

37. "Worthy to Face Passport Showdown," *Baltimore Afro-American*, February 16, 1957, 1.

38. "Indictment of William Worthy," U.S. District Court, Southern District of Florida, April 24, 1962. William Worthy Papers, box 10.1, Department of Rare Books and Manuscripts, Sheridan Libraries, Johns Hopkins University.

39. For example, see "William Worthy speaking on the Cuban revolution: a recent look," Friends Service Association for the Delaware Valley, 1962, hand bill; and "The Cuban Revolution: Wave of the Future," The George Orwell Forum, 1962, hand bill; William Worthy Papers, box. 3.4, Department of Rare Books and Manuscripts, Sheridan Libraries, Johns Hopkins University.

40. U.S. Senate, Internal Security Subcommittee, *Communist Threat to the United States through the Caribbean*, 87th Congress, 2nd session, 1961, 791.

41. Frazier, *East Is Black*; and Broussard, *African American Foreign Correspondents*. Despite his journalistic legend and the ubiquity of his reportage in the footnotes of scholarship on the global civil rights era, Worthy has only recently been examined as a historical actor in his own right.

42. Tietchen, *Cubalogues*, 113.

43. FBI, "Venceremos Brigade (BRIGADE) aka American Brigade, C and C Associates, Brigada Venceremos," file no. NY 100-166943, June 7, 1971, 44. Obtained via FOIA by the author, April 2008.

44. Ibid., 15.

45. Ibid., 8–10; and "Venceremos Brigade (BRIGADE) aka American Brigade, C and C Associates and Brigada Venceremos," file no. HQ 105–195696, September 28, 1973, 12–13. For commentary on a discussion within the Brigade regarding the importance of keeping FBI infiltrators out of the group, see "Venceremos Brigade (BRIGADE) aka American Brigade, C and C Associates and Brigada Venceremos," file no. NY 100-166943, June 7, 1971, 6–7. Obtained via FOIA by the author, April 2008.

46. See FBI, "Venceremos Brigade (BRIGADE) aka American Brigade, C and C Associates and Brigada Venceremos," file no. NY 100-166943, June 7, 1971, 23. Obtained via FOIA by the author, April 2008.

47. Davies, *Left of Karl Marx*, 207.

48. Cole, "What's a Metaphor?," 7. Randall's writings on Cuba, which have emphasized the experiences of Cuban women and gender as a category of analysis, have been groundbreaking. See, for instance, Randall, *Cuban Women Now*; Randall, *Breaking the Silences*; and Randall, *Che On My Mind*.

49. Quoted in Cole, "What's a Metaphor?," 5; James F. Clarity and Warren Weaver Jr., "Plea on Writer's Exclusion," *NYT*, October 28, 1985.

50. FBI, "Venceremos Brigade (BRIGADE) aka American Brigade, C and C Associates and Brigada Venceremos," file no. NY 100-166943, February 14, 1972, 7. Obtained via FOIA by the author, April 2008.

51. "The Venceremos Brigade, Fidel Castro's Sugar Cane Cutters," *Human Events*, October 14, 1972, transcribed and reproduced within FBI, "Venceremos Brigade (BRIGADE) aka American Brigade, C and C Associates and Brigada Venceremos," file no. HQ 105-195696, September 28, 1973, p. 3 and 4. Obtained via FOIA by the author, April 2008.

52. Although the Center for Cuban Studies in New York maintained a large collection of

materials on the Brigade as part of its Lourdes Casal Library until 2008, the archive did not surpass the holdings of the FBI in size or scope.

53. Davies, *Left of Karl Marx*, 207–8.

54. House Committee on Internal Security, *Theory and Practice of Communism, Venceremos Brigade: Hearings*, 7820.

55. Ibid., 7857.

56. Ibid., 7858.

57. FBI, "Venceremos Brigade (BRIGADE) aka American Brigade, C and C Associates and Brigada Venceremos," file no. NY 100-166943, February 14, 1972, 25. Obtained via FOIA by the author, April 2008.

58. House Committee on Internal Security, *Theory and Practice of Communism, Venceremos Brigade: Hearings*, 7825–26.

59. Ibid., 7826.

60. FBI report, "Venceremos Brigade (BRIGADE) aka American Brigade, C and C Associates and Brigada Venceremos," file no. NY 100-166943, October 16, 1972, 6. Obtained via FOIA by the author, April 2008.

61. FBI, "Venceremos Brigade," file no. NY 100-166943, October 23, 1970, 7. Obtained via FOIA by the author, April 2008. The accuracy of this statement cannot be verified. However, a similar statement from Nichamin was reprinted in the Brigade's 1971 book, *Venceremos Brigade*: "The only people who could set an example for doing this work in a Communist way were the Cubans. So, if you looked at it in that sense, there was no way of conceiving of American leadership of the Venceremos Brigade." It is possible that the FBI version is a paraphrasing of the original. Brightman and Levinson, *Venceremos Brigade*, 174.

62. U.S. State Department, "American volunteers for PAIGC," Message to American Embassy, Lisbon, Portugal, June 26, 1973. Obtained via FOIA by the author, September 2010.

63. CIA, report, "Cuba: Castro's Propaganda Apparatus and Foreign Policy," November 1984, 14.

64. I borrow this notion of fantasy projection from scholar Mike Davis, who characterized the 1980s gang scares of southern California as "an imaginary class relationship, a terrain of pseudo-knowledge and fantasy projection," in which racialized public and official fears about gangs grew out of proportion to the actual threat, yet were informed by prevailing fears about race and crime. See Davis, *City of Quartz*, 270.

65. See, for instance, Juan Marrero and Juana Carrasco, "Representatives of the Venceremos Brigade hold press conference," *Granma*, English edition, April 5, 1970.

66. "The Castro Declaration," *NYT*, July 27, 1964, 2.

67. Mills, *Listen, Yankee*, 166.

68. "Encuentro fraternal en el campamento cañero," *Verde Olivo* 10, no. 51, December 21, 1969, 10.

69. U.S. Embassy in Lisbon, "American volunteers for PAIGC?," Message to U.S. Secretary of State, Washington, DC, June 19, 1973, 1.

70. For a history of Cuba's involvement in the independence movement, see Gleijeses, "First Ambassadors."

71. Author's interview with Charlie Hill, September 7, 2012, Havana.

72. Ibid. Amílcar Cabral insisted in 1967 that PAIGC would not accept foreign volunteers — although it had already accepted Cubans — because their presence would compromise the opportunity of the nation to assert its sovereignty and claim its history. Gleijeses, "First Ambassadors," 60.

73. U.S. Embassy in Lisbon, "American volunteers for PAIGC?," Message to U.S. Secretary of State, Washington, DC, June 19, 1973, 1. Obtained via FOIA by the author, September 2010.

74. U.S. Secretary of State, Washington, D.C., "American volunteers for PAIGC?," Message to U.S. Embassy in Lisbon, June 26, 1973, 2–3.

75. Gleijeses, *Conflicting Missions*; LeoGrande and Kornbluh, *Back Channel to Cuba*.

76. U.S. Embassy in Lagos, "Reported Meeting in Cuba Between American Organizations and MPLA," Message to U.S. Secretary of State, March 1976. Obtained via FOIA by the author, September 2010.

77. James E. Bristol, "Report on Seminar in Havana, Cuba, February 26–29, 1976" (Philadelphia: American Friends Service Committee, 1976), *The African Activist Archive* online collection: http://africanactivist.msu.edu/document_metadata.php?objectid=32-130-130A.

78. Michael Kazin, "Cuba, Que Linda Es Cuba? Notes on a Revolutionary Sojourn, 1969," *Dissent Magazine*, August 17, 2015.

79. House Committee on Internal Security, *Theory and Practice of Communism, Venceremos Brigade: Hearings*, 7829.

80. Ibid., 7899.

81. Ibid.

82. Informant testimony. FBI, report, "Venceremos Brigade (BRIGADE) aka American Brigade, C and C Associates, Brigada Venceremos," NY 100-166943, October 16, 1972, 14. Obtained via FOIA by the author, April 2008.

83. Brightman and Levinson, *Venceremos Brigade*, 321.

84. FBI report, "Venceremos Brigade (BRIGADE) aka American Brigade, C and C Associates and Brigada Venceremos," February 14, 1972, 25. Obtained via FOIA by the author, April 2008.

85. Author's interview with Tony Ryan, October 9, 2007. See also Mark Rudd, "Che and Me," a revised version of a talk given April 10, 2008 at Oregon State University: http://www.markrudd.com/?violence-and-non-violence/che-and-me.html.

86. Author's interview with Hugo Govín, November 16, 2015, Havana.

87. Ibid.

88. Author's interview with Tony Ryan, October 9, 2007.

89. The radio transcript appears to be a paraphrasing, not a verbatim transcript. FBI, report, "Venceremos Brigade (BRIGADE) aka American Brigade, C and C Associates, Brigada Venceremos," file no. NY 100-166943, February 14, 1972, 46. Obtained via FOIA by the author, April 2008.

90. FBI report, "Venceremos Brigade," file no. NY 100-166943, October 23, 1970, 29. Obtained via FOIA by the author, April 2008.

91. Ibid.

92. "Communiqué by the Venceremos Brigade on the first anniversary of Ho Chi Minh's death," *Granma*, English edition, September 18, 1970, 4.

93. See FBI, *Foreign Influence—Weather Underground Organization*, report, August 20, 1976, 176–85. See also Berger, *Outlaws of America*, 133–34, 164–65. Berger's monograph includes reprints of the organization's communiqués.

94. FBI, *Foreign Influence—Weather Underground Organization*, report, August 20, 1976, iii, v, and throughout.

95. Nicholas M. Horrock, "FBI Asserts Cuba Aided Weathermen," *NYT*, October 9, 1977.

96. NARA, Records of CIA, Audio Recordings of Monitored Broadcasts from Havana and Port-au-Prince, 1968–1973. Havana International Service In English.

97. Sandweiss, "Spying on Solidarity," 73.

98. FBI, *Foreign Influence—Weather Underground Organization*, report, August 20, 1976, 2.

99. Nicholas M. Horrock, "FBI Asserts Cuba Aided Weathermen," *NYT*, October 9, 1977.

100. See Carroll, *Odyssey of the Abraham Lincoln Brigade*.
101. See Gosse, *Where the Boys Are*.
102. Scott, "Black Nationalism and the Italo-Ethiopian Conflict 1934–1936," 128–29.
103. See chapters 3 and 5 for more detailed discussions of this topic.
104. This legacy of American volunteer fighters abroad is explored in greater depth in chapter 1.
105. Schoultz, *That Infernal Little Cuban Republic*, 271. A year earlier, the U.S.-Cuba antihijacking agreement had raised hopes of a reexamination of hostilities between the two nations, but to no avail: in a report to the U.S. Congress by Richard Nixon, the president reiterated his claim that Cuba continued to present a threat because of Havana's hemispheric meddling and its military ties to the Soviet Union. See Morley, *Imperial State and Revolution*, 250.
106. Hearings before the Subcommittee on Inter-American Affairs of the Committee on Foreign Affairs, House of Representatives, 93rd U.S. Cong., 1st sess., February 20, 1973, 9.
107. *Tricontinental* 12 (May-June 1969): reverse of back cover.
108. Schoultz, *That Infernal Little Cuban Republic*, 5.
109. These accusations were leveled by Major Claudio Rey Mariña, Head of the Delegation of the Republic of Cuba, in a speech at the XVII Special Assembly of the International Civil Aviation Organization, Montreal, Canada, June 1970. Mariña, *Hijacking of Aircraft*.
110. Quoted in Randall, *Exporting Revolution*, 1–2.
111. Schoultz, *That Infernal Little Cuban Republic*, 110–15.
112. See, for example, Saney, "African Stalingrad"; Gleijeses, *Conflicting Missions*; and Schoultz, *That Infernal Little Cuban Republic*.
113. FBI, *Foreign Influence — Weather Underground Organization*, report, August 20, 1976, 29.
114. Ibid., 33–34.
115. While this quotation is widely attributed to Hoover, its primary source is rarely cited. See, for example, Austin, *Up against the Wall*, xxvii.
116. Self, *American Babylon*, 229.
117. Bloom and Martin, *Black against Empire*, 21.
118. Huey P. Newton, "Letter to the National Liberation Front of South Vietnam," August 29, 1970, in Newton, *To Die for the People*, 180–83.
119. Nguyen Thi Dinh, "A Reply: Letter from Nguyen Thi Dinh, October 31, 1970," in Newton, *To Die for the People*, 184–87. The North Vietnamese government had previously offered to release American prisoners of war in exchange for the release of imprisoned Black Panther leaders Huey Newton and Bobby Seale. "Panther Political Prisoners for U.S. Prisoners of War," *Black Panther*, November 22, 1969, 3.
120. Gleijeses was interviewed regarding this subject by Tom Hayden, and a short account of it appears in Hayden, *Listen, Yankee!*, 132–33.
121. Sallah and Weiss, *Yankee Comandante*; Shetterly, *Americano*.
122. For a recent analysis of the BPP's community health programs see Nelson, *Body and Soul*.
123. Cleaver, *Soul on Fire*, 107.
124. Ibid., 107.
125. Reitan, *Rise and Decline of an Alliance*, xv, 131. Reitan's assertion is based upon interviews conducted with Eldridge Cleaver in 1996.
126. Ibid., 105, 130, 131. According to Tom Hayden, Pyongyang also offered weapons and training to the Weather Underground via Bernardine Dohrn. See Hayden, *Listen, Yankee!*, 114.
127. Reitan, *Rise and Decline of an Alliance*, 105.
128. Gates and Cleaver, "Cuban Experience," 49.

129. The mixed motivations underpinning Cuban internationalism are best understood with regard to Cuban foreign policy in Africa and Cuban medical internationalism. See, for instance, Gleijeses, *Conflicting Missions*; and Feinsilver, *Healing the Masses*.

130. Prashad, *Darker Nations*, 107. Italics in original.

131. Gleijeses, *Visions of Freedom*, 25.

132. LeoGrande and Kornbluh, *Back Channel to Cuba*, 112.

133. Author's interview with Tomás Fernández Robaina, Havana, June 28, 2013.

134. U.S. Congress, *Tricontinental Conference of African, Asian and Latin American Peoples: A Staff Study*, 1.

135. Ernesto Che Guevara, "Message to the Tricontinental," 1967, in Guevara, *Guerrilla Warfare*, 173.

136. Gates and Cleaver, "Cuban Experience," 48–49.

137. Ríos, *Cuba*, 435.

138. For Murray, see *Tricontinental* 10, January-February 1969, 96–111; for Newton, no. 11, March-April 1969, 101–4.

139. See, for instance, Bloom and Martin, *Black against Empire*, 349–51.

140. Reitan, *Rise and Decline of an Alliance*.

141. Guevara, "Message to the Tricontinental."

142. Transcript of speech, *The Black Panther*, October 12, 1968, 14.

143. Debray, *Revolution in the Revolution?* See also Childs, "Historical Critique of the Emergence and Evolution," 593–624.

144. Reitan, "Cuba, the Black Panther Party," 219; Reitan, *Rise and Decline of an Alliance*.

145. Quoted in Gleijeses, *Conflicting Missions*, 23.

146. Carmichael, *Ready for Revolution*, 587–88. Historian Tomás Fernández Robaina contends that Cuba's policy of internationalism had, since its inception, focused upon Third World nations that had significant movements of national liberation or were viewed as having appropriate conditions for their growth. These conditions never existed in the United States, and so Cuba's aid to movements there was primarily "moral support." Author's interview with Tomás Fernández Robaina, June 28, 2013, Havana.

147. Stephanie Harrington, "Quiet Evening in a Revolutionary Life," *Village Voice*, October 19, 1967, 35.

148. U.S. Congressional Record, Senate, April 17, 1975, 10549.

149. Ibid.

150. Ibid.

151. Ibid.

152. Ibid., 10550.

153. Ibid.

154. Hoover quote is from U.S. Congress, *Hearings Before the Committee on Internal Security*, 2193.

155. "Hear [sic] 2 Cuba Envoys Denied Visas by U.S.," *Chicago Tribune*, April 5, 1969.

156. Georgie Ann Greyer and Keyes Beech, "Castro's UN Mission Here Hangout for Riot Leaders," *Long Island Press*, October 17, 1970.

157. "Rap Brown Balks Police at Cuban U.N. Mission," *NYT*, January 11, 1968.

158. Hayden, *Listen, Yankee!*, 28.

159. "Bomb Rocks Cuban U.N. Mission," *The Dispatch*, December 8, 1979, 2.

160. See Schoultz, *That Infernal Little Cuban Republic*.

161. See Alfonso Chardy and Oscar Corral, "Cuban Americans Foresee Rise of a Climate of

Fear," *MH*, January 15, 2006; "Statement by Ana Belen Montes, who received 25-year sentence for spying for Cuba," *MH*, October 16, 2002.

162. Saul Landau, "Infiltrating Alpha 66: An Interview with Gerardo Hernandez, Leader of the Cuban Five," *Counterpunch*, April 17–20, 2009.

163. James C. McKinley Jr., "Fate of 5 in U.S. Prisons Weighs on Cubans' Minds," *NYT*, August 5, 2007.

164. Tim Weiner, "Cuban Exile Could Test U.S. Definition of Terrorist," *NYT*, May 9, 2005.

165. I use the word "terrorism" to describe the purposeful violent targeting of civilians and noncombatants to achieve political ends.

166. "5 Cubans Convicted in Plot to Spy on U.S.," *NYT*, June 9, 2001.

167. Brett Kramarsic, FBI Agent, "Affidavit in Support of Criminal Complaint and Arrest Warrant," 2009, 10. Available at *Cryptome* online: http://cryptome.org/myers/myers-004.pdf.

168. CNN, "Former State Department official sentenced to life for spying for Cuba," July 16, 2010. http://www.cnn.com/2010/CRIME/07/16/spy.couple.sentenced/.

169. Ibid.

170. Toby Harnden, "Spying for Fidel: The Inside Story of Kendall and Gwen Myers," *Washingtonian*, October 2009.

171. See, for example, "FBI Questions American Travelers To Cuba," *Huffington Post*, May 30, 2010. http://www.huffingtonpost.com/2010/03/30/travelers-to-cuba-are-bei_n_519215.html.

172. Nicholas M. Horrock, "FBI Asserts Cuba Aided Weathermen," *NYT*, October 9, 1977.

173. Ibid.

174. U.S. Congressional Record, Senate, April 17, 1975, 10550.

175. Ibid.

176. Ibid. This claim is repeated, or perhaps originated in testimony that was later included in a 1980 documentary entitled *The KGB Connections: An Investigation Into Soviet Operations in North America*, in which a masked man identified as a Cuban intelligence defector, speaking in Spanish, is translated as stating "every time that a Venceremos Brigade contingent arrived in Cuba, all the operationals [sic] of the DGI had to drop what they were doing and go to work on the Venceremos Brigade. We had to investigate, collect background, to see who could be recruited, what information could be obtained."

177. U.S. Congressional Record, Senate, April 17, 1975, 10550.

178. Ibid.

179. Georgie Ann Greyer and Keyes Beech, "Castro's UN Mission Here Hangout for Riot Leaders," *Long Island Press*, October 17, 1970.

180. Kevin Gillies, "The Last Radical," *Vancouver Magazine*, November 1998.

Chapter 3

1. Robert T. Holden counts 137 hijackings of flights between 1968 and 1972 by persons who boarded in the United States; of these, 90 were "transportation attempts" to Cuba, while 21 were attempts to reach other countries. Mexico, the next most popular destination for American hijackers, was the desired destination for 4 hijacking attempts. See Holden, "Contagiousness of Aircraft Hijacking," 874, 879.

2. Over a dozen hijackings were also orchestrated by Cuban exiles seeking to return to the island and, in at least two cases, by American citizens protesting *against* the Castro government. However, the overwhelming majority of hijackings were committed by U.S. citizens

who articulated identifiable left-wing ideals and held generally favorable views of Cuba. It is these hijackers that are the focus of this chapter.

3. Brent, *Long Time Gone*, 134.

4. *U.S. News and World Report*, December 9, 1968.

5. Alfred E. Lewis and Jay Mathews, "Father, Son Give Up in '72 Killings," *WP*, July 8, 1975.

6. National Advisory Committee on Criminal Justice Standards and Goals, *Disorders and Terrorism*, 515.

7. NBC, January 30, 1969.

8. As quoted by the Swiss Ambassador, who had spoken with Castro. Memorandum, Secretary of State Rogers to the President, "Hijacking of Aircraft," February 6, 1969. U.S. Department of State online archive, Foreign Relations, 1969–1976, Volume E-1, Documents on Global Issues, 1969–1972, http://2001-2009.state.gov/r/pa/ho/frus/nixon/e1/45587.htm.

9. Representations of Cuba in the American imaginary over time are examined most lucidly in Pérez, *Cuba in the American Imagination*.

10. The diplomatic dimensions of the hijacking surge that began in 1968 have been explored only cursorily in published scholarship. See, for example, Domínguez, *To Make a World Safe for Revolution*, 122, 226–27; and Schoultz, *That Infernal Little Cuban Republic*. María Cristina García includes a brief mention of the episode in García, *Havana USA*, 138.

11. See, for example, Morley, *Imperial State and Revolution*; and Pérez, *Cuba and the United States*. See Suri, *Power and Protest*, for an analysis of the influence of global social movements on government diplomacy during the 1960s.

12. See Guridy, *Forging Diaspora*; Gronbeck-Tedesco, *Cuba, the United States, and Cultures of the Transnational Left*; Brock and Fuertes, *Between Race and Empire*; Greenbaum, *More Than Black*; and James, *Holding aloft the Banner of Ethiopia*.

13. The two scholars who have examined African American relations with Cuba after 1961 most thoroughly are Ruth Reitan and Mark Q. Sawyer. Although they do not devote significant attention to hijacking, their work reveals the larger contours of African American relations with Cuba during the period. See Reitan, *Rise and Decline of an Alliance*; and Sawyer, *Racial Politics in Post-Revolutionary Cuba*.

14. While these studies are not concerned with the questions addressed in this chapter, they provide useful data that has been incorporated where appropriate. See, especially Dugan, LaFree, and Piquero, "Testing a Rational Choice Model of Airline Hijackings."

15. Holden, "Contagiousness of Aircraft Hijacking."

16. Dugan, LaFree, and Piquero, "Testing a Rational Choice Model of Airline Hijackings."

17. Some of their findings have been incorporated into this chapter, as well as newer books on hijacking. Representative works include Arey, *Sky Pirates*; and Philips, *Skyjack*. More recent work on hijacking has been framed by the aftermath of the 9/11 hijacking attacks, including Killen, *1973 Nervous Breakdown*. Air hijacking in the United States was also the focus of several memoirs by former hijackers, and they have been referenced here where appropriate. The best known is Brent, *Long Time Gone*. See also Bryant, *Hijack*; and Fitzgerald, *Tamsin*.

18. One useful journalistic account that resists this polarization is Koerner's *Skies Belong to Us*. For a study of the hijacking outbreak from a counterterrorism perspective, see Feste, *Terminate Terrorism*.

19. Koerner, *Skies Belong to Us*, 37–38.

20. LeoGrande and Kornbluh, *Back Channel to Cuba*, 124.

21. John F. Kennedy, "The President's News Conference," August 10, 1961. Available online at *The American Presidency Project*, http://www.presidency.ucsb.edu/ws/?pid=8276.

22. Cuba's earlier history and encounters with a variety of non-state actors, including sea

pirates and filibusterers, show compelling parallels with air piracy and contributed to Cuba's place in the "long" American imaginary as an island refuge for bandits — a space of lawlessness and agency for foreigners. See Pérez, *Cuba in the American Imagination*; and Greenberg, *Manifest Manhood*. For an analysis of African American perceptions of Cuba before the 1950s, see Guridy, *Forging Diaspora*.

23. Gosse, *Where the Boys Are*, 1–5.

24. See Benson, "Cuba Calls"; Young, *Soul Power*, 18–53; Gosse, "The African-American Press Greets the Cuban Revolution," in Brock and Fuertes, eds., *Between Race and Empire*, 266; Moore, *Pichón*; and Guy, "Castro in New York," 10.

25. Although African American perceptions of Cuba's racial climate in the 1960s were due primarily to changes wrought by the 1959 revolution, perceptions of Cuba as a racial haven existed well before the 1950s. See Guridy, *Forging Diaspora*. For the impact of Castro's famed visit to Harlem, see Plummer, "Castro in Harlem," 133–53.

26 See Tyson, *Radio Free Dixie*.

27. Fidel Castro, speech, Chaplin Theater, Havana, October 4, 1965. LANIC, Castro Speech Database. A slightly different translation of this speech appears in Deutschmann, *Fidel Castro Reader*, 279, which lists the speech as occurring on October 3.

28. For Ghana, see Gaines, *American Africans in Ghana*.

29. Quoted in Díaz-Cotto, *Gender, Ethnicity, and the State*, 78.

30. Bornemann, *Surviving Mexico's Dirty War*, 99–117.

31. "Castroites Hijack Air Liner," *Chicago Tribune*, Aug 7, 1967.

32. "Skyjacking, to Catch a Thief," *Time Magazine*, February 14, 1969.

33. More research is needed to adequately understand hijacking to Cuba from Latin America and overseas during this period.

34. CBS News, *Rebels of the Sierra Maestra: The Story of Cuba's Jungle Fighters*, 1957. The boys' participation was also chronicled in the *New York Times*, March 8 and 24, 1957; April 22, 1957; and May 10, 1957. See Gosse, *Where the Boys Are*, 84.

35. Donald Soldini, interviewed by Van Gosse. In Gosse, *Where the Boys Are*, 91.

36. "Bringing Skyjackers Down to Earth," *Time Magazine*, October 4, 1971.

37. *The Sun*, February 22, 1968.

38. *Time Magazine*, December 6, 1968.

39. "Douglas Robinson, "Hijacking Victims Term Treatment by Cuban Hosts Royal, but Tiresome," *NYT*, February 9, 1969, 79.

40. *Time Magazine*, December 6, 1968.

41. Cleaver, *Soul on Ice*, 140.

42. For a European aviation security perspective, see Alexander and Sochor, *Aerial Piracy and Aviation Security*.

43. David Briscoe, "4 Await Sentencing, 1 Hijacker in Cuba," *Deseret News*, July 4, 1972.

44. "Jet Hijacked To Cuba," *NYT*, May 7, 1972.

45. "Hijacking Suspect Returned By Cuba," *NYT*, June 15, 1975; "Accused Hijacker Held by F.B.I. after Release by Cuban Government," *MH*, June 15, 1975.

46. Alfred E. Lewis and Jay Mathews, "Father, Son Give Up in '72 Killings," *WP*, July 8, 1975.

47. Ibid.

48. See, for example, Paul L. Montgomery, "4 Kill Texas Airline Aide and Hijack a Jet to Cuba," *NYT*, October 30, 1972.

49. Alfred E. Lewis and Jay Mathews, "Father, Son Give Up in '72 Killings," *WP*, July 8, 1975.

50. For instance, according to then U.S. Congressman Bill Richardson, who visited Cuba in 1996, officials there knew that Charles Hill and Michael Finney, Republic of New Afrika

members living as exiles in Cuba, were hijackers, but maintained that they were unaware that the two men were wanted for the slaying of a U.S. police officer. Don Bullis, "NMSP Officer's Killers Remain Free in Cuba," *Rio Rancho Observer*, May 10, 2006.

51. Major Claudio Rey Mariña, Head of the Delegation of the Republic of Cuba, speech at the XVII Special Assembly of the International Civil Aviation Organization, Montreal, Canada, June 1970. See Mariña, *Hijacking of Aircraft*.

52. See L.C. Green, "Hijacking and the Right of Asylum," in McWhinney, *Aerial Piracy and International Law*.

53. Mariña, "Hijacking of Aircraft."

54. Reitan, *Rise and Decline of an Alliance*, 107.

55. Brent, *Long Time Gone*, 119–20.

56. According to Brent, Huey Newton personally reinstated him back into the Black Panther Party in 1975, when Newton was staying in Havana as a political asylee. Brent, *Long Time Gone*, 235–36.

57. Hilliard, *This Side of Glory*, 157–58.

58. Ibid., 162.

59. Sawyer, *Racial Politics in Post-Revolutionary Cuba*, xvii.

60. See de la Fuente, *Nation for All*, especially 259–96; and Sawyer, *Racial Politics in Post-Revolutionary Cuba*.

61. See de la Fuente, "Race, National Discourse and Politics in Cuba," 44. See also de la Fuente, *Nation for All*; Ferrer, *Insurgent Cuba*; and Helg, *Our Rightful Share*.

62. The idea is most often associated with the 1928 Communist International ("Comintern"), which declared the "Black Belt" in the southern United States to be a colonized "nation within a nation." See Solomon, *Cry Was Unity*; and Kelley, *Hammer and Hoe*. See also Singh, "The Black Panthers and the 'Underdeveloped Country' of the Left," in Jones, *Black Panther Party Reconsidered*, 57–105.

63. Obadele, *War in America*.

64. Berger, "Malcolm X Doctrine." See also Singh, "Black Panthers and the 'Underdeveloped Country' of the Left."

65. Robert F. Williams, a political asylee in Cuba during the early 1960s, assumed the RNA's title of Chief of State in 1968. See Cohen, *Black Crusader*.

66. These three factors were commonly invoked by hijackers interviewed by U.S. media. See, for example, Martin Schram and John Wallach, "Unhappy Landings," *Penthouse*, October 1973.

67. Hijackers who expected to be welcomed in Cuba include ex-Black Panthers William Lee Brent, Raymond Johnson, Farland Jesus Grant, and Richard Duwayne Witt, who had volunteered for the Panthers but never joined. See Schram and Wallach, "Unhappy Landings," *Penthouse*, October 1973.

68. Gates and Cleaver, "Cuban Experience," 48–49.

69. Athelia Knight and Ron Shaffer, "Tullers Chose to Risk Jail Rather Than Live in Cuba," *WP*, July 15, 1975.

70. "Hijacking Suspect Returned By Cuba," *NYT*, June 15, 1975, 37; "Cuba Offers Return of Air Ransom," *Milwaukee Journal*, June 17, 1975.

71. Bryant, *Hijack*, 8.

72. Alan Díaz, "Tony Bryant, Cuban Exiles' Hero," *Sun-Sentinel*, December 19, 1999.

73. Summary Calendar, United States Court of Appeals, Fifth Circuit, Appeal from the United States District Court for the Eastern District of Louisiana, Raymond Johnson, pro se, July 22, 1987.

74. Fenton Wheeler, "Life Worse in Cuba, Unhappy Black Panthers Wail," *MH*, June 26, 1969.

75. Brent, *Long Time Gone*, 174.

76. Fenton Wheeler, "Life Worse in Cuba, Unhappy Black Panthers Wail," *MH*, June 26, 1969. Charlie Hill, for his part, suggests that Johnson, who had never traveled outside of the United States before, was unprepared for life in Cuba and resented the Cuban government's detention of hijackers for security clearance. Hill, interview by the author, September 9, 2012, Havana.

77. See Benson, "Cuba Calls," and Rodríguez, "'De la Esclavitud Yanqui a la Libertad Cubana,'" 62–87.

78. For his part, Michael Finney repeatedly declined interviews with U.S. press outlets after growing to resent the tendency of reporters to use hijackers' perceptions of life in Cuba to slander the Cuban government. Author's interview with Esther Finney, widow of Michael Finney, June 26, 2013, Havana.

79. Brent, *Long Time Gone*, 167–88. While in Cuba, Brent would meet a number of other would-be American revolutionaries seeking military training in Cuba.

80. One of the hijackers was rumored in 1973 to be teaching at the University of Havana. See Martin Schram and John Wallach, "Unhappy Landings," *Penthouse*, October 1973.

81. Jay Mathews, "Hijacker, Wanted in Murder, Enjoys Cuba Life," *WP*, January 7, 1975.

82. Charlie Hill, interview by the author, September 7, 9, 2012, Havana. Other African American visitors to Cuba during the period made similar reports. See, especially, Clytus, *Black Man in Red Cuba*. Brent alleges that Eldridge Cleaver ran afoul of Cuban officials when he attempted to organize a chapter of the Black Panther Party in Cuba.

83. *Democracy Now*, "William Lee Brent 1930–2006: A 1998 Conversation in Havana with the Former Black Panther on His Plane Hijacking, Life in Cuba and Much More," November 22, 2006. See also Larry Rohter, "Havana Journal; 25 Years an Exile: An Old Black Panther Sums Up," *NYT*, April 9, 1996. Brent died of pneumonia in a Havana hospital in 2006 at the age of seventy-five.

84. Brent, *Long Time Gone*, 235.

85. Hill, interview by the author, September 9, 2012, Havana. Hill's companions, Michael Finney and Ralph Lawrence Goodwin, are now deceased: Goodwin, according to some reports, drowned at a beach while trying to rescue a drowning survivor; Finney, who spent many years working at Radio Havana Cuba, died of lung cancer in 2005. See also Eugene Robinson, "Exiles," *WP*, July 18, 2004.

86. Charlie Hill, interview by the author, September 7, 2012, Havana.

87. Memorandum, Secretary of State Rogers to The President, "Hijacking of Aircraft," February 6, 1969. U.S. Department of State online archive, Foreign Relations, 1969–1976, Volume E-1, Documents on Global Issues, 1969–1972, http://2001-2009.state.gov/r/pa/ho/frus/nixon/e1/45587.htm.

88. Ibid.

89. "Pilots May Strike if U.N. Doesn't Act on Hijacking," *NYT*, June 9, 1972, 1.

90. U.S. Congress, House of Representatives, *Hearings on Aircraft Hijacking, Committee on Foreign Affairs*, 115–16.

91. "U.S. Jury Indicts Five in $1 Million Hijack," *WP*, August 4, 1972.

92. "Hijacking Bicyclist Gets Ransom, Shot by FBI," *WP*, August 19, 1972.

93. Gray, *Skyjack*, 2011.

94. Robert Lindsey, "2-Million Ransom Imperils Airline," *NYT*, November 16, 1972, 1.

95. Ibid.

96. Feste, *Terminate Terrorism*, 80.

97. "Rising Cost of Piracy," *Time Magazine*, January 1, 1973.

98. See, for example, Georgie Ann Greyer and Keyes Beech, "Cuba, School for U.S. Radicals," *Long Island Press*, October 15, 1970.

99. Bernard Gwertzman, "U.S. Says Pact with Cuba to Curb Hijacking is Near," *NYT*, February 14, 1973. See also Memorandum, Henry Kissinger to the President, "Secretary Rogers to See Swiss Ambassador to Cuba on Monday to Hand Him U.S. Draft Proposal on Hijacking," December 3, 1972. U.S. Department of State online archive, Foreign Relations, 1969–1976, Volume E-1, Documents on Global Issues, 1969–1972, http://2001-2009.state.gov/r/pa/ho/frus/nixon/e1/45625.htm.

100. U.S. Congress, House of Representatives, *Hearing before the Subcommittee on Inter-American Affairs of the Committee on Foreign Affairs*, 16.

101. Domínguez, *To Make a World Safe for Revolution*, 122.

102. "After 87 Hijackings, an Agreement," *WP*, February 16, 1973.

103. Law no. 1226, Osvaldo Dorticós Torrado, President of the Republic of Cuba, "Cuban Hijacking Law," September 16, 1969, translated to English by U.S. Department of State and published in *International Legal Materials* 8, no. 6 (November 1969): 1175–77.

104. Ibid.

105. Memorandum, Henry Kissinger to The President, "Aircraft Hijacking," February 7, 1969. U.S. Department of State online archive, Foreign Relations, 1969–1976, Volume E-1, Documents on Global Issues, 1969–1972, http://2001-2009.state.gov/r/pa/ho/frus/nixon/e1/45587.htm.

106. Mariña, *Hijacking of Aircraft*, 7.

107. Law no. 1226, Osvaldo Dorticós Torrado, President of the Republic of Cuba, "Cuban Hijacking Law," September 16, 1969, translated to English by U.S. Department of State and published in *International Legal Materials* 8, no. 6 (November 1969): 1175.

108. Schoultz, *That Infernal Little Cuban Republic*, 258.

109. Domínguez, *To Make a World Safe for Revolution*, 227.

110. Memorandum, Henry Kissinger for Peter Flanigan, "Possible Actions Against Countries Which Are Uncooperative on Hijacking," October 31, 1970. U.S. Department of State online archive, Foreign Relations, 1969–1976, Volume E-1, Documents on Global Issues, 1969–1972, http://2001-2009.state.gov/r/pa/ho/frus/nixon/e1/45411.htm.

111. See Pérez, *Cuba in the American Imagination*; Schoultz, *That Infernal Little Cuban Republic*.

112. Memorandum, Henry Kissinger for Peter Flanigan, "Possible Actions Against Countries Which Are Uncooperative on Hijacking," October 31, 1970. U.S. Department of State online archive, Foreign Relations, 1969–1976, Volume E-1, Documents on Global Issues, 1969–1972, http://2001-2009.state.gov/r/pa/ho/frus/nixon/e1/45411.htm.

113. See "'Good' v. 'Bad' Hijackers," *Time Magazine*, September 28, 1970. Talks in 1969 and 1970 had foundered upon the problem of reciprocity, with the Cuban government demanding that the United States return some of the Cuban exiles, including hijackers, who had illegally traveled to the United States, in return for tougher measures against U.S. hijackers. See "Air Pirates: Castro Pulls Welcome Mat," *U.S. News and World Report*, December 4, 1972.

114. "The Cuban Dilemma," *Time Magazine*, January 15, 1973.

115. See "Cuba-United States Memorandum of Understanding on Hijacking."

116. "Cuba-United States Memorandum of Understanding on Hijacking of Aircraft and Vessels and Other Offenses," February 15, 1973. See also Bernard Gwertzman, "U.S. and Cuba Hijack Pact But That's All Now," *NYT*, February 18, 1973. For analysis from the U.S. gov-

ernment side, see Serban Vallimarescu, Memorandum for General Scowcroft, "Hijacking Agreement with Cuba," National Security Council, February 13, 1973.

117. U.S. Congress, House of Representatives, *Hearing before the Subcommittee on Inter-American Affairs of the Committee on Foreign Affairs*, 3.

118. See, for example, García, *Havana USA*, 138.

119. Morley, *Imperial State and Revolution*, 250.

120. Schoultz, *That Infernal Little Cuban Republic*, 259.

121. Domínguez, *To Make a World Safe for Revolution*, 122, 230.

122. See Rediker, *Villains of All Nations*.

123. See Hobsbawm, *Bandits*. Although Hobsbawm does not examine air hijacking, the timing of the book's publication in 1969 coincided with the explosion of U.S.-Cuba air piracy.

124. Fanon, *Wretched of the Earth*, 130. Singh, in particular, examines the import of Fanon's idea to the Panthers. See Singh, "Black Panthers and the 'Underdeveloped Country' of the Left." For an analysis of discourses about the role and romanticization of criminality within radical social change movements of the 1960s see, for example, Cummings, *Rise and Fall of California's Radical Prison Movement*.

Chapter 4

1. The term "Cuban American" was not yet in wide circulation in the 1970s, as most Cubans in the United States still regarded their geographic and national status as transitory, and their dislocation from the island as temporary. Cubans arriving in the United States during this period also tended to see themselves as exiles rather than immigrants: people who had been forcibly displaced by the political, social, and economic changes initiated by the Cuban Revolution.

2. Although many of the publication's members hailed from Miami, *Areíto* was soon headquartered in the less hostile environs of New York.

3. FBI, Memo to Director. File no. not provided. Untitled, March 10, 1983, 1. Obtained via FOIA request by the author, February 2009. All files are heavily redacted, and in almost all cases, the file numbers are obscured or not provided. The bureau's reports on the Maceo Brigade frequently referenced the earlier Venceremos Brigade, upon which the group was partially modeled.

4. Dagmaris Cabezas, "The Cuban Exiles: You Can Go Home Again," *Nation*, June 7, 1980, 680. According to María de los Ángeles Torres, Omega 7 claimed responsibility for Varela's murder. See de los Ángeles Torres, *Lost Apple*, 222.

5. See Michael J. Bustamante, "Anti-Communist Anti-Imperialism?"

6. One excellent summary is available in García, *Havana USA*. For another brief but perceptive examination, see López, *Impossible Returns*.

7. De los Ángeles Torres, *In the Land of Mirrors*, 94. Like most scholars who have written about the Maceo Brigade, de los Ángeles Torres is a past member of the group, and I have incorporated the work of these participant-scholars as the necessary foundation for any analysis of the group's history. See also de la Campa, *Cuba on My Mind*; de los Ángeles Torres, "Beyond the Rupture: Reconciling with Our Enemies, Reconciling with Ourselves," in Behar, *Bridges to Cuba/Puentes a Cuba*; and de los Ángeles Torres, *Lost Apple*. Also important is the range of autobiographical material by Cuban Americans who returned to Cuba independently. See, for instance, Risech, "Political and Cultural Cross-Dressing." Other summaries can be found in García, *Havana USA*.

8. Robert Levine's useful study of the covert diplomacy of Bernardo Benes gives the Maceo

Brigade barely a mention. Although Levine's book is concerned primarily with Benes's secret negotiations with high-level Cuban officials, including Fidel Castro, talks conducted to secure the release of Cuban prisoners and reunify diasporic Cuban families, the omission of the Maceo Brigade within the larger scope of the narrative overlooks an important area of context. See Levine, *Secret Missions to Cuba*.

9. See Young, *Soul Power*.

10. See Daulatzai, *Black Star, Crescent Moon*.

11. *Tricontinental* 19–20, July–October 1970, 150.

12. Pérez-Stable, "Field of Cuban Studies," 239–50.

13. Risech, "Political and Cultural Cross-Dressing," 533.

14. See de los Ángeles Torres, *In the Land of Mirrors*, 84–85.

15. Ibid., 88.

16. See Lourdes Casal, "Cubans in the United States: Their Impact on U.S.-Cuba Relations," in Weinstein, *Revolutionary Cuba in the World Arena*, 126.

17. On the Cuban side, the University of Havana created a professorship in U.S. History in 1972, followed a year later by a working group for U.S. Studies in the university's Faculty of Humanities, and a visit to Cuba, organized by the University of Havana, that year by academics associated with the New York–based Center for Cuban Studies. For an overview of U.S.-Cuba academic collaboration, see Martínez, "Academic Exchange between Cuba and the United States."

18. Espinosa, an early supporter of dialogue, later reversed his position and campaigned against "*dialogueros*" on Miami radio stations, repudiating them as agents of Castro.

19. For example, a 1975 survey published in the *Miami Herald* found that in the sample group aged over sixty, 84 percent of Cubans in Miami opposed resumption of diplomatic ties between the United States and Cuba, while 49 percent opposed them in the 26–39 age bracket, and only 27 percent of respondents opposed them in the 16–25 age bracket. *MH*, December 29, 1975.

20. Quoted by Sonia Rivera-Valdéz, in Behar, *Bridges to Cuba/Puentes a Cuba*, 226.

21. Editorial, *Joven Cuba* 1 (February 1974): 1. All translations of *Joven Cuba* from Spanish are my own.

22. Editorial, *Joven Cuba* 1 (February 1974): 1.

23. "Cuba opens up to the children who went away 20 years ago," *Guardian*, January 12, 1979, 6.

24. Lourdes Casal, "Race Relations in Contemporary Cuba," in Dzidizienyo and Casal, *The Position of Blacks in Brazilian and Cuban Society*, 21.

25. Casal, "Race Relations in Contemporary Cuba," 12–13.

26. DRE claimed responsibility for the attack, and the perpetrators were pictured smiling on page two of the *New York Times*. "Young Cubans Relate Details of Attack Near Havana," *NYT*, August 27, 1962, 2.

27. Author's email correspondence with Albor Ruíz, September 2015.

28. Marifeli Pérez-Stable, from personal statement on her website, as it appeared April 2013. While the website is not available as of June 2017, much of the statement is reproduced in Marifeli Pérez-Stable, "Can We Honor the Fallen of Both Sides?," *MH*, October 22, 2009. http://archive.thedialogue.org/page.cfm?pageID=32&pubID=2133.

29. Grupo Areíto, *Contra Viento y Marea*, 53. Translation is mine. Unless indicated otherwise, all translations of *Contra Viento y Marea* from Spanish are my own. See also a reflection by Manolo Gomez, a member of the original Brigade: "A Cuban returns 'home,'" *New York Amsterdam News*, June 17, 1978, 15; and *Areíto* 4, nos. 3 & 4 (Spring 1978).

30. Grupo Areíto, *Contra Viento y Marea*, 54.
31. For examples of this specific interplay between civil rights and the movement in opposition to the Vietnam War, as well as the way in which black political movements in the early 1960s provided a frame through which whites and other groups began to view other injustices, see Anderson, *Movement and the Sixties*.
32. Risech, "Political and Cultural Cross-Dressing," 530.
33. Grupo Areíto, *Contra Viento y Marea*, 55. See also *Areíto* 4, nos. 3 & 4 (Spring 1978).
34. See, for example, María de los Ángeles Torres's recollection of her interactions with members of the Venceremos Brigade in "Beyond the Rupture: Reconciling with Our Enemies, Reconciling with Ourselves," in Behar, *Bridges to Cuba/Puentes a Cuba*.
35. Díaz, *De la Patria y el Exilio*, 92–93. Quoted in Pedraza, *Political Disaffection in Cuba's Revolution and Exodus*, 141. Interviewed in the film *55 Hermanos*, Marifeli Pérez-Stable relates a similar encounter with Venceremos Brigade members.
36. María Nodarse-Pérez, "The Diary of Maria Nodarse-Perez," *MH*, March 30, 1980.
37. LeoGrande and Kornbluh, *Back Channel to Cuba*.
38. See García, *Havana USA*, 138. Cuba later abrogated the agreement in 1976 in response to the bombing of Cubana de Aviación flight 455. Although Cuba continued to honor the agreement in practice, both Fidel and Raúl Castro informed George McGovern, who traveled to Cuba in April 1977 to discuss the U.S.-Cuba relationship, that Cuba's continuing cooperation on the issue of hijacking depended upon the lifting of the trade embargo, and upon tighter U.S. control of anti-Castro Cuban American militant groups operating in Florida. See "McGovern, Back from Cuba, Says He Will Seek the End of Trade Ban," *NYT*, April 12, 1977.
39. Public statement given March 1, 1975, in Houston. Quoted in David Binder, "U.S. and Cubans Discussed Links in Talks in 1975," *NYT*, March 29, 1977. Cuba also extradited an airline hijacker who had fled to Cuba in 1972 with $2 million in ransom cash.
40. Quoted in Schoultz, *That Infernal Little Cuban Republic*, 298.
41. Hearing Before the Committee on Foreign Relations, United States Senate, 95th Cong., 1st sess., *Nomination of Hon. Cyrus R. Vance To Be Secretary of State*, January 11, 1977, 17. Vance's remark came in response to questioning by Senator George McGovern, who asked why Washington's prevailing position of détente with China, the Soviet Union, and Vietnam should not also apply to Cuba.
42. "Relations with the United States," *Granma International*, May 22, 1977.
43. This marked the first time a U.S. sports team had visited the island since 1960. "McGovern, Back from Cuba, Says He Will Seek the End of Trade Ban," *NYT*, April 12, 1977.
44. One has to wonder whether Church, who had witnessed the dark underbelly of illegal U.S. government campaigns against domestic dissidents and foreign governments, believed his own assurances. See Rudy Abramson, "U.S. Won't Subvert Cuba, Senator Says: Church Arrives in Havana, Gives Assurance on Administration Policy," *LAT*, August 9, 1977. The 1975–1976 Church Committee Hearings, as they were known, investigated campaigns of spying, disruption, and slander against U.S. dissidents, ostensibly conducted in the name of national security from domestic and foreign threats.
45. "Cuban-U.S. talks on fishing zones and maritime limits," *Granma International*, April 17, 1977.
46. "U.S. and Cuban Scholars Hold a Quiet Conference," *NYT*, November 9, 1977. Henry Kissinger had personally denied visas to eight Cuban scholars to attend a meeting of the Latin American Studies Association the year before. See also Martínez, "Academic Exchange between Cuba and the United States," 29–42.
47. See, for example, David Lachenbruch, "Curiosity Goes on a Cuban Tour," *LAT*,

March 19, 1978, E12; "250 Yanks taking small boats to Cuba," *Chicago Tribune*, May 13, 1978. U.S. airlines did not resume scheduled flights to Cuba; American tourists to Cuba arrived by way of specially chartered flights or through third countries. Coverage of tourism in Cuba noted the industry's potential for growth as other opportunities for economic development declined: "Tourism is an industry with a future," *Granma International* noted. See "Tourism in Cuba growing by leaps and bounds," *Granma International*, December 10, 1978.

48. Gabriel Molina and Miguel Hernández, "Fidel sees off U.S. swimmer who tried to swim from Cuba to Florida," *Granma International*, July 23, 1978.

49. Castro was described in the *Los Angeles Times* as "the hit and chief Cuba resource"; John Lenker, a vice president at Pillsbury, recalled that Castro "evoked a real high in the people." "Thaw in Relations with U.S.: GE Plans Business Seminar in Cuba," *LAT*, January 3, 1978. For sea cooperation see, for example, "Despite Africa Friction, Sea Accord with Cuba Eyed," *WP*, January 22, 1978; for an overview of these topics, see Morley, *Imperial State and Revolution*, 287–97.

50. Graham Hovey, "U.S. and Cuban Missions Opened In a Step to Resuming Relations," *NYT*, September 2, 1977.

51. Jorge Domínguez, "Cuban Foreign Policy," *Foreign Affairs*, fall 1978.

52. See Senate Subcommittee to Administer the Internal Security Act and Other National Security Laws, *Cuban Connection in Puerto Rico; Castro's Hand in Puerto Rican and U.S. Terrorism*.

53. David Binder, "U.S. and Cubans Discussed Links in Talks in 1975," *NYT*, March 29, 1977, 8. See also Morley, *Imperial State and Revolution*, 253–55.

54. Schoultz, *That Infernal Little Cuban Republic*, 304–20.

55. Carter, however, predicted an eventual U.S. victory of influence in the region, invoking America's longstanding effort to best the Soviet Union's reputation in the global battle for hearts and minds in the arena of racial equality and Third World self-determination, an area in which the Soviets had often won. The U.S. victory, Carter maintained, would be based upon "our own relationship with the African people, our absence of racism against black people now, our commitment to economic aid rather than military aid, would be a very significant factor." Bernard Gwertzman, "Carter Sharply Attacks Cuba, Saying Use of Troops Hurts Peace Moves," *NYT*, May 14, 1978.

56. Francoise Raitberger, "U.S. Rapprochement With Cuba Seen Likely," *WP*, February 9, 1977.

57. Fidel Castro, speech. Reprinted in *Granma International*, January 1, 1978.

58. Ibid.

59. Among the most credible studies on the issue of political prisoners in Cuba was issued by Amnesty International. In its 1975–1976 Annual Report (p. 54), the group condemned Cuba's repression against political dissidents, noting that, "[t]he persistence of fear, real or imagined of counterrevolutionary conspiracies was primarily responsible for the excesses in the treatment of political prisoners." Declining fear within Cuba in the 1970s, as the government continued to consolidate its revolution and became less concerned with U.S. intervention, had led to a lessoning of repression. Quoted in Gómez, *Human Rights in Cuba, El Salvador and Nicaragua*, 87.

60. "Exiles see Fidel," *Guardian*, September 8, 1978. See also, "Castro Seeks Increased Contact with Cuban Exiles Living in U.S.," *WP*, September 8, 1978. Earlier in the year, the U.S. State Department had authorized a one-time sale of less than $80,000 worth of medical supplies to Cuba. See "Despite Africa Friction, Sea Accord with Cuba Eyed," *WP*, January 22, 1978.

61. Fidel Castro, speech, Havana, December 24, 1977, in *Granma International*, January 1, 1978. Quoted in Schoultz, *That Infernal Little Cuban Republic*, 322. *Granma International*, too, featured stories on imprisonment in the United States that charged human rights violations, including one article focusing on an American Medical Association report that had revealed widespread lack of adequate health care for the imprisoned. Yolanda Gómez, "Human rights in U.S. prisons?," *Granma International*, March 13, 1977.

62. Juan Marrero, "Look Homeward, Mr. Carter," *Granma International*, July 3, 1977.

63. Oscar Ferrer, "Political prisoners in the United States," *Granma International*, December 31, 1978. The cited book, Goodell's *Political Prisoners in America*, examines political imprisonment, from repression against Quaker pacifists during the American Revolutionary War to the targeting of the Black Panther Party in the early 1970s.

64. "Exiles see Fidel," *Guardian*, September 8, 1978.

65. Spencer Rich, "Castro Spokesman Asks Exile's Help in Mending Ties," *WP*, November 5, 1978.

66. Author's email correspondence with Raúl Alzaga, September 2015.

67. Casal does not appear to have written about her role in the formation of the Brigade. However, the key role she played is verified elsewhere. See, for instance, Pedraza, *Political Disaffection in Cuba's Revolution and Exodus*, 139–40.

68. Author's email correspondence with Raúl Alzaga, September 2015.

69. See Ferrer, *Insurgent Cuba*.

70. FBI, Memorandum, ADIC New York to FBI Director, "Antonio Maceo Brigade," December 6, 1984, 3. File number not provided. Obtained via FOIA request by the author, February 2009.

71. de la Campa, "Latino Diaspora in the United States," 295. According to Pedraza, Casal "named it after Antonio Maceo . . . because he was black and thus often ignored in Cuban history." See Pedraza, *Political Disaffection in Cuba's Revolution and Exodus*, 140.

72. It is interesting to note here that, aside from Casal, the *Areíto* collective and the Maceo Brigade's organizing committee was composed almost entirely of white and light-skinned Cubans. "Por Que Antonio Maceo?," *Areíto* 4, nos. 3 & 4 (Spring 1978): 5. Unless indicated otherwise, all translations of *Areíto* from Spanish are my own.

73. "Declaración de la Brigada Antonio Maceo," *Areíto* 4, nos. 3 & 4 (Spring 1978): 4.

74. Ibid.

75. According to María de los Ángeles Torres, who interviewed a member of the Ministry. *In the Land of Mirrors*, 92.

76. Ronald Smothers, "Cuban Exiles Visiting Home Find Identity," *NYT*, February 14, 1978.

77. The experiences of the participants of the first Maceo Brigade in Cuba are chronicled in a special edition of *Areíto* 4, nos. 3 & 4 (Spring 1978): 1–83; and in Jesús Díaz, *55 Hermanos*, Instituto Cubano del Arte e Industria Cinematográficos, 1978.

78. Manolo Gómez, "A Cuban returns 'home,'" *New York Amsterdam News*, June 17, 1978.

79. María Nodarse-Pérez, "The Diary of Maria Nodarse-Perez," *MH*, March 30, 1980.

80. FBI, Memorandum, SAC San Antonio, Tex., to FBI Director, "Brigada Antonio Maceo," December 11, 1978, 1. File no. not provided. Obtained via FOIA request by the author, February 2009. The memorandum characterized the Brigade as "a United States–Cuba relations group."

81. Pedraza, *Political Disaffection in Cuba's Revolution and Exodus*, 141.

82. Risech, "Political and Cultural Cross-Dressing," 527–28.

83. Reprinted in *Granma International*. Frank González, "The Cuban Community Moves Toward Dialogue," *Granma International*, November 26, 1978.

84. "Nicolás Guillén Meets with Representatives of Areíto Group," *Granma International*, April 9, 1978.

85. Author's interview with Orlaida Cabrera, Havana, Cuba, November 17, 2015.

86. Image reproduced in "Cuba as seen by the Maceítos," *Granma International*, November 26, 1978.

87. For more on the politics of childhood for Cuban exiles, see Casavantes Bradford, *Revolution Is for the Children*.

88. "Statement on Youth in Our America Special Award and 11th Festival Declaration Read by Haydée Santamaría," *Granma International*, February 19, 1978. In 1981, Casa de Las Americas awarded the literary prize to Lourdes Casal's book *Palabras Juntan Revolución — Words Foment Revolution*.

89. "Nicolás Guillén Meets with Representatives of Areíto Group," *Granma International*, April 9, 1978. World Youth Festivals were organized beginning in 1947 with the intention of uniting global leftist youth after the destruction of World War II. The festivals soon became oriented toward communism and influenced by organizations from the Soviet Union. For a summary of the festival's trajectory, see Krekola and Mikkonen, "Backlash of the Free World."

90. FBI, Memorandum, Boston SAC to FBI Director, "Antonio Maceo Brigade," October 25, 1979, 2. File no. not provided. Obtained via FOIA request by the author, February 2009.

91. Levine, *Secret Missions to Cuba*, 114.

92. Karen DeYoung, "Castro, Exiles Reach Accord on Release of 3,000 Cubans," *WP*, December 10, 1978.

93. Reprinted in *Baraguá* 1, no. 1 (March 1979); transcribed by FBI in FBI, memorandum, "Antonio Maceo Brigade," June 4, 1979. File number not provided. Obtained via FOIA request by the author, February 2009.

94. Robert M. Levine examines these negotiations in detail in *Secret Missions to Cuba: Fidel Castro, Bernardo Benes, and Cuban Miami*. Benefitting from more recently declassified documents, Lars Schoultz also examines the prisoner agreement in Schoultz, *That Infernal Little Cuban Republic*, 320–25.

95. De los Ángeles Torres, *In the Land of Mirrors*, 95.

96. Holly Ackerman, "Different Diasporas: Cubans in Venezuela, 1959–1998," in Herrera, *Cuba*.

97. Karen DeYoung, "Castro, Exiles Reach Accord on Release of 3,000 Cubans," *WP*, December 10, 1978. An article in the *Chicago Tribune* on November 22, 1978, was entitled "Castro to release 3,000; dares U.S. to take them."

98. Bernardo Benes, confidential memorandum to President Jimmy Carter: "The issuance of parole visas to 5,000 ex-political prisoners of Cuba," September 21, 1979, 1–2. Bernardo Benes Papers, Cuban Heritage Collection, University of Miami, Box 14, folder 116.

99. Levine, *Secret Missions to Cuba*, 119.

100. Fidel Castro, quoted in *Granma International*. "Fidel's press conference on the dialogue with the Cuban community abroad," *Granma International*, December 3, 1978.

101. "A bridge of life from Miami to Havana," *Guardian*, January 11, 1979.

102. Karen DeYoung, "Exiles' Visit is Political, Public Relations Coup for Castro," *WP*, December 15, 1978.

103. Gabriel Molina, "46 Ex-prisoners and Prisoners Released by Cuban Government Travel to Miami," *Granma International*, November 5, 1978.

104. Gayle Reaves, "UT students return to Cuba," *American Statesman*, December 1978.

105. "A bridge of life from Miami to Havana," *Guardian*, January 11, 1979.

106. Karen DeYoung, "Exiles' Visit is Political, Public Relations Coup for Castro," *WP*, December 15, 1978.
107. See Levine, *Secret Missions to Cuba*, 2002.
108. "Cuba Frees Four U.S. Prisoners," *WP*, September 18, 1979.
109. Jimmy Carter: "Puerto Rican Nationalists Announcement of the President's Commutation of Sentences," September 6, 1979. Online at *The American Presidency Project*. http://www.presidency.ucsb.edu/ws/?pid=32827.
110. Quoted in Levine, *Secret Missions to Cuba*, 111.
111. Ibid., 90.
112. For its part, the FBI reported that the topics discussed during the November 1978 talks, which included political prisoners, the reunification of families, and permission for exiles to visit Cuba "were presented in the form of a dialogue as opposed to negotiations." FBI, ADIC New York to FBI Director, "Antonio Maceo Brigade," December 6, 1984, 16. File number not provided. Obtained via FOIA request by the author, February 2009.
113. María de los Ángeles Torres, who participated in the Havana dialogues as a member of the Maceo Brigade, contends that, "for the Cuban government the exile community would become an arena in which they could attempt to manipulate Washington." See de los Ángeles Torres, *In the Land of Mirrors*, 96.
114. See de los Ángeles Torres, *In the Land of Mirrors*, 96–97.
115. María Nodarse-Pérez, "The Diary of Maria Nodarse-Perez," *MH*, March 30, 1980.
116. See, for example, Ron Buchanan, "An uncertain welcome for Cuba's prodigal sons," *Guardian*, February 6, 1979.
117. María Nodarse-Pérez, "The Diary of Maria Nodarse-Perez."
118. A *Miami News* article printed on the first day of the meetings included short bios of the 54 delegates scheduled to participate in the first section. Helga Silva, "54 exiles begin 'dialogue' with Castro," *Miami News*, November 20, 1978.
119. Karen DeYoung, "Exiles' Visit is Political, Public Relations Coup for Castro," *WP*, December 15, 1978.
120. Reported in *MH*, April 6, 1991.
121. Levine, *Secret Missions to Cuba*, 220.
122. Meg Laughlin, "A Letter from Samara," *Tropic*, November 6, 1994. Quoted in Pedraza, *Political Disaffection in Cuba's Revolution and Exodus*, 146.
123. Quoted by Ann Louise Bardach, "Our Man in Miami," *New Republic*, October 3, 1994.
124. Roberta Salper, "Counter-revolutionaries strike new blow," *Claridad*, April 8, 1973.
125. Patrick Doyle and John Murphy, "Times Square Blast Injures 5," *Daily News*, July 25, 1973.
126. "Protests Close Expo Cuba a Day Early," *NYT*, July 29, 1973.
127. "No. 1 Topic in Little Havana: Possibility of Visiting Cuba," *NYT*, April 8, 1977. A significant majority of the violence targeted progressive Cubans, although some victims were right-wing casualties of rivalries within the militant community. See, for example, Arguelles, "US National Security State," 299.
128. Sources on Bosch's activities include files held by the National Security Archive. See, for instance: http://nsarchive.gwu.edu/NSAEBB/NSAEBB157/.
129. Quoted in Arguelles, "US National Security State," 300.
130. "Cuba exiles claim three bombings in East," *Chicago Tribune*, March 26, 1979.
131. Les Ledbetter, "Explosion Damages Cuban Mission to U.N.; Three Persons Hurt Slightly," *NYT*, October 28, 1979.

132. CIA, Intelligence Information Cable, "Activities of Cuban Exile Leader Orlando Bosch during his Stay in Venezuela," October 14, 1976, National Security Archive online, http://nsarchive.gwu.edu/NSAEBB/NSAEBB334/.

133. See McPherson, "Terror on Embassy Row."

134. Quoted by Eduardo Santana Castellón and Raúl Alzaga Manresa, "The first exiles travel and a martyr is born," *Progreso Weekly*, June 10, 2009. The circumstances surrounding Varela's assassination are detailed in Arboleya, Alzaga, and del Valle, *La contrarrevolucion cubana en Puerto Rico*.

135. Jesús Díaz, *55 Hermanos*, Instituto Cubano del Arte e Industria Cinematográficos, 1978.

136. Quoted by Eduardo Santana Castellón and Raúl Alzaga Manresa, "The first exiles travel and a martyr is born," *Progreso Weekly*, June 10, 2009.

137. This relationship is traced in Raul Álzaga, "Puerto Rico: Actividades terroristas de Estados Unidos, 1898–2005," *El Correo*, January 9, 2009. http://www.elcorreo.eu.org/Puerto-RicoActividades-terroristas-de-Estados-Unidos-1898-2005?lang=fr. See also Osoria, "Pro-State Violence in Puerto Rico."

138. "Miami Seeks Help to Combat Terror," *NYT*, March 2, 1975.

139. David Vidal, "In Union City, the Memories of the Bay of Pigs Don't Die," *NYT*, December 2, 1979.

140. David Vidal, "U.S. Inquiry Is Sought by Expatriate Cubans on 'Systematic Terror': 'They Fear Normalization,'" *NYT*, November 27, 1979.

141. The National Security Archive provides a useful collection of sources on Carriles. See http://nsarchive.gwu.edu/NSAEBB/NSAEBB153/.

142. Arnold H. Lubasch, "Judge Sentences Omega 7 Leader to Life in Prison," *NYT*, November 10, 1984.

143. "12-Year Term for Assassin of Chilean Envoy," *NYT*, September 13, 1991.

144. "2 Cuban Exiles Acquitted at Retrial of Letelier Murder," *NYT*, May 31, 1981.

145. FBI, Memorandum, SAC Boston to FBI Director, "Antonio Maceo Brigade," December 26, 1979, 3. File number not provided. Obtained via FOIA request by the author, February 2009.

146. The FBI's reports on the Antonio Maceo Brigade also contain abstracts and mini-reports on groups that maintained relationships with the Maceo Brigade. These included the Venceremos Brigade, the United States–Cuba Health Exchange, the Christian Cuban Society for Family Reunification, the Circle of Cuban Culture, the Cuban American Committee for the Normalization of Relations with Cuba, and émigré-run travel agencies such as Marazul Charters, Southern Tours, Inc., and Viajes Varadero, some of which were also alleged to be run by "DGI agents," that is, agents of the Cuban intelligence service.

147. FBI, Memorandum, Director, FBI. Untitled, March 10, 1983, 1. File number not provided. Obtained via FOIA request by the author, February 2009.

148. FBI, ADIC New York to FBI Director, "Antonio Maceo Brigade," December 6, 1984, 6. File number not provided. Obtained via FOIA request by the author, February 2009.

149. Ibid.
150. Ibid.
151. Ibid.
152. Ibid., 7.
153. Ibid., 6–7.
154. Ibid., 7.

155. FBI, Intelligence request, Washington Field Office to Director, "Cuban Interests Section," December 16, 1982, 5. Obtained via FOIA request by the author, February 2009. Emphasis mine.

156. Furthermore, the FBI had Benes under surveillance in order to protect him from assassination attempts in Miami. See Levine, *Secret Missions to Cuba*, 192–98. A later FBI report gets it right, concluding that the talks focused on political prisoners, the reunification of families, and Cuban exile visits to Cuba. FBI, ADIC New York to FBI Director, "Antonio Maceo Brigade," December 6, 1984, 16. File number not provided. Obtained via FOIA request by the author, February 2009.

157. 1993 interview, quoted in Alfonso Chardy and Oscar Corral, "One of two accused spies was Maceo Brigade member," *MH*, January 13, 2006.

158. See Martin, *Other Eighties*.

159. The group also continued to publish *Areíto*, whose pages included significant coverage of Latin America and the Caribbean in the 1980s, as well as Cuba.

160. For an analysis of Cuban American voting patterns, see Bishin and Klofstad, "Political Incorporation of Cuban Americans."

161. Eduardo Santana Castellón and Raúl Alzaga Manresa, *Progreso Weekly*, June 10, 2009.

162. Eduardo Santana Castellón and Raúl Alzaga Manresa, "The murder cover-up," *Progreso Weekly*, June 17, 2009.

163. Eduardo Santana Castellón and Raúl Alzaga Manresa, "The first exiles travel and a martyr is born," *Progreso Weekly*, June 10, 2009. For a masterful account of Varela's life and death, see Arboleya, Alzaga, and del Valle, *La contrarrevolucion cubana en Puerto Rico*.

Chapter 5

1. Media and law enforcement sources used several spellings of Shakur's birth name, including "Joanne," and "JoAnne." Here the spellings have been left as they appear in the original sources.

2. Robert Hanley, "Miss Chesimard Flees Jersey Prison, Helped By 3 Armed 'Visitors,'" *NYT*, November 3, 1979. The prison break occurred on Black Solidarity Day, founded by activists in 1969 and set to occur on the Monday preceding national elections.

3. Although an analysis of Shakur's legal case is beyond the scope of this chapter, the available evidence strongly points to her innocence. Shakur's legal cases are detailed in a book by her aunt, attorney Evelyn A. Williams, who acted as co-counsel. See Williams, *Inadmissible Evidence*.

4. Rev. Herbert Daughtry, "Run hard sister, run hard," *New York Amsterdam News*, December 1, 1979.

5. The most iconic of the posters show a black and white photo of a smiling Shakur wearing small hoop earrings; in the corner of the poster are printed the words "Republic of New Afrika." Oakland Museum of California, All Of Us Or None Archive: http://collections.museumca.org/?q=collection-item/2010547354. Although the poster is dated "c. 1975," before Shakur's break from prison, the poster was also widely used after her escape.

6. See, for example, "Ms. Chesimard breaks prison," *Baltimore Afro-American*, November 10, 1979.

7. Jane Rosen, "Black Lib woman shot in battle," *Guardian*, May 4, 1973.

8. For the early 1960s, see Tyson, *Radio Free Dixie*. For the late 1960s, see Latner, "Take Me to Havana!"

9. Paul Brinkley-Rogers, "People on run finding selves at home abroad with Castro," *MH*, March 10, 2001.

10. Assata Shakur, "An Open Letter from Assata Shakur," *Canadian Dimension*, 32.4 (July 1998): 17, 21.

11. See Price, *Maroon Societies*. For a history of palenques in Cuba specifically, see Corza, *Runaway Slave Settlements in Cuba*.

12. See, for instance, Benson, "Cuba Calls"; Guy, "Castro in New York"; Latner, "Take Me to Havana!"; Reitan, *Rise and Decline of an Alliance*; Rodriguez, "'De la Esclavitud Yanqui a la Libertad Cubana'"; Seidman, "Tricontinental Routes of Solidarity"; and Young, *Soul Power*.

13. For Cuban internationalism, see, for instance, Gleijeses, *Conflicting Missions*; Morley, *Imperial State and Revolution*; and Schoultz, *That Infernal Little Cuban Republic*. The global reverberations of the U.S. civil rights movement have been examined most thoroughly during the period preceding the 1970s. See, for instance, Anderson, *Eyes off the Prize*; Borstelmann, *Cold War and the Color Line*; Dudziak, *Cold War Civil Rights*; Von Eschen, *Race against Empire*; Gaines, *American Africans in Ghana*; Gore, *Radicalism at the Crossroads*; and Tyson, *Radio Free Dixie*. The global reach and imagination of the later era of the African American freedom struggle is examined in various forms within a range of scholarship. See Bloom and Martin, *Black against Empire*; Gore, *Radicalism at the Crossroads*; Joseph, *Waiting 'Til the Midnight Hour*; and Kelley, *Freedom Dreams*.

14. James, *Black Jacobins*, 391.

15. "Political asylum" is here used to indicate the granting of sanctuary and protection to persons fearing significant political, racial, or ideological persecution in their home country. As seen in chapter 3, political asylum has been a highly contested idea throughout the history of U.S.-Cuba relations, as Havana and Washington staked competing claims about what constituted legitimate repression or persecution, and who was deserving of asylum.

16. Cuba has also provided formal sanctuary to at least two U.S.-born Puerto Rican nationalists. New York–born William Morales, a member of the Fuerzas Armadas Liberación Nacional, alleged to have constructed the explosive devices used in dozens of bombings, was assembling a bomb on July 12, 1978, when it exploded in his hands, severely injuring him. Escaping from the prison ward of Bellevue Hospital in New York, apparently with the aid of members of the Black Liberation Army, Morales fled to Mexico but was captured with the help of the FBI in 1983 and sentenced to prison in Mexico. The government of Mexico refused to extradite him to the United States, however, and in 1988 Morales was permitted to emigrate to Cuba, where he was granted political asylum. Víctor Manuel Gerena, also born in New York and a member of Los Macheteros, is alleged in 1983 to have single-handedly pulled off the robbery of a West Hartford, Connecticut, Wells Fargo depot on September 12, the birthday of Puerto Rican revolutionary nationalist Pedro Albízu Campos. The heist netted $7 million. Disappearing with the aid of his organization, Gerena was spirited to Mexico and then flew to Cuba, where he has apparently remained, likely under formal political asylum. Cuba has also provided variations on political sanctuary for a number of white Americans. However, there have often been important differences between their presence on the island and that of African American and U.S.-born Puerto Rican exiles. First, all known white political exiles in Cuba arrived as air hijackers between 1968 and 1973. Once there, the Cuban government refused to extradite them back to the United States to face hijacking and other charges, and permitted many of them the opportunity to live in Cuba. However, none are known to have stayed in Cuba longer than a few years. As a result, their presence in Cuba is best examined through the phenomenon of the 1968–73 hijackings. Second, white hijackers who claimed political repression in the United States appear to have been lone actors, not affiliates of well-known political organizations such as the RNA and the BPP. As a result, their presence in Cuba did not become permanently linked, both in the American public imagination and through the machinations of U.S. law enforcement and diplomacy, to the U.S. left beyond the 1968–73 hijacking surge. Certainly, a number of white Americans have relocated to Cuba voluntarily, living in Cuba

not as political asylees but as voluntary expatriates. They include Jane McManus, a writer who arrived in Cuba in 1968 to work for the Cuban government, eventually marrying William Lee Brent; and Lorna Burdsall, a dancer from upstate New York who married Manuel Piñeiro in the mid-1950s and subsequently moved to Cuba. Piñeiro went on to head Cuba's intelligence service, while Burdsall headed Cuba's premier dance agency. Neither McManus nor Burdsall faced criminal charges in the United States at the time they emigrated to Cuba and, despite their marriages to men who became notorious in U.S. law enforcement and diplomatic circles, appear to have traveled openly between Cuba and the United States on several occasions. While beyond the scope of this chapter, the lives of both women, as well as other U.S. expatriates living voluntarily in Cuba, should be the subject of further study.

17. Gleijeses, *Conflicting Missions*.

18. Saney, "Homeland of Humanity"; Saney, "African Stalingrad."

19. A notable exception is Joy James, "Framing the Panther: Assata Shakur and Black Female Agency," in Gore, Theoharis, and Woodard, *Want to Start a Revolution?* Short discussions of Shakur are included in a number of works. See, for instance, Allen, "Looking Black at Revolutionary Cuba"; and Greenberg, "Of Black Revolutionaries and Whig Histories."

20. Rodríguez, *Forced Passages*, 61.

21. James, "Framing the Panther," 141.

22. LeoGrande and Kornbluh, *Back Channel to Cuba*.

23. See Tyson, *Radio Free Dixie*.

24. Fidel Castro, speech, Chaplin Theater, Havana, October 3, 1965. Quoted in Deutschmann, *Fidel Castro Reader*, 279. A slightly different translation appears in LANIC, Castro Speech Database, which lists speech as occurring on October 4.

25. Ibid.

26. United Nations, Article 14, *Universal Declaration of Human Rights*, adopted by the General Assembly, December 1948.

27. UN General Assembly, *Declaration on Territorial Asylum*, December 14, 1967, A/RES/2312(XXII), available at: http://www.refworld.org/docid/3b00f05a2c.html.

28. Activist Tom Hayden relates that around the time of the signing of the Declaration on Territorial Asylum in December 1967, Cuban ambassador to Cambodia Raúl Valdés Vivó arranged visas for three U.S. prisoners of war who had been held in Vietnam, in case they wanted to defect to Cuba. Hayden, *Listen, Yankee!*, 100–101.

29. "Racistas contra la Religión," *Bohemia*, vol. 57, no. 8, February 19, 1965, 88; "La Policía me Hirío," *Bohemia*, vol. 57, no. 10, March 5, 1965, 85.

30. In one extensive article, for instance, a corruption scandal in Chicago was used to impugn the honesty of police forces throughout the nation: "La Corrupción de la Policía Norteamericana," *Verde Olivo*, November 9, 1969, 53–57; "Violencia racial in the fuerzes armadas yanquis," *Verde Olivo*, October 5, 1969, 10.

31. Clytus, *Black Man in Red Cuba*, 24.

32. "La vida de un hombre vale un dollar," *Verde Olivo*, October 12, 1969.

33. "Fifth anniversary of the black rebellion in Watts," *Granma*, English edition, August 28, 1970, 11.

34. "Fueron 5 los Panteras Negras heridos en el asalto policíaco de Los Angeles," *Granma*, December 10, 1969, 1; "Condena la OSPAAAL política agresiva en E.U. contra el Partido Pantera Negra," *Granma*, December 12, 1969, 1.

35. Brent, *Long Time Gone*, 131.

36. Images of these posters may be viewed at the online archive of *Docs Populi*: www.docspopuli.org.

37. "Solidarity with Afro-Americans," *Tricontinental*, September-October 1968, 138.

38. Sutherland Martínez, *The Youngest Revolution*, 154.

39. The posters can be viewed at www.ospaaal.com.

40. See *Pensamiento Crítico* 17, July 1968.

41. See *Tricontinental* 1 (August 1967): 15–22 (Carmichael); no. 8 (September-October 1968): 135–36 (Hutchings); no. 10 (January-February 1969): 96–111 (Murray); no. 11 (March-April 1969): 101–4 (Newton). For Williams, see Tyson, *Radio Free Dixie*, 227.

42. *Tricontinental* 1 (August 1967).

43. Among the African American exiles who attended the Tricontinental Conference was Josephine Baker, who sang for conference's audience.

44. Yolanda Gómez, "Human rights in U.S. prisons?," *Granma*, English edition, March 13, 1977.

45. Yolanda Gómez, "The rights of blacks in the United States," *Granma*, English edition, May 1, 1977.

46. *Granma International*, May 22, 1977; *Granma International*, May 1, 1977.

47. Lennox Hinds, a member of Assata Shakur's legal defense team during her 1977 trial, served as National Director of the National Conference of Black Lawyers at the time of the filing. Focusing on violations of the rights of African Americans, Puerto Ricans, Native Americans, and Mexican Americans, the petition cited the cases of U.S. political prisoners, including well-known cases such as the Wilmington Ten civil rights activists, Dennis Banks of the American Indian Movement, Assata Shakur, and five Puerto Rican *independistas*, whose release Fidel Castro had advocated for personally. See Simon Anekwe, "Carter challenged by petition," *New York Amsterdam News*, December 23, 1978.

48. Oscar Ferrer, "Political prisoners in the United States," *Granma*, English edition, December 31, 1978.

49. For a detailed account of Williams and the Black Armed Guard, see Tyson, *Radio Free Dixie*.

50. See, for instance, Cobb Jr., *This Nonviolent Stuff'll Get You Killed*; Hill, *Deacons for Defense*; Umoja, *We Will Shoot Back*; and Wendt, *Spirit and the Shotgun*.

51. Tyson, *Radio Free Dixie*, 228–30.

52. Ibid.

53. "Black Power," *Tricontinental* 2, September-October 1967, 172.

54. U.S. radicals seeking advice and validation interacted with Cuban officers and officials in venues such as Cuba's U.N. Mission, during private meetings set up for visiting delegations, including SDS and the Black Panther Party, and more informally, in the solidarity camps of the Venceremos Brigades.

55. Quoted in King, *Threshold of a New Decade*.

56. "Fifth anniversary of the black rebellion in Watts," *Granma*, English edition, August 28, 1970, 11.

57. Transcript of speech, printed in *Black Panther*, October 12, 1968, 14.

58. Author's interview with Charlie Hill, September 7, 2012, Havana.

59. Author's interview with Nehanda Abiodun, September 10, 2012, Havana.

60. Author's interview with Nehanda Abiodun, September 19, 2012, Havana.

61. Author's interview with Charlie Hill, September 7, 2012, Havana. Williams Potts, who arrived in Cuba in 1984 hoping to be trained and sent to South Africa to fight against apartheid, reports a similar result. Author's interview with Antonio Pérez, September 21, 2012, Havana; author's interview with Tomás Fernández Robaina, June 28, 2013, Havana.

62. For instance, Domingo Amuchastegui, former Cuban intelligence officer, interviewed by Ruth Reitan, March 23, 1995, Miami, obtained by the author from Reitan.

63. For a concise summary of the guerrilla phase of the revolutionary war, see Gott, *Cuba*, 154–64.

64. See, for example, Berger, *Outlaws of America*.

65. In 1987 *Newsday* journalist Ron Howell claimed that in addition to the 1973 New Jersey turnpike shooting, Shakur had also been shot in the stomach the year previous in a Manhattan hotel. According to Howell, a former BLA member had alleged that the incident stemmed from the group's efforts to "intimidate and steal money from drug dealers," and that police had classified the incident as "an attempted robbery by Shakur." Ron Howell, "On the Run With Assata Shakur: From Cuba, an Interview with the Black Liberation Army's Fugitive 'Soul,'" *Newsday*, October 11, 1987.

66. Coordinating Committee, Black Liberation Army, "Message to the Black Movement: A Political Statement from the Black Underground," 1976.

67. Coordinating Committee, Black Liberation Army, "Message to the Black Movement: A Political Statement from the Black Underground," 1976, 20. The BLA focused particularly upon the necessity of receiving foreign support from African nations, where a number of former Panthers and RNA members had taken refuge, namely in Algeria and Tanzania. For Tanzania, see the case of Pete O'Neal, a former chairman in the Black Panther Party in Kansas City, who fled to Algeria and then settled permanently in Tanzania, cofounding the United African Alliance Community Center with his wife Charlotte O'Neal, also an ex-Panther, in a village near Arusha. See Mathews, *Panther in Africa*. Curiously, although a number of ex-Panthers and RNA comrades had taken refuge in Cuba, the island was not mentioned in the BLA's communiqué.

68. Shakur, *Assata*, 242.

69. Despite the BLA's notoriety as one of the only expressions of armed black revolutionary struggle during the post-Emancipation period of African American history, little scholarship has examined the group. Among the exceptions are Akinyele Omowale Umoja, "The Black Liberation Army and the Radical Legacy of the Black Panther Party," in Jeffries, *Black Power in the Belly of the Beast*; Umoja, "Repression Breeds Resistance: The Black Liberation Army and the Radical Legacy of the Black Panther Party," in Cleaver and Katsiaficas, *Liberation, Imagination, and the Black Panther Party*; and Berger, *Captive Nation*, especially 248–49. Like the BLA, the FALN has similarly eluded scholarly attention. Brief discussions of the group appear in several publications, for instance, Susler, "More Than 25 Years," 26–27. Academic treatments of both organizations, including from writers who have produced nuanced studies of Black Power and Puerto Rican nationalism, have generally not been sympathetic. In *Waiting 'Til The Midnight Hour*, Peniel E. Joseph includes a single mention of the BLA in the book: "Loosely organized and united principally by the belief that the time for guerrilla warfare had come, ex-Panthers who joined the BLA engaged in clandestine warfare against the police — convinced, even after the incarceration and the death of many colleagues, that they could start the revolution themselves." Joseph, *Waiting 'Til The Midnight Hour*, 269. Journalist Juan González, a founding member of the New York branch of the Young Lords Party, similarly includes a single mention of the FALN in his book *Harvest of Empire*. According to González, clandestine left-wing Latino groups in the United States such as the FALN were hopelessly "divorced . . . from the everyday reality that Latinos were facing. All failed to understand that despite the inequality and stubborn racism that Latinos faced in the United States, conditions here, even for the most destitute, were substantially better than in the Latin American nations from which they'd

emigrated, a reality that to this day has doomed revolutionary Marxist movements in our country to tiny followings." González, *Harvest of Empire*, 176.

70. These portraits of American asylees in Cuba are reconstructed from a combination of news reports, oral history, and U.S. government documents. My understanding of the lives of Americans in Cuba has also been aided by formal and informal interviews with Cubans who knew them as friends, coworkers, lovers, or spouses. See the bibliography for a complete list of interviews.

71. Eldridge Cleaver, "Slow Boat to Cuba," 1, undated, unpublished. Eldridge Cleaver Papers, Bancroft Library, University of California, Berkeley, folder 31, carton 2.

72. See Hilliard, *This Side of Glory*. Although Cleaver's revised account of the ambush is now well established and corroborated, some scholarship on the incident continues to reproduce the BPP's original claim—which Cleaver repeats in *Soul on Fire*—that police initiated the confrontation. See, for instance, Gwendolyn L. Shelton, "Bobby James Hutton (1950–1968)," *Arkansas Encyclopedia of History and Culture* online, http://www.encyclopediaofarkansas.net/encyclopedia/entry-detail.aspx?entryID=6040, accessed October 18, 2013.

73. See, for instance, Kate Coleman, "Souled Out: Eldridge Cleaver Admits He Ambushed Those Cops," *New West*, May 19, 1980.

74. Interview with Henry Louis Gates, *Frontline*, spring 1997. http://www.pbs.org/wgbh/pages/frontline/shows/race/interviews/ecleaver.html?, accessed October 18, 2013. In the interview, Cleaver describes the events as follows: "[W]e saw it coming while the police were acting so we decided to get down first. So we started the fight. There were 14 of us. We went down into the area of Oakland where the violence was the worst a few blocks away from where Huey Newton had killed that cop so we dealt with them when they came upon us. We were well armed, and we had a shootout that lasted an hour and a half."

75. Cleaver, *Soul on Fire*, 141.

76. Ibid., 142.

77. Eldridge Cleaver, "Slow Boat to Cuba," 2, undated, unpublished. Eldridge Cleaver Papers, Bancroft Library, University of California, Berkeley, folder 31, carton 2.

78. Cleaver, *Soul on Fire*, 138.

79. For a discussion of Cleaver's claims about the site, see chapter 2.

80. See Tyson, *Radio Free Dixie*.

81. Cleaver, *Soul on Fire*, 138.

82. Lockwood, *Conversation with Eldridge Cleaver*, 17–18.

83. Rout, *Eldridge Cleaver*, 108.

84. Ibid., 102–3. Cleaver resented the Cuban government's stalling especially after the death of Carter, who was killed by members of Ron Karenga's US Organization in Los Angeles on January 17, 1969, purportedly when Carter would have been in Cuba had he not been delayed. See Gates and Cleaver, "Cuban Experience," 34. However, Lee Lockwood, who talked at length with Cleaver in Havana, believed that Cleaver's suspicions that Cuban officials were holding up communications between both Panther leaders and Cleaver's wife, Kathleen Cleaver, were unjustified. Lockwood, *Conversation with Eldridge Cleaver*, 18.

85. Gates and Cleaver, "Cuban Experience," 40. Charlie Hill disputes the claim that the Cuban government actively discouraged natural hairstyles in the early 1970s. Author's interview with Charlie Hill, September 19, 2012.

86. Likely the Biblioteca Nacional de José Martí in Havana.

87. Gates and Cleaver, "Cuban Experience," 33.

88. See, for instance, Cleaver, *Soul on Fire*, 139.

89. Gates and Cleaver, "Cuban Experience," 34. For more on Cleaver's involvement with the hijackers, see chapter 3.
90. Gates and Cleaver, "Cuban Experience," 35.
91. Ibid.
92. See chapter 3 for background on Johnson.
93. Lockwood, *Conversation with Eldridge Cleaver*, 21.
94. See Kathleen Cleaver, "Back to Africa," in Jones, *Black Panther Party Reconsidered*.
95. See de la Fuente, *Nation for All*; Moore, *Castro, the Blacks, and Africa*; and Sawyer, *Racial Politics in Post-Revolutionary Cuba*.
96. Gates and Cleaver, "Cuban Experience," 37. See also Lockwood, *Conversation with Eldridge Cleaver*, 20–21.
97. According to Lockwood, Cleaver was asked to leave Cuba for Algeria, with the promise that he could return quietly at a later point. Lockwood, *Conversation with Eldridge Cleaver*, 23.
98. For an account of Cleaver's travels beyond Cuba, see Malloy, "Uptight in Babylon."
99. Cleaver, *Soul on Fire*, 143.
100. Quoted in Marable, "Race and Revolution in Cuba," in Marable, ed., *Dispatches from the Ebony Tower*, 101.
101. Cleaver, *Soul on Fire*, 144.
102. See chapter 3 for an account of the incident.
103. Brent, *Long Time Gone*, 134.
104. Ibid., 131.
105. "OSPAAAL on Black American Revolution," *Black Panther*, September 7, 1968, 10.
106. FBI, Miami to Las Vegas & San Francisco, Memorandum, file no. 164–244, untitled, June 18, 1969, 2. Obtained via FOIA request by the author; FBI, SPC (redacted) to SAC, Memorandum, file no. 164-2421, "William Lee Brent, Fugitive," June 20, 1969, 1. Obtained via FOIA request by the author.
107. "FBI Tries to Track Hijacker," *Oakland Tribune*, June 18, 1969.
108. Margaret Randall, for instance, spent much of her eleven years in Cuba employed by El Instituto Cubano del Libro, while her husband worked for Radio Havana Cuba. Randall, *To Change the World*.
109. FBI, SAC San Francisco, file no. 164-248, "William Lee Brent," August 17, 1971, 1. Obtained via FOIA request by the author.
110. Report, FBI, WFO to FBI Director, file no. not provided, "William Lee Brent," November 10, 1980, 1. Obtained via FOIA request by the author.
111. Brent, *Long Time Gone*, 173.
112. "Possible Helper in Hijack Ready to Come Home," *Spartanburg Herald*, June 24, 1970, 5. Coincidentally, Gastonia is not far from Monroe, where Robert F. Williams had confronted the Ku Klux Klan. The *Spartanburg Herald* story appears next to an article reporting that a federal district judge had dismissed a complaint filed against Williams for "carrying a firearm across state lines while under indictment" while on his way to testify before the U.S. Senate Internal Security subcommittee. See Tyson, *Radio Free Dixie*.
113. FBI, San Francisco field office, file no. 164-24-173, "William Lee Brent," January 27, 1977, 1–2. Obtained via FOIA request by the author. Meeks was later declared mentally incompetent to stand trial; McKinney, a minor at the time of the hijacking, was deemed an unwilling participant in the crime and avoided charges. "Hijacking suspect freed," *Wilmington Morning Star*, December 8, 1976, 28.

114. FBI, report, file no. 164-24-115, "William Lee Brent," March 27, 1970, 2. Obtained via FOIA by the author, July 2010.

115. Memorandum, FBI, SAC Las Vegas, "NCIC Validation Check of Fugitive Files," October 25, 1974, 3. Obtained via FOIA by the author, July 2010.

116. Report, SAC San Francisco to FBI Director, file no. not provided, "William Brent," June 21, 1983, 2. Obtained via FOIA by the author, July 2010.

117. Report, SAC San Francisco to FBI Director, file number not provided, "William Brent," July 3, 1984, 2. Obtained via FOIA by the author, July 2010.

118. Brent, *Long Time Gone*, 116–17.

119. See Domínguez, *To Make a World Safe for Revolution*.

120. Brent, *Long Time Gone*, 275.

121. Arthur Allen, "Long Times Gone: A black militant's exile in Castro's Cuba," *Salon*, April 6, 1996. Available online: http://www.salon.com/1996/04/06/cuba1/.

122. I am grateful to John Gronbeck-Tedesco, who knew Brent during his final weeks, for criticizing this section and sharing his recollections of Brent.

123. This biographical sketch draws from interviews with Hill conducted in 2012, 2013, 2015, and 2016. Although Finney has been deceased since 2005, the author interviewed Finney's widow in June 2013.

124. See Obadele, *Foundations of the Black Nation*; Berger, "Malcolm X Doctrine"; Donald Cunnigen, "Republic of New Africa in Mississippi," in Jones, *Black Power in the Belly of the Beast*; Farmer, "Mothers of Pan-Africanism."

125. For a history of these confrontations, see Lumumba, "Short History of the U.S. War on the R.N.A."

126. Author's interview with Charlie Hill, September 9, 2012, Havana.

127. According to Hill's version of the incident, one of the three men — he has never publicly revealed which one — shot the officer after he attempted to draw his gun. Reporter DeWayne Wickham quotes Hill in 2009: "I regret that a life was lost, but it had to be that way. He drew his gun and he was going to kill us." DeWayne Wickham, "Fugitives have good reason to fear closer ties to Cuba," *Miami Times*, October 21, 2009.

128. Author's interview with Charlie Hill, September 19, 2012, Havana; "New Mexico Man Charged," *Reading Eagle*, December 1, 1971.

129. "3 Suspects in Slaying Hijack Jetliner to Cuba," *LAT*, November 28, 1971.

130. See Tyson, *Radio Free Dixie*.

131. Author's interview with Charlie Hill, September 9, 2012, Havana.

132. Author's interview with Charlie Hill, September 7, 2012, Havana.

133. Author's interview with Charlie Hill, September 19, 2012, Havana.

134. Author's interview with Charlie Hill, September 7, 2012, Havana.

135. Officially, the house was known in Havana as a "Casa de los Extranjeros de Residentes," one of several facilities in the city where foreign hijackers and other immigrants were housed.

136. For more on Bryant, see chapter 3.

137. Brett Skakun, "Black Panther: Hijacker Settles Into Life in Cuba," *LAT*, July 5, 1981. See also Jo Thomas, "Havana Releases 33 Americans, And All but Three Return to U.S.," *NYT*, October 28, 1980.

138. Mark Kurlansky, "No escape from Cuba haven for US fugitive," *The Guardian*, July 8, 1985.

139. "Three Hijackers Hoped to Reach Africa," *Chicago Tribune*, November 29, 1971. According to the reporter, a stewardess told the hijackers that they would be "well received in Cuba."

140. Mark Kurlansky, "No escape from Cuba haven for US fugitive," *Guardian*, July 8, 1985. According to Charlie Hill, the two men never left the plane.
141. Author's interview with Charlie Hill, September 9, 2012, Havana.
142. Gary Moore, "Hijacker Remains in Cuba: Michael Finney Talks of Exile," *MH*, October 30, 1980.
143. This portrait of Finney has been supplemented by information provided by the author's interview with Finney's widow, Esther Finney, June 26, 2013, Havana.
144. Ron Howell, "On the Run With Assata Shakur: From Cuba, an Interview with the Black Liberation Army's Fugitive 'Soul,'" *Newsday*, October 11, 1987.
145. According to an anonymous source interviewed by the author, Shakur came under invitation of the Comité Central of the Cuban communist party. Author's interview, September 19, 2012, Havana.
146. Assata Shakur, interview, *Fight Racism! Fight Imperialism!* newspaper, published June/July 1996. Available online: http://www.revolutionarycommunist.org/index.php/fight-racism/2413-assata-shakur.
147. The child's father, Kamau Sadiki, was one of Shakur's co-defendants.
148. Assata Shakur, interview, *Fight Racism! Fight Imperialism!* newspaper, published June/July 1996. http://www.revolutionarycommunist.org/index.php/fight-racism/2413-assata-shakur; Assata Shakur, interviewed by Paul Davidson, November 6, 2000, Havana. http://www.fantompowa.net/Flame/assata_interview.htm.
149. Assata Shakur, interviewed by Paul Davidson, November 6, 2000, Havana. http://www.fantompowa.net/Flame/assata_interview.htm.
150. After the *Newsday* story broke, the New Jersey FBI office and New Jersey State Police released a joint statement maintaining that "recent public statements" about Shakur's presence in Cuba had "confirmed previously known task force information." Nick Ravo, "Officials Can't Confirm Chesimard Is in Havana," *NYT*, October 13, 1987.
151. Although Lawrence Hills Books published *Assata* in the United States and Canada, the book's copyright was held by Zed Books in the United Kingdom in order to circumvent U.S. "Son of Sam" laws preventing persons convicted of crimes from monetarily profiting from published works. Shakur's aunt and longtime attorney, Evelyn A. Williams, who visited Cuba several times, acted as Shakur's intermediary. See Nick Ravo, "Officials Can't Confirm Chesimard Is in Havana," *NYT*, October 13, 1987.
152. See also an interview with Shakur in Pepper, *Through the Wall*.
153. Ron Howell, "On the Run With Assata Shakur: From Cuba, an Interview with the Black Liberation Army's Fugitive 'Soul,'" *Newsday*, October 11, 1987. Shakur would eventually earn a master's degree in social sciences.
154. Lawrence Hill, president of Lawrence Hill Books, quoted in John T. McQuiston, "Fugitive Murderer Reported in Cuba," *NYT*, October 12, 1987. The book's official publication date was January 15, 1988.
155. Shakur's writings and interviews, produced before she arrived in Cuba, were widely disseminated before the publication of *Assata*. The best known was a 1973 letter published in *The Black Scholar*. See Shakur, "To My People."
156. Shakur, *Assata*, 268. Lowercase text in original.
157. Shakur's work in this regard is confirmed by Nehanda Abiodun. Author's interview with Nehanda Abiodun, September 15, 2012, Havana.
158. Author's interview with Nehanda Abiodun, June 24, 2013, Havana. However, even unofficial meetings could provoke censure. See, for instance, Robin Hemley, "Why My Students and I Met With a Potentially Violent Fugitive in Cuba," *Observer*, February 7, 2015.

159. Quoted in Holmes, *A Joyous Revolt*, 179.

160. Manning Marable, "The Color Line: Black Political Prisoners: The Case of Assata Shakur," *Los Angeles Sentinel*, May 7, 1998, A7. An interview with Shakur, entitled "Assata Shakur: The Continuity of Struggle," was published by *Souls: A Critical Journal of Black Politics, Culture, and Society* (Spring 1999) edited by Marable. One academic delegation, organized by the Black Scholar Press and including Toni Cade Bambara, traveled to Havana in January 1985 but appears to have been unaware of Shakur's presence in the city.

161. Shakur, public presentation, World Youth Festival, Havana, August 3, 1997, http://www.youtube.com/watch?v=WJU4b_5LyUY.

162. See, for example, Perkins, *Autobiography as Activism*; and Matthews, "'No One Ever Asks What a Man's Role in the Revolution Is.'"

163. Nisa Islam Muhammad, "Assata Shakur: From exile with love," *Final Call*, June 11, 2002.

164. Rolando, *Eyes of the Rainbow*.

165. Several studies of Cuban hip-hop have examined the significant role played by Black August. See, for instance, Perry, *Negro Soy Yo*.

166. Assata Shakur was a close friend of Afeni Shakur while the two were members of the Black Panther Party. In characteristic Panther internationalism, Tupac Amaru Shakur is named for the Peruvian indigenous leader who led an uprising against the Spanish in 1780.

167. For instance, a search of the hip-hop internet database www.rapgenius.com in 2013 reveals 37 songs with lyrics containing a reference to Assata Shakur by name, 38 to Harriet Tubman, 22 to Angela Davis, 22 to Sojourner Truth, and 8 to Ida B. Wells.

168. James, "Framing the Panther," 138.

169. Welfare Poets, "The Bullet," *Project Blues*.

170. Cheryll Y. Greene, "Word from a Sister in Exile," *Essence*, February 1988, 60.

171. Rick Hepp, "Feds Are Offering a $1 Million Reward to Snare Chesimard, Now in Cuba," *Star-Ledger*, May 2, 2005.

172. Assata Shakur, interviewed by Paul Davidson, November 6, 2000, Havana. http://www.fantompowa.net/Flame/assata_interview.htm.

173. Ibid.

174. Although beyond the scope of this scholarship, discussions of the Black Liberation Army's involvement in clandestine actions in the United States have been summarized in a variety of law enforcement documents. See, for instance, Maryland State Police, Criminal Intelligence Division, "The Black Liberation Army: Understanding, Monitoring, Controlling," October 1991, https://www.ncjrs.gov/pdffiles1/Digitization/136568NCJRS.pdf, and https://www.fbi.gov/wanted/dt/cheri-laverne-dalton.

175. Marc D. Perry provides a useful account of this engagement. See Perry, *Negro Soy Yo*.

176. Author's interview with Nehanda Abiodun, September 10, 2012, Havana.

177. Author's interview with Nehanda Abiodun, November 16, 2015, Havana.

178. Author's interview with Nehanda Abiodun, September 10, 2012.

179. Ibid.

180. Author's interview with Nehanda Abiodun, September 11, 2012.

181. Abiodun's middle name, Isoke, was given to her by U.S. comrades visiting Cuba in the early 1990s. Her first name, inspired by Zimbabwean anticolonial leader Nehanda Nyakasikana, and her Yoruba last name, meaning "born at a time of war," had been given to her by comrades the occasion of her 30th birthday while still in the United States.

182. Author's interview with Nehanda Abiodun, September 10, 2012.

183. Ibid.

184. Author's interview with Nehanda Abiodun, June 24, 2013, Havana. However, even un-

official meetings could provoke censure. See, for instance, Robin Hemley, "Why My Students and I Met With a Potentially Violent Fugitive in Cuba," *Observer*, February 7, 2015.

185. Author's interview with Nehanda Abiodun, June 24, 2013.
186. Author's interview with Nehanda Abiodun, September 15, 2012.
187. Ibid. Scholar Marc D. Perry recounts what appears to be the same incident. Perry, *Negro Soy Yo*, 79–81.
188. Author's interview with Nehanda Abiodun, September 10, 2012.
189. Author's interview with Nehanda Abiodun, September 15, 2012.
190. Author's interview with Nehanda Abiodun, September 19, 2012.
191. Author's interview with Nehanda Abiodun, September 15, 2012.
192. Ibid.
193. Ibid.
194. Ibid.
195. Author's interview with Tomás Fernández Robaina, June 28, 2013. A discussion and first-person ethnography of Robaina's classes can be found in Perry, *Negro Soy Yo*, chapter four.
196. An account of Abiodun's living room sessions appears in Perry, *Negro Soy Yo*, 136–39.
197. Author's interview with Nehanda Abiodun, September 15, 2012.
198. Allen, *¡Venceremos?*
199. These reflections were communicated to the author by several U.S. students during informal conversations, Havana, September 2012.
200. See, for instance, Marc Lacey, "Cuba's Rap Vanguard Reaches Beyond the Party Line," *NYT*, December 15, 2006.
201. See Perry, *Negro Soy Yo*.
202. For a discussion of these delicate politics, see Fernandes, *Cuba Represent!*
203. Black August came into being in the California prison system in 1979 as a holiday commemorating the deaths of black prison activists, including George Jackson. For a concise history, see Berger, *Captive Nation*, 261–67.
204. The encounters in Cuba and South Africa are chronicled in dream hampton's 2010 film *The Black August Hip Hop Project*.
205. See hampton, *Black August Hip Hop Project*.
206. See especially Baker, *Buena Vista in the Club*; Perry, *Negro Soy Yo*; Allen, *¡Venceremos?*
207. See, for instance, Allen, *¡Venceremos?*; and Stout, *After Love*.
208. Author's interview with Nehanda Abiodun, June 24, 2013.
209. Ibid.
210. Ibid.
211. Ibid.
212. The designation was preceded by hearings before the U.S. Senate Subcommittee on Security and Terrorism in February and March entitled, "The Role of Cuba in International Terrorism and Subversion."
213. Quoted in Sullivan, "Cuba and the State Sponsors of Terrorism List," 3.
214. Domínguez, *To Make a World Safe for Revolution*.
215. Ibid.
216. Nick Ravo, "Officials Can't Confirm Chesimard Is in Havana," *NYT*, October 13, 1987.
217. Author's interview with William Potts, Havana, September 13 and 19, 2012. Released from prison, Potts became a farmer in Cuba and remained supportive of the Cuban Revolution despite his imprisonment. He returned to the United States to face trial for the hijacking charges in 2013.
218. LaBeet was later released from prison and allowed to start a life for himself in Havana,

where he remains as of 2017. The Cuban government has refused U.S. extradition requests. It is not clear whether the refusal was due to the Cuban government's belief in LaBeet's innocence, its doubts about whether he received a fair trial, or its unwillingness to participate in extradition without reciprocity from Washington. He is the subject of the 2017 film *The SkyJacker's Tale*, directed by Jamie Kastner.

219. Ron Howell, "On the Run With Assata Shakur: From Cuba, an Interview with the Black Liberation Army's Fugitive 'Soul,'" *Newsday*, October 11, 1987.

220. See LeoGrande and Kornbluh, *Back Channel to Cuba*.

221. P.L. 104-114, Cuban Liberty and Democratic Solidarity (Libertad) Act of 1996, 104th Cong., March 12, 1996.

222. P.L. 104-114, Cuban Liberty and Democratic Solidarity (Libertad) Act of 1996, 104th Cong., March 12, 1996, Section 113.

223. "N.J. cops enlist pope; Seek help in getting fugitive out of Cuba," *Chicago Sun-Times*, December 28, 1997, 34. The text of the letter has never been released publicly.

224. Shakur, telephone interview *Democracy Now*, quoted by David Hinkley, "Fugitive Finds Injustice in Ch. 4 Profile," *New York Daily News*, March 12, 1998.

225. The rebuttal was republished in *Covert Action Quarterly*, October 26, 1998.

226. State Department Spokesman James Rubin contended that the extraditions were legally feasible under a 1905 treaty that had never been voided. "State Department Seeks Extradition of Chesimard," *NYT*, July 3, 1998.

227. H. Con. Res. 244, 105th Cong., 2nd sess., proposed, March 17, 1998.

228. H. Con. Res. 254, 105th Cong., 2nd sess., March 30, 1998. The resolution was passed in the House on September 14, and in the Senate on October 21. The bill cited an FBI report alleging that Cuba was providing sanctuary to ninety-one Americans fleeing criminal prosecution in the United States.

229. H. Con. Res. 254, 105th Cong., 2nd sess., March 30, 1998. The resolution was passed in the House on September 14, and in the Senate on October 21.

230. H. Con. Res. 254, markup hearing before the Subcommittee on the Western Hemisphere, House Committee on International Relations, 105th Cong., 2nd sess., May 13, 1998.

231. Michelle Crouch, "Cuba Denies N.J. Request For Fugitive Joanne Chesimard Fled While Serving Time For Murder," *Philadelphia Inquirer*, April 3, 1998.

232. H. Con. Res. 254, 105th Cong., 2nd sess., March 30, 1998.

233. Michael Ratner, "Immoral Bounty for Assata," *Covert Action Quarterly*, October 27, 1998.

234. Maxine Waters, Letter to Fidel Castro, September 29, 1998. http://www.afrocubaweb.com/assata5.htm#Water's%20letter, accessed October 18, 2013.

235. Shakur, Letter to Pope John Paul II, March 1998. The letter was printed in New York's black news daily, *Daily Challenge*, and translated into several languages. Reprinted in Shakur, *Assata: In Her Own Words*, 37–42.

236. The pope continued: "In the international community, we thus see a small number of countries growing exceedingly rich at the cost of the increasing impoverishment of a great number of other countries; as a result the wealthy grow ever wealthier, while the poor grow ever poorer." Pope John Paul II, Holy Mass, José Martí Plaza, January 25, 1998. https://w2.vatican.va/content/john-paul-ii/en/homilies/1998/documents/hf_jp-ii_hom_19980125_la habana.html.

237. See, for instance, Anthony Lappé, "Fugitive From Time," *NYT*, May 23, 1999.

238. H. R. 2292, "No Safe Haven in Cuba Act," U.S. House of Representatives, June 21, 2001.

239. "Three Years for 1971 Hijacking," *CBS News*, June 12, 2002.
240. "Panther Days Over: Radical Out of Prison and Back Home in Bx," *New York Daily News*, June 29, 2003.
241. The *New York Times* ran a full length article on Critton's capture on the morning of September 11, 2001. See C.J. Chivers, "Traced on Internet, Teacher Is Charged In '71 Jet Hijacking," *NYT*, September 11, 2001.
242. "Panther Days Over: Radical Out of Prison and Back Home in Bx," *New York Daily News*, June 29, 2003.
243. "Finney, other political fighters still safe in Cuba," *AFP*, April 3, 2002.
244. This is the sentence that begins the report's section entitled State Sponsors of Terrorism Overview. U.S. Department of State, *Country Reports on Terrorism 2004*, Office of the Coordinator for Counterterrorism, April 2005, 88.
245. The State Department's 2002 and 2003 *Patterns of Global Terrorism* reports acknowledged that Colombia had publicly agreed to Cuba's mediation with the ELN.
246. U.S. Department of State, *Country Reports on Terrorism 2004*, Office of the Coordinator for Counterterrorism, April 2005, 88. Emphasis mine.
247. On May 13, 1985, Philadelphia police dropped a military grade C-4 explosive device on the neighborhood headquarters of the Move Organization after the group had refused to cooperate with an eviction notice and armed itself against police assault. Eleven of the group's members, including five children, were killed in the resulting fire which police allowed to burn until it had destroyed fifty other homes in the predominantly African American neighborhood in West Philadelphia. Some critics of the police action characterized the incident as an act of state terrorism. See Wagner-Pacifici, *Discourse and Destruction*.
248. Mark P. Sullivan, "Cuba and the State Sponsors of Terrorism List," CRS Report for Congress, Congressional Research Service, Library of Congress, May 13, 2005, 9.
249. FBI, wanted poster, "Joanne Deborah Chesimard," color, c. 2005.
250. Author's interview with Charlie Hill, September 9, 2012, Havana.
251. This information was provided by friends of Shakur living in Havana. The author interviewed these individuals, who wish to remain anonymous for the security of Shakur, in Havana in September 2012 and June 2013.
252. Wayne Parry, "Feds Offer $1 Million Reward for JoAnne Chesimard (Assata Shakur)," *Sun Sentinel*, May 3, 2005.
253. John Rice, "Castro Defends Fugitive Sought by U.S.," Associated Press, May 11, 2005.
254. Kathleen Cleaver, "Why Has the FBI Placed a Million-Dollar Bounty on Assata Shakur?," *Indypendent* 73 (July 20, 2005).
255. Mos Def, "Assata Shakur: The government's terrorist is our community's heroine," www.allhiphop.com, May 18, 2005. https://allhiphop.com/2005/05/17/assata-shakur-the-governments-terrorist-is-our-communitys-heroine/.
256. Karen W. Arenson, "CUNY Chief Orders Names Stripped From Student Center," *NYT*, December 13, 2006.
257. Assembly Resolution no. 232, State of New Jersey, 212th Legislature, Introduced January 4, 2007.
258. Marc Lacey, "U.S. Fugitives Worry About a Cuba Without Castro," *NYT*, May 12, 2007.
259. Olguín, "Assata," in *At the Risk of Seeming Ridiculous: Poems from Cuba Libre*, 67–69.
260. See, for instance, DeWayne Wickham, "Fugitives have good reason to fear closer ties to Cuba," *Miami Times*, October 21, 2009, 2A.
261. Sean T. Kean, Letter to Barack Obama, April 17, 2009. Author's collection. http://blog.nj.com/ledgerupdates_impact/2009/04/LettertoPresObamaSenatorKean.pdf.

262. Sara Just, "Common Controversy Comes to White House Poetry Night; Cops, Conservatives Cry Foul at Some of His Past Work," ABCNews.com, May 11, 2011. http://abcnews.go.com/blogs/politics/2011/05/common-controversy-comes-to-white-house-poetry-night-cops-conservatives-cry-foul-at-some-of-his-past-work/.

263. Rep. Scott Garrett, letter to Barack Obama, May 13, 2011.

264. FBI, "New Most Wanted Terrorist: Joanne Chesimard First Woman Added to List," FBI website, May 2, 2013, accessed August 20, 2013. Author's collection.

265. FBI, Newark Office, press release, "Joanne Chesimard, Convicted Murderer and Fugitive, Named to FBI Most Wanted Terrorists List, with $1 Million FBI Reward Offered for Information Leading to Her Capture and Return," May 2, 2013. Website access 9/3/2013: http://www.fbi.gov/newark/press-releases/2013/joanne-chesimard-convicted-murderer-and-fugitive-named-to-fbi-most-wanted-terrorists-list-with-1-million-fbi-reward-offered-for-information-leading-to-her-capture-and-return.

266. Author's interview with Tomás Fernández Robaina, June 28, 2013, Havana.

267. Carla Baranauckas, "Christie to Obama: Demand Cuba return cop killer Joanne Chesimard," *Record*, December 21, 2014.

268. Michael Isikoff, "Castro government: We will never return fugitive cop killer to U.S.," *Yahoo News*, March 2, 2015. https://www.yahoo.com/news/castro-government—we-will-never-return-fugitive-cop-killer-to-u-s-203643115.html.

Epilogue

1. Martin Luther King Jr., "Beyond Vietnam," Riverside Church, New York, April 4, 1967.

2. Benson, *Antiracism in Cuba*; de la Fuente, *A Nation for All*. See also Sawyer, *Racial Politics in Post-Revolutionary Cuba*; and Allen, *¡Venceremos?*

3. For an assessment of the early period of the Cuban Revolution, see Chase, *Revolution within the Revolution*.

4. See Allen, *¡Venceremos?*; Bejel, *Gay Cuban Nation*; Stout, *After Love*; and Lumsden, *Machos Maricones and Gays*.

5. Allen, *¡Venceremos?*, 1–2.

6. Griffin, "Para las chicas Cubanas," 74.

7. Ibid., 77.

8. Ibid. This racialization of sex work is also not unique to Cuba.

9. Allen, "Looking Black at Revolutionary Cuba," 54. Samuel Farber, writing from an avowedly socialist yet highly critical perspective, provides a vigorous critique of this tendency within the U.S. Left in *Cuba since the Revolution of 1959*.

10. I borrow this conceptualization of the arc of U.S.-Cuba ties from Louis A. Pérez. See Pérez, *Cuba and the United States*.

11. Center for Cuban Studies Website, accessed 11/2/2013, http://centerforcubanstudies.org/about/.

12. For a concise overview, see Margaret Randall, *Exporting Revolution*.

13. For a recent overview of the Cuban health system, see Burke, *Health Travels*.

14. For an incisive critique of these policies, see Farber, *Cuba since the Revolution of 1959*. For a more mixed assessment, see Taylor, *Inside El Barrio*.

15. This tension is evident at times in Allen, *¡Venceremos?*

Bibliography

Archives

The African Activist Archive Project, online collection, Michigan State University, East Lansing, Mich.
The American Presidency Project, Papers of John F. Kennedy, University of California, Santa Barbara
Bancroft Library, Special Collections, University of California, Berkeley
Biblioteca Nacional de Cuba José Martí, Havana, Cuba
Contemporary Culture Collection, Samuel L. Paley Library, Temple University, Philadelphia, Pa.
Cuban Heritage Collection, Special Collections, University of Miami, Miami, Fla.
Latin American Network Information Center (LANIC), LLILAS Benson Digital Collections, University of Texas Libraries
Lourdes Casal Library, Center for Cuban Studies, New York, N.Y.
National Archives and Records Administration at College Park, College Park, Md.
National Security Archive, George Washington University, online collection, Washington, D.C.
Oakland Museum of California, Oakland, Calif.
Research Collections, New York Public Library for the Performing Arts
Special Collections, New York Public Library
Special Collections and Archives, DePaul University, Chicago, Ill.
Special Collections and Archives, Langson Library, University of California, Irvine
Special Collections and Archives, Milton S. Eisenhower Library, The Johns Hopkins University, Baltimore, Md.
Tamiment Library and Robert F. Wagner Labor Archives, New York University
U.S. Department of State, online archives

Cuban Newspapers and Periodicals

Bohemia
El Caimán Barbudo
Granma
Granma (English edition)
Granma International
Juventud Rebelde
Pensamiento Crítico
Prensa Latina

Tricontinental
Verde Olivo

Newspapers and Periodicals

Afro-American Red Star
Against the Current
American Statesman
Areíto
Atlanta Daily World
Baltimore Afro-American
Baraguá
Berkeley Tribe
The Black Panther
Chicago Daily News
Chicago Sun-Times
Chicago Tribune
Claridad
Columbia Forum
Covert Action Quarterly
Cuba Internacional
Cuba Va
The Crusader
Daily Challenge
The Deseret News
The Dispatch
Dissent Magazine
Essence
Evergreen Review
The Final Call
Foreign Affairs
Frontline
The Guardian
Huffington Post
Human Events
International Socialist Review
Joven Cuba
Liberation News Service
Long Island Press
Los Angeles Sentinel
Los Angeles Times
Miami Herald
Miami Times
The Militant
Milwaukee Journal
The Movement

The Nation
The New Republic
Newsday
New West
New York Amsterdam News
New York Daily News
New York Times
Oakland Tribune
Observer
The Participant
Penthouse
Philadelphia Inquirer
Ramparts
Reading Eagle
The Record
The Rio Rancho Observer
Spartanburg Herald
The Sun
Sun-Sentinel
Third World Information Service
Time Magazine
Tropic
U.S. News and World Report
Vancouver Magazine
The Village Voice
The Washingtonian
Washington Post
Wilmington Morning Star
Z Magazine

Online Media Sources

ABC
AFP
Allhiphop
Associated Press
BBC
Counterpunch
Democracy Now
Examiner
The Indypendent
NBC
PBS
Progreso Weekly
Salon
Yahoo News

Music

Common. *Like Water for Chocolate*. MCA, 2000, CD.
Ochs, Phil. *All the News That's Fit to Sing*. Elektra, 1964, LP.
Welfare Poets. *Project Blues*. Raymond Ramirez, 2000, CD.

Files Obtained under the Freedom of Information Act (FOIA)

CENTRAL INTELLIGENCE AGENCY
Venceremos Brigade
Center for Cuban Studies

U.S. STATE DEPARTMENT
Venceremos Brigade
Center for Cuban Studies

FEDERAL BUREAU OF INVESTIGATION
Antonio Maceo Brigade
William Lee Brent
Center for Cuban Studies
Cuban Mission to the United Nations in New York
Carlos Muñiz Varela
Venceremos Brigade
Weather Underground Organization

U.S. Government Publications and Declassified Documents

"Foreign Influence: Weather Underground Organization (WUO)." United States Department of Justice, Federal Bureau of Investigation (FBI). Chicago, Ill., August 20, 1976. File no. CG 100-40903, pp. i–viii; 1-410. National Advisory Committee on Criminal Justice Standards and Goals. *Disorders and Terrorism, Report of the Task Force on Disorders and Terrorism*. Washington, D.C.: U.S. Government Printing Office, 1976.

National Archives and Records Administration. *Records of the Central Intelligence Agency (CIA), 1894–2002*. Audio Recordings of Monitored Broadcasts from Havana and Port-au-Prince, 1968–1973. Havana International Service In English. Sullivan, Mark P. "Cuba and the State Sponsors of Terrorism List." CRS Report for Congress, Library of Congress. Washington, D.C.: Congressional Research Service, May 13, 2005.

U.S. Congress. House of Representatives. *Hearings before the Committee on Internal Security*. 93rd Cong., 1st sess., Oct. 17–18, 1973. Washington, D.C.: U.S. Government Printing Office, 1973.

———. House Committee on Foreign Affairs. *Hearings on Aircraft Hijacking*. 91st Cong., 2nd sess., Sept. 17, 22, 23, and 30, 1970. Washington, D.C.: U.S. Government Printing Office, 1970.

———. House Committee on Internal Security. *Theory and Practice of Communism, Venceremos Brigade*. 92nd Cong., 2nd sess., Oct. 16, 18, and 19, 1972. Washington, D.C.: U.S. Government Printing Office, 1972.

———. House Subcommittee on Inter-American Affairs of the Committee on Foreign Affairs. *United States Relations with Panama: Hearings*. 93rd Cong., 1st sess., Feb. 20, 1973. Washington, D.C.: U.S. Government Printing Office, 1973.

U.S. Congress. Senate Subcommittee to Administer the Internal Security Act and Other National Security Laws, Committee on the Judiciary. *The Cuban Connection in Puerto Rico; Castro's Hand in Puerto Rican and U.S. Terrorism: Hearings.* 94th Cong., 1st sess., July 30, 1975. Washington, D.C.: U.S. Government Printing Office, 1975.

———. Senate Subcommittee to Investigate the Administration of the Internal Security Act and Other Internal Security Laws. *Fair Play for Cuba Committee: Hearings.* 87th Cong., 1st sess., Apr. 29, May 5, and Oct. 10, 1960. Washington, D.C.: U.S. Government Printing Office, 1961.

———. Senate Select Committee to Study Governmental Operations with Respect to Intelligence Activities. *Final Report.* 94th Cong., 2nd sess. Washington, D.C.: U.S. Government Printing Office, 1976.

———. Senate Committee on Foreign Relations. *Nomination of Hon. Cyrus R. Vance to be Secretary of State: Hearing.* 95th Cong., 1st sess., Jan. 11, 1977. Washington, D.C.: U.S. Government Printing Office, 1977.

———. Senate Subcommittee on Security and Terrorism of the Committee on the Judiciary. *The Role of Cuba in International Terrorism and Subversion: Hearings.* 97th Cong., 2nd sess., Feb. 26 and Mar. 4, 11, and 12, 1982. Washington, D.C.: United States Government Printing Office, 1982.

———. Senate Subcommittee to Investigate the Administration of the Internal Security Act and Other Internal Security Laws of the Committee on the Judiciary. *The Tricontinental Conference of African, Asian and Latin American Peoples: A Staff Study.* 89th Cong., 2nd sess. Washington, D.C.: United States Government Printing Office, 1966.

U.S. Department of State. Office of the Coordinator for Counterterrorism. *Country Reports on Terrorism 2004.* Washington, D.C.: Office of the Coordinator for Counterterrorism, April 2005.

Interviews

All interviews conducted in person by the author unless otherwise noted.
Anonymous, Havana, Cuba (six interviewees requested anonymity)
Nehanda Abiodun, Havana, Cuba
Domingo Amuchastegui, interviewed by Ruth Reitan, Miami, FL
Rafael Betancourt, Havana, Cuba
Martha Insoa Brindis, Havana, Cuba
Orlaida Cabrera, Havana, Cuba
Jesús Arboleya Cervera, Havana, Cuba
Esther Finney, Havana, Cuba
Hugo Andres Govín Díaz, Havana, Cuba
José Estévez Hernández, Havana, Cuba
Charlie Hill, Havana, Cuba
Antonio Perez, Havana, Cuba
William Potts, Havana, Cuba
Tomás Fernández Robaina, Havana, Cuba
Tony Ryan, Oakland, Calif. (telephone)
Louis Segal, Berkeley, Calif. (telephone)
Irma Tamayo, Havana, Cuba
René Trujillo Tamayo, Havana, Cuba
Roberto Zurbano, Havana, Cuba

Published Interviews

Gates, Skip, and Eldridge Cleaver. "Cuban Experience: Eldridge Cleaver on Ice." *Transition* 49 (1975).
Shakur, Assata. "Assata Shakur, Former Black Panther, Speaks from Exile in Cuba." *Fight Racism! Fight Imperialism!* 131 (June/July 1996).
Shakur, Assata. "Interview with Assata Shakur." By Paul Davidson. *Flame 6*, November 6, 2000. http://www.fantompowa.net/Flame/assata_interview.htm.

Correspondence

Raúl Alzaga, email correspondence with author.
Dennis Duncanwood, email correspondence with author.
Albor Ruíz, email correspondence with author.

Autobiographies and Memoirs

Adler, Margot. *Heretic's Heart: A Journey Through Spirit and Revolution*. Boston: Beacon Press, 1997.
Ayers, Bill. *Fugitive Days: Memoirs of an Anti-war Activist*. Boston: Beacon Press, 2001.
Baraka, Amiri. *The Autobiography of LeRoi Jones*. Chicago: Lawrence Hill, 1984.
Bornemann, Alberto Ulloa. *Surviving Mexico's Dirty War: A Political Prisoner's Memoir*. Edited by Arthur Schmidt and Aurora Camacho de Schmidt. Philadelphia: Temple University Press, 2007.
Brent, William Lee. *Long Time Gone: A Black Panther's True-Life Story of His Hijacking and Twenty-Five Years in Cuba*. New York: Times Books, 1996.
Brightman, Carol, and Sandra Levinson, eds. *The Venceremos Brigade: Young Americans Sharing the Life and Work of Revolutionary Cuba*. New York: Simon and Schuster, 1971.
Bryant, Anthony. *Hijack*. Fort Lauderdale: Freedom Press International, 1984.
Carmichael, Stokely (Kwame Ture), with Ekwueme Michael Thelwell. *Ready For Revolution: The Life and Struggles of Stokely Carmichael (Kwame Ture)*. New York: Scribner, 2003.
Carmichael, Stokely (Kwame Ture). *Stokely Speaks: From Black Power to Pan-Africanism*. Chicago: Chicago Review Press, 2007.
Cleaver, Eldridge. *Soul on Fire*. Waco: Word Books, 1978.
———. *Soul on Ice*. New York: McGraw-Hill, 1968.
Cleaver, Kathleen, and George Katsiaficas, eds. *Liberation, Imagination, and the Black Panther Party: A New Look at the Panthers and Their Legacy*. London: Routledge, 2001.
Cluster, Dick. "The Venceremos Brigade: A 60s Political Journey," *ReVista: Harvard Review of Latin America* 8 (Winter 2009): 30–31.
Clytus, John. *Black Man in Red Cuba*. Miami: University of Miami Press, 1970.
Davis, Angela. *Angela Davis, an Autobiography*. New York: Random House, 1974.
Dunbar-Ortiz, Roxanne. *Outlaw Woman: A Memoir of the War Years, 1960–1975*. San Francisco: City Lights Books, 2001.
Fitzgerald, Tamsin. *Tamsin*. New York: Dial Press, 1973.
Gitlin, Todd. *The Sixties: Years of Hope, Days of Rage*. New York: Bantam Books, 1987.
Grupo Areíto. *Contra Viento y Marea: Jóvenes Cubanos Hablan Desde Su Exilio en Estados Unidos*. Mexico D.F.: Siglo Veintiuno Editores, 1978.

Guevara, Ernesto. *The Motorcycle Diaries: Notes on a Latin American Journey.* Melbourne: Ocean Press, 1997.
Hilliard, David. *This Side of Glory: The Autobiography of David Hilliard and the Story of the Black Panther Party.* Chicago: Lawrence Hill Books, 2001.
Moore, Carlos. *Pichón: Race and Revolution in Castro's Cuba: a Memoir.* Chicago: Chicago Review Press, 2008.
Oglesby, Carl. *Ravens in the Storm: A Personal History of the 1960s Antiwar Movement.* New York: Scribner, 2008.
Pepper, Margot. *Through the Wall: A Year in Havana.* San Francisco: Freedom Voices, 2005.
Randall, Margaret. *To Change the World: My Years in Cuba.* New Brunswick: Rutgers University Press, 2009.
Shakur, Assata. *Assata: An Autobiography.* London: Zed Books, 1987.

Film and Television

Álvarez, Santiago. *79 primaveras.* Havana: Instituto Cubano del Arte e Industria Cinematográficos (ICAIC), 1969.
CBS News. *Rebels of the Sierra Maestra: The Story of Cuba's Jungle Fighters.* 1957.
Díaz, Jesús. *55 Hermanos.* Instituto Cubano del Arte e Industria Cinematográficos, 1978.
Dickson, Sandra, and Churchill Roberts. *Negroes With Guns: Rob Williams and Black Power.* Burlington: California Newsreel, 2005.
hampton, dream. *The Black August Hip Hop Project.* New York: Malcolm X Grassroots Movement, 2010.
Mathews, Aaron. *A Panther in Africa.* New York: Filmmakers Library, 2004.
Rogers Communications, Inc. *The KGB Connections: An Investigation into Soviet Operations in North America.* Westlake: American Media, 1980.
Rolando, Gloria. *The Eyes of the Rainbow: A Documentary Film with Assata Shakur.* Havana: Grupo Vocal Baobab; Grupo Folklórico Alafia, 1997.

Books and Articles

Alexander, Yonah, and Eugene Sochor. *Aerial Piracy and Aviation Security.* Dordrecht: Nijhoff, 1990.
Allen, Jafari Sinclaire. "Looking Black at Revolutionary Cuba." *Latin American Perspectives* 36, no. 1 (2009): 53–62.
———. *¡Venceremos? The Erotics of Black Self-Making in Cuba.* Durham: Duke University Press, 2011.
Anderson, Carol. *Eyes off the Prize: The United Nations and the African-American Struggle for Human Rights, 1944–1955.* Cambridge: Cambridge University Press, 2003.
Anderson, Jon Lee. *Che Guevara: A Revolutionary Life.* New York: Grove Press, 1997.
Anderson, Terry H. *The Movement and the Sixties.* Oxford: Oxford University Press, 1995.
Arboleya Cervera, Jesus, Raul Alzaga Manresa, and Ricardo Fraga del Valle. *La contrarrevolucion cubana en Puerto Rico y el caso de Carlos Muñiz Varela.* San Juan: Ediciones Callejon, 2016.
Arey, James A. *The Sky Pirates.* New York: Scribner, 1972.
Arguelles, Lourdes. "The US National Security State: The CIA and Cuban Émigré Terrorism." *Race & Class* 23 (April 1982): 287–304.
Artaraz, Kepa. *Cuba and Western Intellectuals since 1959.* New York: Palgrave Macmillan, 2009.

Asch, Chris Myers. *The Senator and the Sharecropper: The Freedom Struggles of James O. Eastland and Fannie Lou Hamer.* New York: New Press, 2008.
Austin, Curtis J. *Up against the Wall: Violence in the Making and Unmaking of the Black Panther Party.* Fayetteville: University of Arkansas Press, 2006.
Baker, Geoffrey. *Buena Vista in the Club: Rap, Reggaetón, and Revolution in Havana.* Durham: Duke University Press, 2011.
Behar, Ruth, ed. *Bridges to Cuba/Puentes a Cuba: Cuban and Cuban American Artists, Writers, and Scholars Explore Identity, Nationality, and Homeland.* Ann Arbor: University of Michigan Press, 1995.
Bejel, Emilio. *Gay Cuban Nation.* Chicago: University of Chicago Press, 2001.
Benson, Devyn Spence. *Antiracism in Cuba: The Unfinished Revolution.* Chapel Hill: University of North Carolina Press, 2015.
———. "Cuba Calls: African American Tourism, Race, and the Cuban Revolution, 1959–1961." *Hispanic American Historical Review* 93, no. 2 (2013): 239–71.
Berger, Dan. *Captive Nation: Black Prison Organizing in the Civil Rights Era.* Chapel Hill: University of North Carolina Press, 2014.
———. "The Malcolm X Doctrine: The Republic of New Afrika and National Liberation on US Soil." In *New World Coming: The Sixties and the Shaping of Global Consciousness*, edited by Karen Dubinsky, Catherine Krull, Susan Lord, Sean Mills, and Scott Rutherford. Toronto: Between the Lines Press, 2009.
———. *Outlaws of America: The Weather Underground and the Politics of Solidarity.* Oakland: AK Press, 2005.
Bernardo, Robert M. "Moral Stimulation as a Nonmarket Mode of Labor Allocation in Cuba." *Studies in Comparative International Development* 6, no. 6 (1970).
Bishin, Benjamin G., and Casey A. Klofstad. "The Political Incorporation of Cuban Americans: Why Won't Little Havana Turn Blue?" *Political Research Quarterly* 20, no. 10 (2011): 1–14.
Bloom, Joshua, and Waldo E. Martin. *Black Against Empire: The History and Politics of the Black Panther Party.* Berkeley: University of California Press, 2013.
Borstelmann, Thomas. *The Cold War and the Color Line: American Race Relations in the Global Arena.* Cambridge: Harvard University Press, 2001.
Brock, Lisa, and Digna Castañeda Fuertes, eds. *Between Race and Empire: African-Americans and Cubans before the Cuban Revolution.* Philadelphia: Temple University Press, 1998.
Broussard, Jinx Coleman. *African American Foreign Correspondents: A History.* Baton Rouge: Louisiana State University Press, 2013.
Burke, Nancy J., ed. *Health Travels: Cuban Health(care) on and off the Island.* San Francisco: University of California Medical Humanities Press, 2013.
Bustamante, Michael J. "Anti-Communist Anti-Imperialism? Agrupación Abdala and the Shifting Contours of Cuban Exile Politics, 1968–1986." *Journal of American Ethnic History* 35, no. 1 (Fall 2015): 71–99.
Cardenal, Ernesto. *En Cuba.* Barcelona: Editorial Pomaire, 1977.
Carmichael, Stokely. *Black Power and the Third World.* Thornhill, Ont.: Third World Information Service, n.d.
Carroll, Peter. *The Odyssey of the Abraham Lincoln Brigade: Americans in the Spanish Civil War.* Stanford: Stanford University Press, 1994.
Casal, Lourdes. *Palabras Juntan Revolución — Words Foment Revolution.* Havana: Casa de las Américas, 1981.

Casavantes Bradford, Anita. *The Revolution Is for the Children: The Politics of Childhood in Havana and Miami, 1959–1962*. Chapel Hill: University of North Carolina Press, 2014.

Castro, Fidel. Speech, Chaplin Theater, Havana, August 10, 1967. English translation reprinted in *International Socialist Review* 28, no. 6 (November-December 1967): 11–32.

Chanan, Michael. *Cuban Cinema*. Minneapolis: University of Minnesota Press, 2004.

Chase, Michelle. *Revolution within the Revolution: Women and Gender Politics in Cuba, 1952–1962*. Chapel Hill: University of North Carolina Press, 2015.

Childs, Matt D. "An Historical Critique of the Emergence and Evolution of Ernesto Che Guevara's Foco Theory." *Journal of Latin American Studies* 27, no. 3 (October 1995): 593–624.

Cobb, Charles E., Jr. *This Nonviolent Stuff'll Get You Killed: How Guns Made the Civil Rights Movement Possible*. New York: Basic Books, 2014.

Cohen, Robert Carl. *Black Crusader: A Biography of Robert Franklin Williams*. Secaucus: Lyle Stuart, 1972.

Cole, David. "What's a Metaphor? The Deportation of a Poet." *Yale Journal of Law and Liberation* 1, no. 1 (1989): 5–15.

Collier-Thomas, Bettye, and V.P. Franklin, eds. *Sisters in the Struggle: African-American Women in the Civil Rights–Black Power Movement*. New York: New York University Press, 2001.

Corza, Gabino La Rosa. *Runaway Slave Settlements in Cuba: Resistance and Repression*. Chapel Hill: University of North Carolina Press, 2003.

"Cuba — United States: Memorandum of Understanding on the Hijacking of Aircraft and Vessels." *International Legal Materials* 12, no. 2 (1973): 370–76.

Cummings, Eric. *The Rise and Fall of California's Radical Prison Movement*. Stanford: Stanford University Press, 1994.

Cunnigen, Donald. "The Republic of New Africa in Mississippi." In *Black Power in the Belly of the Beast*, edited by Judson Jeffries. Champaign: University of Illinois Press, 2006.

Daulatzai, Sohail. *Black Star, Crescent Moon: The Muslim International and Black Freedom beyond America*. Minneapolis: University of Minnesota Press, 2012.

Davies, Carole Boyce. *Left of Karl Marx: The Political Life of Black Communist Claudia Jones*. Durham: Duke University Press, 2008.

Davis, Mike. *City of Quartz: Excavating the Future in Los Angeles*. New York: Verso, 2006.

Debray, Régis. *Revolution in the Revolution?* New York: Grove Press, 1967.

de la Campa, Román. *Cuba on My Mind: Journeys to a Severed Nation*. New York: Verso, 2000.

———. "The Latino Diaspora in the United States: Sojourns from a Cuban Past." *Public Culture* 6, no. 2 (1994): 293–317.

de la Fuente, Alejandro. *A Nation for All: Race, Inequality, and Politics in Twentieth-Century Cuba*. Chapel Hill: University of North Carolina Press, 2001.

———. "Race and Inequality in Cuba, 1899–1981." *Journal of Contemporary History* 30, no. 1 (1995): 131–68.

———. "Race, National Discourse and Politics in Cuba." *Latin American Perspectives* 25, no. 3 (1998): 43–69.

de los Ángeles Torres, María. *In the Land of Mirrors: Cuban Exile Politics in the United States*. Ann Arbor: University of Michigan Press, 1999.

———. *The Lost Apple: Operation Pedro Pan, Cuban Children in the U.S., and the Promise of a Better Future*. Boston: Beacon Press, 2003.

Deutschmann, David. *Fidel Castro Reader*. Melbourne: Ocean Press, 2007.
Díaz, Jesús. *De la Patria y el Exilio*. Havana: Unión de Escritores y Artistas de Cuba, 1979.
Díaz-Cotto, Juanita. *Gender, Ethnicity, and the State: Latina and Latino Prison Politics*. Albany: State University of New York Press, 1996.
Domínguez, Jorge. *To Make a World Safe for Revolution: Cuba's Foreign Policy*. Cambridge: Harvard University Press, 1989.
Dorticós Torrado, Osvaldo. Law No. 1226, "Cuban Hijacking Law," September 16, 1969. Translated to English by U.S. Department of State. *International Legal Materials* 8, no. 6 (1969): 1175–77.
Dubinsky, Karen, Catherine Krull, Susan Lord, Sean Mills, and Scott Rutherford, eds. *New World Coming: The Sixties and the Shaping of Global Consciousness*. Toronto: Between the Lines Press, 2009.
Dudziak, Mary L. *Cold War Civil Rights: Race and the Image of American Democracy*. Princeton: Princeton University Press, 2000.
Dugan, Laura, Gary LaFree, and Alex Piquero. "Testing a Rational Choice Model of Airline Hijackings." *Criminology* 43, no. 4 (2005): 1031–65.
Dzidzienyo, Anani, and Lourdes Casal. *The Position of Blacks in Brazilian and Cuban Society*. London: Minority Rights Group, 1979.
Elbaum, Max. *Revolution in the Air: Sixties Radicals Turn to Lenin, Mao, and Che*. New York: Verso, 2002.
Enck-Wanzer, Darrel. *The Young Lords: A Reader*. New York: New York University Press, 2010.
Fanon, Frantz. *The Wretched of the Earth*. New York: Grove Press, 1963.
Farber, David. *The Age of Great Dreams: America in the 1960s*. New York: Hill and Wang, 1994.
Farber, Samuel. *Cuba since the Revolution of 1959: A Critical Assessment*. Chicago: Haymarket Books, 2011.
Farmer, Ashley D. "Mothers of Pan-Africanism: Audley Moore and Dara Abubakari." *Women, Gender, and Families of Color* 4, no. 2 (2016): 274–95.
Feinsilver, Julie M. *Healing the Masses: Cuban Health Politics at Home and Abroad*. Berkeley: University of California Press, 1993.
Fernandes, Sujatha. *Cuba Represent!: Cuban Arts, State Power, and the Making of New Revolutionary Cultures*. Durham: Duke University Press, 2006.
Ferrer, Ada. *Insurgent Cuba: Race, Nation and Revolution, 1868–98*. Chapel Hill: University of North Carolina Press, 1999.
Feste, Karen A. *Terminate Terrorism: Framing, Gaming, and Negotiating Conflicts*. Boulder: Paradigm, 2010.
Firestone, Shulamith, and Anne Koedt, eds. *Notes from the Second Year: Women's Liberation: Major Writings of the Radical Feminists*. New York: Radical Feminism, 1970.
Foner, Philip Sheldon. *The Black Panthers Speak*. Philadelphia: Lippincott, 1970.
Frazier, Robeson Taj. *The East Is Black: Cold War China in the Black Radical Imagination*. Durham: Duke University Press, 2014.
Gaines, Kevin. *American Africans in Ghana: Black Expatriates in the Civil Rights Era*. Chapel Hill: University of North Carolina Press, 2006.
García, María Cristina. *Havana USA: Cuban Exiles and Cuban Americans in South Florida, 1959–1994*. Berkeley: University of California Press, 1996.
Gerassi, John, ed. *Venceremos! The Speeches and Writings of Ernesto Che Guevara*. New York: Simon and Schuster, 1968.

Ginsberg, Allen. *Spontaneous Mind: Selected Interviews, 1958–1996*. New York: Harper Collins, 2001.
Gleijeses, Piero. *Conflicting Missions: Havana, Washington, and Africa, 1959–1976*. Chapel Hill: University of North Carolina Press, 2001.
———. "Cuba's First Venture in Africa: Algeria, 1961–1965." *Journal of Latin American Studies* 28, no. 1 (1996): 159–95.
———. "The First Ambassadors: Cuba's Contribution to Guinea-Bissau's War of Independence." *Journal of Latin American Studies* 29, no. 1 (1997): 45–88.
———. *Visions of Freedom: Havana, Washington, Pretoria, and the Struggle for Southern Africa, 1976–1991*. Chapel Hill: University of North Carolina Press, 2013.
Gómez, Mayra. *Human Rights in Cuba, El Salvador and Nicaragua: A Sociological Perspective on Human Rights Abuse*. New York: Routledge, 2003.
González, Juan. *Harvest of Empire: A History of Latinos in America*. New York: Penguin Books, 2001.
Goodell, Charles. *Political Prisoners in America*. New York: Random House, 1973.
Gordy, Katherine A. *Living Ideology in Cuba: Socialism in Principle and Practice*. Ann Arbor: University of Michigan Press, 2015.
Gore, Dayo. *Radicalism at the Crossroads: African American Women Activists in the Cold War*. New York: New York University Press, 2011.
Gore, Dayo, Jeanne Theoharis, and Komozi Woodard, eds. *Want to Start a Revolution? Radical Women in the Black Freedom Struggle*. New York: New York University Press, 2009.
Gosse, Van. "Active Engagement: The Legacy of Central American Solidarity." *NACLA Report on the Americas* 28, no. 5 (1995): 22–29.
———. *Rethinking the New Left: An Interpretive History*. New York: Palgrave Macmillan, 2005.
———. *Where the Boys Are: Cuba, Cold War America, and the Making of a New Left*. New York: Verso, 1993.
Gott, Richard. *Cuba: A New History*. New Haven: Yale University Press, 2004.
Gray, Geoffrey. *Skyjack: The Hunt for D. B. Cooper*. New York: Crown, 2011.
Greenbaum, Susan D. *More Than Black: Afro-Cubans in Tampa*. Gainesville: University Press of Florida, 2002.
Greenberg, Amy S. *Manifest Manhood and the Antebellum American Empire*. University Park: Pennsylvania State University Press, 2005.
Greenberg, Cheryl. "Of Black Revolutionaries and Whig Histories: Using *Assata* in the Classroom." *Journal of American Ethnic History* 32, no. 1 (2012): 90–94.
Griffin, Farah Jasmine. "Para las Chicas Cubanas." *Callaloo* 26, no. 1 (2003): 74–82.
Gronbeck-Tedesco, John A. *Cuba, the United States, and Cultures of the Transnational Left, 1930–1975*. New York: Cambridge University Press, 2015.
Guerra, Lillian. *Visions of Power in Cuba: Revolution, Redemption, and Resistance, 1959–1971*. Chapel Hill: University of North Carolina Press, 2014.
Guevara, Ernesto Che. *Guerrilla Warfare*. Lincoln: Bison Books, 1998.
Guridy, Frank Andre. *Forging Diaspora: Afro-Cubans and African Americans in a World of Empire and Jim Crow*. Chapel Hill: University of North Carolina Press, 2010.
Guy, Rosa. "Castro in New York." *Black renaissance/Renaissance noire* 1, no. 1 (1996): 10–19.
Hayden, Tom. *Listen, Yankee!: Why Cuba Matters*. New York: Seven Stories Press, 2015.
Helg, Aline. *Our Rightful Share: The Afro-Cuban Struggle for Equality, 1886–1912*. Chapel Hill: University of North Carolina Press, 1995.

Herrera, Andrea O'Reilly, ed. *Cuba: Idea of a Nation Displaced*. Albany: State University of New York Press, 2007.
Hill, Lance. *Deacons for Defense: Armed Resistance and the Civil Rights Movement*. Chapel Hill: University of North Carolina Press, 2006.
Hobsbawm, Eric. *Bandits*. Rev. ed. New York: New Press, 2000.
Holden, Robert T. "The Contagiousness of Aircraft Hijacking." *American Journal of Sociology* 91, no. 4 (1986): 874–904.
Holmes, Linda Janet. *A Joyous Revolt: Toni Cade Bambara, Writer and Activist*. Santa Barbara: Praeger, 2014.
Huberman, Leo, and Paul M. Sweezy. *Cuba: Anatomy of a Revolution*. New York: Monthly Review Press, 1960.
———. *Socialism in Cuba*. New York: Monthly Review Press, 1969.
James, C. L. R. *The Black Jacobins*. New York: Vintage, 1989.
James, Winston. *Holding Aloft the Banner of Ethiopia: Caribbean Radicalism in Early Twentieth-Century America*. New York: Verso, 1998.
Jameson, Fredric. "Periodizing the 60s." *Social Text* 9/10 (Spring-Summer 1984): 178–209.
Jeffries, Judson L., ed. *Black Power in the Belly of the Beast*. Champaign: University of Illinois Press, 2006.
Jones, Charles E., ed. *The Black Panther Party Reconsidered: Reflections and Scholarship*. Baltimore: Black Classic Press, 1998.
Jones, LeRoi. "Cuba Libre." *Evergreen Review* 4, no. 15 (November-December 1960): 139–59.
Joseph, Peniel E. *Stokely: A Life*. New York: Basic Civitas, 2014.
———. *The Black Power Movement: Rethinking the Civil Rights-Black Power Era*. New York: Routledge, 2006.
———. *Waiting 'Til the Midnight Hour: A Narrative History of Black Power in America*. New York: Henry Holt, 2006.
Karl, Terry. "Work Incentives in Cuba." *Latin American Perspectives* 2, no. 4 (1975): 21–41.
Katsiaficas, George. *The Imagination of the New Left: A Global Analysis of 1968*. Cambridge: South End Press, 1987.
Kelley, Robin D. G. *Freedom Dreams: The Black Radical Imagination*. Boston: Beacon Press, 2003.
———. *Hammer and Hoe: Alabama Communists During the Great Depression*. Chapel Hill: University of North Carolina Press, 1990.
Killen, Andreas. *1973 Nervous Breakdown: Watergate, Warhol, and the Birth of Post-Sixties America*. New York: Bloomsbury, 2006.
King, Martin Luther, Jr. *Threshold of a New Decade, January 1959–December 1960*. Vol. 5 of *The Papers of Martin Luther King, Jr.* Berkeley: University of California Press, 2005.
Klein, Jeffrey. "In Cuba with the Second Venceremos Brigade." *Columbia Forum* 13, no. 4 (Winter 1970): 23–33.
Klimke, Martin. *The Other Alliance: Student Protest in West Germany and the United States in the Global Sixties*. Princeton: Princeton University Press, 2011.
Koerner, Brendan I. *The Skies Belong to Us: Love and Terror in the Golden Age of Hijacking*. New York: Crown, 2013.
Kozol, Jonathan. *Children of the Revolution: A Yankee Teacher in the Cuban Schools*. New York: Dell, 1978.
Krekola, Joni, and Simo Mikkonen. "Backlash of the Free World: the U.S. Presence at the World Youth Festival in Helsinki, 1962." *Scandinavian Journal of History* 36, no. 2 (2011): 230–55.

Latner, Teishan. "Take Me to Havana! Airline Hijacking, U.S.-Cuba Relations, and Political Protest in Late 1960s America." *Diplomatic History* 39, no. 1 (2015): 16–44.
Lekus, Ian. "Queer Harvests: Homosexuality, the U.S. New Left, and the Venceremos Brigades to Cuba." *Radical History Review* 89 (2004): 57–91.
LeoGrande, William M., and Peter Kornbluh. *Back Channel to Cuba: The Hidden History of Negotiations between Washington and Havana.* Chapel Hill: University of North Carolina Press, 2014.
Levine, Robert M. *Secret Missions to Cuba: Fidel Castro, Bernardo Benes, and Cuban Miami.* New York: Palgrave Macmillan, 2001.
Lockwood, Lee. *Conversation with Eldridge Cleaver, Algiers.* New York: McGraw-Hill, 1970.
López, Iraida H. *Impossible Returns: Narratives of the Cuban Diaspora.* Gainesville: University Press of Florida, 2015.
Lumsden, Ian. *Machos, Maricones, and Gays: Cuba and Homosexuality.* Philadelphia: Temple University Press, 1996.
Lumumba, Chokwe. "Short History of the U.S. War on the R.N.A." *The Black Scholar* 12, no. 1 (January/February 1981): 72–81.
Malitsky, Joshua. *Post-Revolution Nonfiction Film: Building the Soviet and Cuban Nations.* Bloomington: Indiana University Press, 2013.
Malloy, Sean L. "Uptight in Babylon: Eldridge Cleaver's Cold War." *Diplomatic History* 37, no. 3 (2013): 538–71.
Marable, Manning, ed. *Dispatches from the Ebony Tower: Intellectuals Confront the African American Experience.* New York: Columbia University Press, 2000.
———. *Malcolm X: A Life of Reinvention.* New York: Viking Press, 2011.
Mariña, Claudio Rey. *Hijacking of Aircraft: A Boomerang Hurled at Cuba by the Imperialist Government of the United States of America.* Havana: Abel Santamaria Printing Office, 1970.
Martin, Bradford. *The Other Eighties: A Secret History of America in the Age of Reagan.* New York: Hill and Wang, 2011.
Martinez, Elizabeth. "The Venceremos Brigade Still Means 'We Shall Overcome.'" *Z Magazine* (July/August 1999): 56–62.
Martínez, Elizabeth Sutherland. *The Youngest Revolution: a Personal Report on Cuba.* New York: Dial Press, 1969.
Martínez, Milagros. "Academic Exchange between Cuba and the United States: a Brief Overview." *Latin American Perspectives* 33, no. 29 (2006): 29–42.
Matthews, Tracye E. "'No One Ever Asks What a Man's Role in the Revolution Is': Gender Politics and Leadership in the Black Panther Party, 1966–71." In *Sisters in the Struggle: African-American Women in the Civil Rights–Black Power Movement,* edited by Bettye Collier-Thomas and V. P. Franklin. New York: New York University Press, 2001.
McPherson, Alan. "Terror on Embassy Row, Revisited." *NACLA Report on the Americas* 48, no. 3 (2016): 286–91.
McWhinney, Edward, ed. *Aerial Piracy and International Law.* New York: Oceana Publications, 1971.
Mesa-Lago, Carmelo. *The Labor Sector and Socialist Distribution in Cuba.* Stanford: Hoover Institution on War, Revolution and Peace, 1968.
Mills, C. Wright. *Listen, Yankee: The Revolution in Cuba.* New York: Ballantine Books, 1961.
Mills, Sean. *The Empire Within: Postcolonial Thought and Political Activism in Sixties Montreal.* Montreal: McGill-Queens University Press, 2010.

Moore, Carlos. *Castro, the Blacks, and Africa*. Los Angeles: Center for Afro-American Studies, University of California, Los Angeles, 1988.
———. *Pichón: Race and Revolution in Castro's Cuba: A Memoir*. Chicago: Chicago Review Press, 2008.
Morley, Morris H. *Imperial State and Revolution: The United States and Cuba, 1952–1986*. Cambridge: Cambridge University Press, 1987.
Nelson, Alondra. *Body and Soul: The Black Panther Party and the Fight against Medical Discrimination*. Minneapolis: University of Minnesota Press, 2011.
Newton, Huey P. *To Die for the People*. Edited by Toni Morrison. San Francisco: City Lights, 2009.
Obadele, Gaidi (Obadele, Imari Abubakar). *War in America*. Detroit: Gaidi Obadele, 1967.
Obadele, Imari Abubakar. *Foundations of the Black Nation*. Detroit: House of Songhay, 1975.
Olguín, B. V. *At the Risk of Seeming Ridiculous: Poems from Cuba Libre*. San Antonio: Aztlan Libre Press, 2014.
Osoria, José M. Atiles. "Pro-State Violence in Puerto Rico: Cuban and Puerto Rican Right-Wing Terrorism from the 1960s to the 1990s." *Socialism and Democracy* 26, no. 1 (March 2012): 127–42.
Pedraza, Silvia. *Political Disaffection in Cuba's Revolution and Exodus*. Cambridge: Cambridge University Press, 2007.
Pérez, Louis A. *Cuba in the American Imagination: Metaphor and the Imperial Ethos*. Chapel Hill: University of North Carolina Press, 2008.
———. *Cuba and the United States: Ties of Singular Intimacy*. 3rd ed. Athens: University of Georgia Press, 2013.
———. *Cuba: Between Reform and Revolution*. 4th ed. Oxford: Oxford University Press, 2011.
Pérez-Stable, Marifeli. "The Field of Cuban Studies." *Latin American Research Review* 26, no. 1 (1991): 239–50.
Perkins, Margo V. *Autobiography as Activism: Three Black Women of the Sixties*. Jackson: University Press of Mississippi, 2000.
Perry, Marc D. *Negro Soy Yo: Hip Hop and Raced Citizenship in Neoliberal Cuba*. Durham: Duke University Press, 2016.
Philips, David. *Skyjack: The Story of Air Piracy*. London: Harrap, 1973.
Plummer, Brenda Gayle. "Castro in Harlem: A Cold War Watershed." In *Re-Thinking the Cold War*, edited by Allen Hunter, 133–55. Philadelphia: Temple University Press, 1997.
———. *In Search of Power: African Americans in the Era of Decolonization, 1956–1974*. Cambridge: Cambridge University Press, 2013.
———. *Rising Wind: Black Americans and U.S. Foreign Affairs, 1935–1960*. Chapel Hill: University of North Carolina Press, 1996.
Prashad, Vijay. *The Darker Nations: A People's History of the Third World*. New York: New Press, 2007.
Price, Richard, ed. *Maroon Societies: Rebel Slave Communities in the Americas*. 3rd ed. Baltimore: Johns Hopkins University Press, 1996.
Pulido, Laura. *Black, Brown, Yellow, and Left: Radical Activism in Los Angeles*. Berkeley: University of California Press, 2006.
Ramos, Ana. *Cuba Resource Center Newsletter*, vol. 2, no. 2, March 1972.
Randall, Margaret. *Breaking the Silences: 20th Century Poetry by Cuban Women*. Vancouver: Pulp Press, 1982.

———. *Che on My Mind*. Durham: Duke University Press, 2013.
———. *Cuban Women Now*. Toronto: The Women's Press, 1974.
———. *Exporting Revolution: Cuba's Foreign Policy*. Durham: Duke University Press, 2017.
———. *Women in Cuba: 20 Years Later*. New York: Smyrna Press, 1981.
Reckord, Barry. *Does Fidel Eat More Than Your Father? Conversations in Cuba*. New York: Harper Collins, 1971.
Rediker, Marcus. *Villains of All Nations: Atlantic Pirates in the Golden Age*. Boston: Beacon Press, 2004.
Reitan, Ruth. "Cuba, the Black Panther Party and the US Black Movement in the 1960s: Issues of Security." *New Political Science* 21, no. 2 (1999): 217–30.
———. *The Rise and Decline of an Alliance: Cuba and African American Leaders in the 1960s*. East Lansing: Michigan State University Press, 1999.
Ríos, Baldomero Alvarez, ed. *Cuba: Revolución e imperialismo: apuntes, cifras y fragmentos*. Havana: Instituto del Libro, 1969.
Risech, Flavio. "Political and Cultural Cross-Dressing: Negotiating a Second Generation Cuban-American Identity." *Michigan Quarterly Review* 33, no. 3 (1994): 526–40.
Rodriguez, Besenia. "'De la Esclavitud Yanqui a la Libertad Cubana': U.S. Black Radicals, the Cuban Revolution, and the Formation of a Tricontinental Ideology." *Radical History Review*, 92 (Spring 2005): 62–87.
Rodríguez, Dylan. *Forced Passages: Imprisoned Radical Intellectuals and the U.S. Prison Regime*. Minneapolis: University of Minnesota Press, 2006.
Rojas, Rafael. *Fighting over Fidel: The New York Intellectuals and the Cuban Revolution*. Princeton: Princeton University Press, 2015.
Rout, Kathleen. *Eldridge Cleaver*. Boston: Twayne, 1991.
Sale, Kirkpatrick. *SDS: The Rise and Development of the Students for a Democratic Society*. New York: Random House, 1973.
Sallah, Michael, and Mitch Weiss. *The Yankee Comandante: The Untold Story of Courage, Passion, and One American's Fight to Liberate Cuba*. Guilford: Lyons Press, 2015.
Sandweiss, Stephen. "Spying on Solidarity: The FBI's investigations of the Venceremos Brigade and CISPES." Master's thesis, San Francisco State University, 1990.
Saney, Isaac. "African Stalingrad: The Cuban Revolution, Internationalism, and the End of Apartheid." *Latin American Perspectives* 33, no. 5 (September 2006): 81–117.
———. *Cuba: A Revolution in Motion*. London: Zed Books, 2004.
———. "Homeland of Humanity: Internationalism within the Cuban Revolution." *Latin American Perspectives* 36, no. 1, January (2009): 111–23.
Sawyer, Mark Q. *Racial Politics in Post-Revolutionary Cuba*. Cambridge: Cambridge University Press, 2005.
Scheer, Robert, and Maurice Zeitlin. *Cuba: An American Tragedy*. London: Penguin, 1964.
Schoultz, Lars. *That Infernal Little Cuban Republic: The United States and the Cuban Revolution*. Chapel Hill: University of North Carolina Press, 2011.
Scott, William R. "Black Nationalism and the Italo-Ethiopian Conflict 1934–1936." *Journal of Negro History* 63, no. 2 (1978): 118–34.
Seidman, Sarah. "Tricontinental Routes of Solidarity: Stokely Carmichael in Cuba." *Journal of Transnational American Studies* 4, no. 2 (2012): 1–25.
Self, Robert O. *American Babylon: Race and the Struggle for Postwar Oakland*. Princeton: Princeton University Press, 2003.

Shakur, Assata. *Assata: In Her Own Words*. Stone Mountain: Talking Drum Collective, 2009.
———. "The Continuity of Struggle." *Souls: A Critical Journal of Black Politics, Culture and Society* 93, no. 1 (Spring 1999): 93–100.
———. "An Open Letter from Assata Shakur." *Canadian Dimension* 32, no. 4 (July 1998): 17–21.
———. "To My People." *The Black Scholar* 5, no. 2 (October 1973): 16–18.
Shetterly, Aran. *The Americano: Fighting with Castro for Cuba's Freedom*. Chapel Hill: Algonquin Books, 2007.
Solomon, Mark. *The Cry Was Unity: Communists and African Americans, 1917–1936*. Jackson: University Press of Mississippi, 1998.
Springer, Kimberly. *Living for the Revolution: Black Feminist Organizations, 1968–1980*. Durham: Duke University Press, 2005.
Stout, Noelle M. *After Love: Queer Intimacy and Erotic Economies in Post-Soviet Cuba*. Durham: Duke University Press, 2014.
Suri, Jeremi. *Power and Protest: Global Revolution and the Rise of Détente*. Cambridge: Harvard University Press, 2003.
Susler, Jan. "More Than 25 Years: Puerto Rican Political Prisoners." *NACLA Report on the Americas* 40, no. 6 (November/December 2007): 26–27.
Taylor, Henry Louis. *Inside El Barrio: A Bottom-Up View of Neighborhood Life in Castro's Cuba*. Sterling: Kumarian Press, 2009.
Tietchen, Todd F. *The Cubalogues: Beat Writers in Revolutionary Havana*. Gainesville: University Press of Florida, 2010.
Torres, Andrés, and José E. Velázquez, eds. *The Puerto Rican Movement: Voices from the Diaspora*. Philadelphia: Temple University Press, 1998.
Tyson, Timothy B. *Radio Free Dixie: Robert F. Williams and the Roots of Black Power*. Chapel Hill: University of North Carolina Press, 1999.
Umoja, Akinyele Omowale. "The Black Liberation Army and the Radical Legacy of the Black Panther Party." In *Black Power in the Belly of the Beast*, edited by Judson Jeffries. Champaign: University of Illinois Press, 2006.
———. *We Will Shoot Back: Armed Resistance in the Mississippi Freedom Movement*. New York: New York University Press, 2013.
U.S. Peace Council. *Sandy Pollack: Her Life*. New Haven: U.S. Peace Council, 1985.
Venceremos Brigade. *Democracy in Cuba*. Venceremos Brigade Educational Commission, 1976.
Von Eschen, Penny. *Race against Empire: Black Americans and Anticolonialism*. Ithaca: Cornell University Press, 1997.
———. *Satchmo Blows Up the World: Jazz Ambassadors Play the Cold War*. Cambridge: Harvard University Press, 2006.
Wagner-Pacifici, Robin. *Discourse and Destruction: The City of Philadelphia Versus MOVE*. Chicago: University of Chicago Press, 1994.
Walsh, Daniel C. *An Air War with Cuba: The United States Radio Campaign against Castro*. Jefferson: McFarland, 2012.
Weinstein, Martin, ed. *Revolutionary Cuba in the World Arena*. Philadelphia: Institute for the Study of Human Issues, 1979.
Wendt, Simon. *The Spirit and the Shotgun: Armed Resistance and the Struggle for Civil Rights*. Gainesville: University Press of Florida, 2007.

Westad, Odd Arne. *The Global Cold War: Third World Interventions and the Making of our Times*. Cambridge: Cambridge University Press, 2006.
Williams, Evelyn A. *Inadmissible Evidence: The Story of the African-American Trial Lawyer Who Defended the Black Liberation Army*. Chicago: Lawrence Hill Books, 1993.
Wu, Judy Tzu-Chun. *Radicals on the Road: Internationalism, Orientalism, and Feminism during the Vietnam Era*. Ithaca: Cornell University Press, 2013.
Young, Allen. *Gays under the Cuban Revolution*. San Francisco: Grey Fox Press, 1981.
Young, Cynthia A. *Soul Power: Culture, Radicalism, and the Making of a U.S. Third World Left*. Durham: Duke University Press, 2006.

Index

Page numbers in italics refer to illustrations.

Abbot, Tarnel, 54
Abiodun, Nehanda Isoke, 128, 217–18, 221, 238, 242–51, *246*, 312n181
Abortion, 4, 65
Abourezk, James, 119
Abraham Lincoln Brigade, 107
Abreu, Lázaro, *220*
Academics, Cuban, 158, 296n17
Ackerman, Holly, 182
Adler, Margot, 57
Advertisements: FPCC and, 18, 80–81; in *Ramparts*, 27; satirical, 52, *52–53*
Africa and Cuba, 96–98, 168–69, 177, 185, 211, 251, 298n55. *See also specific African countries*
African Americans: Cuban revolution and, 1–3, 14–15, 22–23; as hijackers, 125–26, 134–36, 290n13; as revolutionary leaders, 110–13; revolution in America and, 215–20, 242; struggle connections to Cuba of, 48–49. *See also* Black freedom movement; *specific African Americans and African American groups*
African Party for the Independence of Guinea and Cape Verde (PAIGC), 96–97, 285n72
Afro-Cubans: benefits of Revolution to, 2, 136; Cuban government opposition to political initiatives of, 23, 135, 136, 223–24; racial solidarity and, 135, 225; racism and, 23, 60–61
Agency for International Development, U.S., 247
Airlines, 123–24, 131, 132, 143–44, 298n47
Air piracy. *See* hijacking
Alarcón, Ricardo, 117
Albright, Madeleine K., 254
Algeria, 51, 97, 106, 112, 225, 307n67
Ali, Ishmael Muslim, 252, 313–14n218

Allen, Ernie, 19
Allen, Jafari S., 249, 267, 268
Allen, James, 115
Alliance for Progress, 23, 28
Almeida, Juan, 16, 47
Alpha 66, 117, 118
Álvarez, Santiago, 49–50, 81
Álzaga, Raúl, 191, 197
American fighters in foreign theaters, 102–3, 106–7, 130
American Journal of Sociology, 126
Amnesty International, 169, 298n59
Amuchástegui, Domingo, 112
Angola, 3, 71, 97, 168, 177, 251
Angola: African Giron, 71
Anti-apartheid, 235, 252
Anti-Castroism, 169; CIA and, 94, 161, 169; in Cuban American communities, 10–11, 25, 155; espionage and, 117, 118, 196; terrorism and, 25, 117, 188–92. *See also specific anti-Castro groups*
Anticolonial movement: African American radicals and, 15, 102–3, 106–7, 108, 112, 203, 211; Cuban media and cultural production and, 49, 103, 211; Cuban support to, 3, 51, 96, 97, 109, 168, 203, 251; hijackings and, 132; political asylum and, 206; Puerto Rico and, 186, 219; U.S. concerns and efforts to thwart, 89–90, 109–10; U.S. Left and, 13, 23, 28, 29–30, 35, 91–92, 105
Antihijacking agreement, 22, 24–25, 104, 125, 144–50, 166, 287n105, 297n38
Antihijacking Law No. 1226 of Cuba, 134, 145, 146, 207
Anti-imperialism. *See* Anticolonial movement
Anti–Vietnam War movement, 10, 53–54, 79, 84, 115, 163, 208

Antonio Maceo Brigade, *178–79*; anti-Castro violence and, 190–91; Cuba and, 11, 171–73, 177; "the dialogue" and, 170–71, 180–82, 187; emergence of, 158–65; FBI and, 154, 172, 175, 192–96, 295n3, 302n146, 303n156; first brigade of, 174–75, 299n72; name origin of, 171–72, 299n71; overview of, 25, 153–57, 196–97; second brigade of, 176, 191; today, 269
Apartheid, 3, 53, 235, 237, 252
Árbenz, Jacobo, 109
Ardizones, Javier, 37
Areíto, 162–64, *164*, 197, 295n2, 299n72, 303n159; *Contra Viento y Marea* and, 162, 163–64, 179–80; "the dialogue" and, 180; Maceo Brigade and, 153, 171, 172–73, 299n77
Armed self-defense, 16, 216
Arocena, Eduardo, 192
Assata: An Autobiography (Shakur), 199, 237, 311n151, 311nn154–55
Assembly of the International Civil Aviation Organization, 146, 287n109
Asylum, political: for African American activists, 2, 4, 200–207, 219; Cuban international, 203, 304n16; Cuban press and, 214–15; Cuban racial sanctuary image and, 128; defined, 304n15; hijacking and, 10, 125, 133, 135–36, 145, 149–50, 151, 207; legal basis for, 206–7; for overthrown Batista government, 205; overview of Cuba granting, 11–12, 122, 218, 304n16; relations and diplomacy and, 11–12, 22, 252–53, 263, 269; U.N. declarations on, 133, 206–7; U.S. House Congressional Resolution 254 and, 254–55. *See also* Exile profiles; Extradition
Athletic and cultural college-exchange program, 166–67, 297n43

Baez, Joan, 81
Baker, Josephine, 306n43
"Ballad of William Worthy" (Ochs), 86
"Ballot and the bullet," 15, 240, 274n34
Bambara, Toni Cade, 16, 238–39, 312n160
Banks, Dennis, 306n47
Ban on travel to Cuba, U.S., 4, 27, 28–29, 44, 45, 85–86, 166–67

Baraguá, 172
Baraka, Amiri, 15, 47, 231. *See also* Jones, LeRoi
Batista, Fulgencio, 12, 17
Bay of Pigs invasion, 13, 46, 162
Bay of Pigs veterans, 182, 185, 188
Beech, Keyes, 77, 282n8
Benedetti, Mario, 104
Benes, Bernardo, 181–83, 185, 186, 188, 195, 303n156
Ben Tre, Cuba, 50
Bến Tre, South Vietnam, 50–51
Bertrand Russell Peace Foundation, 84
Betancourt, Rafael, 160
Bevel, James, 208
Biblioteca Nacional de José Marti, 248
Billboards, *vi*, 39, 49, 50, 51
Black Armed Guard, 215
Black August Collective (BAC), 239, 249–50
Black August hip-hop festivals, 250
Black August Hip Hop Project, The (hampton), 313n204
Black August initiative, 249, 313n203
Black freedom movement: Cuban American Left and, 163; Cuban policy and support of, 113–14, 134, 136, 203, 215; Cuban press and cultural production and, 81, 207–15, 212; political asylum and, 263; Shakur and, 202. *See also specific groups of*
Black Liberation Army (BLA), 199, 218, 219–20, 259, 304n16, 307n67, 307n69
Black Lives Matter movement, 204
Black Panther, The, 8, 227
Black Panther Party, 7–8, 107; Brent and, 226–27; Cuba and, 4, 79, 99–100, 111, 116, 134, 200, 202; Cuban press and cultural production and, 209, 210; Cuban and international sections of, 139, 224–25; Cuban press and cultural production and, 209, 210; as hijackers, 138–41, 151, 293n67, 293n76; internationalism of, 106, 112, 287n119; Los Angeles Police Department and, 27; Oakland police shoot-out and, 221–22, 308n72, 308n74; revolution in America and, 217, 220; training for, 24, 96, 107, 223; U.S. government and, 25–26, 33–34, 76, 77, 105–6, 107, 112; whites and, 35. *See also specific members of*

Black Power movement: Carmichael and, 1; Cuba and, 202, 223; Cuban American Left and, 163; Cuban press and cultural production and, 82, 135, 208–9, 210, 216; homophobia and, 66; Shakur and, 239
Black Scholar, The, 10, 72, 97, 311n155
Black Solidarity Day, 303n2
Bohemia, 44, 81, 208, 214
Bolivia, 87, 103, 104, 111–12
Bombings, political, 101, 117, 150, 154, 188–92, 219
Boorstein, Edward, 71–72
Boorstein, Reggie, 72
Bornemann, Ulloa, 129
Bosch, Orlando, 189, 190, 192, 255
Bounty on Assata Shakur, 204, 240, 259–60, 261, 262
Brent, William Lee: exile profile of, 140, 141–42, 209, 221, 226–31, 292n56, 293n79, 293nn82–83; *Long Time Gone*, 199, 229, 230, 253, 292n56; San Francisco police shoot-out and, 134–35
Brigada Antonio Maceo. *See* Antonio Maceo Brigade
Brigadistas. *See* Venceremos Brigade
Brightman, Carol, 68, 70
Brothers to the Rescue, 118, 253
Brown, H. Rap, 117, 216, 231
Bryant, Anthony, 138, 234
Brzezinski, Zbigniew, 184
Buffalo Evening News, 149
"Bullet, The" (Welfare Poets), 240
Bunke, Haydee Tamara, 39, 277n37
Burdsall, Lorna, 305n16
Bush, George W., 257, 258

Cabral, Amílcar, 96, 107, 265, 285n72
Cabrera, Orlaida, 43–44, 58, 60
Calendar, rearranged, 31
Camarano, Chris, 51–52
Camp Lejeune incidents, 208
Canada: Black Panther training in, 96, 107, 108; as a route to Cuba, 46, 283n34
"Canción para Ángela Davis" (Milanés), 209, 261
Cannon, Terry, 71–72
Capitalism: Cuba's replacement of, 5, 28, 51; racism and, 52, 61, 208, 210

Cardenal, Ernesto, 179–80
Carmichael, Stokely: Castro and, 114, 202; Cuba and, 2–4, 223; global revolution and, 47–48, 107; OLAS speech of, 1–2, 36; *Tricontinental* and, 8, 211; U.S. government and, 2, 83
Carriles, Luis Posada, 118, 190, 192, 259
Carter, Alprentice "Bunchy," 223, 308n84
Carter, Jimmy, 166–67, 169, 185–86, 298n55; administration of, 10, 22, 166–69, 170, 183, 185–86, 213
Casa de las Américas, 8, 64, 179–80, 238, 248, 300n88
Casa de los Extranjeros de Residentes, 140–41, 227, 228, 233, 310n135
Casal, Lourdes, 159, 160–62, 171, 299n67, 299n71, 300n88
Castro, Fidel: Africa and, 177; black freedom movement and, 82; Black radicals and, 15, 259–60; Carmichael and, 2, 114; communism and, 13–14; "Declaration of Santiago" and, 95; "the dialogue" and, 154, 170–71, 180, 182, 183–85; hijacking and, 124, 127, 145, 234; homosexuality and, 68; John Paul II and, 256; Maceo Brigade and, 154, 178–79, 180; political asylum and, 128, 202, 205–6, 260; racism and, 3, 61, 226; revolution tenth anniversary speech of, 31; scholarship and press on, 12, 17, 95; Shakur and, 259; Soviets and, 5, 104; U.S. relations and diplomacy and, 104, 166–67, 169–70, 182–87, 298n49, 299n61; Venceremos Brigades and sugar harvest and, 40, 40, 42–43, 44, 71, 92, 276n13, 278n57
Castro, Mariela, 266, 281n157
Castro, Ramón, 174, *178*
Castro, Raúl, 40, 260, 266, 297n38
Caucuses within work camps, 59–61, 99
Censorship, 5, 66, 136
Center for Cuban Studies, 10, 189, 194, 269, 284–85n52, 296n17
Center for Democracy in the Americas, 269
Central Committee of the Communist Party, 214, 238, 244, 311n145
Central Committee of Venceremos Brigades, 66
Centro Nacional de Educación Sexual (CENESEX), 266

Chesimard, JoAnne. *See* Shakur, Assata
Children of anticommunist Cubans seeking reconciliation, 10, 153–54, 159, 177–79
Chrisman, Robert, 72
Christian Evangelical Reformed Church, 159
Christians for Justice and Freedom, 158
Christie, Chris, 263
Chullima Riders Volunteer Workers Brigade, 39
Church, Frank, 167, 297n44
Church Committee hearings, 297n44
CIA, 116, 167; anti-Castro violence and, 161, 189, 190; "Cuba: Castro's Propaganda Apparatus and Foreign Policy" report of, 94; foreign subversion and, 9, 76, 78, 82–84, 94; investigations of, 24, 67, 100; Miami University station of, 109, 169; *Patterns of International Terrorism* report of, 251; sabotage campaigns of, 28, 109, 112; U.S. Left and, 76, 78–79; Venceremos Brigade and, 28, 46, 77, 100, 117
Cienfuegos, Osmani, 98
City College in New York, 260
Civil rights movement. *See* Black freedom movement
Clark, Mark, 209
Clarke, John Henrik, 15
Cleaver, Eldridge, 4, 110, 112; Black Panthers in Cuba and, 107–8, 293n82; exile profile of, 202, 221–26, 308n84; on hijacking, 137–38, 224; Oakland police shoot-out and, 221–22, 308n72, 308n74; *Soul on Fire*, 107, 222, 226; *Soul on Ice*, 131, 221, 225
Cleaver, Kathleen, 260, 308n84
Clinton administration, 254, 255
Clytus, John, 208
Cold War: Cuba and, 11, 12, 21, 150–51, 156, 203; foreign subversion and, 88; hijacking and, 125, 150–51; racial politics and, 23, 80; Reagan administration and, 196; Venceremos Brigade and, 28
Cole, Johnnetta, 71–72
Collazo, Oscar, 186
Collectivity, 5, 38–39, 41, 56, 93
Colombia, 258, 315n245
Comando Cero, 189
Comandos L, 138, 183

Comintern, 292n62
Comité Central (of Cuban communist party), 214, 238, 244, 311n145
Committee of 75, 183, 191
Committee on Foreign Relations, Senate, 115
Committee on Internal Security, U.S. House of Representatives, 90, 92, 129
Committees for the Defense of the Revolution (CDRs), 42, 44, 71, 140
Common, 239, 240, 261
Communism, 3, 13, 76, 93
Communist International, 292n62
Communist Party U.S.A. (CPUSA), 8, 10, 13–14, 19
Communities, Cuban American, 10–11, 158–59
Congo, Democratic Republic of, 97, 211
Congressional Black Caucus, U.S., 255
Congressional Research Service, 258–59
Constant, Emmanuel, 255
Contra Viento y Marea, 162, 163–64, 179–80
Convictions of anti-Castro terrorists, 192
Cooper, D. B., 143
Coordination of United Revolutionary Organizations, 117, 190
Costs of hijacking, 143–44
Counter Intelligence Program of FBI ("Cointelpro"), 78
Country Reports on Terrorism, 258, 315n244
Crews, Dwight Douglass, 91, 98–99
Criminology, 126
Critton, Patrick, 257
Crombet, Jaime, 42, 278n52
Crusade for Justice, 157
Cruse, Harold, 13, 15
Cuba: aid to foreign revolutions by, 108–10, 288n129; antihijacking Law No. 1226 of, 134, 145, 146, 207; current state of, 265–67, 270–71; demographics of, 176–77; economic reforms of, 270; as a haven to outlaws and political refugees, 127–28, 144, 205–6, 290–91n22; outmigration of, 177; as a revolution mecca, 7–8
Cuba: An American Tragedy (Zeitlin), 12
"Cuba: School for U.S. Radicals" (Beech and Greyer), 77, 116–17, 282n8
"Cuba and the American Negro" report, 86

Cuba Coordinating Committee (CCC), 229–30
Cubana de Aviación flight 455, 150, 190, 191, 192, 255, 259, 297n38
Cuban American, term of, 295n1
Cuban American Left. *See* Left, Cuban American
Cuban American National Foundation, 118
Cuban Communist Party, 113, 122, 237, 311n145
Cuban Institute for Friendship Among the People (ICAP), 16, 35, 97, 141; Cabrera and, 43–44; exiles and, 233, 238, 244; Maceo Brigade and, 174, 193, 194; Venceremos Brigades and, 29, 43, 57, 58, 60, 62, 66, 86, 99–100
Cuban Liberty and Democratic Solidarity (Liberated) Act, 253, 257
Cuban Mission to the United Nations, 101, 116–17, 119, 121, 190, 193
Cuban Refugee Adjustment Act, 125, 146, 148
Cuban Revolution: background and overview of, 2–8, 12–14, 20–21, 218; humanistic ethos of, 265; unfinished portions of, 266–67
Cuban Studies, 157
Cuban Studies/Estudios Cubanos, 158
Cuban Women Now (Randall), 63
Cuba-United States Memorandum of Understanding on Hijacking of Aircraft and Vessels and Other Offenses, 22, 24–25, 104, 125, 144–50, 166, 287n105, 297n38
Cuba Va, 70
Cuesta, Tony, 183, 184
Cultural Congress of Havana, 32
Cultural production, Cuban: black freedom movement and, 111, 207, 209–11, 212–13; gay liberation and, 67; revolution ideology and, 8, 85, 103, 274n35; U.S. dissidents and, *vi*, 209; Vietnam War and, 49–50. *See also* Media

Dalton, Cheri Laverne. *See* Abiodun, Nehanda Isoke
Daulatzai, Sohail, 156
Davidson, Carl, 32, 276n13
Davidson, Robert, 72

Davies, Carole Boyce, 88–89, 90
Davis, Angela, *vi*, 4, 19, 48, 51, 202, 209, 261, 278n73
Davis, Fania E., 73
Davis, Mike, 285n64
Day of Solidarity, 210
Debray, Régis, 113, 114
Declaration of Asylum, U.N., 133
"Declaration of Santiago," 95
Declaration of Territorial Asylum, U.N., 206–7
Decolonization, 2, 3, 7, 14, 201, 217
Defectors, U.S. military, 207, 305n28
De la Fuente, Alejandro, 72, 266
Dellinger, David, 32, 83
Dellums, Ronald V., 72
Democracy in Cuba, 71
Democracy promotion initiatives of U.S., 269
Democratic Party, 197
Détente in U.S.-Cuba relations, 10, 11, 154
De Zayas, Eduardo, 191
"Dialogue, the": background and overview of, 154, 165; backlash for, 188–92; Cuban readiness for, 170–71; FBI and, 195, 301n112, 303n156; Maceo Brigade and, 156, 180; meetings of, 180–83, 301n118; post meeting efforts and effects of, 183–87, 197, 301n113
Dialogueros, 159, 296n18
Díaz, Alvin Ross, 192
Díaz, Ariel Fernández, 250
Díaz, Pablo, 16
Díaz-Miranda, Mariano, 184
Diplomacy, U.S.-Cuba: hijacking and, 10, 22, 125, 126–27, 145–51, 149, 290n10; political asylum and, 201, 205, 230, 252–55, 263; political prisoners and, 185–86; reciprocity and, 22, 148, 185, 205, 294n113; U.S. Left and, 153, 156, 158–59, 165–66, 169–70, 182, 269; Venceremos Brigades and, 28, 70. *See also* Relations, U.S.-Cuba
Diplomatic exceptionalism, 29, 125, 147, 207, 208, 255
Directorio Revolucionario Estudiantil (DRE), 161, 296n26
Disillusionment with Cuba, 224, 225–26, 228, 230–31, 245, 270

Domínguez, Jorge, 145, 147, 168
Douglas, Emory, 210, 220
Dreke, Víctor, 109
Drug trade, Latin American, 194
Dunbar-Ortiz, Roxanne, 27, 39–40, 73
Dylan, Bob, 81

Eastland, James O., 75, 76, 77, 80, 86, 94, 122, 129
Economic reforms of Cuba, 270
Economist, The, 52
Educational Commission of Venceremos Brigades, 70–71
Elbaum, Max, 73
El Caimán Barbudo, 81
El Conjunto Folklórico Nacional de Cuba, 37, 243–44
El Diario-LaPrensa, 186
Electoral participation, 71
Ellison, Ella Mae, 211
El Salvador, 21, 23, 73, 87
Embargo, trade. *See* Trade embargo
Émigrés, Cuban: Cuba portrayal of, 140, 154, 177, 182; "the dialogue" and, 180–81, 184, 188; extradition and, 253–55; hijacking and, 146, 148; political homogeneity facade of, 155, 158, 164–65; reconciliation seeking children of, 10, 153–54, 159, 177–79; as refugees, 125. *See also* Left, Cuban American
Emulation, 38, 41, 93
Encounter groups, 68
Entitlement, 267
Escartín, Ricardo, 174
Escobar, Jiménez, 116
Escuela Latinoamericana de Medicina (ELAM), 249, 270
Escuela Superior del Patido, 237
Espín, Mariela Castro, 266, 281n157
Espín, Vilma, 246
Espinosa, Manuel, 159, 180, 296n18
Espionage, 9; by American-borns, 118–20; anti-Castro organizations and, 117, 118; Black Panther Party and, 24; by Cuban-borns, 116; Cuban Mission to the U.N. and, 116–17; Maceo Brigade and, 195–96; U.S. convictions for, 117–18; Venceremos Brigades and, 84–85, 99, 115–18, 120–21, 196, 289n176
Esquivel, José Dionisio Suárez, 192
Essence, 240
Ethiopia, 102, 107, 168, 185, 251
Exile groups, Cuban, 117, 118, 154. *See also specific groups*
Exile profiles: of Abiodun, 221, 242–51; of Brent, 221, 226–31; of Cleaver, 221–26, 308n84; of Finney and Hill, 221, 231–35, 310n127, 310n139; overview of, 220–21, 308n70; of Shakur, 220–21, 236–42, 311n145, 311n151, 311n153
Exiles. *See* Asylum, political; Émigrés, Cuban; Exile groups, Cuban; Exile profiles; Extradition; *specific exiles*
Expatriates voluntarily living in Cuba, 227, 304–5n16
Expo Cuba, 189
Extradition: of American fugitives, 22, 200–201, 252–54, 256–63, 314n218, 314n226, 314nn228–29; of foreign fugitives, 192, 234, 314n218
Eyes of the Rainbow (Rolando), 239

Fair Play for Cuba Committee (FPCC), 13, 15, 18–19, 38, 47, 74, 80–81, 165
Fanon, Frantz, 151, 211
FBI, 24, 46, 75, 118, 205; Abiodun and, 242–43; Black Panther Party and, 105–6, 107; Brent and, 227–29; charges of U.S. Left-Cuba ties by, 9, 24, 76, 86–87, 92–94, 105, 282n7; Cointelpro and, 78; "the dialogue" and, 192, 301n112; guerrilla arming and training and, 98–103; Maceo Brigade and, 154, 172, 175, 192–96, 295n3, 302n146, 303n156; Shakur and, 199–200, 204, 237, 259, 261, 262, 311n150; Venceremos Brigades and, 58, 78–80, 84–90, 92, 98–99, 106, 120
Federación de Mujeres Cubanas (FMC), 71, 246–47
Federal Aviation Administration, 144
Feminism: Abiodun and Shakur and, 204, 239–40, 243, 246–47; Cuban women and, 63–65; Venceremos Brigades and, 62, 74
F4 Commandos, 117, 118
Fidel (Landau), 33, 92

55 Hermanos, 175, 191
Fighters in foreign theaters, American, 102–3, 106–7, 130
Final Call, The, 239
Finney, Michael, 291–92n50, 293n78, 293n85; exile profile of, 221, 231–35, 258; hijacking and shooting incident and, 96, 310n127, 310n139
Five, The, 118
Florida International University poll, 188
FMC (Federación de Mujeres Cubanas), 71, 246–47
Foco theory of revolution, 113
Ford, Gerald, 168
Ford administration, 150, 166, 211–13, 251
Foreign Affairs, 168
Foreign Influence — Weather Underground Organization report (FBI), 101, 105, 120, 282n7
Foreign subversion in U.S.: Africa and, 96–98; African Americans and Black Panther Party and, 106–8, 113–14; CIA scandals and, 82–84; Cuban goal of U.S. disruption and, 109–11, 114, 288n146; guerrilla arming and training and, 94–96, 98–103, 107–8, 114; overview of, 75–80; propaganda and, 80–82, 85–94; Venceremos Brigade and, 84–85; Weather Underground and, 105
Fountain Valley Massacre, 252
Franks, Robert, 254
Free and Equal (Cannon and Cole), 71–72
Free Breakfast for School Children Program, 107
Freedom of Information Act, 58, 80
Fuentes, Rick, 240
Fuerzas Armadas de Liberación Nacional Puertorriqueña (FALN), 168, 218–19, 260, 304n16, 307n69

Gaines, Kevin, 14
García, Raúl Roa, 190, 192
Garland, Phyl, 72
Garrett, Scott, 261
Gates, Henry Louis, 108, 138
Gay Liberation Movement, 67
Gender: Cuban inequality of, 6, 63–65, 266, 268; Venceremos Brigades and, 62–65

General Directorate of Intelligence (DGI), 115–16, 120, 121, 193–95, 289n176
Gerena, Víctor Manuel, 219, 259, 304n16
Ghana, 14, 128
Ginsberg, Allen, 13, 66, 67
Gitlin, Todd, 17, 32, 54
Gleijeses, Piero, 107, 109, 203
Goals of book, 20–23
Gómez, Andrés, 195, 197
Gómez, Manolo, 175
González, Alejandro, 255
González, Corky, 157
González, Israel P., 133
González, Juan, 307–8n69
González, Reinol, 185
González-Pando, Miguel, 185
Goodwin, Ralph Lawrence, 232, 233, 293n85
Goodwin, Richard, 127
Gorman, Cleo, 51
Gosse, Van, 12, 127, 130
Gott, Richard, 7
Government of Fulgencio Batista, 205
Govin, Hugo, 57, 58, 60, 99–100, 278n65
Graham, William White, 132–33, 141
Granma: black freedom movement and, 208–9, 211, 213–14, 217; gender and, 65; Kent State University killings and, 81–82; Venceremos Brigade and, 27–28, 42, 59, 60, 63, 100–101, 275n2, 278n52
Granma International, 170, 177, 213, 299n61
Grant, Farland Jesus, 292n67
Grathwohl, Larry, 101–2
Gray period, 6
Greyer, Georgie Ann, 77, 282n8
Griffin, Farah Jasmine, 267–68
Guantánamo, U.S. Naval Base in, 146
Guardian, The, 160, 184
Guatemala, 21, 73, 103, 109
Guerra, Lillian, 67
Guerrilla arming and training: Black Panther Party and, 107–8, 222; CIA and FBI accusations of, 94–96, 98–103, 114
Guerrilla training camp, 98
Guerrilleros de Bolivia "millionaire brigade," 39
Guevara, Ernesto "Che": collectivity and, 38–39; death of, 104, 111–12; doctrine of, 112, 113; Guatemala and, 109; hijacking

and, 127; "Message to the Tricontinental," 109–10; quotes of, 27, 75; on revolution in U.S., 115; sugarcane harvest and, 40; U.S. Left and, 17–18, 127; Vietnam War and, 79
Guinea-Bissau, 96–97, 107, 211
Guthrie, Woodie, 81

Hairstyles, natural, 139, 223, 308n85
Hall, Gus, 13–14
Hampton, Fred, 209
Hansen, Michael Lynn, 132, 138
Harrington, Stephanie, 115
Havana Libre hotel, 32, 131
Hayden, Tom, 17, 32, 117, 276n13, 287n126, 305n28
Health care, 4, 63, 71, 92, 270
Helms, Jesse, 115
Helms-Burton Act, 253, 257
Hernandez, Gerardo, 118
Hernández, Valentín, 192
Herrera, Pablo, 249–50
Hijack House, 140–41, 227, 228, 233, 310n135
Hijacking: black liberation organizations and, 96, 134–36; Brent and, 226–27; Cleaver and, 224; costs of, 143–44; Critten and, 257, 313n217; Cuba as a haven and, 127–28; Cuban national security and, 133–34, 291–92n50; Cuban treatment of those who commit, 137–42, 144, 145, 202, 207, 252, 292n67, 293n80, 304n16; diplomacy and, 144–51, 294n113; espionage and, 135; by foreigners, 129–30, 291n33; global solidarity and, 142; negotiating power of, 131–32; for overthrown Batista government exiles, 205; overview of, 10, 22, 24–25, 114, 123–27, 289–90nn1-2; people who commit, characteristics of, 123–24, 126–27, 131, 151; Potts and, 252; pre-1968, 127; press coverage of, 130–31, 149; ransom for, 143–44, 148, 297n39; return of planes from, 147–48, 205, 294n113; scholarship on, 126, 290n10, 290n13, 290n17; as social protests, 132–33; U.S. acceptance of from Cuba, 146–48
Hill, Charles, 96, 142, 217–18, 291–92n50, 293n76, 308n85; exile profile of, 221, 231–35, 236, 310n127, 310n139
Hilliard, David, 134–35, 222, 226

Hinds, Lennox, 306n47
Hip-hop, 239–40, 245, 249–50, 261, 312n167
Hobsbawm, Eric, 151, 295n123
Holden, Robert T., 289n1
Holy Family Church, 191
Homosexuality, 6, 65–68, 74, 247–48, 250, 271, 281n157
Hoover, J. Edgar, 105, 116, 287n115
Horne, Lena, 81
House Congressional Resolution 254, 254–55
Howell, Ron, 237, 307n65
Hubbard, Stanley, 133
Huberman, Leo, 12
Hughes, Bernard, 62
Human Events, 90
Human rights, 4, 133, 169–70, 186, 211–13, 250, 256, 299n61
"Human rights in U.S. prisons?," 211
Hurwitch, Robert A., 103, 144–45, 150
Hutchings, Phil, 211
Hutton, Bobby, 221
Huỳnh Văn Ba, 54

"I Ain't Singing Charlie or What to Do When the FBI Calls" pamphlet, 88
ICAP. *See* Cuban Institute for Friendship Among the People (ICAP)
Identity: Cuban, 34, 49, 172, 201–2; politics of, 57, 102; Venceremos Brigades and, 68; youth émigrés and, 159–60
Imaginaries: African American political, 239, 240; Cuban internationalist, 203; Cuban nationalist, 3, 172; Cuba outlaw mystique, 24; of U.S. radicals, 6, 7, 8, 14–15, 20, 29, 245, 265, 270
Immigration and Nationality Act, 86
Immigration policy, Cuban, 137
Immigration policy, U.S., 86, 125, 148
Imperialism, 105, 111, *111*
Incarcerations, U.S., 169–70, 208, 211, *212*, 214, 299n61, 306n47
Individualism, 5, 34, 55, 56
Indoctrination, 24, 114
Institute for Policy Studies, 269
Instituto Cubano de Amistad con los Pueblos (ICAP). *See* Cuban Institute for Friendship Among the People (ICAP)

Instituto Cubano del Arte e Industria Cinematográficos (ICAIC), 174–75
Instituto de Estudios Cubanos, 158, 171
Intelligence: American-born agents for, 118–20; anti-Castro organizations and, 117–18; DGI and, 116–17, 120, 289n176; Maceo Brigades and, 193–96; provided by Cubans, 118; Venceremos Brigades and, 115–16, 117. *See also* Espionage
Inter-American Affairs Subcommittee of U.S. House of Representatives, 103, 144–45, 150
Interests Sections, 167, 174, 228, 259
Internal colony thesis, 59, 110, 137, 201, 292n62
Internal Security Subcommittee of U.S. Senate, 86, 110, 120, 121, 168
"International Connections of U.S. Peace Groups" report (CIA), 83–87, 283n25
Internationalism: African Americans and, 106–7; Black Panther Party and, 106, 287n119; Cuba and, 4–5, 49, 108–10, 203, 225, 240, 288n129, 288n146; foreign subversion in U.S. and, 78, 79; political asylum and, 201; Tricontinental Conference and, 7; U.S. Left and, 30, 201, 237–38; Venceremos Brigade and, 30
Internationalist iconography, 8
International Women's Day, 64
Iraq, 258

Jackson, George, 82, 210, 213
Jackson, Jimmie Lee, 208
Jacobs, John, 122
James, C. L. R., 201–2
James, Joy, 205, 239–40
Jameson, Fredric, 13
Jehovah's Witnesses, 6
Jiménez, Cha Cha, 157
JMWAVE, 169
John Paul II (pope), 254, 256, 314n236
Johnson, Raymond, 139–40, 224, 292n67, 293n76
Johnson administration, 45
Jones, Claudia, 89, 90
Jones, Jeff, 116–17
Jones, LeRoi, 15–16, 47, 215, 278n70. *See also* Baraka, Amiri

Jordan, Fania, 48
José Martí Mausoleum, *178*
Joseph, Peniel E., 307n69
Joven Cuba, 159–60, 171
Julio Antonio Mella International Camp, 171, 174
Juventud Rebelde, 103, 279n79

Karenga, Maulana, 231
Kastner, Jamie, 314n218
Kazin, Michael, 73, 98
Kean, Sean T., 261
Kennedy, John F., 45, 127
Kennedy administration, 28
Kent State University killings, 81–82, 163
KGB, 116
KGB Connections, The, 289n176
King, Martin Luther, Jr., 105, 215, 216, 265
Kissinger, Henry, 103, 115, 145–46, 147, 166, 297n46
Kochiyama, Yuri, 73
Kornbluh, Peter, 109
Kouri, Raúl Roa, 81
Kozol, Jonathan, 51
Kunstler, William, 252

LaBeet, Ishmael, 252, 313–14n218
Landau, Saul, 33, 92
"La Policía me Hirió," 208
La Reunion de Residentes Norteamericanos, 227
Latin American School of Medicine (ELAM), 249, 270
Latin American Studies Association, 167, 297n46
Law No. 1226 of Cuba, antihijacking, 134, 145, 146, 207
Lawrence Hill Books, 237, 311n151
Lazo, Jesús, 192
Lebrón, Lolita, 186
Left, Cuban American: demographics of, 159, 296n19; emergence of, 158–65; overview of, 153–58. *See also* Antonio Maceo Brigade
Left, U.S.: Cuban influence on, 8, 14, 76–77; Cuban relationship with, 5, 6, 19, 221, 263, 268–70; current concerns with Cuba of, 271–72; federal government and, 78–79,

97; view of Cuban revolution of, 6–7, 12. *See also specific groups of*
Lekus, Ian, 66
LeoGrande, William M., 109
Letelier, Orlando, 190, 192
Levine, Robert, 183, 186, 188, 295–96n8
Levinson, Sandra, 68, 70, 189
Life magazine, 32
"Life Worse in Cuba, Unhappy Black Panthers Wail" article, 139
Lincoln Detox Center, 243
Listen, Yankee: The Revolution in Cuba (Mills), 12, 95
Lockwood, Lee, 123, 223, 308n84, 309n97
Long Island Press, 77, 116–17, 282n8
Long Time Gone (Brent), 199, 229, 230, 253, 292n56
Lorie, Jorge Roblejo, 180
Los Angeles, Calif., gay harassment in, 67–68
Los Angeles Police Department, 27
Los Angeles Times, 234, 298n49
Los Macheteros, 168, 218, 304n16
Louie, Miriam Ching, 49, 53–54
Luis Arcos Bergnes, 36, 46, 55
Lumumba, Patrice, 211
Lunes de Revloución, 211

Maceitos, 179
Maceo, Antonio, 164, 172–73, 174, 223–24
Maceo Brigade. *See* Antonio Maceo Brigade
Macheteros, 168, 218, 304n16
Machín, Gustavo, 263
Madruga, Salvador, 185, 188
Malcolm X, 14–15, 231, 240, 274n34
Malcolm X Grassroots Movement (MXGM), 239, 249
Marable, Manning, 239, 312n160
Mariel emigration crisis, 177
Mariña, Claudio Rey, 287n109
Márquez, Gabriel García, 256
Marti, José, 3, 153, 172, 223
Martin, Bradford, 196
Martínez, Elizabeth Sutherland, 9, 14, 47, 73, 210
Martínez, Isidro, 41–42
Martínez, Milagros, 158
Martin Luther King Labor Center, 189

Marxism, 13, 73, 76, 92, 93, 102
Masculinist body politic of Cuba, 6
Massiah, Louis, 16
Matthews, Herbert, 17, 129
Maurer, Harry, 56–57
Mayfield, Julian, 14, 15
McCarran-Walter Act, 89
McGovern, George, 166–67, 297n38, 297n41
McKinley, William, 54
McKinney, Diane, 228, 309n113
McManus, Jane, 142, 227, 305n16
McNamara, Robert, 51
Media: African Americans and, 217; Black Panther Party and, 226–27; Cuban émigrés and, 140; Cuban Revolution and, 18; "the dialogue" and, 188, 301n118; hijackers and, 139, 140, 293n78; human rights and, 170; international revolution and, 94, 103; U.S. exiles and, 253; U.S. social movements and, 2, 27–28, 81–82, 207–15, 305n30; Venceremos Brigades and, 9, 27–28, 39, 55–56, 277n38; Vietnam War and, 49, 278–79n79. *See also specific newspapers and magazines*
Medical diplomacy of Cuba, 269–70
Medical experimentation, 208, 211
Medical supplies to Cuba, 169, 298n60
Meeks, Ira, 228, 309n113
Mena, Fernando, 184–85
Menendez, Robert, 255, 263
"Message to the Tricontinental" (Guevara), 79, 109–10, 112
Mexico, 32, 45–46, 176, 289n1, 304n16
Miami, political violence in, 189
Miami Herald, 139, 140, 187, 296n19
Miami News, 301n118
Milanés, Pablo, 209, 261
Militant, The, 35
Military units to aid production labor camps, 6, 66, 281n151
Mills, C. Wright, 12, 95
Mills, Leroy, 48–49
Ministry of the Interior, Cuban, 173, 223
Miranda, Rafael Cancel, 186
Moffitt, Ronni, 190
Montes, Ana Belén, 118
Morales, William Guillermo, 219, 259, 260, 304n16

Morality drives, 66
Mos Def, 239, 250, 260
"Most Wanted Terrorists" list, 204, 261, 262
Motorcycle Diaries, The (Guevara), 18
Move, 258, 315n247
Movement, The, 93
Movimento Popular de Libertaçãi de Angola (MPLA), 71, 97, 168
Movimiento Pro Independencia, 69
Muhammad, Nisa Islam, 239
Muñiz Varela, Carlos, 154, 190–91, 197
Murray, George, 111, 112, 211, 217, 226
Myers, Kendall and Gwendolyn S., 118–20
My Lai Massacre, 279n79

Namibia, 3, 203, 251
Nation, The, 56–57
National Committee of Students for a Democratic Society, 32
National Committee of Venceremos Brigades, 33, 34, 59, 61, 66, 69, 73
National Conference of Black Lawyers, 213, 306n47
National Congress of Black Lawyers, 97
National Endowment for Democracy, 247
Nationalism, black, 3, 135, 136, 225, 246
Nationalism, Cuban, 3, 136–37, 172, 223
National Lawyers Guild, 88
National Liberation Army (ELN), 258, 315n245
National Liberation Army of Vietnam, 100
National Mobilization Committee to End the War in Vietnam, 83
Native Americans, 48–49
NBC News, 124
Negrín, Eulalio José, 154, 191–92
Neto, Agostinho, 97
New Jersey State Police, 240, 252, 254, 260, 261, 262, 311n150
New Jersey turnpike shooting, 11, 25, 199, 303n3, 306n47
New Left, 13–14, 17–18, 21, 30, 35, 66. *See also* Students for a Democratic Society (SDS); Venceremos Brigade
New Mexico State police officer shooting, 232, 234, 310n127
New Nigerian, 97

Newsday, 200, 237, 253, 307n65
Newton, Huey P.: Brent and, 142, 292n56; internationalism and, 106; political asylum of, 4, 107, 202; as a political prisoner, 212, 226–27, 287n119; *Tricontinental* and, 111, 211; Venceremos Brigade and, 35
New York Amsterdam News, 175, 199–200
New York Daily News, 2
New York Times: advertisements in, 18, 80–81; anti-Castro violence and, 189, 296n26; articles sympathetic to Cuba in, 16, 17; Castro interview in, 129; on CIA and FBI, 82–83, 101, 102; on Cuban intelligence, 120; on hijacking, 143; on Shakur, 199; Walker and, 16; on WUO, 101, 102
Nguyen Miah Phoung, 100
Nguyen Thi Dinh, 106
Nguyễn Văn Trỗi, 51
Nicaragua, 21, 23, 89, 104, 196, 251
Nichamin, Julie, 34, 93, 95–96, 105, 285n61
Nieves, Luciano, 191, 192
Nixon, Richard, 67, 80, 287n105
Nixon administration, 82, 150, 166
Nkrumah, Kwame, 128
Nodarse-Pérez, María, 165
Normalization of U.S.-Cuba relations: Carter administration and, 10, 166–69, 170; Cuban Americans and, 10–11, 158, 159, 165, 296n19; "the dialogue" and, 184; Helms-Burton Act and, 253; Maceo Brigade and, 155, 173, 176, 193; Obama administration and, 261; political asylum and, 11, 25; Shakur and, 201, 263; trend favoring, 25, 197, 269
Northwest Airlines, 143
No Safe Haven in Cuba Act, 257
Now (Álvarez), 81
Nuestra América Brigade, 141, 233

Oakland police shoot-out, 221–22, 308n72, 308n74
OAS (Organization of American States), 46, 115, 147
Obama, Barack, 263
Obama administration, 261–62
Obsesión, 249
Ochs, Phil, 86
Oglesby, Carl, 32–33, 276n15

OLAS (Organization of Latin American Solidarity), 1–2, 36, 47
Olatunji, Fela. *See* Hill, Charles
Old Left, 12, 13–14, 282n7
Olguín, Ben V., 73, 260–61
Omega 7, 154, 189–90, 191, 295n4
Only the People Can Perform Miracles, 71
On the Ten Millions Trail, 8, 42
Open spaces classes, 247–48
Operation Pedro Pan, 179
Optimism, 242
Organization of American States (OAS), 46, 115, 147
Organization of Latin American Solidarity (OLAS), 1–2, 36, 47
Organization of Solidarity with the People of Asia, Africa, and Latin America (OSPAAAL): civil rights movement and, 82; conferences of, 112, 217, 226; cultural production of, 8, 85, 111, 209–10, 212–13, 220; Guevara and, 79; sexuality and, 67–68. See also *Tricontinental*
Organized protest ban in Cuba, 247
Ortega, Juanito, 99
Ortiz, Antulio Ramírez, 127
OSPAAAL. *See* Organization of Solidarity with the People of Asia, Africa, and Latin America (OSPAAAL)
Oswald, Lee Harvey, 18
Oughten, Diana, 101
Outlaw Woman (Dunbar-Ortiz), 27
Overview of book, 19–26

Padilla, Herberto, 6
Palenque, Cuba as a, 25, 201, 202, 240
Pan-Africanists, U.S., 15, 125–26
"Para las chicas Cubanas" (Griffin), 267–68
Parodi, Rámon Sánchez, 167, 171
Pastors for Peace, 242
Patria Es Humanidad, 203
Patterns of International Terrorism report, 251
Payments to hijackers, 143–44, 148, 297n39
Pedraza, Silvia, 299n71
Pensamiento Crítico, 210
Penza, Ralph, 254
Peoples Committee for Solidarity with American People, South Vietnamese, 110
People's Movement for the Liberation of Angola (MPLA), 71, 97, 168
Pepper, Claude, 90
Pérez, Louis A., 8, 38, 147
Pérez-Stable, Marifeli, 157, 162, 165
Pilot strike threat, 124, 143
Piñeiro, Manuel, 305n16
Pinochet, Augusto, 190
Policy, Cuban foreign, 103, 112–14, 133, 167–68, 196, 203, 251–52
Policy on Cuba, U.S.: hijacking and, 145, 147, 150–51; immigration and, 125, 207; Maceo Brigade and, 196; overview of, 22; political exiles and, 253–54, 257–58; state sponsored terror and, 103–4; on travel, 28–29, 45; Venceremos Brigade and, 28, 73
Political asylum. *See* Asylum, political
Poll on "the dialogue," 188
"Por Qué Antonio Maceo," 172–73
Port Huron Statement of SDS, 18
Potts, Williams, 252, 306n61, 313n217
Prairie Fire, 105
Prashad, Vijay, 109
Prensa Latina, 72, 177
Preyer, Richardson, 99
Prisoners, release of political, 165–66, 169–70, 180–86, 187, 234, 298n59, 306n47
Prison population, U.S., 169–70, 208, 211, 212, 214, 299n61
Profiles of exiles. *See* Exile profiles
Progressive Labor Party, 19
Propaganda, Cuban: Maceo Brigade and, 194; revolutionary, 50–53; U.S. foreign subversion and, 80–82, 85, 92–94, 95–96, 111
Protest of Baraguá, 172, 173
Provisional Revolutionary Government of the Republic of South Vietnam, 100, 106
Public education campaigns of Venceremos Brigades, 92
Puerto Rican Caucus of Venceremos Brigades, 59
Puerto Rican Socialist Party, 41, 97
Puerto Rico: Cuban émigrés in, 177–79; independence movement of, 153, 156, 168, 186, 191, 218–19; Maceo Brigade and, 154–55
Pulido, Laura, 17, 59

Queen Mother Moore, 231

Racial climate of Cuba, 223, 225
Racial equality: Cuba and, 23, 61, 136, 241–42, 268, 271; hijackers and, 140; Maceo Brigade and, 171–72
Racial war of 1912, 161
Racism: in Cuba, 2–3, 61, 71, 136, 245–47, 266; Cuba as a sanctuary from, 128, 291n25. *See also* Racial equality
"Racistas contra la Religión, 208
Radical Education Project, 83
Radicalism, U.S.: black, 201, 215, 239, 306n54; Cuban influence on, 9, 45, 76–77; foreign subversion and, 80, 94; Maceo Brigade and, 171, 193; overview of, 12–19; political asylum and, 263; Venceremos Brigade and, 49, 74, 86. *See also specific radical people and groups*
Radicalization of Cuban Americans, 162–64
Radical orientalism, 55
Radio Free Dixie (Williams), 8, 222, 232
Radio Havana Cuba: Brent and, 142, 227; Finney and, 235; programs for North American allies, 8, 42, 222, 232; Shakur and, 238; Venceremos Brigades and, 42, 100, 102, 277n50
Ramparts, 8, 27
Randall, Margaret, 41, 61, 63, 64–65, 89, 284n48, 309n108
Ransom to hijackers, 143–44, 148, 297n39
Rap music, 239–40, 245, 249–50, 261, 312n167
Ratner, Michael, 73, 255
Reagan administration, 11, 196, 230, 251–52
"Rebels of the Sierra Maestra," 130
Reconciliation with Cuban Government. *See* Normalization of U.S.-Cuba relations
Recruitment by Venceremos Brigade, 37–38, 48, 69
Rediker, Marcus, 151
Regla de Ochá, 233–34
Reitan, Ruth, 108, 112, 113, 290n13
Relations, U.S.-Cuba: under Carter administration, 154, 166–69, 297n38; under Clinton administration, 256–57; Cold War and, 21–22; "the dialogue" and, 185–86; under George W. Bush Administration, 258; political asylum and, 201, 204, 304n15; political prisoner release and, 165–66; U.S. radicals and, 269. *See also* Détente in U.S.-Cuba relations; Diplomacy, U.S.-Cuba; Normalization of U.S.-Cuba relations
Relations between Cuba and the Cuban diaspora, 186
Religion in Cuba, 256
Religious organizations, 158–59
Reproductive rights, 65
Republican Party, 10, 196–97
Republic of New Afrika (RNA), 96, 137, 200, 202, 231–32, 249, 257
Revolutionary Action Movement, 19
Revolution in America, 215–20, 306n54
Reyes, Manolo, 92, 98–99
Richardson, Bill, 291–92n50
Risech, Flavio, 176
Rizo, Julian, 41, 53, 58
Roa, Raúl, 42, 81
Robaina, Tomás Fernández, 109, 248, 263, 288n146
Rodríguez, Alexey, 249
Rodríguez, Carlos Rafael, 32–33
Rodríguez, Dylan, 204
Rodríguez, Félix García, 190, 192
Rodríguez, Irving Flores, 186
Rodríguez, Silvio, 209
Rodríguez-Trías, Helen, 72
Rogers, William, 96–97, 143
Rojas, Rafael, 67
Rolando, Gloria, 239
Romero, Virgilio Paz, 192
Rubin, James, 314n226
Rubin, Jerry, 83
Rubio, Rubén Batista, 82
Ruckert, Pat, 54
Rudd, Mark, 116–17

Sadiki, Kamau, 311n147
Sale, Kirkpatrick, 14, 68
Sampol, Guillermo Novo, 192
Sanchez, Sonia, 239
Sanctuary, political. *See* Asylum, political
Sandinista Front for National Liberation (FSLN), 251
Sandinista Revolution, 21, 104, 251
Saney, Isaac, 203

San Francisco police shoot-out, 134–35
Santamaria, Haydée, 64–65
Santería, 233–34
Sawyer, Mark Q., 136
Scheer, Robert, 12
Scholarship: on BLA and FALN, 307n69; on Cuban Revolution, 78, 157, 158; on hijacking, 126, 290n10, 290n13, 290n17; Maceo Brigade and, 155, 156, 197, 295–96nn7–8; on social movements, 20
Schoultz, Lars, 103, 147
Seale, Bobby, 106, 223, 226, 287n119
Seeger, Pete, 81
Segal, Louis, 50
Segregation, 1, 71, 128, 136
Self, Robert O., 105
Self-determination, 3, 7, 14, 28, 34, 50, 203, 298n55
79 primaveras (Álvarez), 49–50
Sex economy of Cuba, underground, 268
Sexual equality, 266
Sexuality, 65, 67, 247. *See also* Homosexuality
Shabazz, Betty, 231
Shakur, Afeni, 242, 312n166
Shakur, Assata, 219, 253, 303n5, 307n65, 312n166; *Assata: An Autobiography*, 199, 237, 311n151, 311nn154–55; current hiding and bounty of, 204, 240, 259–60, 261, 262, 315n251; exile profile of, 200–205, 219, 220–21, 236–42, 241, 311n145, 311n151, 311n153; extradition and, 200–201, 252–56, 258–59, 263; *Granma* on, 213–14; New Jersey turnpike shooting and, 25, 254, 303n3, 306n47; prison break of, 199–200, 303n2
Shakur, Tupac, 204, 239, 242, 312n166
Shoot-down of Cessna aircrafts, 253
Sierra Maestra Hotel shelling, 161, 296n26
Situation Information Report of CIA, 84, 283n34
Skyjacker's Tale, The (Kastner), 314n218
Skyjacking. *See* Hijacking
Sky marshals, 127, 144
Slavery as a metaphor, 240–41
Smith, Robert, 117
Social banditry, 151
Socialism, Cuban, 4, 16, 62, 63, 242, 266–67, 271

Socialist Workers Party (SWP), 8, 35
Soldini, Donald, 130
Solidarity travel, 38, 47, 69, 70, 172
Somalia, 168
Somoza, Anastasio, 251
"Song for Assata, A" (Common), 240, 261
Sontag, Susan, 54, 281n151
Soul on Fire (Cleaver), 107, 222, 226
Soul on Ice (Cleaver), 131, 221, 225
Soul Students Advisory Council, 19
Southern Airways, 143, 148
Soviet Union: Africa and, 168–69, 298n55; break up of, 252; Cold War doctrine of, 108–9; Cuba and, 5, 13, 32, 67, 112, 113; DGI and, 116
Spanish Civil War, 102
Spartanburg Herald, 309n112
Special Period, 230, 234, 235, 253, 271
Spies. *See* Espionage
Stanford, Max, 19
Stanton, Jacquelyn, 72
State sponsors of terrorism: Cuba as, 11, 25, 204, 230, 251, 257, 258–59, 313n212; U.S. as, 103–4
Stone, Richard, 115
Student Nonviolent Coordinating Committee (SNCC), 1, 4, 7–8, 33, 79, 89, 117, 216
Student Revolutionary Directorate, 161, 296n26
Students for a Democratic Society (SDS): background and overview of, 7–8, 14, 18; CIA and FBI and, 76, 83, 84, 100; Cuban Mission to U.N. and, 116–17; Venceremos Brigade and, 27–28, 32–34, 129, 276n13, 276n15
Sugar, 31–32
Sugar harvest: SDS and, 32; Venceremos Brigades and, 27, 29, 36, 36–43, 40, 44, 50, 56, 62–63
Sun, The, 131
Sun Sentinel, 259
Surveillance: by CIA, 82; of Maceo Brigade, 193; of Venceremos Brigades, 46, 78, 79–80, 88, 90, 121, 283n14
Survival of the American Indian Association, 48
Sweezy, Paul, 12

Taber, Robert, 130
Talmadge, Herman, 115
Tania La Guerrillera, 39, 277n37
Tanzania, 307n67
Tarnoff, Peter, 186
Telephone directories, 121
10 million tons harvest. *See* Sugar harvest
Terrorism: accusations of Venceremos Brigades of, 98, 100; anti-Castro, 104, 188–92; Carriles and, 118; defined, 289n165; list of accused committers of, 260, 261, 262; political asylum and, 204; war on, 204, 258, 262. *See also* Hijacking; State sponsors of terrorism
Theft in work camps, 57, 58
"Theory and Practice of Communism" hearings, 90, 98–99
"Third World: Our World" (Carmichael), 211
Third World Caucus of Venceremos Brigade, 61
Third World Left, U.S., 14, 33, 37–38, 47, 74, 156–57, 172
Third World revolution, 14, 20, 30, 92, 156, 218, 251
Third World Women's Alliance, 74, 89
Tietchen, Todd, 87, 274n35
Time magazine, 130–31
Torrado, Osvaldo Dorticós, 110–11
Torres, María de los Ángeles, 155–56, 158, 295n7, 301n113
Totalitarianism, 13
To The Point, 96
Tourism, Cuban, 167, 187, 256, 271, 298n47
Trade embargo: activists and, 269; "the dialogue" and, 184, 185; diplomacy and, 10, 167, 169, 253, 297n38, 298n49; hijacking and, 143; Maceo Brigade and, 173, 176; propaganda and, 85; Venceremos Brigades and, 28, 44, 70, 92
Trading with the Enemy Act, 28–29
Training, guerrilla. *See* Guerrilla arming and training
Training of anti-Castro exiles, U.S., 94, 95
Transformational power of travel to Cuba, 46–49
Travel to Cuba: American activists', 7, 24, 32, 69; by exiles for "the dialogue," 187; as a threat to U.S. security, 9; U.S. ban on, 4, 27, 28–29, 44, 45, 85–86, 166–67; Venceremos Brigades and, 46–47, 48–49, 69, 74, 278n69
Tricontinental, 8, 52, 69, 103; Black Panthers and, 111; Carmichael in, 2, 8; coverage of U.S. social movements by, 81, 156–57, 207, 210–11, 215–16; Guevara and, 79; homosexuality and, 67, 68; satire in, 52, 52; Venceremos Brigades and, 69
Tricontinental Conference of 1966, 7, 79
Tri-Continental Information Center, 83
Tropical Marxism, 13
Trujillo, Rafael, 127
Tuller, Bryce, 132–33, 138, 141, 148
Tuller, Charles A., 132–33, 138, 141, 148
Tuller, Jonathan, 132–33, 138, 141, 148
Tuller gang, 132–33, 138, 141, 148
Turquino, 69, 89
Tuskegee syphilis experiments, 211

Unidades Militares de Ayuda a la Producción, 6, 66, 281n151
Unión de Escritores y Artistas de Cuba (UNEAC), 248
United African Alliance Community Center, 307n67
United Nations: Cuban Mission to, 101, 116–17, 119, 121, 190, 193; human rights and, 28, 133, 206
U.S.-Cuba relations. See Relations, U.S.-Cuba
U.S. Third World Left, 14, 33, 37–38, 47, 74, 156–57, 172
Universal Declaration of Human Rights, U.N., 28, 133, 206
University of Havana, 13, 43–44, 296n17

Values of Cuban revolutionaries, 5
Vance, Cyrus, 166, 297n41
Venceremitos, 179
Venceremos, 70
Venceremos Brigade, 36, 40, 87; background and overview of, 8–9, 10, 23–24, 27–31, 72–74, 129; building of, 31–36, 276n15; challenges of, 56–58, 68; espionage and, 115–16, 117, 118, 120–21, 196, 289n176; FBI and, 58, 78–80, 84–90, 92, 98–99, 106,

120; financing of, 81, 194–95; foreign subversion in U.S. and, 75–76, 77–78, 84–85, 283n34; gender and, 62–65; global revolution and, 49–55, 97, 98, 100; guerrilla arming and training and, 94, 98–99; as guests of Cuba, 44–45; Guevara and, 79; homosexuals and, 65–68; impact and legacy of, 43–44, 68–69, 73–74; labor and, 36–44; PAIGC and, 96–97; print culture of, 69–72, 89–90, 91–92; public education campaigns of, 92; racial tensions and, 57, 59–62; recruitment by, 37–38, 48, 69; today, 269; transition to second group of, 55–56; travel to Cuba and, 46–47, 48–49, 69, 74, 278n69

Venceremos Brigade: Young Americans Sharing the Life and Work of Revolutionary Cuba (Venceremos Brigades), 69, 91, 285n61

"¡Venceremos!" slogan, 267

¡Venceremos? The Erotics of Black Self-Making in Cuba (Allen), 249

Verde Olivo, 95–96, 208, 279n79

Viajes Varadero Travel Agency bombings, 190–91, 302n146

Viera, José, 117

Vietnamese communist revolutionaries, 53–54

Vietnamese National Liberation Front, 49, 50, 53, 87, 106

Vietnam War: Black Panther Party and, 106, 287n119; Cuba and, 4, 109–10; global revolution and, 49–51, 53–54, 278–79n79; Guevara and, 79; hijacking and, 132; protests against, 34, 53–54; Soviet Union and, 108–9; Weather Underground and, 101, 105, 218–19

Village Voice, 115

Violence: to repress political dissidents, 81; by right-wing anti-Castro groups, 117, 154, 188–92, 301n127; by Weather Underground and FALN, 101, 219

Vivó, Raúl Valdés, 305n28

Voluntary expatriates living in Cuba, 227, 304–5n16

Volunteerism, 28, 38, 42

W. E. B. Du Bois Clubs of America, 83
Wald, Karen Lee, 276n15
Walker, Alice, 16
War on Terror, 204, 258, 262
War Resistors League, 83–84
Washington Committee on Africa, 97
Washington Post, 141, 145
Waters, Maxine, 255–56
Watts Riots, 210, 215
Weather Underground Organization (WUO), 76, 79, 94, 99, 101–2, 105, 218
Welfare Poets, 240
Wells Fargo robbery, 259, 304n16
Westad, Odd Arne, 30
"What to Do When the Hijacker Comes," 131
Whitman, Christine Todd, 254, 255
Wickham, DeWayne, 310n127
Widener, Daniel, 73
Williams, Carl, 254
Williams, Evelyn A., 303n3, 311n151
Williams, Mabel, 128, 205–6
Williams, Robert F., 15, 211; armed self-defense and, 215, 216, 309n112; indictment of, 309n112; political asylum of, 16, 19, 128, 202, 205–6, 215; *Radio Free Dixie* and, 8, 222, 232; RNA and, 231, 232, 292n65
Wilmington Ten, 212, 306n47
Witt, Richard Duwayne, 292n67
WNBC-TV, 254
Women: equality of, 246–47, 271; status of Cuban, 4, 63–65; sugar harvest and, 62–63. *See also* Feminism
Women's agricultural battalion, 39
Women's International League for Peace and Freedom, 97
Women's Liberation, 4, 62, 63
Women Strike for Peace, 83
Work camps: for political dissidents and antisocials, 6, 66; radicalism and, 86–87; Venceremos Brigades and, 36–37, 48, 49, 53, 57–62, 68, 120
World Festival of Youth and Students, 180, 300n89
Worthy, William, 86, 284n41
Wretched of the Earth, The (Fanon), 151

Wright, Sarah, 15
Writers Guild of America, East, 239
Wu, Judy Tzu-Chun, 55
WUO. *See* Weather Underground Organization (WUO)

Yahoo News, 263
Yale University academic conference, 167
Yedra, Reynaldo Castro, 37, 276n28
Young, Allen, 282n7
Young, Cynthia A., 14, 74, 156

Young Communist League, 37, 42
Youngest Revolution, The (Martínez), 14, 47
Young Lords Party, 7–8, 157
Youth Centennial Column, 39

Zafra de los diez millones. *See* Sugar harvest
Zapatista movement, 21
Zed Books, 311n151
Zeitlin, Maurice, 12
Zenni, Chafik Sakar, 116

www.ingramcontent.com/pod-product-compliance
Lightning Source LLC
Chambersburg PA
CBHW032012300426
44117CB00008B/1005